The US–China Trade Dispute

To Nisreen and Danny

The US–China Trade Dispute

Facts, Figures and Myths

Imad Moosa

Professor of Finance, Royal Melbourne Institute of Technology (RMIT), Australia

Edward Elgar

Cheltenham, UK • Northampton, MA, USA

Published by
Edward Elgar Publishing Limited
The Lypiatts
15 Lansdown Road
Cheltenham
Glos GL50 2JA
UK

Edward Elgar Publishing, Inc.
William Pratt House
9 Dewey Court
Northampton
Massachusetts 01060
USA

A catalogue record for this book
is available from the British Library

Library of Congress Control Number: 2012930611

MIX
Paper from responsible sources
FSC® C018575
FSC www.fsc.org

ISBN 978 1 78100 154 7 (cased)

Typeset by Servis Filmsetting Ltd, Stockport, Cheshire
Printed and bound by MPG Books Group, UK

Contents

Abbreviations

ASEAN	Association of Southeast Asian Nations
BEER	Behavioural Equilibrium Exchange Rate
BIS	Bank for International Settlements
CAD	Canadian Dollar
CBO	Congressional Budget Office
CDO	Collateralized Debt Obligation
CDS	Credit Default Swap
CNY	Chinese Yuan
CPI	Consumer Price Index
CRS	Congressional Research Service
DEER	Desired Equilibrium Exchange Rate
DHS	Department of Homeland Security
EMS	European Monetary System
FDI	Foreign Direct Investment
FEER	Fundamental Equilibrium Exchange Rate
G7	Group of Seven Countries
GBP	British Pound
GDP	Gross Domestic Product
GM	General Motors
IC	Import Certificate
IMF	International Monetary Fund
IOU	I Owe You
ITMEER	Intermediate-Term Model-Based Equilibrium Exchange Rate
JPY	Japanese yen
KBR	Kellogg, Brown and Root
LCH	Life Cycle Hypothesis
LOP	Law of One Price
LTCM	Long-Term Capital Management
METI	Ministry of Economy, Trade and Industry
MITI	Ministry of International Trade and Industry
NAIRU	Non-Accelerating Inflation Rate of Unemployment
NATREX	Natural Real Equilibrium Exchange Rate
NEER	Nominal Effective Exchange Rate

OECD	Organisation for Economic Co-operation and Development
OPEC	Organization of Petroleum Exporting Countries
PEER	Permanent Equilibrium Exchange Rate
PPP	Purchasing Power Parity
RMB	Renminbi
S&P	Standard and Poor's
SCM	Subsidies and Countervailing Duties (Agreement)
SDR	Special Drawing Rights
SOE	State-Owned Enterprise
STIC	Standard International Trade Classification
USD	US Dollar
WTI	West Texas Intermediate
WTO	World Trade Organization

Preface

The US is accusing China of playing a "dirty game" involving currency manipulation and mercantilism, claiming that these policies have created the massive bilateral trade deficit and destroyed America's manufacturing industry. China is also accused of causing the global financial crisis, impeding the recovery of the world economy from the great recession, perpetuating higher oil (and copper) prices, aggressively buying up the corporate world, and threatening American security. These unsubstantiated and exaggerated allegations are typical products of the blame-it-on-foreigners and do-as-I-say culture. Furthermore, the US is ambivalent towards China's accumulation of foreign reserves (mostly US Treasury securities). China's accumulation of reserves is taken to be indicative of an undervalued currency and a threat to the US; meanwhile America is apprehensive about the possibility that China may stop buying Treasury securities, effectively cutting America's credit lines. As a result, China finds itself in a classic damned-if-you-do, damned-if-you-don't position.

Just before the completion of the manuscript in September 2011, I was visiting the Beijing Institute of Technology where I presented a paper on why revaluation of the yuan will not work. The visit was rather informative with respect to some of the issues addressed in this book. The claim that the Chinese do not spend enough gave me a different impression from what I saw: luxury cars, busy restaurants and bustling shopping malls. I also found out how generous the Chinese are with guests. Generosity and not spending do not go together. The Chinese, I would say, spend adequately while striking a balance with saving. And they do not have the habit of spending money that they have not yet earned. I also observed examples that are counterintuitive with respect to the claim that things are cheap in China because of an undervalued currency. A ride on the subway in Beijing costs 2 yuan – about 1/20th the cost in my home city, Melbourne. I am not sure how the cost of a subway ride is related to the exchange rate – it is not. These are just two observations that have reinforced my belief in what is written in this book.

While this book is mostly about the bilateral trade deficit of the US with China and the consequent trade dispute, it also deals with all matters arising from Sinophobia. It addresses the three pillars of the current debate. The first is whether or not the Chinese yuan is undervalued. The second is whether or not the presumed undervaluation of the yuan is the cause of the massive US trade deficit with China. If so the revaluation of the yuan is the means whereby the trade balance can be corrected. The third is whether or not Chinese exchange rate and trade policies are illegal and/or immoral. The thorough analysis presented in this book leads us to the following conclusions. First, the yuan may or may not be undervalued – claims of undervaluation are motivated by political agenda rather than sound economics. Second, even if the yuan was undervalued, its revaluation will not affect the trade deficit, just like the appreciation of the yen from over 300 to under 80 has not made any difference to the US deficit with Japan. Third, Chinese economic policies are not immoral and do not violate the rules of the World Trade Organization (WTO) and the International Monetary Fund (IMF). It is also concluded that the US trade deficit with China is an American problem that America must deal with decisively.

Following an introductory chapter in which the issues under consideration are discussed briefly, Chapters 2 and 3 deal with the history and structure of the international monetary system and international financial and trading relations. The discussion is helpful for putting the underlying issues into perspective. For example, to deal with the accusation that China is pursuing mercantilist policies, it is helpful to understand the concept of mercantilism and how it has evolved. And a discussion of the issue regarding whether or not China is violating IMF rules by adopting a fixed exchange rate regime requires some understanding of the current rules and regulations governing exchange rate regime choice.

Chapter 4 is about exchange rate misalignment and the measurement of the equilibrium exchange rate. It is demonstrated that there are no reliable estimates of the equilibrium exchange rate – hence no one knows whether or not the yuan is undervalued. In Chapters 5, 6 and 7 we will see why the relation between the exchange rate and the trade balance is not as straightforward as it is typically portrayed to be. Several factors impede the transmission of the effect of changes in the exchange rate to prices, volumes and consequently the trade balance. Chapter 8 presents an evaluation of Chinese policies and what China is accused of. Chapters 9 and 10 portray the US trade deficit as an American problem resulting from too much debt-financed spending, too little saving, the demise of manufacturing industry, and the dominance of the financial sector. Concluding thoughts are presented in Chapter 11.

Writing this book would not have been possible without the help and encouragement I received from family, friends and colleagues. My utmost gratitude must go to my wife and children who had to bear the opportunity cost of writing this book. My gratitude also goes to Lee Smith who is my source of due diligence. She read the whole manuscript word for word and came up with numerous suggestions that have made the book more readable. I am grateful to Ming Ma for the hospitality I was accorded while visiting the Beijing Institute of Technology in September 2011.

I would also like to thank my colleagues and friends at RMIT, particularly Tony Naughton, Larry Li, Terry Hallahan, George Tawadros, Vikash Ramiah, Bruce Cowling, Michael Schwartz, Marie-Anne Cam and Mark Stewart. I have benefited greatly from discussions with John Vaz and Kelly Burns, to whom I am grateful. I should not forget the people I socialize with, including Liam Lenten, Theo Gazos, Brien McDonald, Wayne Geerling, Steffen Joeris and Rumi Khan. I must say that I benefited greatly from Steffen's knowledge of history as we discussed the fall of the Roman Empire and the evolution of mercantilism in more recent times.

In preparing the manuscript, I benefited from an exchange of ideas with members of the Table 14 Discussion Group, and for this reason I would like to thank Bob Parsons, Greg O'Brien, Greg Bailey, Bill Breen, Rodney Adams, Paul Rule, Peter Murphy, Bob Brownlee and Tony Paligaro. I am particularly grateful to Paul Rule for reading the manuscript and making some interesting comments. My thanks also go to friends and former colleagues who live far away but provide help via means of telecommunication, including Kevin Dowd (to whom I owe an intellectual debt), Razzaque Bhatti, Ron Ripple, Bob Sedgwick, Sean Holly, Dave Chappell, Dan Hemmings and Ian Baxter.

Naturally, I am the only one responsible for any errors and omissions that may be found in this book. It is dedicated to my beloved children, Nisreen and Danny.

Imad A. Moosa
September, 2011

1. An overview

THE COLD TRADE WAR

In 1930, in the midst of the Great Depression, the US raised tariffs on imported goods as a result of the implementation of the Smoot–Hawley Act. That action triggered a tit-for-tat reaction from other countries, resulting in the destruction of international trade and making the Great Depression even greater. Since about 2005 the threat of a trade war has become real, symbolized by calls for the imposition of tariffs on US imports from China. On this occasion no one knows how China will react, should the US declare a trade war, but history tells us that trade hostilities are not one-sided.

In May 2005 a bill was introduced into the US Congress to impose a 27.5 per cent tariff on all US imports from China unless the Chinese currency is revalued substantially. Twice a year the US Secretary of the Treasury is required to determine whether or not other countries are manipulating their currencies and if so they will be "named and shamed". On 29 September 2010, the US House of Representatives passed legislation to punish China for "undervaluing its currency", thereby "harming the competitiveness of US manufacturers and exporters". The legislation would allow the US government to use estimates of exchange rate misalignment to calculate duties on imports from China. On 11 October 2011 the Senate passed the Currency Exchange Rate Oversight Reform Act, which would allow any "fundamentally misaligned currency" to be labelled a subsidy subject to countervailing duties. Unless and until these bills are signed into laws and implemented, a trade war remains a mere (but serious) threat, something that resembles a cold trade war. Therefore it is refreshing to realize that since 2003 bills of this sort have failed, in the sense that they did not become laws.

Trade wars (or disputes) and resorting to protectionism are quite common despite the rhetoric about the benefits of free international trade (a typical example of countries, and people, not practising what they preach). There are indeed similarities between a trade war and a military war. In a military war, as in a trade war, countries exchange accusations on who started offensive action, claiming that their action is a reaction that is necessary to defend the homeland (which may include a pre-emptive strike). This is what we can clearly observe these days as the US is threatening to impose tariffs on Chinese imports in self-defence (against Chinese currency manipulation).

While trade disputes could arise any time, they are more common when economic conditions are bad. In 1997, when conditions in the US were rosy, American politicians were complaining about the Japanese current account surplus although Japan was going through rather turbulent economic conditions as the country struggled against the deflation that followed the boom of the 1980s. During a visit to Japan in April 1997, the then US Treasury Secretary, Robert Rubin, said: "it is critical that Japan's current account surplus not rise again to a level that is detrimental to global growth, that causes trade frictions with Japan's trading partners and that could fuel protectionist sentiments around the world" (Moosa, 2010a). As we know, in the aftermath of the global financial crisis, wise judgement is not one of Rubin's virtues. At the same time that he was warning Japan, Rubin was sowing the seeds of the global financial crisis as he opposed fiercely the proposed regulation of over-the-counter derivatives. To his own personal benefit, Rubin was also the driving force behind the abolition of the Glass–Steagall Act, a deregulatory measure that allowed banks to grow bigger and do as they please.

Trade friction between the US and Japan actually goes back to 1970 when rising competition from Japan led to a political phenomenon known as "Japan-bashing". The US repeatedly threatened Japan with trade sanctions, demanding yen appreciation and the imposition of "voluntary" constraints on particular exports to the US. In the 1980s Japan gave in to pressure and participated in concerted central bank intervention that helped push the yen up from 360 in August 1971 to 80 in April 1995. McKinnon and Ohno (1997) demonstrate that the strong yen caused a deflationary slump in the Japanese economy with a zero interest rate liquidity trap. That, however, did not turn Japan's current account surplus into deficit, which shows the impotence of exchange rate-based expenditure switching policies that the US is currently demanding from China.

China has replaced Japan as the culprit, and this is why McKinnon (2007) argues that "the current US–China trade frictions are reminiscent of the US–Japan frictions from the 1970s through to 1995". China is accused (by the US) of exchange rate manipulation, of taking deliberate policy actions to boost its competitive position (making its products more competitive, price-wise, than those of its trading partners, particularly the US). Zakaria (2010) describes the September 2010 bill as "at best pointless posturing and at worst dangerous demagoguery", adding that "it won't solve the problem it seeks to fix" and that "more worrying, it is part of growing anti-Chinese sentiment in the US that misses the real challenge of China's next phase of development". He goes on to say that the real challenge is that "China is beginning to move up the value chain into industries and jobs that were until recently considered the prerogative of the Western world", suggesting that this challenge "is not being produced by Beijing's currency manipulation or hidden subsidies but by strategic investment and hard work". Hence, according to Zakaria, "the best and most effective response to the Chinese challenge is not threats and tariffs but deep structural reforms and major new investments to make the US economy dynamic and its workers competitive".

The passing of the anti-Chinese legislation in 2010 came in response to pressure from groups believing that the undervalued Chinese currency is the cause of the US trade deficit with China. In the aftermath of the global financial crisis and the Great Recession, a view emerged that "China's cheap currency" is "an illegal subsidy" that is hampering the recovery of the US economy. Some observers question the morality and legality of Chinese policies, allegedly designed to dominate the world economy as the largest exporter, an objective that is accomplished by "crooked means", including the manipulation of the exchange rate. It is even claimed that Chinese policies are hampering the recovery of the world economy at large. President Obama joined the bandwagon by expressing the view that "Beijing is keeping the yuan artificially low to give Chinese exports an unfair advantage" (McNally, 2010). Tim Geithner, the US Treasury Secretary, made it so dramatic by declaring that "China's unwillingness to allow the yuan to rise created a 'dangerous dynamic' of 'competitive non-appreciation' in emerging economies" and that "excess accumulation of reserves is leading to 'serious distortions' in the world economy" (*The Economist*, 2010a).

Accusing China of being the culprit in a potential trade war (that will not benefit anyone) rests on three propositions. The first is that the yuan is undervalued. The second is that undervaluation of the yuan is the cause of the US trade deficit with China, implying that revaluation of the yuan would be the cure. And the third is that Chinese growth and exchange rate policies are questionable on moral and legal grounds (allegedly because these policies hurt other countries and violate international rules). This book examines these three propositions and presents counter arguments to the underlying allegations. Specifically, it is argued that the propositions that the Chinese currency is undervalued and that it is the cause of the US trade deficit are neither substantiated by sound theoretical reasoning (not even by intuition) nor are they supported by solid empirical evidence. This book provides answers, backed by extensive research, to two questions posed by Goldstein and Lardy (2008): (i) given the wide range of estimates of the yuan's undervaluation, can one be confident that it is seriously undervalued?; and (ii) if China did choose to implement a sizeable revaluation/appreciation of the yuan, will it be effective in reducing substantially China's large global current account deficit?

Another question this book examines is also raised by Goldstein and Lardy (2008): should the IMF have regarded China's "large-scale, prolonged, one-way" intervention in the foreign exchange market as currency manipulation, and how should the IMF exchange rate surveillance be conducted going forward? This question is one of many that cast doubt on the legality and/or morality of Chinese economic policies. In this book it is argued that there is nothing illegal or immoral about Chinese economic policies and that lecturing China on the (altruistic) economic policies it should pursue is out of order, to say the least. It is also argued that any country has the sovereign right to pursue macroeconomic, development and industrial policies the way it sees fit and appropriate for its domestic economic conditions. In the remainder of this chapter a brief overview of the issues under consideration is presented. The discussion is expanded significantly in the chapters that follow.

UNDERVALUATION OF THE YUAN: ANYBODY'S GUESS

US policy and law makers have been arguing that "the Chinese currency is undervalued by as much as 40 per cent against the dollar" and that China's exchange rate policy is designed "to depress the value of the yuan and push cheap Chinese goods into US markets" (Wolverson, 2010). For some reason, 40 per cent is the preferred round number used in an ad hoc manner by those claiming that the yuan is undervalued. Nouriel Roubini, one of the few economists acknowledged to have predicted the global financial crisis, agrees with the proposition that the yuan is "grossly" undervalued, suggesting that the Chinese surplus and massive foreign exchange reserves balances are indicative of exchange rate misalignment – that is, the yuan is undervalued (Roubini, 2007). He also suggests that the yuan would appreciate sharply if it were not for the intervention of the Chinese authorities in the foreign exchange market.

Likewise, Bergsten (2010a) argues that the Chinese currency is undervalued by about 25 per cent on a trade-weighted basis and by about 40 per cent against the dollar. He points out that the Chinese authorities buy about $1 billion daily to avoid appreciation of the yuan. By the way, Bergsten heads the Peterson Institute for International Economics, a Washington-based "think tank" whose members hold extreme anti-Chinese views that we will come across throughout this book.

Ahearne et al. (2007) reach the conclusion that the yuan must appreciate by 5–25 per cent to reduce China's global current account deficit by 3.5–6.5 per cent. Crockett (2008) suggests that there is wide agreement that the yuan is undervalued but admits that there is little agreement on the size of the undervaluation and how to correct it. Goldstein and Lardy (2008) argue that "any reasonable back-of-the envelope calculation aimed at finding the level of the renminbi that would eliminate China's global current account surplus would generate a large (and growing) estimate of the renminbi undervaluation". We can already see significant dispersion in the estimates of the extent of yuan undervaluation, but more is coming.

In October 2010 *The Economist*'s Big Mac index indicated that the yuan is undervalued by 40 per cent against the dollar, exactly the figure that Bergsten has in mind (which may not be a coincidence). The reason why the yuan is undervalued by this magical number is simple: a Big Mac costs 14.5 yuan in China and $3.71 in the US, which means that the equilibrium exchange rate should be 3.91 (*The Economist*, 2010b). The problem is that Big Mac analysis ignores the fact that factors of production are much cheaper in China than in the US and that the index is based on the heroic assumption that a trader can make a profit by buying Big Macs in Shanghai and selling them in New York, in accordance with what economists call the "law of one price". It should be mentioned here that there is no such thing as "law" in economics, despite what most economists like to believe (Boyle's Law is a law that holds universally whereas Okun's Law is not a law, it is an empirical observation that varies across space and time). In its 30 July 2011 issue, *The Economist* presented a modified Big Mac index that takes into account differences in the levels of per capita income. This modified Big Mac index shows that the yuan is neither undervalued nor overvalued (*The Economist*, 2011a).

Arbitrary round and nice-looking numbers are typically used to describe the extent of the undervaluation of the Chinese currency. The problem is that these (unreliable) estimates would be used as the basis of the impending trade war with China because implementing the latest anti-Chinese legislation requires estimates of exchange rate misalignment (provided, of course, that "misalignment" means undervaluation of the yuan). However, it has also been established that "it is almost impossible to be sure when a currency is misaligned, let alone by how much" (*The Economist*, 2007a). Even Paul Krugman, who describes China as "really the bad guy in currency war", admits that "we don't know the RMB fair value" (Krugman, 2010a). However, he uses some twisted logic to indict China by arguing that "the right way to judge is not the value of the renminbi but rather the scale of currency intervention China must effect to keep its peg in place". In legal terms, Krugman is trying to use circumstantial evidence to obtain a guilty verdict against China. Even if circumstantial evidence were admissible, China has not committed any offence by intervening in the foreign exchange market.

Evidence on the misalignment of the yuan/dollar exchange rate is a mixed bag and is highly unreliable. Again, this is economics, not physics, despite what the majority of economists would like to think – that economics is as rigorous as physics. Unlike physics, empirical estimates in economics are not produced from experiments conducted under controlled conditions but rather from invariably faulty data using ad hoc methods (that, to some, look scientific) to produce results that confirm preconceived ideas. Take, for example, the estimates of the undervaluation of the yuan in 2003 as reported by the Congressional Research Service (CRS) to Congress (Morrison and Labonte, 2008). The yuan was undervalued by 40 per cent according to Manufacturer's Alliance, by 15–25 per cent according to the Institute for International Economics, and by 9.5–15 per cent according to Goldman Sachs. The report describes these figures as "back of the envelope calculations, none of them based on theoretically grounded, econometrically estimated economic models". But even estimates based on "sophisticated" theory and econometrics are not reliable because the underlying procedures lend themselves to significant subjective manipulation. The IMF (2004) concluded that "it is difficult to find persuasive evidence that the renminbi is undervalued". By the way, Goldman Sachs has been producing figures that are more favourable to China – a smart move, given the potential business opportunities.

Those empirical studies that found evidence for the undervaluation of the yuan place the extent of undervaluation in a very wide range, providing evidence for the sensitivity of the estimates to a number of factors. Dunaway et al. (2006) concluded that "small changes in model specifications, explanatory variable definitions, and time periods for estimation can lead to very substantial differences in equilibrium real exchange rate estimates". They found that the choice of sample period, equation specification, and variable definition can lead to large variations in the results. Consequently, estimates of misalignment must surely be all over the place. Some studies found that the yuan was either not undervalued or indeed overvalued. Chinn et al. (2006) cast doubt on the proposition that the yuan is undervalued by suggesting "why the Renminbi might be overvalued (but probably isn't)". Wang (2004) found a 1 per cent negative current account gap, suggesting that the yuan was actually overvalued. Research conducted at Morgan Stanley showed that the yuan is undervalued by 1 per cent only, a result described by *The Economist* (2007a) as "not the answer Congress wants". This variation in the results, and the views based upon them, leads to the inevitable consequence of "cherry picking" by those who are ideologically motivated to prove that China is the culprit causing the trade imbalance. It is often the case that some economists produce numbers that suit their political agendas, and this can easily be done by manipulating their models (which cannot happen in physics). In the current debate, it seems that model manipulation, not exchange rate manipulation, is a more likely source of concern.

There are those who argue that the yuan is undervalued without putting a number on the extent of undervaluation – they simply use "circumstantial evidence" to substantiate the claim that the yuan is undervalued. The evidence for undervaluation is taken to be China's foreign exchange reserves, its current account surplus, and the fact that things are cheaper in China than in America. Starting with reserves, *The Economist* (2010b) suggests that a country that runs sizeable trade surpluses, resulting in a rapid build-up of foreign assets, "probably [only probably] has an undervalued exchange rate". This would be a conclusion that may be supported by a misalignment model based on the proposition that the equilibrium exchange rate stabilizes foreign assets and liabilities at a "reasonable level". However, China's rapid accumulation of foreign exchange reserves is not only a consequence of the trade surplus but also a product of capital inflows propelled by expectations of yuan revaluation. There is some sort of vicious circle here: US political arguments for revaluation encourage speculative capital flows, triggered by those hoping to profit from such a revaluation, which in turn boost foreign exchange reserves. Then a surplus with one trading partner does not prove that the currency of the surplus country is undervalued.

The claim that the yuan would appreciate significantly if it were not for intervention in the foreign exchange market is also flawed. It has been firmly established that, because of the sheer size of the foreign exchange market, intervention is ineffective unless it works in the same direction as a market trend (which is exactly what happened in 1985 following the Plaza meeting). One billion dollars, which is presumably the value of the daily Chinese intervention, is a drop in the ocean relative to the size of the foreign exchange market (and even that part of the foreign exchange market that involves trading the yuan against the dollar). If market forces dictate a stronger yuan, central bank intervention will be ineffective.

As for the current account as an indication of undervaluation, *The Economist* (2009a) suggests that "it is wrong to define the yuan's fair value by the revaluation required to eliminate current account surplus" and that "China's surplus partly reflects its high saving rate". It is noteworthy that the anti-Chinese Peterson Institute for International Economics uses this notion to produce its regular estimates of exchange rate misalignment (for example, Cline and Williamson, 2011). The argument that the Chinese currency is undervalued because things are cheaper in China is rather silly, because we should expect nothing but that. The costs of production are lower in China, and Chinese firms do not have to factor in the real possibility of being wiped out by a lawsuit as in the American tradition. We will discuss these points in more detail in Chapter 4.

UNDERVALUATION AND REVALUATION AS THE CAUSE AND CURE

The US–China trade imbalance is invariably attributed to exchange rate misalignment, which makes currency revaluation the optimal (or only) solution to the problem. However, this view has more to do with dogmatic ideology than with sound economics. The US trade deficit has less to do with the value of the yuan and more to do with Chinese saving and American profligacy. While China has a high saving rate, a combination of cheap money and weak regulation in the US led to bubbles and temporary capital gains that reduced savings. Cheap foreign money (combined with cheap Chinese land, energy and natural resources) has driven down the prices of "Made-in-China products". Furthermore, China's international competitiveness is not due to an undervalued currency as much as it is caused by low costs of production in China.

McKinnon (2007) argues that US politicians are targeting China on the basis of what he calls the "mistaken presumption" that the appreciation of the yuan would reduce China's trade surplus with the US. He also argues that "blaming foreigners for misaligned exchange rates is easier than facing up to the problem of inadequate private saving and large structural fiscal deficits in the United States". This is similar to the argument of Miller (2008) who refers to "politicians looking for quick fixes to perceived US economic ills" and that of Persaud (2010) who suggests that "the US obsession with the Chinese exchange rate is a classic example of blaming foreigners for domestic woes" and that "blaming foreigners for domestic woes is the sad but unsurprising cardinal rule of politics, followed by even the most ardent internationalist". More importantly, however, McKinnon does not attribute this state of affairs only to "political populism" but also to "bad economic theorizing". He attributes the US trade deficit not to exchange rate misalignment but to the structural fiscal deficit and low personal saving rate in the US.

In a testimony before a hearing of the Senate Committee on Banking, Housing and Urban Affairs, Nicholas Lardy argued that "China's emergence as a large surplus country reflects the rise of domestic savings relative to investment" and that "the very large US deficits reflected our [US] low national savings relative to our national investment" (Lardy, 2010). He concluded that "it may appear that the renewed focus by the US Congress on China's currency and its external imbalance is misplaced". Cappiello and Ferrucci (2008) argue that "structural factors affecting the intertemporal choices of consumption, saving and investment have been key determinants of China's widening trade surplus". They cast serious doubt on the role of the pegged exchange rate in promoting Chinese exports by suggesting that "whether it [the pegged exchange rate] has also promoted external trade in the context of China's so-called export-led growth model is still open to debate".

Roubini (2007) disputes the view that the exchange rate is irrelevant, arguing that while the US fiscal deficit and the Chinese high saving rate have been important drivers of the growing US trade deficit, the Chinese exchange rate policy has also been a crucial factor. He points out that "a persistently weak RMB has made imports expensive and exports cheap, which has reduced, in relative terms, both overall consumption and consumption of imports". Some observers go as far as to claim that "a change in China's exchange rate policy is a critical element in the world economy's recovery" because "the reality is that China with a large trade surplus sells substantially more to the rest of the world than it purchases, and therefore, it continues to subtract significantly from world demand" (Dunaway, 2010). According to those embracing these views, appreciation of the yuan will materially change trade imbalances. This belief is not supported by a recent IMF report on China, in which it is stated explicitly that "a substantial appreciation of the Chinese renminbi would have little effect on trade and growth in the rest of the world even if accompanied by other economic liberalization" (Beattie, 2011). Specifically, the report points out that a 20 per cent trade-weighted appreciation of the Chinese currency would boost growth in the US economy by between 0.05 and 0.07 per cent, too little to make any fuss about.

In 2005 Alan Greenspan urged the Senate Finance Committee to avoid protectionist measures (Goldkorn, 2005). He argued that he was "aware of no credible evidence that an increase in the value of the yuan relative to the US dollar would significantly increase manufacturing activity and jobs in the United States which some mistakenly believe". Greenspan went on to say that "US imports of textiles . . . assembled computers, toys and similar products would in part shift from China as the final assembler to other emerging-market economies in Asia and perhaps in Latin America, as well . . . Few, if any, American jobs would be protected."

Those who believe that revaluation of the yuan will eliminate the US trade deficit with China choose to overlook the fact that the yuan has appreciated by 50 per cent in real terms since 2005 (*The Economist*, 2010c).

Yet nothing has happened in response, although it seems plausible to argue that a small dose of an effective remedy should produce some results (albeit less than what is desired). Zakaria (2010) argues that making Chinese goods more expensive through revaluation (if at all possible) will not make American factories more competitive. The most likely outcome, he says, is that "it would help other low-wage economies like Vietnam, India and Bangladesh, which make many of the same goods as China". He refers to what happened in the 1980s when Japan was forced to let the yen appreciate against the dollar, saying that "the subsequent 50% increase did little to make American goods more competitive".

Those who believe that revaluation of the yuan can reduce or eliminate China's trade surplus with the US envisage a process that works as follows: (i) revaluation of the yuan leads to a higher dollar price of Chinese exports and a lower yuan price of Chinese imports; (ii) changes in prices lead to changes in volumes; and (iii) higher export revenue and lower import expenditure for the US lead to a reduction in the deficit. This process, according to Moosa (2011a), will not work for seven reasons that include the following: (i) distribution mark-ups and importers' profit margins; (ii) producers' profit margins; (iii) the use of the dollar as the currency of invoicing; (iv) inelastic demand for Chinese exports; (v) inelastic supply of US exports; (vi) the offsetting effects of other factors; and (vii) the fact that the deficit is an American problem. These points will be discussed in detail in Chapters 5, 6 and 7.

Even if revaluation worked it would, according to Miller (2008), benefit "those few manufacturers that compete directly with Chinese firms and hurt many others, including the producers who use Chinese imports in their US production processes, and American consumers buying Chinese goods". He adds: "an inflated renminbi won't punish the Chinese; it will, on balance, punish Americans". For the American economy as a whole, Miller considers an undervalued yuan (if it is) to be a source of double benefit because "we get both more goods and services, and more investment capital to help our economy grow and keep our unemployment rate low".

THE MORALITY AND LEGALITY OF CHINESE POLICIES

It has been suggested that the Chinese exchange rate and growth policies hurt the rest of the world (hence they are immoral) and could be illegal as judged by the IMF and WTO rules. Some economists have accordingly suggested that China should change its policies in such a way as to serve the interests of the US and the rest of the world, as if a planet Earth without China would be more prosperous. It is even claimed that Chinese policies are not good for China itself. For example, Goldstein (2004) claims that China's exchange rate policy is working against efforts to rein in an excessive growth of bank lending, handicapping efforts to bring an end to the overheating of the economy and to keep inflation down. He warns that the policy could interrupt the market access that China now enjoys for its exports and weaken popular support for further trade liberalization within China.

Whether Chinese policies are immoral and/or illegal is debatable. On one side, it is argued that focusing on a revaluation of the Chinese currency is unjustified by the prevailing rules of the international economic order – meaning that there is no legitimacy in putting pressure on China to change its exchange rate policy (Keidel, 2005). On the other hand, it is claimed that a "competitive undervaluation of the Chinese currency" is a "blatant form of protectionism" because it subsidizes Chinese exports by the extent of the misalignment, hence it is equivalent to a tariff on imports (Bergsten, 2010a). Bergsten, who is definitely one of the top ten China bashers, even argues that "it would thus be incorrect to characterize as protectionist a policy response to the Chinese actions by the United States or other countries" and that "such actions should more properly be viewed as anti-protectionist". This argument amounts to stretching the meaning of "protectionism" far beyond any reasonable limit, and it is the trade war equivalent of a military pre-emptive strike under the pretext of self-defence.

The question here is whether or not what China is doing (including foreign exchange market intervention) is illegal, as judged by the IMF and WTO rules, and whether or not the US is justified in threatening China with retaliatory measures. The "smoking gun" argument (the proposition that the trade deficit indicates an unfair exchange rate) does not meet the common sense test for fairness. What is not fair is to sanction a country because it has a small deficit or a large surplus. According to the IMF guidelines, countries can intervene in the foreign exchange market "to counter disorderly conditions" characterized by "disruptive short-term movements in exchange value of its currency", which is exactly what China is experiencing in the aftermath of the global financial crisis. Intervention is not a malpractice – it is rather a means for preserving the exchange rate regime chosen by a country in accordance with the post-Bretton Woods IMF rules. And then why is it that China is singled out as the perpetrator of abuse of the international economic order because it intervenes in the foreign exchange market? In reality, China is not the only big intervener because other countries have been intervening more vigorously. In terms of the tendency to accumulate foreign reserves, Singapore, Korea, Thailand and Malaysia have outperformed China when reserves are measured as a percentage of the monetary base (*The Economist*, 2010d). It is quite legitimate for these countries, including China, to resort to foreign exchange market intervention in response to a consequence of the global financial crisis – this being the enormous pressure exerted on their currencies to appreciate rapidly. There is indeed a big difference between this practice and competitive devaluation, and this is why Bergsten (2010a) got it wrong.

A former chief economist of the IMF, Michael Mussa, insists that China's exchange rate policy violates Article IV of the IMF Articles of Agreement (Mussa, 2007). He refers to the "catastrophic failure of Fund surveillance in the critical case of China" because "since 2002, the Chinese authorities have used massive, largely sterilized, official intervention to resist substantial, economically-warranted appreciation of the yuan". Therefore, according to Mussa, the Chinese have an undervalued currency that is kept weak by intervention and they have a policy "operating strongly in the opposite direction". This travesty is an unnecessary dramatization of a normal state of affairs that boils down to Mussa's dissatisfaction with the performance of his former boss, the IMF's Managing Director, as he refrained from telling China what to do. Mussa describes as "incomprehensible incompetence" the Managing Director's agreement with the Chinese view that a government has unilateral authority to determine its exchange rate (he also describes as "fools" those who disagree with his views on this issue). The IMF, we have to remember, has an advisory role, and it stops at that. Not accepting the Fund's advice is not a violation of any rule that requires the imposition of sanctions or expulsion, at least as things stand now. Incidentally, Liu (2005a) makes a very interesting point about the role of the IMF, arguing that "the IMF which has been ferocious in imposing draconian fiscal and monetary conditionalities on all debtor nations everywhere in the decade after the Cold War, is nowhere to be seen on the scene in the world's most flagrantly irresponsible debtor nation". This nation, as we all know, is the US.

China's decision to peg its currency to the dollar is not inconsistent with the IMF rules (adopted following the collapse of the Bretton Woods system) that allow countries to choose the exchange rate regimes they deem suitable for their economies. In reality, however, countries go as far as declaring one exchange rate regime while following another, which has been accepted as a common practice resulting from the so-called "fear of floating" or "fear of pegging" (Calvo and Reinhart, 2002). While the IMF is aware of this phenomenon, no country has been punished or even reprimanded for indulging in this kind of behaviour. Going back to Mussa's argument, declaring an exchange rate regime while practising another one is perhaps more of a violation of IMF rules than China's fixed exchange rate regime and the foreign exchange market intervention necessary to maintain the regime.

It is also claimed that China's exchange rate policy is as much a violation of the WTO rules as the Chinese violation of intellectual property rights (Dunaway, 2010). This is the same idea put forward by Bergsten (2010a), postulating that an undervalued currency works as an import tax and export subsidy. It follows from these arguments that China is violating the WTO rules as enshrined in the Agreement on Subsidies and Countervailing Duties (SCM Agreement). Ahn (2010) argues that, for China to violate the SCM Agreement, its exchange rate policy must constitute a subsidy under Article 1 of the SCM, which requires the following conditions to be satisfied: (i) there must be a financial contribution by the government, (ii) benefit is conferred, and (iii) the subsidy must be specific. This means that the financial contribution is made by a direct transfer of funds, forgone government revenue, the provision or purchase of goods or services other than general infrastructure, or payment to a funding mechanism. Obviously, none of these conditions are satisfied in this case, and it will be rather hard to convince anyone with any degree of objectivity that China is indeed violating the WTO rules by pursuing a particular exchange rate policy. The possibility that China may be violating WTO rules in other ways, such as intellectual property rights, is a different matter that we are not concerned with here. And if that is the case, China is not alone in violating the WTO rules, one way or another.

Because China is perceived as inflicting damage on the world economy and the international monetary system, some of those obsessed with Sinophobia have put forward suggestions on how China should proceed to change its "harmful" policies. It has been suggested that China should move away from heavy reliance on investment and exports to generate growth towards greater reliance on consumption, which will not be accomplished "unless greater flexibility and an appreciation of the exchange rate are permitted" (Dunaway, 2010). Economic growth models emphasize the importance of investment, while the export-led growth hypothesis highlights the role of exports. I have not yet come across anything that remotely resembles a consumption-based growth model. Then how would China boost consumption? We must not overlook the fact that the saving phenomenon is symptomatic across "catching-up economies", and China is one such economy. We must remember that, in its early stages of development, America relied on investment as a source of growth.

It is also suggested that Chinese manufacturing must shift from export-led growth to domestic demand-led growth (Dunaway, 2010). But there is nothing illegal or immoral about pursuing a policy of export-led growth, which was the model followed by Japan, Korea and even Britain when it was the "workshop of the world". While some would argue that the export-led growth model contributes to trade imbalances, it is the export-led growth model that has made China a global manufacturing powerhouse. In this capacity China has contributed to the suppression of world inflation and, therefore, to the so-called "great moderation". Ironically, the same free marketeers who are condemning China have been promoting the notion of the "great moderation" (at least up to the onset of the global financial crisis) as the outcome of free-market capitalism and globalization.

What is ludicrous is that those who call for a drastic shift in Chinese economic policies claim that they are doing so for China's sake. For example, Goldstein and Lardy (2008) claim that the Chinese fixed exchange rate system "has diminished the effectiveness of monetary policy" and that "currency flexibility is needed to reduce the risks of macroeconomic instability". Prasad (2008) identifies the consequences of fixed exchange rates in the case of China as "financial repression and a relatively closed capital account", which result in "a low real rate of return to savers, provision of cheap credit to inefficient state enterprises, less scope for using monetary policy to combat shocks, slower employment growth and a higher risk of asset price bubbles": in other words, all of the apocalyptic scenarios that one could ever imagine.

Goldstein and Lardy (2008) present some proposals that they claim to be consistent with "President Hu Jintao's emphasis both on creating a harmonious society and on reducing the pace of growth of energy consumption". To make the President's wishes come true they suggest the usual: the promotion of domestic consumption demand by reducing personal taxes and increasing government consumption expenditure, financial reform (whatever that means) and (of course) revaluation of the yuan. Hofman and Kuijs (2008) explain why a more sustainable growth path in China requires "more reliance on services and less on industry, more reliance on factor productivity and less on capital accumulation, and more reliance on domestic demand and less on net exports". The whole story boils down to saying "you will be fine if you follow the American example". While these "experts" have the right to express an opinion as to what China should do, China has the right to say "thanks but no thanks". Macroeconomic policy is a sovereign decision and China has the last say on how to run its economy.

The US trade deficit with China is mostly an American problem that America must deal with effectively. Doing something about the extensive indebtedness in the US economy will be much more fruitful than accusing

China of illegal and immoral policies and demanding drastic changes in Chinese policies that will hurt China, most likely without benefiting the US anyway. It is these issues that we will elaborate on in the coming chapters.

PRELIMINARY NOTES AND CLARIFICATIONS

In this book we use the jargon typically found in the international economics literature. This jargon is often confused, as for example when the words "appreciation" and "revaluation" are used interchangeably, which is wrong. When the US dollar rises in value against the Japanese yen, we say that the dollar has appreciated, which necessarily means that the yen has depreciated. The reason why we use the terms "appreciation" and "depreciation" to describe movements in the yen/dollar exchange rate is that this exchange rate is determined by market forces because it involves two floating currencies. However, the exchange rate between the Chinese currency and the US dollar is determined by the Chinese authorities, because it is fixed – that is, the yuan is pegged to the dollar. Thus when the Chinese authorities allow the yuan to rise in value against the dollar, that is "revaluation" of the yuan. And when the Chinese authorities allow the yuan to fall in value against the dollar, this constitutes "devaluation" of the yuan.

The Americans are therefore calling on the Chinese to revalue the yuan against the US dollar – that is, allowing or rather forcing the exchange rate to fall from the current level. In July 2005 the Chinese revalued the yuan against the dollar. We have to remember that the exchange rate is ultimately determined by market forces. Countries that want to have a fixed exchange rate must overcome pressure from market forces, which they can do through several means such as capital controls, foreign exchange market intervention, and changes in interest rates. Since the Chinese are currently on a fixed exchange rate regime, we will talk about the revaluation of the yuan as a measure of reducing the Chinese surplus, which is equivalent to the US deficit.

However, what the Chinese have been doing since 2005 (with some interruption caused by the global financial crisis) is to allow the yuan to rise in value gradually, perhaps because they have since then adopted a system of crawling peg. In this case it is legitimate to talk about the appreciation of the yuan. Thus, "revaluation" will be used to imply a one-off big rise in the value of the yuan and "appreciation" to represent continuous small upward changes.

Talking about surpluses and deficits must pertain to a particular account of the balance of payments, because the overall balance must be balanced (neither in deficit, nor in surplus). We will invariably refer to the trade balance or trade account, which is the balance of the imports and exports of goods – sometimes known as merchandise trade (hence, the merchandise balance or account). But we will also come across the concept of the current account, which includes the trade balance in addition to trade in services and transfers (such as remittances, interest payments and dividend payments). Because the trade balance is typically the largest component of the current account, a current account surplus is usually associated with a trade balance surplus. This, however, is not always the case with open economies; Australia, for example, typically has a deficit on transfers that is larger than its trade deficit. Moreover, the current account is equal to the change in net foreign assets. A current account deficit implies a corresponding reduction of net foreign assets. The overall balance of payments consists of the current account and the capital (or financial) account, which measures short-term and long-term capital flows (for example, flows of portfolio investment and foreign direct investment). While the US has a current account (and a trade balance) deficit, it has a capital account surplus. It is the other way round for China, which finances the current account deficit of the US by buying Treasury bonds and other US assets.

As noted by Baxter (1995), short-term variations in net exports and in the current account are highly correlated since the discrepancy between these two measures tends to change very slowly over time. For the purposes of forecasting and short-run policy determination, net exports are indeed the relevant concept from the perspective of the national income accounts. Figure 1.1 shows the trade balance and current account for the US, China, Germany and Australia. We can see a big gap between the current account and trade balance in the case of Australia and Germany in the 1990s. For China and the US, the gap between the two balances is small, so we will invariably refer to the trade balance.

We will also distinguish between the bilateral trade balance (one country against another) and the overall trade balance (one country against the rest of the world, or its trading partners). The corresponding exchange rate terms are the bilateral exchange rate (for example, the yuan/dollar exchange rate) and the multilateral or effective exchange rate, which measures the average exchange rate of a currency against the currencies of its trading partners. Distinction is also made between the nominal and real exchange rates, hence between nominal and real appreciation or depreciation. When the yuan/dollar exchange rate declines by 10 per cent, this represents 10 per cent depreciation of the dollar in nominal terms. If, over the same time period, the Chinese inflation rate is 5 per cent higher than the

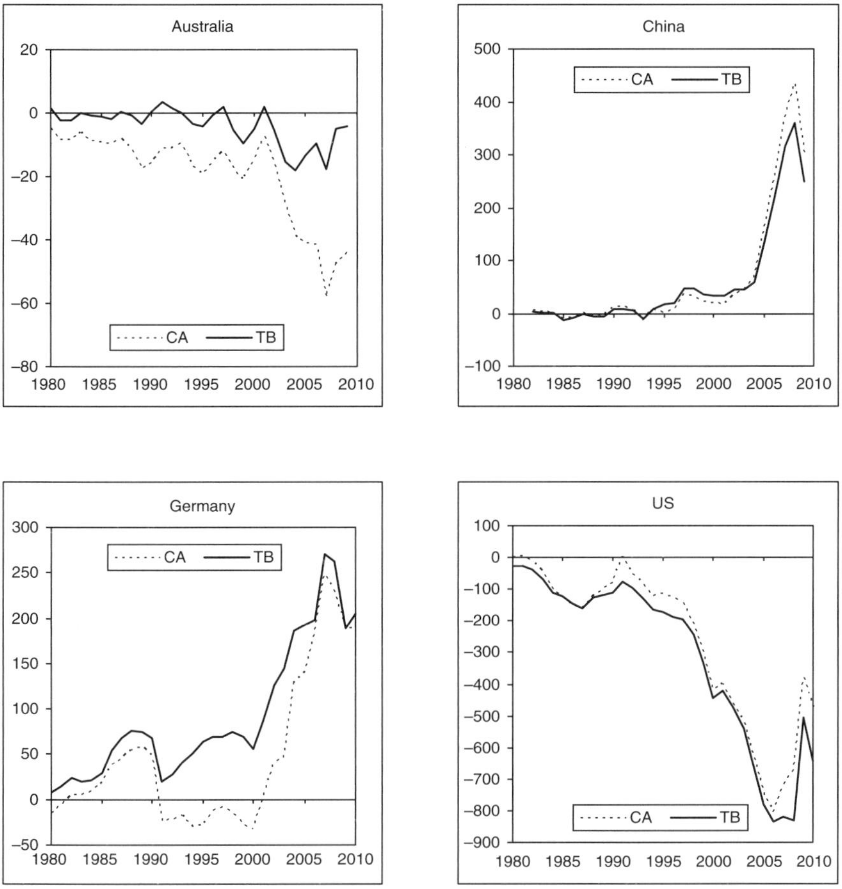

Figure 1.1 Current account (CA) and trade balance (TB) ($ billion)

US inflation rate, the real depreciation of the yuan is 15 per cent. The real exchange rate measures the purchasing power of the domestic currency in foreign markets, which depends on the nominal exchange rate and the price levels or inflation rates in the two countries.

Before we elaborate on the issues discussed briefly in this chapter, we must explore the developments that have led to the present international monetary system and consider international financial relations. This will help us put arguments and issues into perspective.

2. The international monetary system

INTRODUCTION

This chapter is devoted to a study of the structure and history of the international monetary system and exchange rate arrangements for the purpose of putting things into perspective when we discuss Chinese policies in Chapter 8. As we saw in Chapter 1, some economists argue that China is hurting the world economy by adopting an exchange rate arrangement that represents a violation of the IMF rules (Mussa, 2007; Bergsten, 2010a). To answer the question of whether or not China has the right to choose the exchange rate arrangement it deems suitable for its economy, we need to understand the developments that have led to the rules and regulations governing the present international monetary system.

The international monetary system (IMS) is a framework of rules, regulations and conventions that govern financial relations among countries. It is so important and crucial for the world economy and international economic relations that Adam Smith described it as the "Great Wheel" because "when it does not turn well it adversely affects the welfare of nations" (Smith, 1776). Rules and conventions govern the supply of international liquidity and the adjustment of external imbalances as well as exchange rate and capital flow regimes.

CLASSIFICATION OF INTERNATIONAL MONETARY SYSTEMS

International monetary systems can be classified according to two criteria: the nature of the reserves held by central banks and the degree of flexibility of exchange rates. Reserves may be commodities (metals, such as gold and silver, to be precise) or currencies, which presently cannot be converted into gold (the so-called fiat currencies). According to this criterion, international monetary systems can be classified into: (i) pure commodity standards, such as the gold standard and the bimetallic standard (gold and silver) that was in operation in France in the eighteenth century; (ii) pure fiat standards, in which reserves consist entirely of fiat currencies; and (iii) mixed standards, in which reserves consist of fiat currencies as well as commodities, most notably gold. An example of this system is the Bretton Woods system that was in operation during the period 1944–71.

Fixed Exchange Rates

When international monetary systems are classified according to the flexibility of exchange rates several kinds arise. Under a system of fixed exchange rates, the exchange rate is determined by the central bank or the monetary authorities of the country concerned. It is often the case that under such a system the exchange rate is fixed at a level that makes the domestic currency overvalued, although in the current debate China is accused of keeping its currency undervalued. For the central bank to maintain such a regime (by keeping the exchange rate at the fixed level or at least within a narrow margin of the fixed level) it must offset the effect of market forces by imposing capital controls and/or intervening in the foreign exchange market. One reason why some countries abandon fixed exchange rates is the failure to resist market forces, which is exactly what happened to Thailand in 1997 and the UK in 1992. In the 1992 episode the pound was taken out of the European Monetary System of fixed rates due to failure to maintain the predetermined fixed exchange rates against the German mark and other member currencies.

Floating Exchange Rates

The other extreme of the spectrum of exchange rate arrangements is that of perfectly flexible (or floating) exchange rates, where exchange rates change continuously according to the forces of supply and demand in the foreign exchange market. Under a hybrid system of fixed but adjustable exchange rates, countries alter the par value (that is, the declared fixed value) of the exchange rate whenever such a measure is necessary (typically as dictated by the balance of payments position). For example, the value of the currency is reduced (the currency is devalued) when the country has a persistent deficit in its balance of payments. As explained in Chapter 1, the terms "devaluation" and "revaluation" are for fixed exchange rates what "depreciation" and "appreciation" are for flexible exchange rates. However, there are differences. Movements of flexible exchange rates (appreciation and depreciation) are small, continuous and propelled by news events that affect market forces. Conversely, movements of fixed exchange rates (devaluation and revaluation) are large, discrete and initiated by deliberate policy decisions.

Fixed and Flexible within a Band

Under a system of fixed exchange rates and flexible within a band, the exchange rate is flexible within upper and lower limits that comprise a band around the par value – that is, the declared fixed value. However, the exchange rate is fixed otherwise in the sense that it is not allowed (by central bank intervention in the foreign exchange market) to move outside the band (below the lower limit or above the upper limit). Such a system is similar to the European Monetary System (EMS) and the Bretton Woods System.

Sometimes a system of multiple bands is used whereby the exchange rate is allowed to move within a band of a certain width against one or a group of currencies and within a wider band against another group of currencies. An example of a system with two bands is the "Snake in the Tunnel", the predecessor of the EMS, where the exchange rates of member currencies were allowed to fluctuate within a narrow band of ±1.25 per cent (the Snake) against each other and a wider band of ±2.25 per cent (the Tunnel) against the currencies of non-member countries as prescribed by the Smithsonian Agreement of 1971. Within this system, a third, narrower band (called the "Worm") was in operation, as the currencies of the Netherlands and Belgium were allowed to move against each other by ±0.75 per cent.

Crawling Peg

Under a system of crawling peg, where the word "peg" means the fixed or the par value of the exchange rate, the peg is revised periodically according to the average exchange rate over the previous weeks or months, or in relation to an economic indicator such as inflation. There is some indication that China adopted a system of crawling peg against the dollar in July 2005, which was interrupted temporarily by the onset of the global financial crisis (Moosa et al., 2009). Typically, but not necessarily, a country adopts a crawling peg by reducing the value of the domestic currency periodically to maintain its competitive position. China's (undeclared) crawling peg was designed to raise the value of its currency against the dollar slowly as a concession to American demands for currency revaluation.

Dual Exchange Rates

The system of dual exchange rates is a mixed system of fixed and flexible exchange rates. A commercial (fixed) rate is used for imports and exports (current account transactions) and a financial (flexible) rate is used for trading in financial assets (capital account transactions). This system is adopted by countries that wish to insulate commercial transactions from exchange rate fluctuations resulting from speculative capital flows. The capital controls introduced by the Thai authorities in May 1997 created a two-tier market with different exchange rates quoted onshore and offshore. China has also used a dual exchange rate system in recent times. The very fact that countries can adopt a system of dual exchange rates and fix the rate at two different levels is a compelling argument against Mussa's (2007) assertion that no country has the right to determine the level of the exchange on its own terms.

Managed Floating

Under managed floating, which is also called dirty floating as opposed to free floating, exchange rates are basically flexible, but central banks intervene in the market to limit the frequency and amplitude of fluctuations in exchange rates around their long-term trends or to keep the exchange rate within a certain range. Typically central banks do not admit the existence of a target range, either because they cannot maintain it or because they do not want to be perceived as tampering excessively with market forces. This system is adopted because countries in general want to see their currencies neither too strong (because of the adverse effect on the competitive position of the economy) nor too weak (because imports become expensive). The fact that this system is allowed is contrary to the accusation that China manipulates its currency.

Target Zones

The system of target zones arose out of an attempt by major industrial countries to coordinate their exchange rate policies with the objective of eliminating, or at least reducing, exchange rate misalignment. According to this system, major countries establish a set of mutually consistent targets for their real effective exchange rates. Thus, the nominal rates would move continuously to reflect differences in inflation rates. An example of a system of target zones for major currencies, which was suggested in the 1980s by John Williamson, is based on the so-called fundamental equilibrium effective exchange rate, the rate that is supposed to be consistent with a sustainable current account position (Williamson, 1983). This exchange rate is adjusted periodically to reflect changes in economic fundamentals while the actual exchange rate is allowed to fluctuate around this level within a soft-edged band of ±10 per cent. The band is described as "soft-edged" because central banks are not committed to buy or sell the currency if it reaches the upper or lower limit of the band. This, the argument goes, would prevent the creation of a one-way bet for speculators thinking that a weak or strong currency will be bought and sold by the central bank in the process of market intervention. The problem, of course, is how to estimate the fundamental equilibrium exchange rate, as we are going to see in Chapter 4.

THE GOLD STANDARD

The gold standard is often remembered with nostalgia because it is typically associated with a thriving world economy during the period when the system was in operation. The system did not encompass the entire world but only a core of major countries led by Britain. In 1821 Britain went on the gold standard when the Bank of England was legally required to redeem its notes and coins in gold and when the prohibition of the melting of coins and exporting of gold was repealed. In doing so, Britain formally met the conditions of being on the gold standard. By the mid-1870s France had abandoned bimetallism (the use of gold and silver as reserve assets) in favour of gold. In 1870 Germany was still on the silver standard, but war reparations in the form of gold payments from France enabled it to adopt the gold standard. And in 1879 the US returned to the gold standard after the suspension of gold convertibility during the Civil War.

The gold standard is a system of fixed exchange rates whereby the exchange rate is determined by a process requiring central banks to fix the price of gold in terms of the domestic currency, standing ready to buy or sell any amount of gold at that price. This process establishes a fixed exchange rate between any two currencies called the "mint parity", which is equal to the ratio of gold prices in terms of the two currencies. The exchange rate can vary above and below the mint parity only between certain (narrow) limits called the "gold points", determined by the cost of shipping gold between the two countries. The exchange rate cannot go above or below the limits because this would make it profitable to buy gold in one country, ship it to another and sell it for profit. This condition cannot be sustained and it is eliminated by a return of the exchange rate to where it should be – that is, within the narrow limits. The amount of money created by any central bank is determined by its gold reserves, hence the gold standard provides a disciplinary mechanism that prevents excessive monetary creation and consequently inflation. Naturally, quantitative easing cannot be implemented under the gold standard.

One advantage of the gold standard is that the balance of payments adjusts automatically, eliminating surpluses and deficits by the movement of gold flows. For example, if a country has a deficit in the balance of payments it loses gold, leading to a decline in the money supply because it is tied up to gold reserves. As a result of monetary contraction, deflation ensues – that is, prices decline. The idea then is that prices fall in a deficit country and rise in a surplus country. The exports of a deficit country become more competitive than its imports, hence changes in volumes and prices will correct the balance of payments. However, several conditions need to be satisfied for changes in prices to affect volumes, which is an issue that lies at the heart of the current debate. Moreover, at least two conditions must be satisfied for gold flows to affect prices: (i) prices and wages are flexible in both directions (upwards and downwards), and (ii) the monetary authorities do not insulate the money supply from the effect of changes in gold flows via a policy of sterilization (for example, by buying bonds from banks, thus boosting the money supply to offset the effect of gold outflows). The last rule means that a country cannot use monetary policy in the way dictated by domestic macroeconomic conditions.

The gold standard came to an end abruptly in August 1914 when World War I broke out, as the warring countries abolished the convertibility of their currencies into gold and into each other. Since its demise in 1914, there has been one attempt to return to the gold standard in the interwar period. However, calls to return to the gold standard arise every now and then, not only because it provides anti-inflationary discipline but also because currencies have intrinsic values as they are backed by and convertible into gold.

THE INTERWAR PERIOD

In the aftermath of World War I, many countries suffered from hyperinflation because of the tendency to print money to pay off war debt. The German hyperinflation of 1919–23 was the most notorious case, particularly because a clause in the Treaty of Versailles involved war reparations being paid by Germany to the victors, which meant more excessive printing of money. In 1922 the Genoa Conference recommended worldwide adoption of a gold exchange standard, whereby the pound would be convertible into gold and other currencies would be convertible into pounds. In 1925 Britain re-established the convertibility of the pound into gold, signalling the birth of the gold exchange standard. The scarcity of gold after the war at the pre-war exchange rates prevented a return to the pre-war classical gold standard.

One problem with the return to some sort of gold standard was the choice of the appropriate level of exchange rates. For example, Britain set the pound exchange rate at an extremely high level which produced chronic trade deficits, whereas France did the opposite, hoping that a weak franc would boost the international competitiveness of French goods. Confusing political power with economic might, Winston Churchill (then the British finance minister) and Prime Minister Alec Douglas-Home insisted on a strong (overvalued) British currency, choosing the pre-war rate of $4.87 per pound. John Maynard Keynes warned Churchill against overvaluing the pound, but Churchill ignored the advice and referred to the suggestions of Keynes as "feather-brained" (Keynes, 1925). The overvaluation of the pound triggered gold outflows. In 1931 France decided to exchange pound holdings for gold, putting pressure on Britain's gold reserves. Eventually, there was little that Britain could do other than to make the pound inconvertible into gold. That was the end of the gold exchange standard, which was followed by the decade of the Great Depression (1931–9), a period of open economic warfare.

The interwar experiment with the gold exchange standard failed because the world economy had experienced significant changes as a result of the war and the Great Depression. More specifically, the attempt to go back on the gold standard failed because (i) the pre-war exchange rates were inappropriate since there were widely divergent inflation rates; (ii) prices and wages became rigid (particularly downwards); and (iii) countries did not follow the "rules of the game" because of concern about domestic economic instability. In general, circumstances were different, and some of the conditions necessary for the gold standard adjustment process to work smoothly were not in place any more. Because of economic distress, dealing with domestic economic problems became more important than allowing automatic adjustment to take place. Countries did not allow the money supply to change as dictated by gold flows, hence hampering the adjustment process.

Most countries eventually had to leave the gold standard; one of the last countries holding on to the system was the US. President Roosevelt took the US off the gold standard between 1933 and 1934, when the dollar was redefined at a lower parity in terms of gold (from $20.67 to $35 per ounce of gold). By 1933, the overall level of international trade had dropped substantially and most countries experienced depressed economies throughout the decade. Countries experimented with all kinds of exchange rate arrangements. Some of them tried to peg their currencies to a stronger currency (such as the dollar), but ended up devaluing, by necessity (corrective devaluation) or just to gain an advantage (competitive devaluation). Other countries eventually floated their currencies. The intrinsic instability of the period was illustrated by wild reserve fluctuations for pegged currencies and wild exchange rate fluctuations for floating currencies. The whole international payments system fell into chaos, and trade as well as capital flows were curtailed severely.

THE BRETTON WOODS SYSTEM

The Bretton Woods system was born in 1944 in Bretton Woods, a ski resort in New Hampshire. The creation of this system, endorsed by the delegates of 44 countries, was accompanied by the establishment of international institutions, including the International Bank for Reconstruction and Development (presently known as the World Bank) and the International Monetary Fund (IMF). The IMF was entrusted with the supervision of the new international monetary system and the granting of loans to deal with balance of payments difficulties, whereas the World Bank was assigned the task of granting loans for the reconstruction of Europe and for development purposes.

Negotiators at Bretton Woods sought an exchange rate system that would combine the advantages of fixed and flexible exchange rates. The choice was a hybrid system of fixed but adjustable exchange rates, the so-called adjustable peg. Accordingly, the dollar was pegged to gold at the fixed rate of $35/ounce, and the US was prepared to buy and sell unlimited amounts of the metal at this price, although dealings would be restricted to foreign governments and central banks. Other countries were required to declare the rates (par values) of their currencies in terms of gold or the dollar, and to defend the declared rates in the foreign exchange market by buying and selling the dollar – that is, using the dollar as an intervention currency. Exchange rates could only vary within the support or intervention points, initially fixed at 1 per cent.

Figure 2.1 shows the dollar exchange rates of the yen, pound, yuan and Canadian dollar over the period 1957–71, which is part of the Bretton Woods era. We can see that the Japanese yen fluctuated within the limits around the par value of the exchange rate, which was allowed by the system. The Chinese yuan was also fixed to the dollar at the rate of 2.46. The big jump in the GBP/USD exchange rate reflects the 1967 devaluation of the pound, which was approved by the IMF as Britain demonstrated the presence of a persistent balance of payments deficit, but otherwise the behaviour of the exchange rate represents compliance with the Bretton Woods agreement. Canada, however, experimented with floating exchange rates until 1962 – it went back to a fixed exchange rate of 1.08 until 1970, when it started to allow its currency to depreciate against the US dollar. Out of the four countries, therefore, it was Canada, not China, that was non-compliant with the international monetary system in operation at that time.

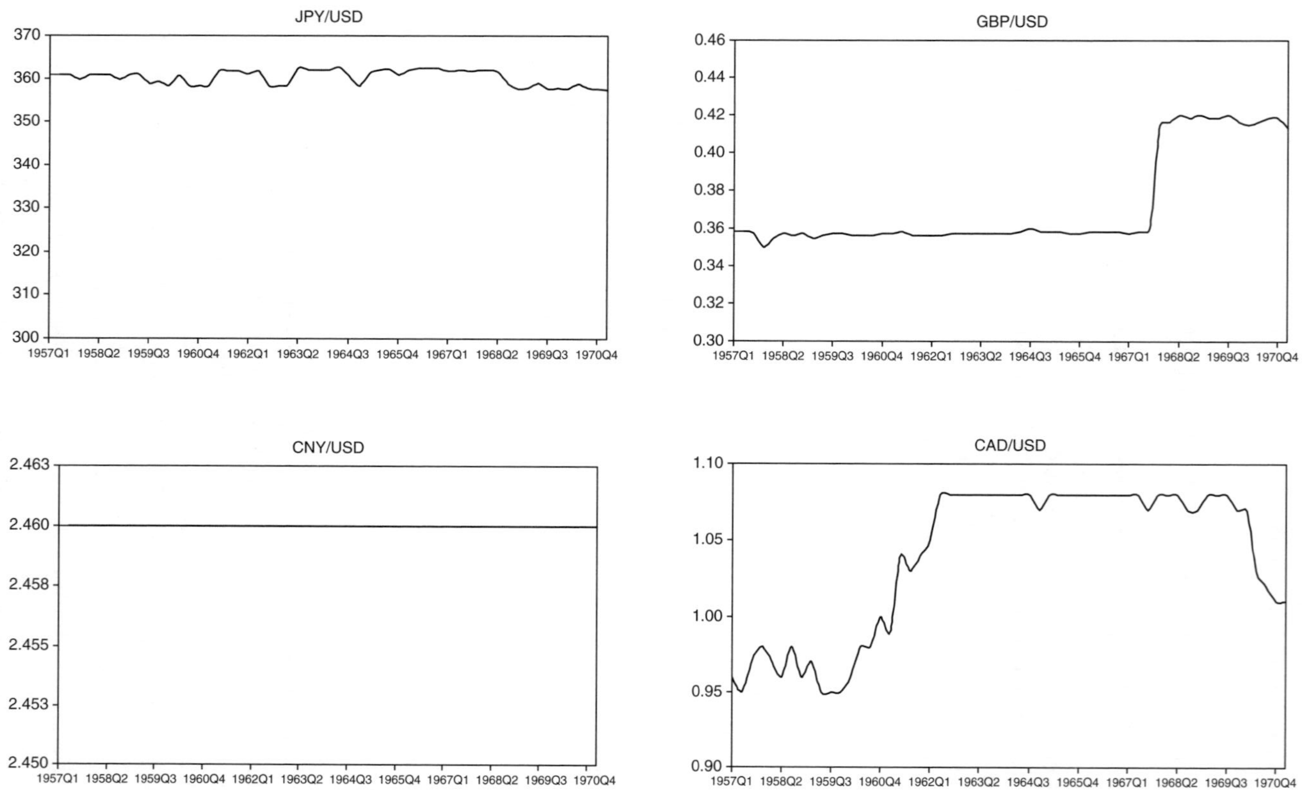

Figure 2.1 Exchange rates under the Bretton Woods system

The Bretton Woods system suffered from a number of problems that led to its eventual collapse. The first of these problems pertains to the adjustment mechanism (of the balance of payments). Governments had to demonstrate the existence of a fundamental disequilibrium in the balance of payments before they could adjust their exchange rates (Britain devalued the pound twice under this kind of arrangement, in 1949 and 1967). The adjustable-peg system lacked the stability, certainty and automaticity of the gold standard, and the flexibility of the free-floating system. The second problem is that under a system of fixed but adjustable exchange rates, speculation can be destabilizing because of the possibility of changing the par values of the currencies. When a currency is under pressure (perhaps because the country concerned is running out of reserves) it can only be devalued, motivating speculators to sell or short sell that currency. This is exactly what George Soros did in 1997 when he short sold (borrowed and sold) the Thai baht on a massive scale.

An important loophole in the Bretton Woods system was defects in the liquidity creation mechanism because it depended on the dollars issued by the US. In the early 1960s the prospect of a global liquidity shortage caused widespread concern in official circles as attention focused on proposals for new reserve creation mechanisms. This problem has led to the emergence of the so-called "Triffin Dilemma" or "Triffin Paradox" (Triffin, 1960). To avoid a liquidity shortage, the US would have to run a balance of payments deficit, and this would have undermined confidence in the dollar. To avoid speculation against the dollar the deficit would have to shrink, which would have created a liquidity shortage. So, it was a vicious circle. One solution to this problem was suggested in 1968, which was the creation of special drawing rights (SDRs) as an international currency. The SDR is a composite currency whose value (exchange rate) is calculated as a weighted average of the exchange rates of the currencies to which it is pegged. It is mainly used as a unit of account in transactions involving the International Monetary Fund. As we are going to see later, the SDR is back in the spotlight as concern mounts over the international role of the dollar as a reserve currency.

The Bretton Woods era can be divided into two periods: (i) the period of dollar shortage, 1944–58; and (ii) the period of dollar glut, 1958–71. The second period was characterized by a significant US balance of payments deficit at a time when the surplus countries (Germany and Japan) were resisting revaluation of their currencies. In 1962 France began to exchange dollars for gold despite the objection of the US. Not only were the French doubtful about the future value of the dollar, they also objected to the prominent role of the US in the Bretton Woods system. The French action led other countries to worry about whether sufficient gold would remain for them after the French had finished selling their dollars. The US felt severely constrained, being unable to change its exchange rate.

On 15 August 1971 the US responded to a record \$30 billion trade deficit by making the dollar inconvertible into gold as announced by President Richard Nixon. This action, similar to the action taken by Britain in 1931, marked the collapse of the Bretton Woods system. As *The Economist* (2011b) puts it, "the [Bretton Woods] system worked well for more than two decades, helped by the post-war economic boom" and that "it broke down because America refused to pay the domestic price for bearing the system's weight". According to *The Economist* (2011c), "Richard Nixon's place in history is secure" because "he was the president who, 40 years ago, severed the link between global currencies and gold and ended the fixed exchange rate system". It seems that the man did not make his reputation only on Watergate and Vietnam.

THE PRESENT SYSTEM

On 18 December 1971 the ten major industrial countries tried to save the Bretton Woods system by signing the Smithsonian Agreement in Washington, DC. The US agreed to raise the official price of gold to \$38/ounce but refused to restore the free convertibility of the dollar into gold. Other countries, in return, agreed to revalue their currencies against the dollar. Moreover, exchange rates were allowed to fluctuate within a wider band of ±2.5 per cent.

The Smithsonian Agreement, however, did not solve any of the fundamental defects of the Bretton Woods system. As a result, floating became widespread in 1973, while European countries experimented with the "Snake in the Tunnel". Floating exchange rates were legalized in January 1976, with ratification coming in 1978 when the Jamaica Accord was signed. The Accord allowed countries the freedom of choice of the exchange rate system they deemed appropriate for their economies, encouraging them not to resort to competitive devaluation. There was also an agreement to pursue domestic economic policies conducive to stability. The official price of gold was abolished, allowing it to fluctuate according to market forces.

A new Article IV of the IMF agreement was instated to deal with exchange rate regime choice and cooperation. This Article still governs exchange rate regime choice, which makes it central to our understanding of the current US–China dispute. Mussa (2007) believes that China is violating Article IV and that the IMF is not doing its job properly by neglecting to tell China that it is not compliant with the provisions of this

Article. The revised Article IV requires member countries (of the IMF) to (i) endeavour to direct their economic and financial policies towards the objective of fostering orderly economic growth and reasonable price stability, with due regard to their circumstances; (ii) promote stability by fostering orderly underlying economic and financial conditions and a monetary system that does not tend to produce erratic disruptions; (iii) avoid manipulating exchange rates or the international monetary system in order to prevent effective balance of payments adjustment or to gain an unfair competitive advantage over other members; and (iv) follow exchange policies that are compatible with these undertakings. Other provisions of Article IV require the following:

1. Each member country shall notify the IMF promptly of changes in its exchange rate arrangement.
2. Exchange rate arrangements may include (i) the maintenance by a member of a value for its currency in terms of the special drawing right or another denominator, other than gold, selected by the member; (ii) cooperative arrangements by which members maintain the value of their currencies in relation to the value of the currency or currencies of other members; and (iii) other exchange arrangements of a member's choice.
3. The IMF shall oversee the international monetary system in order to ensure its effective operation, and shall oversee the compliance of each member with its obligations under this Article.
4. In order to fulfil its functions the IMF shall exercise firm surveillance over the exchange rate policies of member countries, and shall adopt specific principles for the guidance of all members with respect to those policies.
5. Each member country shall provide the IMF with the information necessary for such surveillance and, when requested by the Fund, shall consult with it on the member's exchange rate policies.
6. The principles adopted by the IMF shall be consistent with cooperative arrangements by which members maintain the values of their currencies in relation to the value of the currency or currencies of other members, as well as with other exchange arrangements of a member's choice consistent with the purposes of Article IV.
7. These principles shall respect the domestic social and political policies of members, and in applying these principles the IMF shall pay due regard to the circumstances of members.

A major problem with the provisions of Article IV is the contradiction between the freedom to choose an exchange rate regime that is deemed suitable for the domestic economy and the avoidance of exchange rate "manipulation". If a country chooses a fixed but adjustable exchange rate regime, as under the Bretton Woods system, this country should be allowed to "manipulate" the exchange rate by changing the par value and/or by intervening in the foreign exchange market. Under the Bretton Woods system, intervention was mandatory to keep the exchange rate within the band prescribed by the system, but that was not called "manipulation". The contradiction in Article IV is that it gives countries the right to choose their exchange rate regimes while requiring them to avoid the means whereby the regime can be preserved. In the current debate it is the US Treasury, not the IMF, that has been labelling this or that country a "currency manipulator". It is, however, not "manipulation" that represents the violation of Article IV but rather adopting one arrangement and reporting another to the IMF. Scores of countries have been doing this. Note also that Article IV stresses that domestic circumstances are pivotal for policy formulation and that it does not define explicitly the term "manipulation"; for example, does quantitative easing constitute manipulation?

EXCHANGE RATE ARRANGEMENTS UNDER THE PRESENT SYSTEM

In response to Article IV of the IMF agreement, countries have adopted various exchange rate arrangements. The following is a brief description of the arrangements.

Exchange Arrangements with No Separate Legal Tender

Under this arrangement, the currency of another country circulates as the sole legal tender. Alternatively, a country may belong to a monetary or currency union in which the same legal tender is shared by the members of the union. In both cases this arrangement boils down to a tightly fixed exchange rate. Examples are the European countries using the euro as well as members of other currency unions.

Currency Board Arrangements

A currency board is an arrangement that is based on an explicit legislative commitment to exchange the domestic currency for a specified foreign currency at a fixed exchange rate, combined with restrictions on the issuing authority to ensure the fulfilment of its legal obligation. Until early 2002 Argentina opted for this arrangement, exchanging the peso for the US dollar on a one-to-one basis. Following the 2002 financial crisis in

Argentina, this arrangement was abolished as the peso was floated. Hong Kong and Estonia still have currency boards.

Other Conventional Fixed Peg Arrangements

These arrangements include pegging to a single currency and to a basket of currencies, such as the SDR. Under this arrangement, a country pegs its currency (formally or de facto) at a fixed exchange rate to a single currency or a basket of currencies, allowing the actual exchange rate to fluctuate within a narrow margin around a central rate (the rate determined by the arrangement). Examples are Bahrain (the US dollar) and Kuwait (undeclared basket of currencies). The objective of pegging to a single currency is to stabilize the bilateral exchange rate against that currency (bilateral exchange rates against other currencies remain volatile). Under a basket peg, bilateral exchange rates are volatile but the effective exchange rate is stabilized. An alternative system is that of pegged exchange rates with horizontal bands. In this case, the band within which the exchange rate is allowed to fluctuate is wider than ±1 per cent.

Crawling Pegs and Crawling Bands

Under a crawling peg, the exchange rate is adjusted periodically at a fixed, preannounced small rate or in response to changes in some quantitative indicators such as inflation. An arrangement of crawling bands requires the exchange rate to be maintained within a certain band around a central rate that is adjusted periodically at a fixed preannounced rate or in response to changes in some indicators. A question that may be raised here is whether or not the periodic adjustment constitutes "manipulation".

Managed Floating and Independent Floating

Under managed floating, the exchange rate is determined by market forces but the monetary authority intervenes actively in the foreign exchange market without specifying a path for the exchange rate. Under independent floating the exchange rate is determined by market forces and any intervention in the foreign exchange market aims at curbing exchange rate volatility.

Some Examples

Figure 2.2 shows the exchange rates against the dollar of Japan, Canada, China and Australia over the period covering the present (post-Bretton Woods) system. We can see that Japan and Canada have been on free

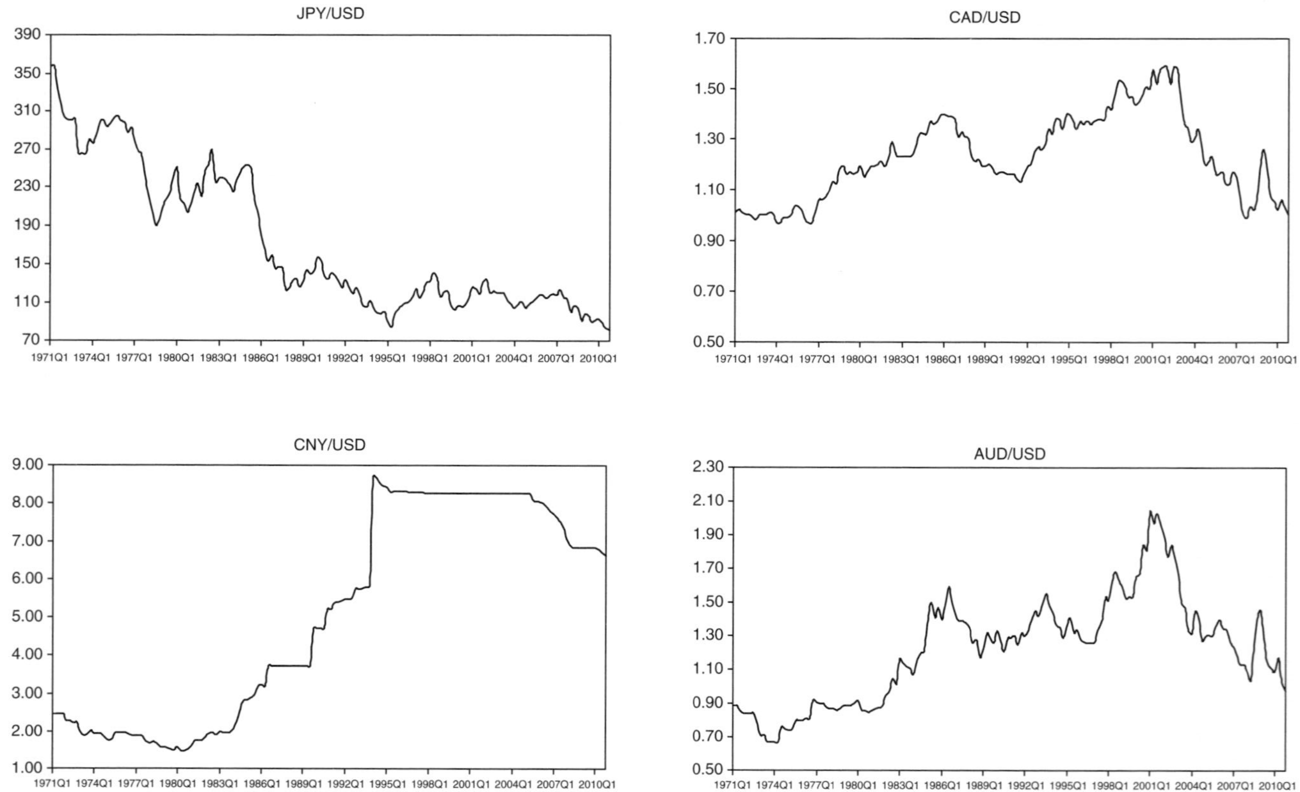

Figure 2.2 Exchange rates post-Bretton Woods

floating for the whole period. The Japanese yen has been appreciating persistently against the dollar, despite the appreciation of the dollar in the first half of the 1980s. In September 1985 the Plaza Accord was signed with the intention of intervening in the foreign exchange market to enforce depreciation of the dollar, and since then the yen has been appreciating persistently. It is this kind of rapid appreciation that China is currently worried about. The Canadian dollar, on the other hand, has been more stable, as the Canadians pursue a monetary policy that is conducive to the achievement of this objective (given that the US is Canada's main trading partner).

China went through a number of exchange rate regimes with three episodes of fixed exchange rates: 1986–9, 1995–2005 and 2008–10. In the third quarter of 2010 China resumed its policy of what resembles a crawling peg by allowing the yuan to appreciate gradually against the dollar. As for Australia, although one may get the impression that it has been on free floating all over the period, free floating was not used until the end of 1983. For a very short period of time the Australian dollar was pegged to the US dollar, but following the floating of major currencies, the Australian dollar was pegged to a basket reflecting trade patterns (hence the objective was to stabilize the trade-weighted effective exchange rate). The important message here is that variation in exchange rate arrangements throughout the period has been quite legitimate and well within the post-Bretton Woods rules.

RECENT DEVELOPMENTS

The currency crises of thc 1990s have led economists and policy makers to seek new designs for the "international financial architecture". In 1999, a group of 29 economists (for example, Paul Krugman), former central bankers (for example, Paul Volcker) and currency traders (for example, George Soros) produced a report sponsored by the US Council on Foreign Relations (Institute for International Economics, 1999). The report contained the following propositions:

- Improving incentives for sound policy by linking IMF loans to crisis-prevention efforts.
- Encouraging the imposition of holding period taxes on short-term capital flows in countries characterized by financial fragility.
- Encouraging private-sector burden sharing by introducing collective-action clauses in sovereign bond contracts, thus effectively making the private sector partly responsible for the consequences of sovereign bond issues.

- Discouraging fixed but adjustable exchange rates in favour of either managed floating or currency boards.
- Directing the IMF to lend less freely and to distinguish between country crises and systemic crises.
- Removing overlapping from the responsibilities of the IMF and the World Bank. The IMF should concentrate on macroeconomic issues, leaving the Bank to deal with structural aspects of development.

The international monetary system that was in place when the global financial crisis struck in 2007–8 was shaped by two main events that took place in the late 1990s: the Asian financial crisis of 1997–8 and the advent of the euro in 1999. This system can be seen as an evolution from the Bretton Woods system and the subsequent system, which was centred on three major floating currencies: US dollar, Japanese yen and German mark. At that time, Japan and Germany were the main creditors, financing the US current account deficit. The Asian financial crisis led to the emergence of a "revitalized US dollar area", encompassing the US and a new group of creditors comprising some Asian countries, particularly China, and the Gulf oil exporters. Dooley et al. (2003) call this arrangement the "revived Bretton Woods" system or "Bretton Woods II". The advent of the euro has provided a credible alternative to the US dollar, which has motivated the quest for a new international monetary system that is less dependent on the dollar.

The global financial crisis has prompted a re-examination of the international monetary system. The debate centres on (i) whether the present international monetary system is conducive to the build-up of global imbalances; (ii) the desirability of maintaining the status of the US dollar as the dominant international currency and the resulting Triffin dilemma; (iii) the need for a multipolar international monetary system based on national currencies or complemented by a global supranational reserve currency; (iv) the accumulation of foreign assets by countries; (v) the global demand for safe debt instruments, believed to be a cause of the global financial crisis; and (vi) excess capital flow volatility and contagion.

FIXED VERSUS FLEXIBLE EXCHANGE RATES

The debate of fixed versus flexible exchange rates is a prominent issue that international economists deal with regularly. No verdict has been reached, but an observer listening to one side of the story can be easily convinced that what has just been heard is the truth. And the "truth" may be that "flexible exchange rates are better" or that "fixed exchange rates are better", depending on which side of the story has just been told. Let us start with the arguments for flexible exchange rates:

- Under flexible exchange rates, adjustment of the balance of payments is smoother and less painful than under fixed rates. Flexible exchange rates move continuously and in small doses to restore equilibrium.
- Since flexible exchange rates move continuously in reaction to disequilibria in the balance of payments, large and persistent deficits do not arise. This in turn boosts confidence in the international monetary system, resulting in fewer attempts to readjust currency portfolios, and this can only result in calmer foreign exchange markets.
- Liquidity problems do not arise (or at least they are not as acute) under flexible exchange rates, because central banks do not need to hold foreign exchange reserves for the purpose of market intervention.
- Flexible exchange rates are more conducive to achieving free international trade because this system maintains equilibrium in the balance of payments, hence tariffs and other trade impediments will not be imposed.
- Flexible exchange rates are conducive to increased independence of policy, in the sense of allowing a country to follow policies that are different from those of its major trading partners. It is also claimed that, under flexible exchange rates, countries are insulated from what happens in other economies.
- Countries with flexible exchange rates are in a better position to cope with currency crises than those with fixed rates.

The arguments against flexible rates are:

- They cause uncertainty and inhibit international trade and investment because they affect the private sector's decision making process.
- Flexible exchange rates cause destabilizing speculation, accentuating the rise and fall of exchange rates.
- They are not suitable for small economies with undiversified export bases.
- They are not appropriate for countries without sophisticated financial systems, as a successful operation of such a system requires developed forward and futures markets.

- They are inflationary in a general sense, whereas fixed exchange rates provide anti-inflationary discipline.
- Flexible exchange rates are unstable in the sense that small moves can grow into extremely large disturbances.
- With flexible exchange rates, serious balance of payments difficulties could lead to a steep fall in the value of the domestic currency, which could adversely affect price stability and output in the short run.

So what is the verdict? The only answer to this question is that the jury is still out. This view is even expressed by the market-loving magazine, *The Economist*. In 1971 the magazine celebrated the demise of the fixed exchange rates system on the grounds that flexible exchange rates are less likely to cause disturbance than fixed rates. This is the same idea that was expressed by Friedman (1953) who argued that, subject to the adoption of "sensible" policies, speculators would act as a stabilizing force. In a re-examination of its welcoming stance towards flexible exchange rates, *The Economist* (2011c) pointed out that "exchange rates have been more volatile than Friedman might have expected". It is concluded that "the lesson of the past 40 years is that neither a fixed nor a floating-rate system is a panacea".

What is typically overlooked in this debate is that the arguments for and against fixed or flexible exchange rates cannot be generalized. A clear-cut conclusion may be reached if the debate is related to a particular country or a group of countries. A related point is that exchange rate regime choice is a sovereign decision that is up to the country concerned. The IMF may provide advice on the suitability or otherwise of a particular exchange rate regime but the country concerned has (or should have) the final decision. The arguments for and against flexible exchange rates will be re-examined in Chapter 8 from a Chinese perspective.

THE FUTURE OF THE INTERNATIONAL MONETARY SYSTEM

The present international monetary system has its loopholes and weaknesses. The future of the system is a hot topic, both in professional and academic circles, but there seems to be no consensus view on the issue. Liu (2002) expresses a very strong view against the current dollar-based international monetary system. He writes:

> World trade is now a game in which the US produces dollars and the rest of the world produces things that dollars can buy. The world's interlinked economies

> no longer trade to capture a comparative advantage; they compete in exports to capture needed dollars to service dollar-denominated foreign debts and to accumulate dollar reserves to sustain the exchange value of their domestic currencies. To prevent speculative and manipulative attacks on their currencies, the world's central banks must acquire and hold dollar reserves in corresponding amounts to their currencies in circulation. The higher the market pressure to devalue a particular currency, the more dollar reserves its central bank must hold. This creates a built-in support for a strong dollar that in turn forces the world's central banks to acquire and hold more dollar reserves, making it stronger. This phenomenon is known as dollar hegemony, which is created by the geopolitically constructed peculiarity that critical commodities, most notably oil, are denominated in dollars. Everyone accepts dollars because dollars can buy oil.

Liu (2002) makes several recommendations "to save the world from the path of impending disaster": (i) promoting awareness that excessive dependence on exports merely to service dollar debt is self-destructive to any economy; (ii) promoting a new global finance architecture away from the dollar hegemony; (iii) promoting the application of the state theory of money (that the value of money is ultimately backed by a government's authority to levy taxes) to provide needed domestic credit for sound economic development; and (iv) restructuring international economic relations towards aggregate demand management away from the current overemphasis on predatory supply expansion through redundant competition.

Choosing Another National Currency?

One solution to the dollar hegemony problem is to use another national currency as the international currency. Cooper (2009) considers this issue and concludes that "none of the other leading currencies in the world today is ready to replace the US dollar in its international role". He disputes the claims about the gains that accrue to the US as the issuer of a national currency that is widely used internationally (what Charles de Gaulle called an "exorbitant privilege"), stressing minor gains from seigniorage: ease of financing deficits and thriving financial markets. The World Bank (2011) estimates the seigniorage benefits accruing to the US to have been about $90 billion in 2010. Liu (2004) believes that "China is in a position to kick start a new international finance architecture that will serve international trade better", which can be done by requiring payment for Chinese exports in yuan, thus making it an alternative reserve currency.

The problem here is that replacing one national currency with another does not address the issue of "an asymmetry in a system that at least formally and legally (as in the United Nations Charter and most international treaties) treats all nations as equal" (Cooper, 2009). Three possible courses of action are available as alternatives to the use of a national reserve currency: returning to the gold standard, extending the role of the SDR and the use of a global currency.

Back to the Gold Standard?

Several factors have contributed to the revival of interest in the gold standard since the 1980s: (i) dissatisfaction with the instability associated with floating; (ii) a greater acceptability of the monetarist theories of inflation; (iii) political attitudes supporting balanced budgets and the operation of market forces; and (iv) the election in 1980 of Ronald Reagan, who in pre-election speeches supported the idea of going back to the gold standard.

In particular, it is believed that the gold standard provides some sort of discipline against excessive monetary expansion and, therefore, inflation. However, it is unlikely that the gold standard will solve the problems of the current international monetary system. In today's multi-financial centre world, short-term capital flows are likely to move erratically in a destabilizing fashion from one centre to another, hindering the balance of payments adjustment mechanism. We have also seen that the classical gold standard did not really work as envisaged in theory, for reasons including non-conformity to the rules of the game. Another problem is that at today's gold prices the amount of gold available may not be adequate to allow countries to convert their dollar reserves into gold reserves. A good point in favour of the gold standard is that it excluded the possibility of countries creating money out of thin air, which is what quantitative easing is all about.

An SDR-Based International Monetary System?

Another course of action is to adopt an SDR-based international monetary system, which requires the promotion of the use of the SDR (leaving it as a currency basket) as a key reserve asset. This proposal is not new; it has triggered a rich debate over the past four decades. A review of the main arguments for and against an enhanced role for the SDR is provided in, for example, Carney (2010) and IMF (2011). The proponents of this course of action point out that, being a basket of major currencies, the SDR would (i) be a more stable store of value and unit of account than its constituent currencies individually; (ii) enhance the process of dealing with exchange rate volatility in a more multipolar currency world; (iii) reduce the likelihood of exchange rate adjustment for currencies pegged to it compared with pegs to national currencies; and (iv) enable the pricing decisions of risky assets to be based on "global" monetary conditions rather than on the monetary policy stance prevailing in an individual economy. For the SDR to develop into a reserve asset, its liquidity must be increased significantly, not only through greater issuance by the IMF but also by developing a private SDR market.

Aiyar (2009) argues that the SDR cannot rival the dollar as a reserve currency for two reasons: (i) it is a derivative of four national currencies (and a derivative is not a currency, as he claims); and (ii) unlike the US government (the issuer of the dollar) the IMF (the issuer of the SDR) has no GDP or taxing power. Williamson (2009) responds to the first argument by correctly pointing out that several national currencies are pegged to baskets or even to single currencies, hence they are derivatives yet acceptable national currencies. He responds to Aiyar's second argument by pointing out that the moneyness of an asset depends on its acceptability as a medium of exchange, not on the ability of the issuer to tax its citizens. Williamson concludes that both the US and China might benefit from an enhanced role for the SDR.

A Supranational Currency?

An option that aims to overcome the limitations of the currency basket is to create a new supranational currency, issued by a supranational central bank and floating against national currencies. This currency would serve as "outside fiat money"; it actually resembles the "bancor", which was proposed by John Maynard Keynes as head of the UK delegation during the Bretton Woods negotiations.

The idea has its pros and cons. The attraction of the concept lies in the undoubted convenience of a single currency, but that comes at the cost of losing the exchange rate as a policy instrument that can be used if, for example, there is an abrupt fall in the demand for exports. In setting the costs against the benefits, the crucial factors are openness to trade and free movement of factors of production. A small open economy has more to gain from the convenience provided by a single currency. Of the many questions surrounding this proposal, those regarding its feasibility stand out most. Would countries be willing to give up part of their monetary sovereignty to a supranational central bank at the global level? Would the incentive to surrender sovereignty differ for large and small countries? What would be a realistic time horizon for the introduction of such a challenging proposal? What intermediate steps would need to be taken, and what further measures would be needed in the long run?

A Chinese Perspective

It may be useful at this stage to consider a Chinese perspective on reforming the international monetary system. In the lead-up to the 2009 G20 London summit, the Chinese government issued a speech by respected central bank governor Zhou Xiaochuan, entitled "Reflections on Reforming the international monetary system" (Zhou, 2009). In the speech, Governor Zhou asserted that the world needs an international currency option "that is disconnected to individual nations and is able to remain stable in the long run, thus removing the inherent deficiencies caused by using credit-based national currencies". The main message of the speech is that it is in the world's interest to reform the international monetary system, namely by strengthening and expanding the role of the SDR as a multilateral reserve currency. Some analysts suggest that the governor's speech is important because it marks the first time the Chinese leadership has publicly issued such a high-profile statement of concern about the international monetary system. The speech provides the first public indication that China is seriously reconsidering its reliance on the dollar and options for reducing its international monetary dependence on the US.

Zhou's speech on reforming the international monetary system focused on the Triffin Dilemma, the root cause of the global financial crisis, according to many Chinese policy makers and academics. Zhou's reading of Triffin is that when the currency of one country is used as the global reserve currency – as is the case with the US dollar – the currency-issuing country faces the dilemma of making decisions on domestic monetary policy that serves national interests at the expense of the global economy. The contention is that an international monetary system based on a national currency cannot simultaneously sustain both the growth of reserves and confidence in the currency. The Chinese view is that these "externalities" contribute to excess liquidity throughout the world, which resulted in overly relaxed US monetary policy and ultimately the global financial crisis. According to Zhou, "although the crisis may not necessarily be an intended result of the issuing authorities, it is an inevitable outcome of the institutional flaws". Thus it is argued that the "dollar standard system" has a tendency to cause imbalances and it lacks an effective adjustment mechanism. Jianye Wang, the chief economist of China Export–Import Bank and a former senior economist at the IMF, suggests that the "institutional drawbacks" of the existing international monetary system have been "a contributing factor" to the global financial crisis (Wang, 2009).

CONCLUDING REMARKS

The future role of the dollar in the international monetary system is uncertain. Perhaps the most troublesome sign is that Zimbabwe, which in early 2009 resorted to using the dollar as legal tender because of hyperinflation, is wondering whether it is time to "ditch" the dollar for fear of importing "America's macroeconomic recklessness" (*The Economist*, 2011d). Zimbabwe is in fact seriously considering a switch to the South African rand. *The Economist* (2011d) correctly argues that "it cannot be a good sign that even Zimbabweans are now considering alternatives".

Irrespective of how the international monetary system will be shaped in the future, current Chinese policies do not constitute a violation of the rules of the present system. What China is doing with respect to exchange rate regime choice is perfectly consistent with the available options under the current IMF rules. Although it is not clear what "manipulation" means, Article IV of the IMF charter gives China the right to choose its current exchange rate regime and to adopt the policies necessary to maintain the regime. This is an issue that we will return to in Chapter 8.

3. International trading and financial relations

INTRODUCTION

In this chapter we examine some of the ideas, doctrines and policies that govern international trading and financial relations and trace their historical origins. These ideas, doctrines and policies are relevant to the current US–China trade dispute. We will consider the concept of "currency war" because the US accuses China of initiating a currency war by preventing the yuan from appreciating, while China accuses the US of indulging in a currency war through quantitative easing. We also consider the related concepts of free trade, protectionism and mercantilism, which acquired renewed interest following the global financial crisis and the Great Recession of 2009. Actually, China has been repeatedly accused of adopting mercantilist, protectionist and anti-free trade policies. However, the fact remains that countries using these terms in rhetoric directed against other countries do not practise what they preach.

CURRENCY WARS

A currency war is also known as "competitive devaluation", "competitive depreciation" and what Tim Geithner calls "competitive non-appreciation", when he once referred to the Chinese reluctance to allow the yuan to appreciate (*The Economist*, 2010a). It is a state of affairs where countries compete against each other to weaken their currencies, hoping that a cheap currency will make exports more competitive internationally. This action is typically taken with the intention of supporting domestic industry, boosting production and alleviating unemployment; whether or not it works is an entirely different matter. The mechanism is not straightforward: changes in exchange rates are supposed to lead to changes in the prices of exports and imports and consequently changes in the volumes of exports and imports. As we are going to see later, many factors inhibit the transmission of the effect from the exchange rate to the volumes of exports and imports and hence to the trade balance.

Furthermore, a weak currency may create problems that outweigh its benefits.

While "competitive devaluation" implies an intentional action taken by a country to reduce the value of its currency by adjusting a fixed exchange rate, "competitive depreciation" implies that no action is taken to oppose market forces or that some action is taken to make market forces work in such a direction as to bring about a decline in the market value of a floating currency. Geithner's term "competitive non-appreciation" is his way of playing with words to make the situation sound more dramatic. What it implies is the act of preventing a floating currency from appreciating as required by market forces. While it may be possible to accelerate currency appreciation or depreciation by policy actions that reinforce market forces, historical experience tells us that trying to prevent appreciation or depreciation when market forces warrant appreciation or depreciation is likely to fail. In other words intervention is more likely to succeed when it is not directed at resisting a change dictated by market forces.

Currency wars have been rare throughout most of modern history as countries typically recognize the problems associated with weak currencies and opt instead to maintain relatively strong currencies. Alternatively, most countries have been content to allow the values of their currencies to be determined by market forces, perhaps because they have realized the impotence of actions taken against market forces. The most widely recognized episode of currency war occurred in the 1930s in the midst of the Great Depression. Opinion is divided on whether or not the world is currently witnessing a currency war that started in 2010 in the aftermath of the global financial crisis. In fact there are those who hold the view that even the 1930s did not witness a currency war.

What is a Currency War?

A currency war has been defined differently and with various degrees of dramatization. In one definition (a Chinese definition), a currency war refers to "the situation where one nation, relying on its strong economic power, buffets its competitors and seizes other nations' wealth through monetary and foreign exchange policies". It is, therefore, "a form of economic warfare with cold premeditation, specific purpose and considerable destructive power" (Xinhuanet, 2010). This is a very strong definition that is unlikely to describe the current state of affairs or even the situation in the 1930s. Although the US has such power under the present international monetary system of dollar hegemony, this power is not related to a currency war. With and without a currency war, the US has the privilege of being able to print dollars without a gold back-up and to exchange those dollars for the goods produced by other countries.

The term "currency war" is sometimes used with meanings that are not related to competitive devaluation. Akita and White (2009) use the term to refer to competition between Japan and China for their currencies to be used as the preferred legal tender in parts of Asia in the years leading up to the Second Sino-Japanese War. In his book, *Currency Wars*, the Chinese economist Hongbing Song uses the term to refer to a "situation where unscrupulous bankers lend to an emerging country and then speculate against its currency, trying to force it down in value" (Song, 2007). In another book that has the same title, John Cooley uses the term to refer to the desire of the monetary authorities of a certain country to protect the domestic currency from forgers, whether they are straightforward criminals or agents of foreign governments, attempting to devalue the currency by flooding markets with counterfeit notes (Cooley, 2008). This is an act of economic sabotage as it can create hyperinflation. It has been reported that, during the period when sanctions and the no-fly zone were imposed on Iraq in 1991–2003, the Americans used the air force to "bomb" Iraq with local currency banknotes for this purpose.

The term "currency war" is typically used in conjunction with the term "beggar thy neighbour", which describes policies aimed at benefiting one country at the expense of other countries. The term was originally devised to characterize policies designed to cure domestic depression and unemployment by shifting effective demand away from imports towards domestic goods, either through restrictions on imports or by competitive devaluation. Thus a moderate definition of a currency war is that it is a state of affairs whereby countries facing internal economic difficulties devalue their currencies to simulate exports and create more jobs. Wang and Fu (2010) define a currency war as "actions countries take to drive down the exchange rate of their own currencies, hoping to gain competitive advantage in export and consequently protect or expand the shares of their related industries in the global market". For the purpose of this book, the term "currency war" is taken to mean a race to the weakest currency; hence it requires a large number of countries to engage in such an endeavour simultaneously.

The Tools of Currency War

A currency war involves forced currency devaluation or depreciation, which means that for a country to be a successful "currency warrior", it must have some control over its exchange rate and the ability to move this exchange rate in the desired direction. This ability depends, in part, on the international monetary system, insofar as it determines exchange rate regimes, and on the prevailing market conditions. For example, a country with a fixed exchange rate can, in theory at least, change the par (or declared) value of its currency directly. Flexible exchange rates, on the other hand, are determined by market forces, which means that for a country to be successful in pushing its currency one way or another it must be able to oppose market forces if they act in the opposite direction to the desired change. The tools used for this purpose include changes in interest rates, foreign exchange market intervention and quantitative easing.

During the 1930s, countries had relatively more direct control over their exchange rates through the actions of their central banks. For one thing, a recognized international monetary system did not exist following the collapse of the gold exchange standard in 1931 when Britain abolished the convertibility of the pound into gold. Furthermore, there were stringent capital controls, segmented markets and not much in the way of speculative capital flows. Direct devaluation of currencies was easy at that time, providing an environment that facilitated the act of currency war. Under the Bretton Woods system, however, countries were on fixed but adjustable exchange rates without a licence to devalue as they wished. A country could devalue its currency only if such an action was approved by the IMF on the grounds that the country could demonstrate that it had a chronic balance of payments deficit and that devaluation was the only way out.

Following the collapse of the Bretton Woods system in the early 1970s, the move towards free-floating currencies gave more power to market forces in determining exchange rates. Unless a country has very strong capital controls, the exchange rate of its currency is essentially set by market forces, which is exactly the reason why a currency war cannot be conducted this way under the present circumstances. However, central banks may resort to foreign exchange market intervention to change the values of their currencies by buying or selling them against other currencies (typically against a key intervention currency such as the US dollar). The post-1971 history tells us that, in the absence of stringent capital controls, market forces dominate, which weakens the effectiveness of intervention.

Starting in 1981, the dollar went on a relentless upward trend, reaching an all-time high in February 1985, despite concerted intervention by the central banks of major countries. Intervention is often portrayed to have succeeded following the Plaza meeting of September 1985, but that success was a success only because of a reversal of market conditions as portfolio managers started to unwind saturated dollar positions, starting in March 1985. By early 1987, the dollar had lost all of the gains it made during the period 1981–5. In 1992, the Bank of England failed to stem the decline of the pound within the European Monetary System despite the loss of most of its reserves and the raising of the interest rate by five percentage points. And we all know what happened when the Thai authorities tried to oppose the market forces unleashed by George Soros in 1997. However, a central bank may be in a position to talk down the value of its currency by hinting at future action that will discourage speculators from betting on the appreciation of the currency. Direct intervention in the foreign exchange market works only if it reinforces an already established market trend, simply because the foreign exchange market is too big for any central bank or a group of central banks.

Another means whereby the value of the domestic currency can be reduced is quantitative easing, which has become common in the aftermath of the global financial crisis and the Great Recession. This practice has been adopted by the US, Japan, the UK and to a lesser extent the Eurozone. Quantitative easing involves the creation of money (by running the printing press faster, just like the Germans did in the 1920s) and injecting the newly created money into the domestic economy, typically by buying securities from banks and other financial institutions. The underlying idea is that the new money will flow (in the form of loans) from banks to other areas of the economy where they are needed, boosting spending, production and investment. Specifically, long-term bonds are bought with newly printed money, pushing up prices and reducing yields, thus providing a boost to growth when short-term interest rates are close to zero. *The Economist* (2011e) describes quantitative easing as "an ugly name for a simple idea".

Countries that are in the best position to indulge in quantitative easing on a large scale are those that have a reserve currency or a currency that is actively traded (the US, Japan, the Eurozone and the UK have the most actively traded currencies), otherwise there is the risk of a speculation-triggered runaway depreciation. For example, issuing excessive amounts of dollars leads to depreciation that is partially offset by demand for the dollar to settle oil transactions or to buy US securities.

Quantitative easing may affect the underlying currency directly, in a process that is simple and intuitive: the more you produce of something the less valuable it becomes. This is why countries producing excessive amounts of money suffer from hyperinflation and rapid currency depreciation. It is a prediction of the monetary model of exchange rates that growth in the money supply leads to a proportional depreciation of the domestic currency (see, for example, Moosa and Bhatti, 2010). Quantitative easing may also lead to currency depreciation in two indirect ways. First, it encourages speculators to believe that the currency will depreciate further if quantitative easing is maintained, particularly if it is well publicized. Acting on this belief, they take short positions on the currency (they borrow the currency and sell it), which brings it down further.

Secondly, the large increase in the domestic money supply reduces domestic interest rates through the so-called liquidity effect (the availability of funds for borrowing reduces the cost of borrowing, that is, interest rates).

The interest rate effect works on the assumption that interest rates in countries indulging in quantitative easing are likely to decline to a lower level than those in countries that are not. The interest rate differential creates the conditions for "carry trade", a financial operation whereby market participants seeking profit borrow a low-interest currency and invest in a high-interest currency (for example, Moosa, 2008a, 2010b). Because the operation involves selling the currency used for quantitative easing, this currency depreciates. Whether or not an increase in the money supply leads to lower interest rates is questionable. A monetary expansion may lead to higher inflation and/or higher inflationary expectations, thereby leading to higher rather than lower interest rates. The direct effect channel sounds more plausible. However, the carry trade argument may still be valid because of the expectation of depreciation of the funding currency, that is, the currency denominating the short position.

Bill Gross, who manages a $237 billion fund, thinks that quantitative easing is like a "Ponzi scheme", arguing that he will not buy Treasuries until the Fed stops doing it (*The Economist*, 2011f). Although the Fed announces when it will end a quantitative easing programme, getting out of it is not that easy. Bringing the programme to an end cannot be achieved by putting an end to the buying of bonds – it must also involve offloading the bonds already bought, otherwise the central bank will have a permanently bigger balance sheet. This is not easy, given the value of the Treasuries the Fed has accumulated, which is estimated by *The Economist* (2011f) to be around $1.3 trillion. In short, it is easy to start quantitative easing but difficult to get out of it.

While there is rampant debate about whether or not quantitative easing works, little attention has been given to the issue of who should do it. Normally it is the central bank, but *The Economist* (2011e) suggests that it can be done by the Treasury and that this was actually tried in 1961 during the presidency of John F. Kennedy. To reduce long-term yields, the government sells short-term bills and uses the proceeds to buy long-term bonds, which brings about a twist in the yield curve. If there is no coordination between the central bank and the Treasury, quantitative easing will not have the desired effect.

The History of Currency War

Throughout history, governments slowly devalued their currencies by reducing their intrinsic values, that is, the actual value of the metal used to mint coins. This was done by reducing the amount of gold in a coin or by switching from gold to cheaper metals. The objective was not to boost exports but rather to exploit the difference between the face value of the currency and its intrinsic value, which is called "seigniorage". For example, switching from a gold dollar coin to a silver dollar coin leaves the face value unchanged (one dollar) but the intrinsic value declines because silver is cheaper than gold. Hence the difference between the intrinsic value and the face value (seigniorage) increases. This kind of practice was used predominantly to finance war or pay off debt; a notable example is the substantial devaluations that occurred during the Napoleonic wars.

A currency war is recognized to have erupted in the 1930s following the abolition of the convertibility of the pound into gold in 1931. Competitive devaluation became prevalent as a means of boosting exports and reducing unemployment. As a result, the currency war of the 1930s had an adverse effect on all countries as exchange rates became highly volatile and international trade plummeted. That currency war was conducted through direct devaluation because the foreign exchange market was not as big then as it is now, and because there were no rules to regulate currency devaluation as under the Bretton Woods system. However, some economists and economic historians dispute the proposition that competitive devaluation was prevalent in the 1930s. Irwin (2011a) argues that "countries did not deliberately devalue their currencies in the 1930s to give their exports a competitive advantage". Instead, he argues, "countries fought the exchange market pressure on their currency by raising interest rates and borrowing emergency reserves from other central banks in a valiant effort to prop up their currency's value". For example, Britain resisted selling pressure on the pound for weeks after decoupling from gold, but eventually decided that it was a losing battle. This view boils down to saying that what happened in the 1930s was a trade war fought by resorting to protectionism rather than currency devaluation.

From the end of World War II until about 1971, the Bretton Woods system of fixed but adjustable exchange rates curtailed the power of individual countries to engage in competitive devaluation, which was one of the design objectives of the system's architects. Under that system, countries were allowed to devalue their currencies only with the approval of the IMF and after demonstrating that the would-be devaluing country suffered from a chronic balance of payments deficit. Furthermore, there was little incentive for major countries to devalue even if it had been possible because global growth was generally strong in that period. Currency wars take place when economic conditions are bad.

While some of the conditions that are conducive to a currency war were in place at various points throughout the post-1973 period, countries generally had contrasting priorities. At no point in time was there an adequate number of countries simultaneously wanting to devalue their currencies for a currency war to break out. While it is tempting to think that the decoupling of the dollar from gold in 1971 and its subsequent devaluation could have triggered a currency war, countries were predominantly attempting to maintain the strength of their currencies in the face of market forces, including the UK in 1992 and Asian countries during the 1997–8 financial crisis. The fact remains that countries want to see their currencies neither too strong nor too weak.

The Asian crisis shattered faith in free market thinking among developing and emerging countries, which subsequently began intervening in the foreign exchange market more actively to build up foreign reserves. No currency war resulted because developed countries were (at least initially) happy to have access to cheap imports of manufactured goods from developing countries. The expanding current account deficit of the US was accepted by free market economists and policy makers such as the former Fed Chairman Alan Greenspan and the then US Treasury Secretary Paul O'Neill. The idea was that the current account deficit was a reflection of the capital account surplus and that as long as countries exporting to the US continued to buy US financial assets (Treasury securities to be precise) there was nothing to worry about.

This state of affairs was labelled by some economists "Bretton Woods II", which is a strange name for a system encompassing flexible exchange rates (Bretton Woods I was a system of fixed exchange rates). The situation was described as a new international system involving interdependence between countries with high savings in Asia lending and exporting to developed countries (Dooley et al., 2003, 2009). Some observers, however, have described "Bretton Woods II" as a "fiction" and called for the elimination of the structural imbalances that underlie it, namely the chronic US current account deficit (for example, Martin Wolf, 2010). Those thinking along these lines typically blame developing countries (most notably China) for trade imbalances, which is outrageous, to say the least. If developed countries, or some of them, decided to give up their manufacturing industry and import manufactured goods from developing countries, they have only themselves to blame.

Mixed Views on the Status Quo

The second major episode of currency war was supposed to have broken out in 2009 or 2010 and continues until the time of writing. On 27 September 2010, Brazil's finance minister, Guido Mantega, said that there were concerns of an "international currency war" (Bloomberg,

2010a). Some financial journalists agree with this view, referring to foreign exchange market intervention by various countries seeking to weaken their currencies (for example, Martin Wolf, 2010).

The former IMF Managing Director, Dominique Strauss-Kahn, and the US Treasury Secretary, Tim Geithner, were reported as saying that the risk of a genuine currency war breaking out was low. However, by early October 2010, Strauss-Kahn was warning that the risk of a currency war was real. He also suggested that "using currencies as weapons is not a solution [and] it can even lead to a very bad situation", and that "there's no domestic solution to a global problem" (Bloomberg, 2010a). What is really happening is an escalating rhetorical conflict between the US and China over the valuation of the yuan.

In the middle of October 2010, finance ministers congregated in Washington DC for an IMF meeting where talk of currency wars was rampant, particularly coming from those believing that weaker currencies would hurt the global economy amidst the global financial crisis and when global growth was already slowing down. As expected, China was the target of criticism for "failing to revalue the yuan rapidly". Canadian Finance Minister Jim Flaherty declared that "this is a crucial time that we need to address the commitment of our leaders to free trade, that we avoid protectionist measures". Tim Geithner added that "global rebalancing is not progressing as well as needed to avoid threats to the global economic recovery", meaning that China should somehow do something about its surplus with the US (Bloomberg, 2010b). Various finance ministers said that the IMF should endeavour to reduce the chance of a currency war by "encouraging initiatives to expand national economies without hurting that of other countries", again implying that China's growth should not hurt the US. The IMF, in turn, urged most developed countries to boost exports and advised some emerging countries (meaning China) to enhance domestic consumption and let their currencies appreciate. Dominique Strauss-Kahn said that the IMF would highlight the linkages between economies as part of a "systemic stability initiative" (Bloomberg, 2010c).

Australia's Federal Treasurer, Wayne Swan, played down rumours of currency war, saying that finance ministers were working in a coordinated way to deal with "exchange rate reform". However, the shadow government's finance minister, Andrew Robb, warned that with some countries (meaning China) deliberately devaluing their currencies, other countries may retaliate, thus initiating a "trade war", and he urged Swan to alert major countries to the "very damaging implications of a currency war" (ABC, 2010). Being "more royal than the royals", Robb was beating the drums of currency war by claiming that China was deliberately devaluing its currency, when China has actually been allowing its currency to appreciate slowly since July 2005. Robb would have been more accurate to blame the Americans for hurting Australian retailers. As a result of quantitative easing and carry trade, the Australian dollar has soared in value against the US dollar, prompting a wave of internet shopping by Australian consumers with adverse consequences for the bottom line of Australian retailers. Unlike Robb, Swan has shown considerable wisdom by recognizing the strategic importance of China for the Australian economy. He reportedly refused to buy the US-sponsored proposition that "the global economy's imbalances were largely Beijing's fault" and declared that "we're not joining Washington's currency war to rescue the US economy" (Stutchbury, 2010).

As of October 2010, the majority view from senior policy makers and journalists is that "currency war" is too strong a phrase for the current situation, though there is a risk of further escalation. We will return to the question of whether or not the world is currently witnessing a currency war, but before doing so we will examine the actions taken by individual countries and the implications for the recent behaviour of exchange rates.

Recent Individual Country Practices

Figure 3.1 shows the exchange rates against the US dollar of the yen, euro, pound, Australian dollar, yuan, Brazilian real, Chilean peso and Thai baht since December 2007. Figure 3.2 shows the exchange rate of the dollar against the SDR and the nominal effective exchange rate (NEER). These graphs will help us put into perspective the forthcoming discussion. It is important to note that in Figure 3.1 the exchange rates are measured in national currency units per dollar, which means that a decline in the exchange rate implies dollar depreciation, and vice versa. The same applies to Figure 3.2.

The US, and to a lesser extent the UK, share a position where they have actively-traded currencies and twin deficits (current account and budget deficits). The belief that weak currencies can eliminate current account deficits led them to engage in quantitative easing on a massive scale, putting downward pressure on their currencies, which depreciated as a result. Geithner has made it clear that a weaker dollar would be in the (US) "national interest" (for example, Butler, 2010). As a result of repeated announcements by the Federal Reserve Chairman Ben Bernanke of the possibility of further easing of US monetary policy, the dollar has been depreciating even against the pound and the euro (and in effective terms, as shown in Figure 3.2). The US must have been engaged in quantitative easing on a more massive scale than the UK and the Eurozone. For example, Buiter and Rahbari (2011) use two measures of quantitative

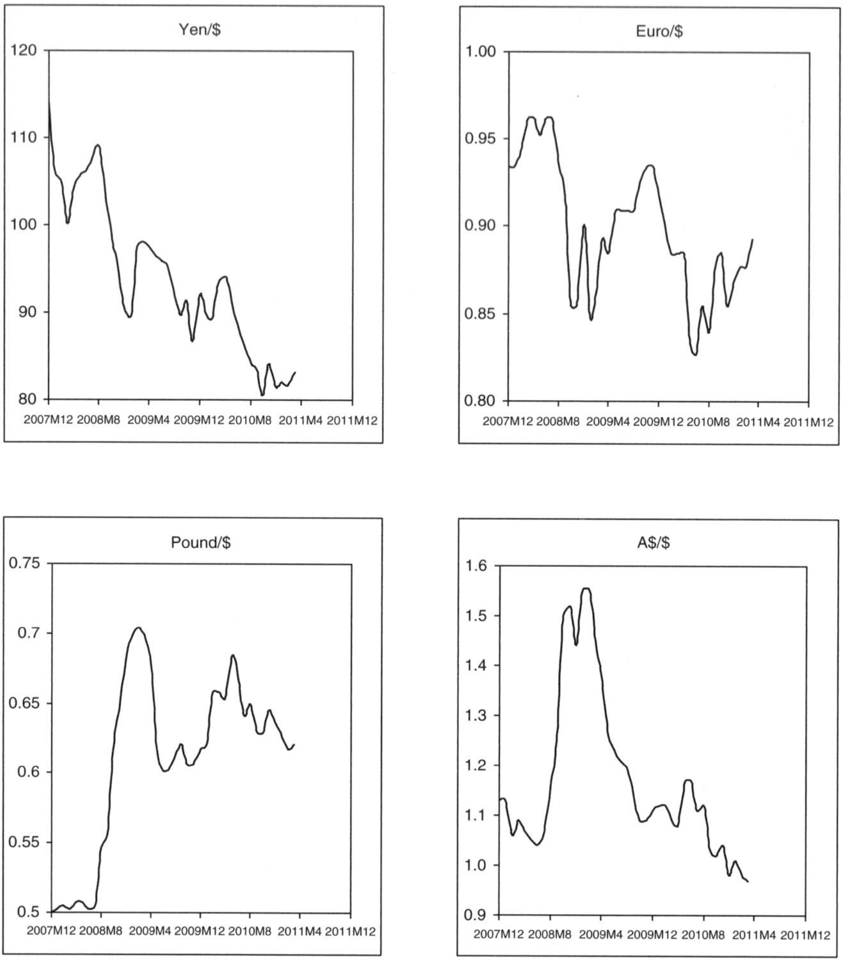

Figure 3.1 Bilateral exchange rates against the US dollar

easing (relative monetary base and relative balance sheet size, both as a percentage of GDP, for the Fed vis-à-vis a trade weighted average of foreign central banks) to show that "the degree of quantitative easing in the US was much higher than in the rest of the world".

It is however against the currencies of Japan, Australia and developing countries that the dollar has depreciated massively. China has since May 2010 resumed its policy of allowing the yuan to appreciate gradually against the dollar, a policy that was initiated in July 2005. Therefore, if anyone is initiating a currency war, it is the US. The danger of such a

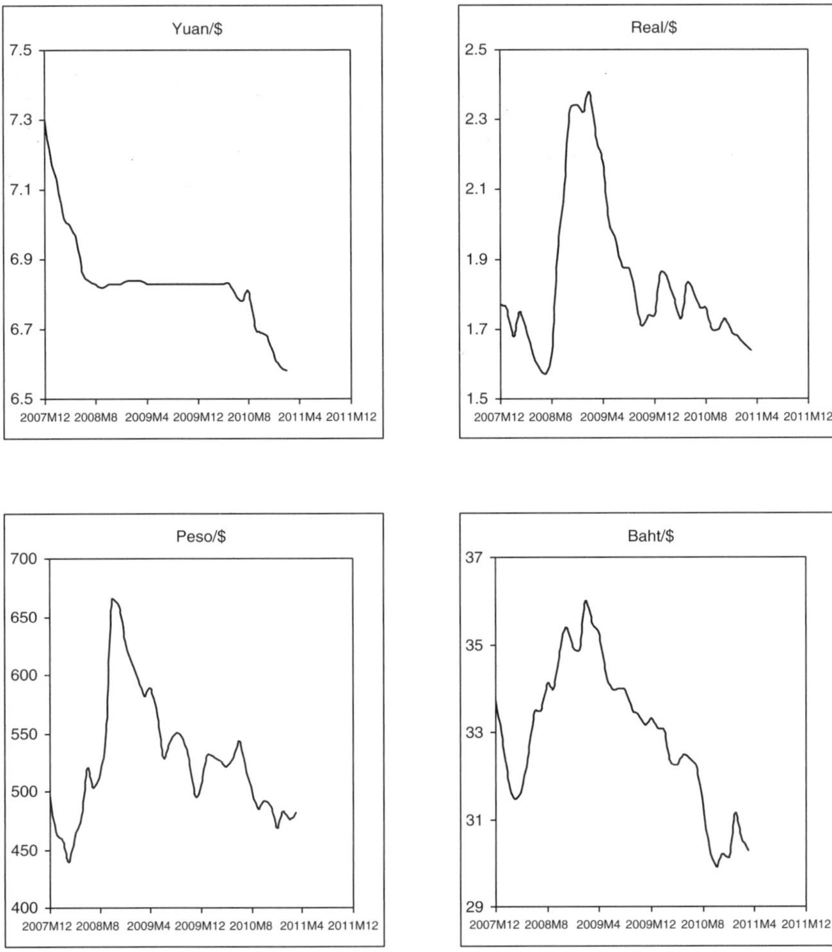

Figure 3.1 (continued)

policy for the US is that an unchecked decline in the value of the dollar could raise the cost of living in the long run and reduce the demand for US debt. The situation will be even worse as a result of the 5 August 2011 downgrading of the US credit rating by Standard and Poor's.

The Cold Currency War

What we are witnessing today is not a fully-fledged currency war, because it does not seem compatible with some stylized facts. To start with,

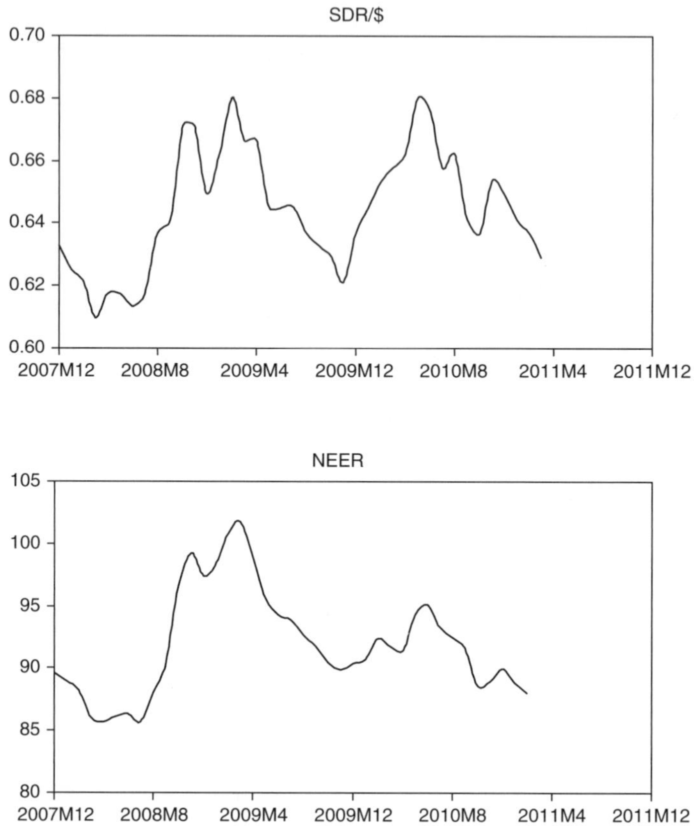

Figure 3.2 Exchange rates of the US dollar

countries typically want to see their currencies neither too weak nor too strong, trying to strike a balance between the benefits and costs of a weak currency, and this is actually why the occurrence of a currency war is rare. While a weak currency is supposed to boost exports, it also makes imports more expensive. A weak domestic currency has a low purchasing power in terms of foreign goods and services, thus it becomes more expensive to import and travel abroad. More expensive imports boost domestic inflation. Furthermore, a weak domestic currency makes international debt servicing more expensive if debt is denominated in foreign currencies. Foreign investors will be discouraged if a weak currency is taken to indicate further weakness. Thus while the positive effect of devaluation or depreciation on the current account is uncertain, it has an adverse effect on the capital account (it encourages capital outflows).

The negative consequences of a weak currency must be weighed against the perceived benefits. One of these benefits is that a country can grow out of high unemployment by boosting exports via currency depreciation, as it is always thought that a weak currency is a necessary condition for export-led growth. This course of action may be attractive if and when other options like increased public spending are ruled out due to high public debt and/or a significant budget deficit. Another benefit lies in the principle that expenditure switching policies can be used to correct a trade imbalance, an argument that lies at the heart of the current US–China trade dispute. Yet another perceived benefit is that a weak currency is conducive to the build-up of foreign exchange reserves, which provide some protection in the event of a financial crisis. This argument, which is typically used against China, is questionable because a weak currency that is expected to depreciate even further does not attract capital inflows and indeed encourages capital outflows. Therefore, for currency devaluation to lead to acceleration in the build-up of foreign reserves, the current account effect must be stronger than the capital account effect, which is unlikely to be the case. The reasoning is very simple: for devaluation to affect the current account, changes in exchange rates must be translated into changes in prices and volumes. Several factors may impede this process, as we are going to see in Chapters 5 and 6. The effect on the capital account is straightforward: an expectation of currency depreciation makes foreign assets more attractive than domestic assets, particularly if currency depreciation is engineered via lower interest rates.

The underlying argument for expenditure switching policies seems to ignore the crucial factor of the currency of invoicing, which is an issue that we will discuss in great detail. If a country invoices its exports in the currencies of its trading partners, the exchange rate becomes irrelevant and changes in the exchange rate will not affect the foreign currency prices of exports. For example, since the US dollar is the currency of invoicing of China's exports to the US and the US exports to China in US dollar terms, only the US can engage in a currency war (against China). Furthermore, many factors are likely to impede the transmission of the effect of changes in the exchange rate to the prices and volumes of exports and imports. Using the jargon of international economics, it is unlikely that there is a high pass-through effect from the exchange rate to prices, which makes expenditure switching policies ineffective. Again these are issues that we will come back to and elaborate on.

Under the present international monetary system and the absence of stringent capital controls, exchange rates are determined by market forces, which means that the ability of a country to force its currency to depreciate depends on whether or not market forces are working in that direction.

Furthermore, for a country to launch a successful currency war, it must have a diversified set of domestic currency invoiced exports and a limited set of imports. For a widespread currency war to occur, a large proportion of significant countries must wish to devalue their currencies at once. The characterization of the current situation as a "currency war" is no more than anti-Chinese rhetoric.

PROTECTIONISM

Protectionism is an economic policy that entails the imposition of restrictions on international trade transactions. These restrictions typically take the form of tariffs, quotas and a variety of other government regulations designed to discourage imports. This policy is closely aligned with anti-globalization and contrasts with free trade, where government-imposed barriers to trade and the movement of capital are kept to a minimum. Protectionism refers in general to doctrines (hence policies) postulating that businesses and workers within a country can be protected by restricting or regulating trade with other countries.

Historically, protectionism was associated with economic doctrines such as mercantilism – the proposition that it is beneficial to maintain a positive trade balance. Most contemporary economists share the belief that protectionism is harmful, that its costs outweigh the benefits, and that it impedes economic growth. Paul Krugman once famously stated that "if there were an Economist's Creed, it would surely contain the affirmations 'I understand the Principle of Comparative Advantage' and 'I advocate Free Trade'" (Krugman, 1987). Recent acts of protectionism in developed countries are typically motivated by the desire to protect politically important domestic industries. At one time mostly blue-collar jobs were lost from developed countries to foreign competition, but in recent years protectionism has been motivated by offshore outsourcing and the loss of white-collar jobs. For example, there has been a lot of talk about Bangalore (India) hijacking a big fraction of the jobs available at the Silicon Valley in California. And, of course, China has been accused of stealing jobs as manufacturers seeking lower costs of production set up business in China (and India).

History of Protectionism

While the US is accusing China of adopting protectionist policies (via an undervalued currency), protectionism has a long history in the US – it was indeed a major reason for the breakout of the American Civil War.

Because of their low-cost manual labour, slave-holding southern states had little need for mechanization, while claiming the right to buy manufactured goods from any country, as opposed to buying from the industrial north. Southern states, therefore, called themselves "free traders". Northern states, on the other hand, sought to develop manufacturing industry, which required the imposition of tariffs to allow their firms to compete with British competitors. In his *Report on Manufactures*, the first US Secretary of the Treasury, Alexander Hamilton, advocated the protection of infant industries by imposing tariffs on imports and using the proceeds to subsidize exports. Thus the US was in the lead with respect to opposition to free trade.

Throughout the nineteenth century, leading US statesmen, including Senator Henry Clay, maintained Hamilton's themes within the Whig Party under a set of policies and doctrines called the "American System". The opposed Southern Democratic Party contested several elections throughout the 1830s, 1840s and 1850s in part over the issue of tariffs and the protection of industry, but southern Democrats were never as strong as the more populated north. The northern Whigs sought and obtained higher protective tariffs, despite the bitter resistance of the south. One southern state precipitated what was called the nullification crisis over the issue of tariffs, arguing that states had the right to ignore federal laws. Abraham Lincoln strongly opposed free trade, implementing a 44 per cent tariff during the Civil War in part to pay for the building of the Union-Pacific Railroad, the war effort, and to protect American industry.

President William McKinley stated the stance of the US under the Republican Party as follows (McKinley, 1892):

> Under free trade the trader is the master and the producer the slave. Protection is but the law of nature, the law of self-preservation, of self-development, of securing the highest and best destiny of the race of man. [It is said] that protection is immoral . . . . Why, if protection builds up and elevates 63 000 000 [the US population] of people, the influence of those 63 000 000 of people elevates the rest of the world. We cannot take a step in the pathway of progress without benefiting mankind everywhere. Well, they say, 'Buy where you can buy the cheapest' . . . . Of course, that applies to labour as to everything else. Let me give you a maxim that is a thousand times better than that, and it is the protection maxim: 'Buy where you can pay the easiest.' And that spot of earth is where labour wins its highest rewards.

Protectionist tendencies were revived in the 1930s, as the Great Depression took its toll on the US economy. Franklin D. Roosevelt attributed the depression to the protectionist policies exemplified by the previous Republican President, Herbert Hoover, who signed the Tariff Act of 1930, also known as the Smoot–Hawley Act, into law. This act has been described as a "shorthand for counter-productive, short-sighted piece of protectionist folly" (*The Economist*, 2011g). In 2009 a Minnesota Republican, Michele Bachmann, declared that the act "took a recession and blew it into a full-scale depression". Back in 1930, some 1000 economists signed a letter asking Hoover to veto the Act as a flawed piece of legislation. Their argument against the Act was that it did not make any sense to protect farmers' incomes by raising duties on things that they did not produce (manufactured products) and therefore had to buy. However Irwin (2011b) argues that monetary and financial factors were more to blame for the Great Depression than the Act. According to Liu (2005a), "the real cause of the Great Depression. . . . was the 1930 Smoot–Hawley tariffs that put world trade into a tailspin from which it did not recover until World War II began".

The Smoot–Hawley Act allowed the US government to impose tariffs on foreign imports, thus triggering "tit-for-tat" measures that destroyed international trade and made the Great Depression even greater. Between 1929 and 1932, US imports fell by 40 per cent, while exports fell by 49 per cent. According to *The Economist* (2011g), the collapse of exports was "at least partly the result of a whole host of measures taken by other countries after Smoot–Hawley that were designed to divert trade away from America". Eichengreen and Irwin (2009) estimate that global trade volumes fell by 25 per cent during the period 1929–33, with about one third of the decline attributable to higher trade barriers. Gregory et al. (2010) argue that "the new protectionist policies often remained in place for many years, blocking the expansion of trade and dragging down growth" and that "despite economic recovery in most countries after 1933, trade volumes failed to reach their 1929 peak by the end of the 1930s".

In 1971 the US resorted to protectionism in the face of economic difficulty using a dual measure of currency devaluation and tariffs. On 15 August 1971, President Richard Nixon abolished the convertibility of the dollar into and devalued it against gold (hence, against other currencies). The US also imposed a 10 per cent surcharge on imports. Between August 1971 and August 2011 the dollar depreciated by 98 per cent against gold (and by a big percentage against the yen).

More recently, US protectionist measures or the threat of adopting them have been directed mostly towards China. In early 2005 two American senators brought a bill to Congress that threatened a tariff of 27.5 per cent on all Chinese imports unless the yuan was revalued by that percentage. On 3 April 2008 the China Currency Manipulation Act was introduced in the US Senate and endorsed by presidential candidates Hillary Clinton and Barack Obama. On 29 September 2010, the House of Representatives passed legislation that would allow the US to use estimates of currency (yuan) undervaluation to calculate duties on imports from China. And on 11 October 2011, the Currency Exchange Rate Oversight Reform Act was passed by the Senate to penalize countries that have "fundamentally misaligned currencies." In February 2007, the US filed a complaint with the WTO against Chinese subsidies, and in late March of the same year the US Department of Commerce announced tariffs of 10–20 per cent on the glossy paper imported from China to offset the impact of alleged government subsidies. The imposition of these tariffs reversed a 23-year-old policy of not imposing countervailing duties on a non-market economy (*The Economist*, 2007b). This sounds exactly like the Smoot–Hawley: imposing tariffs on Chinese goods that have no American substitute, thus making Chinese goods more expensive for American consumers.

Protectionist Policies

Protectionism can be implemented by various means, but the most common tool is tariffs, that is, taxes on imported goods. The effect of tariffs is to raise the price of imported goods and, if demand is responsive to price changes, reduce the volume of imports. Direct quantitative restrictions – that is, import quotas – may be used for the same purpose. Countries may, and do, use various administrative rules to introduce barriers to imports, including food safety, environmental standards and electrical safety. For example, in June 2010, American officials seized a shipment of honey from China because it violated food-safety standards (*The Economist*, 2010e). Restrictive certification procedures on imports are used for the same purpose, including intellectual property, copyright, and patent restrictions that benefit large firms. These provisions have been employed against China in recent years.

Further protectionist measures include anti-dumping legislation, designed to prevent the dumping of cheap foreign goods that would hurt local firms. Government subsidies (in the form of lump-sum payments or cheap loans) may also be granted to local firms that cannot compete well against foreign imports. Export subsidies, which may be financed by the tax revenue received from tariffs, are often used to boost exports by paying exporters a percentage of the value of their exports. And we have exchange rate manipulation, which is what China is accused of – the idea being that a weak currency raises import prices and reduces export prices.

Arguments for Protectionism

Protectionists believe that there is a legitimate need for government restrictions on free trade in order to protect the domestic economy and preserve the standard of living of the citizens. The opposite doctrine of free trade is advocated on the basis of the principle of comparative advantage – that is, all countries will be better off if each country specializes in the production of the goods in which it has a comparative advantage. Advocates of protectionism argue against free trade on the grounds that the principle of comparative advantage does not hold in a world characterized by free capital movements. For example, China attracts capital because it is cheaper to produce in China than in the US, and for the same reason US companies are inclined to shift production from the US to Mexico.

Protectionists believe that allowing foreign goods to enter domestic markets without restrictions puts domestic firms at a disadvantage. Protectionism is also advocated on the grounds that infant industries must be protected so that they grow to a point where they can compete fairly with more mature foreign industries. Another argument rests on international differences in legislation pertaining to child labour, environmental protection, competition, occupational safety and health, equal opportunity, collective bargaining, minimum wage and intellectual property. If domestic legislation is more stringent than it is in other countries, domestic firms will be put at a disadvantage when they compete, both domestically and internationally, with firms exposed to less stringent restrictions.

Arguments Against Protectionism

Arguments against protectionism are essentially arguments for free trade. Most mainstream economists criticize protectionism on the grounds that it harms the people it is supposed to help. These economists argue that protectionism results in a "deadweight loss" – a loss of overall welfare. Despite their ideological differences, Milton Friedman and Paul Krugman believe that free trade helps workers in developing countries, even though they are not subject to the stringent health and labour standards of developed countries. They justify this proposition on the grounds that the growth of the export sector has a ripple effect throughout the economy that creates competition among producers, lifting wages and living standards. Alan Greenspan, the former chair of the Federal Reserve, has criticized protectionist proposals as leading "to an atrophy of our competitive ability", arguing that "if the protectionist route is followed, newer, more efficient industries will have less scope to expand, and overall output and economic welfare will suffer" (Sicilia and Cruikshank, 2000).

Opponents of protectionism also argue that it is a major cause of war, at least historically. Those holding this view attribute the wars of the seventeenth and eighteenth centuries among European countries to protectionist policies. The American Revolution is attributed primarily to British tariffs and taxes. Even World War I and World War II are attributed to the protective policies preceding them. According to Frederic Bastiat, "when goods cannot cross borders, armies will" (Bastiat, 1848). Furthermore, it is argued that protectionism does not promote equal access to domestic resources (human, natural, capital, and so on) for domestic participants and foreign participants alike. More will be said about the pros and cons of free trade (hence the cons and pros of protectionism) later on.

Current World Trends

Since the end of World War II, it has been the stated policy of most developed countries to eliminate protectionism by pursuing the free trade policies enforced by international treaties and organizations such as the World Trade Organization (WTO). In general, however, it has been an attitude of preaching without practising. Some modern protectionist policies even have specific names, such as the "Common Agricultural Policy" in the European Union and the "Buy American" provision in the economic recovery packages in the US.

Protectionism became more rampant in the aftermath of the global financial crisis. In the G20 London summit of 2010, a pledge was taken to abstain from imposing any trade protectionist measures. However, a study conducted by a team of IMF economists showed that "the pace of trade reforms waned from the mid-2000s as protectionist sentiment began to increase" and that "with the onset of the global financial crisis, reform progress not only halted but began to reverse". They showed that the new trade restrictions have had a strong negative impact on trade, estimated at about 0.25 per cent of global trade (Gregory et al., 2010).

Related Terms

Protectionist practices have led to the emergence of some related terms such as "economic nationalism" and "economic patriotism". Economic nationalism is a term used to describe policies that emphasize domestic control of the economy, labour and capital formation, even if it requires the imposition of restrictions on trade and the movement of factors of production (labour and capital). Economic nationalism is embodied in the "American System", a doctrine that played a prominent role in American policy during the first half of the nineteenth century. Rooted in the thoughts of Alexander Hamilton, the doctrine rested on three pillars: (i) the use of tariffs to protect and promote American industry; (ii) the establishment of a national bank to foster commerce; and (iii) the provision of federal subsidies for infrastructure.

Another example is the French doctrine of *dirigisme*, which refers to an economy in which the government exerts strong influence, which may sound more applicable to centrally planned economies or command economies where the state effectively controls production and the allocation of resources. However, when the term was originally used in France, it meant a mainly capitalist economy in which the government played a pivotal role. In this sense most modern economies can be characterized as *dirigiste* to some degree. Yet another example is the power assigned to the now dismantled Ministry of International Trade and Industry (MITI) in Japan. At the height of its influence, MITI effectively ran much of Japanese industrial policy, funded research and directed investment. In 2001, the role of MITI was taken over by the Ministry of Economy, Trade and Industry (METI).

More typical examples of economic nationalism are instances where the government intervenes to prevent the takeover of a domestic firm by foreign firms. Recent examples include the proposed takeover of Arcelor (France and Luxembourg) by Mittal (India), the listing of Danone (France) as a "strategic industry" to pre-empt a potential takeover bid by PepsiCo (US), blocking the takeover of Autostrade (Italy) by the Spanish company Abertis, and the proposed takeover of Suez (France) by Enel (Italy). In the US, examples include Congressional opposition to the takeover bid for Unocal by CNOOC (China) and the subsequent takeover by Chevron (USA); and political opposition in 2006 to sell port management businesses in six major US seaports to DP World, a company based in the United Arab Emirates. One of the accusations against China these days is that the Chinese are buying the corporate world. We will return to this issue in Chapter 8.

Economic patriotism boils down to the coordinated favouring of domestic goods and services. It can be practised either through demand stimulation (encouraging consumers to buy domestic goods and services) or through the protection of domestic firms by imposing trade restrictions. Economic patriotism may also take the form of hostility against potential foreign acquisitions of firms considered to be of "strategic value" to the domestic economy.

Supporters of economic patriotism describe it as a protection of national economic interests. The problem is that consumer preference for local goods gives local producers more market power and allows them to raise prices to boost profit. Consumers may end up being exploited by profit-maximizing local producers. For example, the imposition by the US of tariffs on foreign cars gave Ford and GM market power that allowed them to raise their prices, which adversely affected American consumers and car manufacturers themselves. Another problem is that local firms supported by economic patriotism have an incentive to pass cheap foreign goods off as local goods. This is particularly the case in today's environment where distinguishing between foreign and local goods is not easy. If foreign components are assembled locally to produce a television set, would this be a local or foreign product?

MERCANTILISM

Mercantalism is effectively a form of economic nationalism – the underlying idea being that economic prosperity and well-being depends upon the supply of capital (originally believed to be gold and silver) and that the way to boost the supply of capital is to maintain a positive trade balance with other countries by resorting to the use of export subsidies and import tariffs. Economic policies in Western Europe from the sixteenth to the late-eighteenth century were formulated on the basis of this doctrine. It was the dominant school of thought throughout the late Renaissance and early modern period (from the fifteenth to the eighteenth century). Mercantilism and the resulting policies motivated the many intra-European wars of that period and fuelled European expansion and imperialism until the nineteenth and early twentieth century.

In his *Austria Over All, If She Only Will* of 1684, the Austrian lawyer and scholar, Philipp Wilhelm von Hornick, described a nine-point programme based on mercantilist ideas (Ekelund and Hébert, 1997): (i) every inch of a country's soil must be utilized for agriculture, mining or manufacturing; (ii) all raw materials found in a country should be used in domestic manufacturing industry, since finished goods have a higher value than raw materials; (iii) a large working population should be encouraged; (iv) the export of gold and silver must be prohibited; (v) the imports of foreign goods should be discouraged; (vi) if certain imports are indispensable, they must be obtained in exchange for domestic goods instead of gold and silver; (vii) imports are to be confined to raw materials; (viii) opportunities must be constantly sought for selling surplus manufactured goods for gold and silver; and (ix) the imports of goods that have a domestic substitute should be prohibited. Those advocating mercantilism view the economic system as a zero-sum game, in the sense that any gain by one party implies a corresponding loss by another. Mercantilists' writings were also generally created to rationalize particular practices rather than as investigations into the best policies. The requirement of a large population is necessary to create bigger markets and armies.

Belief in mercantilism began to fade in the late eighteenth century as a result of the views put forward by Adam Smith and the classical economists, and the doctrine was abandoned gradually in favour of the principle of comparative advantage that encourages free trade. Adam Smith saw the mercantilist system as an enormous conspiracy by manufacturers and merchants against consumers. Indeed, much of Adam Smith's *The Wealth of Nations* is an attack on mercantilism. He noted that the core of the mercantilist system was the "popular folly of confusing wealth with money" and that bullion was just the same as any other commodity, hence there was no reason to give it special treatment (Smith, 1776).

Mercantilist regulations were steadily removed over the course of the eighteenth century in Britain, and during the nineteenth century the British government fully embraced free trade and Smith's laissez-faire economics. However, prominent figures continued to favour mercantilism, including Alexander Hamilton and Abraham Lincoln in the US and Thomas Malthus in Britain. At present the word "mercantilism" is often used to attack various forms of protectionism. China's trade and exchange rate policies are often described as being mercantilist. For example, Robert Samuelson argued in the 14 May 2007 issue of *Newsweek* that China was pursuing an essentially mercantilist trade policy that threatened to undermine the post-World War II international economic structure (Samuelson, 2007).

FREE TRADE

Under a system of free trade business is conducted without government intervention. Free trade implies the absence of "distortions" (such as taxes, subsidies, regulations or laws), free access to markets, free access to information, and the free movement of labour and capital between and within countries. Obviously, no country practises free trade as described here, and most countries conduct trade policies that are protectionist to one degree or another. One protectionist policy employed by countries takes the form of agricultural subsidies whereby they attempt to protect their agricultural sectors from outside competition by artificially reducing the prices of their agricultural products.

The literature is rich with extensive work on the theoretical and empirical effects of free trade. Although free trade produces winners and losers, the broad consensus among US economists is that it produces a large and unambiguous net gain for society (Friedman, 1997; Fuller and Geide-Stevenson, 2003). In a 2006 survey of American economists (83 responders), 87.5 per cent agreed that the US should eliminate remaining tariffs and other barriers to trade, while 90.1 per cent disagreed with the suggestion that the US should restrict employers from outsourcing work to foreign countries (Whaples, 2006). Actually, Whaples (2006) states explicitly that free trade is one of the issues that economists agree upon. Mankiw (2006a) argues that "few propositions command as much consensus among professional economists as that open world trade increases economic growth and raises living standards".

However, Deraniyagala and Fine (2001) found that much of the work on free trade was flawed, and concluded that the extent to which free trade benefits economic development is unknown. They believe that the theoretical arguments are largely dependent upon specific empirical assumptions that may or may not hold true. In the empirical literature, many studies suggest that the relation between free trade and growth is ambiguous. Lind (2003) presents a strong criticism of free trade. He argues that "most third world countries grew faster before they abandoned industrial policy tools like import substitution tariffs than in the period in which they followed the advice of the IMF, the World Bank and free-trade evangelists like Jeffrey Sachs, Jagdish Bhagwati and Paul Krugman".

Free trade is often opposed by domestic industries that would have their profits and market shares reduced by competing with imported goods. For Karl Marx, free trade represented the exploitation of workers (for example, Malia, 1998). This is what is written in *The Communist Manifesto*: "The bourgeoisie . . . has set up that single, unconscionable freedom – Free Trade. In one word, for exploitation, veiled by religious and political illusions, it has substituted naked, shameless, direct, brutal exploitation."

Free trade is also opposed by anti-globalization groups, based on the assertion that it does not benefit the poor. To this extent, free trade is seen as the means to circumvent the rules and regulations designed to protect workers. It is seen by some as a form of colonialism or imperialism, a position taken by various proponents of economic nationalism and mercantilism. In the nineteenth century, Britain's call for free trade was seen as a cover for the hidden agenda of expanding the British Empire.

Free Trade as an Ideology

Free trade is sometimes used as an ideology that encompasses not only economics but also politics and even ethics. For example, Liu (2005a) argues that "the US asserts that world trade is a moral imperative and as such promotes democracy, political freedom and respect for human rights in trade participating nations". There is, however, a contradiction in the proposition linking trade with democracy, political freedom, and so on, which Liu calls a "twisted ideological assertion". It is inconsistent with the US practice of imposing trade embargoes and sanctions against countries the US deems too undemocratic, lacking in political freedom and deficient in human rights. Liu argues that "if trade promotes such desirable conditions, such practice of linking trade to freedom is tantamount to denying medicine to the sick".

On the morality of free trade, Liu (2005a) quotes President George Bush II who declared in a speech on 7 May 2001 that "when we promote open trade, we are promoting political freedom", a link that is not that obvious. Liu also quotes Phyllis Schlafly, a conservative columnist, who noted that "the Bible does not instruct us on free trade and it's not one of the Ten Commandments", that "Jesus did not tell us to follow Him along the road to free trade . . . . nor is there anything in the US Constitution that requires us to support free trade and abhor protectionism". She refers to the historical use of tariffs in the US, arguing that "despite the ascendance of neo-imperialism in US foreign policy, protectionism remains strong in US political culture, particularly among conservatives and in the labor movement". Liu adds that "it is clear that political freedom is often the first casualty of a garrison state mentality and such mentality inevitably results from hostile US economic and security policy toward any country the US deems as not free". With respect to China, Liu suggests that "whenever US policy toward China turns hostile . . . political and press freedom inevitably face stricter curbs".

Commenting on the 2003 ministerial meeting of the WTO that was held in Cancun in October 2003, Elliott (2003) wrote the following for *The Guardian*:

> The language of globalisation is all about democracy, free trade and sharing the benefits of technological advance. The reality is about rule by elites, mercantilism and selfishness. As one *Guardian* reader said last week, perpetuation of the status quo means "the rich nations, and those within rich nations, gaining control over a greater and greater proportion of the world's wealth and becoming increasingly ruthless to retain that control, particularly as resources become stretched, pollution mounts and the number of hungry mouths multiplies".

Free trade, it seems, has become no more than a slogan, a tool that is conducive to the achievement of neo-imperialist objectives. Paul Samuelson, who was an ardent supporter of free trade, suggested that China's growing economic might calls into question whether free trade is a win–win game for the US (Samuelson, 2004). He agreed with the view that open trade helped the US economy grow since World War II but argued that competition from abroad drove down wages in lower-skilled jobs. As a result, he thought that China and India could displace US high-tech jobs as well, and more US wages could be forced further down to sustain competitiveness. Samuelson concluded that even though US consumers get cheaper Chinese-made goods, many US citizens could be net losers from such trade.

The Concept of Balanced Trade

An alternative to free trade is balanced trade whereby countries are required to provide a fairly even reciprocal trade pattern, which means that they cannot run large trade deficits. The concept of balanced trade has been suggested by McKeever (1996), who describes the concept as follows:

> Balanced trade is a simple concept which says that a country should import only as much as it exports so that trade and money flows are balanced. A country can balance its trade either on a trading partner basis in which total money flows between two countries are equalized or it can balance the overall trade and money flows so that a trade deficit with one country is balanced by a trade surplus with another country.

Richman et al. (2008) describe balanced trade as "a minimum standard for ensuring that trade does benefit all is that trade should be relatively in balance". Balanced trade is advocated by Buffet (2003a) who suggests a system of "import certificates" (ICs) whereby exporters receive \$1 of ICs for each \$1 of goods they export whereas importers would be required to present \$1 of ICs for every \$1 of goods they import. This system would limit the value of imports to, at most, the value of exports. A market can then evolve for exporters to sell ICs to importers, effectively subsidizing exporters and taxing importers.

The concept of balanced trade was introduced in the US legislatively in the Balanced Trade Restoration Act of 2006. The proposed legislation was sponsored by Senators Byron Dorgan and Russell Feingold, two Democrats in the US Senate. Since then there has been no action on the Bill. It is interesting, however, that Liu (2005b) argues that "the US is waking up from its self delusion about free trade to the reality that free trade never leads to balanced trade".

CONCLUDING REMARKS

Developing countries are under pressure to adopt "good" policies such as free trade to foster economic development. The underlying argument is that developed countries used these same policies a long time ago to move from being developing to developed. Therefore, the idea of developing countries not accepting the economic wisdom of developed countries is rather silly. Specifically, China and developing countries are urged to follow the so-called "Washington Consensus" that, according to Rodrik (2006), involves ten commandments: (i) fiscal discipline; (ii) reorientation of public expenditure; (iii) tax reform; (iv) financial liberalization; (v) unified and competitive exchange rates; (vi) trade liberalization; (vii) openness to FDI; (viii) privatization; (ix) deregulation; and (x) property rights. It can be argued that the US itself is not following the Washington Consensus at least on the basis of the first three commandments.

Chang (2002) argues that "contrary to the conventional wisdom, the historical fact is that the rich countries did not develop on the basis of the policies and institutions that they now recommend to, and often force upon, the developing countries". He suggests that "almost all of today's rich countries used tariff protection and subsidies to develop their industries". For example, it is a myth that the US and UK have developed by adopting free markets and free trade policies – rather they actively resorted to protectionism. Between the Civil War and World War II, the US was the most heavily protected economy in the world. As a matter of fact, the American Civil War broke out because of disagreement on tariffs as much as on slavery. In the 1880s, the Americans realized that Britain had reached the top through protectionism and subsidies and that they needed to do the same if they wanted to reach the top. According to Chang (2002), Ulysses Grant, the US President over the period 1868–76 criticized the preaching by Britain of free trade to the US. However, when the US reached the top after World War II, it too started to preach free trade to developing countries. It is not only Britain and the US – almost all developed countries at present used protectionist measures in earlier stages of development.

The moral of the story is that the developed world is preaching to the developing world what it did not practise in earlier stages of economic development. And even today, those countries preaching free trade indulge in protectionism every now and then. A report prepared by the Congressional Budget Office makes it explicit that "we like free trade if and when it suits us" (CBO, 2000). The report says:

> Since long before the war, the United States had run an almost unbroken string of trade surpluses – that is, an excess of exports over imports – and the war damaged or destroyed much of the most significant international competition for US industry. Consequently, before 1970, US industry seemed to have little to fear and much to gain from free trade. After 1970, however, the almost unbroken string of trade surpluses turned into one of trade deficits, and in the 1980s and 1990s, those deficits grew quite large . . . .Opponents of freer US trade point to the deficits as evidence of mistaken US and unfair foreign trade policies. Many are concerned that the deficits cause a number of economic ills, such as unemployment and slower economic growth, and they therefore support import restrictions and other trade policies intended to reduce or eliminate the deficits.

This is the story of the present time. The US is telling China and other developing countries not to do what the Americans did at one stage or another and what they are doing at present (quantitative easing, for example). While the US became the country it is now after years of protectionism, developing countries are told (by the US) to be "good members of the international community" by accepting and implementing the Washington Consensus and by following the WTO rules and the example set by the "West", whatever the "West" means. Lind (2003) accuses the US and other advanced industrial countries of being "not only selfish but hypocritical" because "they would deny to newly-industrialising countries the very practices that they used in the past to become economic superpowers". Chang (2002), on the other hand, believes that "the WTO rules should be re-written so that the developing countries can more actively use tariffs and subsidies for industrial development". The economic rules set by the "West" are indeed selfish and hypocritical.

4. Exchange rate misalignment

THE CONCEPT OF MISALIGNMENT

The US trade deficit with China is typically attributed to undervaluation of the yuan (hence overvaluation of the dollar). In February 2009, the then managing director of the IMF, Dominique Strauss-Khan, made the undervaluation of the yuan an undisputable fact of life, describing it as "common knowledge". *The Economist* (2009a) correctly argues that "you would assume that such strong claims were backed by solid proof, but the evidence is, in fact, mixed". In July 2011, *The Economist* (2011a) changed its long-held view that the yuan is undervalued by announcing that its modified Big Mac index shows that the yuan is not undervalued against the dollar.

When a currency is overvalued or undervalued, the exchange rate is said to be misaligned. Therefore, exchange rate misalignment is the deviation of the actual exchange rate from its long-run equilibrium level as determined by economic "fundamentals". Measuring misalignment is difficult and inherently imprecise, as it requires estimation of the equilibrium exchange rate, which is not observable. Given the miserable state of exchange rate economics, we simply do not know which fundamentals affect the exchange rate and how they do that (for some, exchange rates are determined by aliens from distant galaxies). Furthermore, when misalignment refers to the real exchange rate, even the actual rate becomes unobservable, as the real exchange rate depends on the price indices used to measure it (the real exchange rate is measured by adjusting the nominal exchange rate for the prevailing price levels in the countries concerned). The equilibrium exchange rate is defined differently, as we are going to find out. For all of these reasons and more, the empirical findings on exchange rate misalignment are controversial and suffer from limitations of simplistic assumptions (Edwards and Savastano, 1999).

We start by exploring the simple methods traditionally used to measure exchange rate misalignment, including the law of one price (LOP) and purchasing power parity (PPP). Then we move to the "sophisticated" methods and concepts that provide the opportunity to produce the results that suit anyone's political agenda. We will find out that measuring exchange rate misalignment is a good example of how most economists are inclined to produce results that politicians want to hear.

THE LAW OF ONE PRICE

The law of one price (LOP) is the basis of the colourful Big Mac index used by *The Economist* magazine (or newspaper as they like to call it) to estimate the extent of undervaluation or overvaluation of currencies. The idea is very simple: the price of a commodity in two countries must be equal when converted to the same currency. Thus the dollar price of a Big Mac in China must be equal to the dollar price of a Big Mac in the US. If this equality does not hold then the exchange rate is misaligned; this means that to restore the common currency price equality, the exchange rate and/or prices must change via the process of commodity arbitrage. If Big Macs are cheaper in China than in the US, commodity arbitragers buy Big Macs in China and sell them in America. Obviously, no one in his or her right mind will contemplate such a silly operation. The law of one price is a law only when it is applied to commodities such as gold, as it explains why gold has the same dollar price anywhere in the world. But to generalize this "law" and use it to measure exchange rate misalignment is rather heroic, to say the least, although it is rather entertaining. Still American politicians cite the Big Mac index to support their demands for a big revaluation of the Chinese currency.

On the basis of comparing the prices of Big Macs in China and the US, *The Economist* (2010b) reached the conclusion that "China's yuan [is] one of the most undervalued currencies in the Big Mac index". The exchange rate that is compatible with the LOP is calculated as the ratio of the yuan price in China to the dollar price in the US. If the actual exchange rate is higher than the LOP-consistent rate, the yuan is considered to be undervalued (remember that the convention is to measure the exchange rate as yuan/dollar, which means that a higher rate implies stronger dollar and weaker yuan, and vice versa). Figure 4.1 shows the extent of the undervaluation of the yuan according to the Big Mac index during the period 1998–2010 – it has varied between a maximum of 59 per cent and a minimum of 48 per cent. Apart from the period immediately after the revaluation of the yuan in 2005, there is little correspondence between the exchange rate and the extent of misalignment, when it is logical to expect the extent of undervaluation to become smaller as the yuan appreciates. Figure 4.2 shows misalignment of the yuan/dollar exchange rate and the actual exchange rate, both measured as indices starting with 100 in 1998.

Estimates of yuan undervaluation as judged by the Big Mac index cannot be taken seriously. A Big Mac costs less in China than in the US,

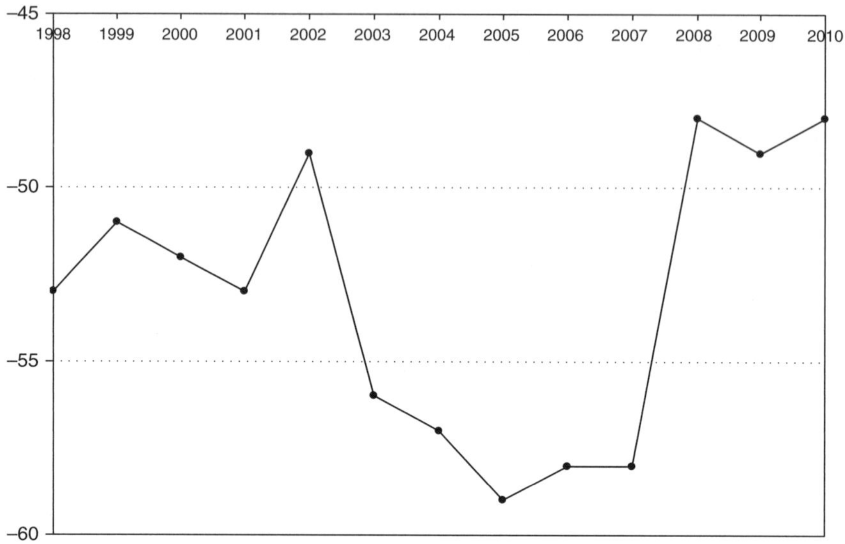

Figure 4.1 Undervaluation of the yuan against the dollar according to the Big Mac index

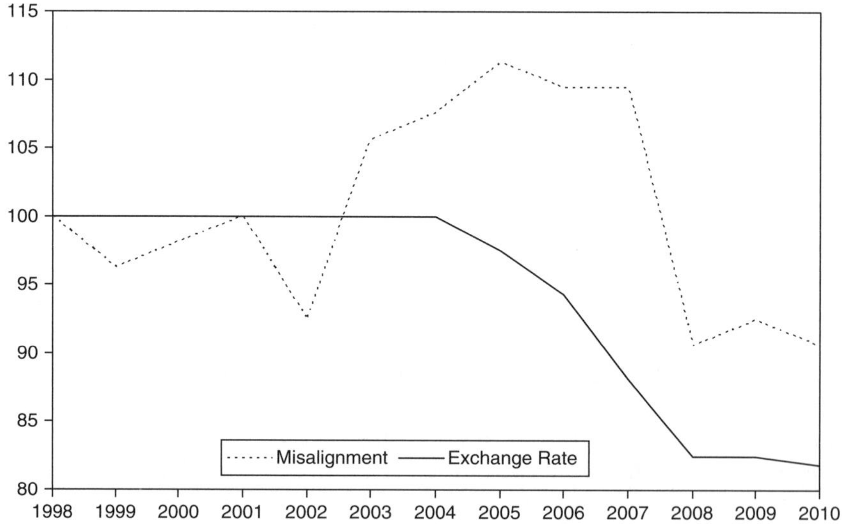

Figure 4.2 Misalignment versus exchange rate (yuan/dollar)

which some would take to indicate an undervalued yuan, not because of the exchange rate but because the lower price in China can be sustained, given a lower level of wages in China than in the US. We have to understand also that it takes a typical Chinese worker a greater number of work hours to earn the price of a Big Mac compared to the average US worker. And while a Big Mac is a cheap meal in the US, it is a luxury imported meal for most people in China. McDonald's operates in China because it is profitable to sell Big Macs at a lower price than in the US. Raising the price when demand is elastic reduces total revenue and hence profit. Thus the difference in the dollar price of the Big Mac has to do more with wages (the prices of factors of production in general) than with exchange rates. Funke and Rahn (2004) point out that with seemingly infinite pools of underemployed workers in the countryside and in inefficient state-owned enterprises, as well as a pitifully low standard of living, China looks like it should be able to out-compete other economies in almost any category of manufacturing with significant labour inputs.

The Modified Big Mac Index

Notwithstanding the fact that the Big Mac index has become the best-known regular feature in *The Economist*, the logic behind it is twisted in its assumption that differences in the prices of Big Macs are due only to exchange rates. Actually, *The Economist* (2009a) argues against its own Big Mac index because the index would tell us that "the currencies of virtually all low-income countries are undervalued, since prices are generally lower in these countries than in rich ones". Positive correlation between the price of a Big Mac and GDP per capita is a solid empirical observation that confirms the Balassa–Samuelson theory, postulating that average prices are higher in rich, high-productivity countries because higher wages push up prices in labour-intensive goods and services. Thus, it is only natural for China's currency to be weaker than what is implied by the LOP. Figure 4.3 shows that the dollar price of a Big Mac is positively related to GDP per capita in a sample of rich and poor countries.

In its issue of 30 July 2011, *The Economist* (2011a) came up with the so-called "gourmet version of the Big Mac index", which suggests that "the yuan is not that undervalued". The gourmet version was prepared by modifying the original Big Mac index to take into account differences in GDP per capita. In July 2011, the average price of a Big Mac in the US was \$4.07, whereas it cost \$2.27 in China. Accordingly the original Big Mac index would tell us that the yuan is undervalued by 44 per cent against the dollar. *The Economist* (2011a) admits that "some find burgernomics hard to swallow" because "burgers cannot easily be traded across borders,

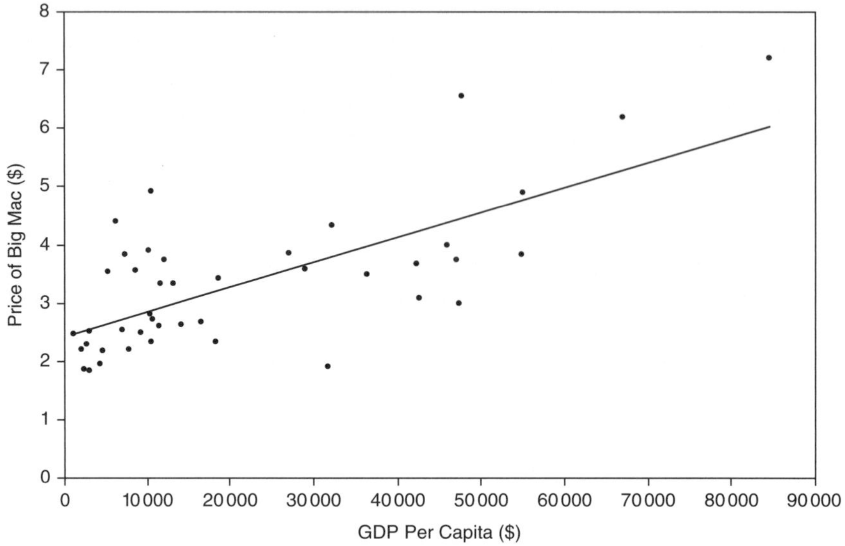

Figure 4.3 The dollar price of a Big Mac in relation to GDP per capita

and prices are distorted by big differences in the cost of non-traded local inputs such as rent and workers' wages". When the original Big Mac index is modified for GDP per capita, the yuan is found to be "close to its fair value against the greenback".

An Alternative Index

It may be useful here to suggest another index based on the cover price of *The Economist* itself, which we call *The Economist* price index. Figure 4.4 shows the extent of misalignment in 2010 using the Big Mac index, as reported by *The Economist*, and *The Economist* price index, as calculated by the author. Obviously there is a stark difference between what the two indices tell us. In the case of China, the yuan appears to be 20 per cent (rather than 48 per cent) undervalued. The Hong Kong dollar is about 17 per cent overvalued as opposed to 48 per cent undervalued. The Malaysian ringgit is 50 per cent overvalued as opposed to 41 per cent undervalued. With the exception of the yuan and the yen, all other currencies judged to be undervalued according to the Big Mac index are overvalued according to *The Economist* price index.

Some formal studies have examined the LOP on the basis of *The Economist*'s cover price. Ghosh and Wolf (1994) investigated the

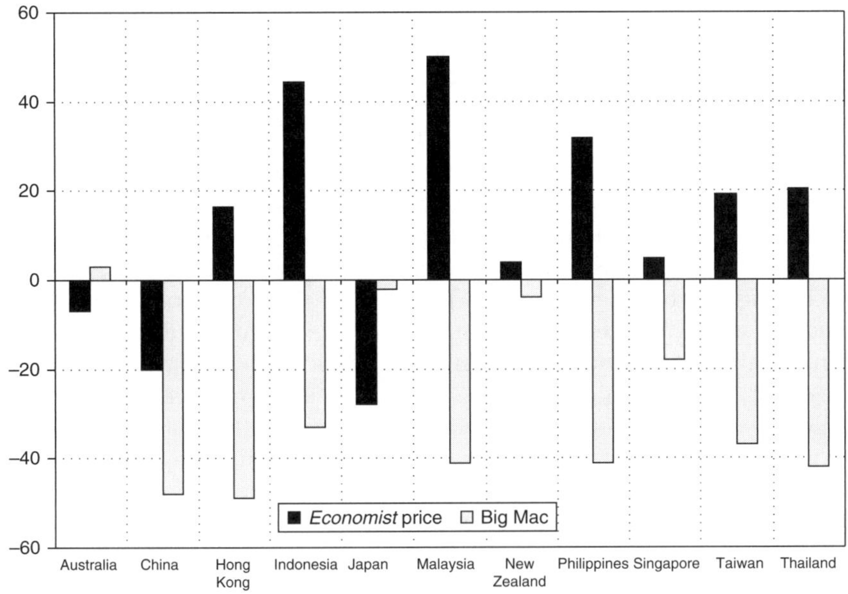

Figure 4.4 Exchange rate misalignment: Big Mac versus The Economist *price indices*

characteristics and determinants of changes in the cover prices of *The Economist* in a sample of 12 countries over the floating rate period. They reached the conclusion that the law of one price fails. The point to be made here is not that one of these indices is better than the other, but rather that these ad hoc measures of misalignment are arbitrary and unreliable, notwithstanding their entertainment value.

Deviation from LOP

The proposition of "pricing to market" can be used to explain cross-country variation in *The Economist* cover price. The basic idea is that the price of an imported good in a particular country does not only depend on the exchange rate but also on the price in the country of origin and profit margins. Export firms tend to stabilize destination market prices in the face of nominal exchange rate changes in order to protect market share. Prices are typically lower in poor countries because exporters aim at maintaining their market shares, which can be accomplished by reducing the profit margin in terms of the exporter's currency. This is why we should expect *The Economist* to cost more in Japan than in Indonesia and more in China than in Mongolia. If profit margins are reduced in response to an adverse change in the exchange rate, the exchange rate will remain looking as if it were misaligned. This phenomenon, which is called "pricing to market", makes mark-ups destination specific, as firms take into account local conditions when setting prices. If these conditions vary, so will prices. Therefore the full impact of any change in the exchange rate may not be fully passed through, implying that the LOP will not hold.

The LOP may not hold because of prices, not because of exchange rates, and there are reasons why exchange rates may be inconsistent with the LOP without being misaligned. The first of these reasons is the existence of trade barriers and transport costs. A non-tradable good is simply an extreme example of this type of friction where transport cost is either infinitely high, or else constitutes a disproportionately high fraction of the cost of the commodity. So long as any of these frictions exists, it is possible for prices to differ across countries by any amount up to the size of the transaction costs. Another reason why the LOP may fail is provided by the nature of the competitive structure of the markets for different goods. Producers may compete on the basis of quality; thus any change in the exchange rate can be offset by adjusting prices.

PURCHASING POWER PARITY

PPP is an extension of the LOP to more than one commodity. According to PPP the equilibrium exchange rate should be at a level that equates the prices of an identical basket of commodities when converted to the same currency. The "ultimate" basket of commodities comprises the goods and services that we consume every day, a basket that has a price represented by the consumer price index (CPI). If the consumer price index represents the general price level in the economy, then inflation is measured as the percentage change in the CPI.

PPP is considered a theory of exchange rate determination under floating exchange rates and a theory of inflation under fixed exchange rates. As a theory of exchange rate determination, PPP tells us that, starting from a particular point in time, the exchange rate should be determined by the inflation rates in the two countries. Specifically, the theory says that the country that has a higher inflation rate (that is, the country in which the prices of goods and services rise faster than in the other) will experience currency depreciation. Thus the equilibrium exchange rate is calculated by adjusting the starting value of the exchange rate for changes in prices.

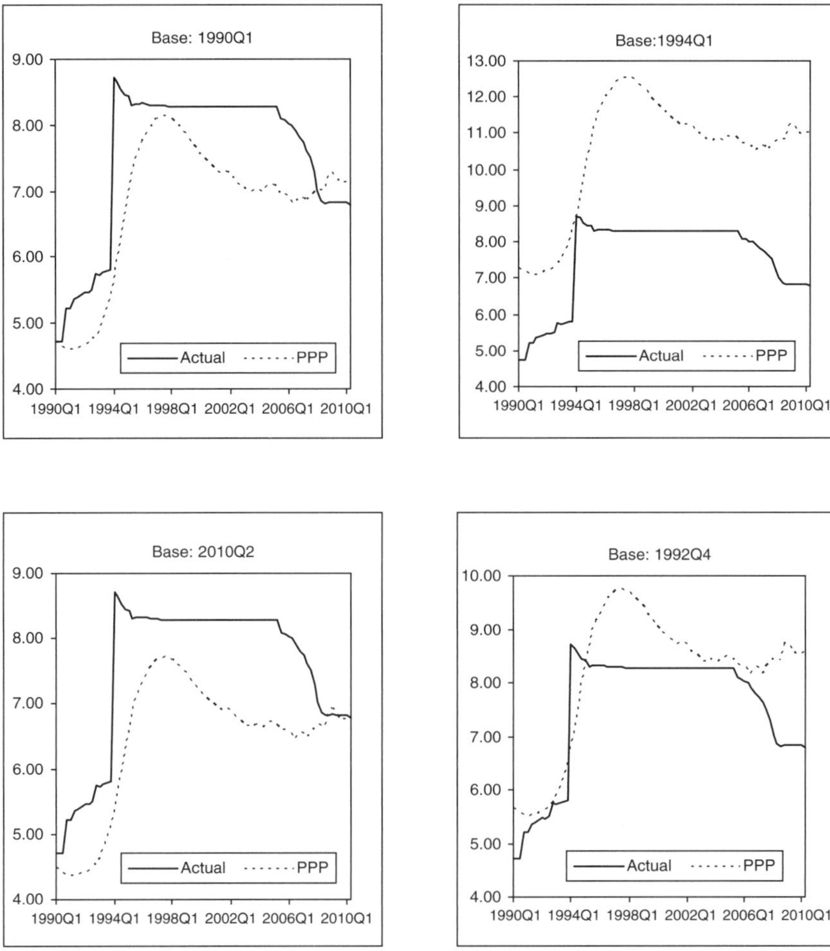

Figure 4.5 *Actual and PPP yuan/dollar exchange rates with different base periods*

Determining the Base Period and Other Problems

A major problem with PPP is how to determine the starting point, because the results are crucially affected by the choice of the base period, which gives leeway to subjective judgement. Consider Figure 4.5, which shows quarterly observations on the yuan/dollar exchange rate over the period 1990–2010. Four different base periods are used for the purpose of calculating the PPP rate: 1990Q1 (base rate 4.72), 1994Q1 (base rate 8.71),

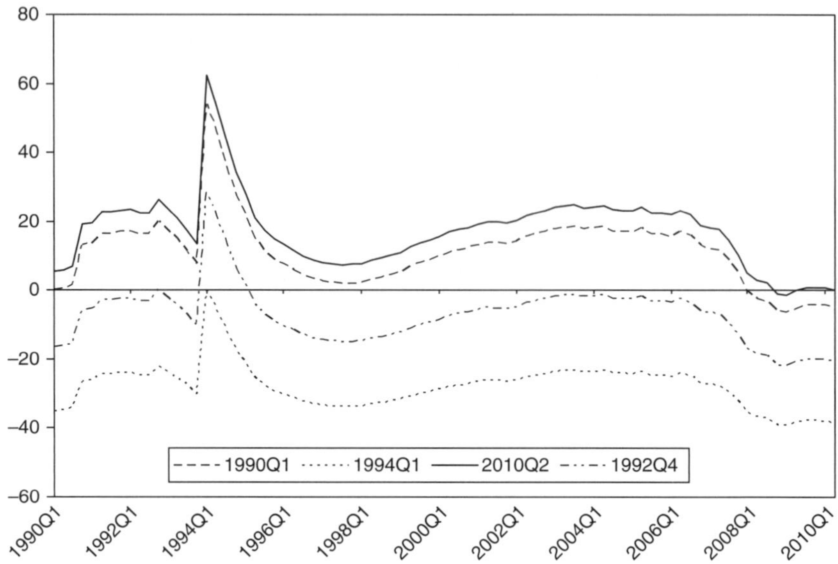

Figure 4.6 Exchange rate (yuan/dollar) misalignment with different base periods

2010Q2 (base rate 6.79) and 1992Q4 (base rate 5.75). In the first case, the yuan is undervalued except for the latter part of the period, with an average misalignment of 11.23 per cent. In the second case, the yuan is consistently overvalued with an average misalignment of 27.17 per cent. In the third case, the yuan is mostly undervalued with an average misalignment of 17.17 per cent. And in the fourth case, it is mixed with an average misalignment of 7.23 per cent. Figure 4.6 shows how estimates of misalignment have changed over time for the four base periods. So, what are we supposed to believe? Well, economists tell us that the base period should be associated with some sort of equilibrium in the trade balance or the current account. If this is the case then the appropriate base period should be 1990Q1, because it was around that time that the Chinese trade balance and current account changed from negative to positive. If this is the case, the yuan (according to PPP) must be overvalued as a result of the 2005 change in the exchange rate regime that brought up a gradual appreciation of the currency.

There are other problems with PPP that cast doubt on the reliability of the estimates of the equilibrium exchange rate. Since the PPP rate is calculated by adjusting the base period exchange rate for price changes proxied by price indices, it follows that cross-country differences in the construction of price indices render the results unreliable. There are certainly differences between how the consumer price index is calculated in the US and China because of significantly different spending and consumption patterns. For this reason the weights of the goods in the consumption basket differ across countries. There are also differences in the quality of goods included in the basket used to calculate the consumer price index – thus we will not be comparing apples with apples (more likely, apples with onions). Furthermore, PPP tells us that the exchange rate is determined by one factor only (the inflation differential), which cannot be true. The problem is that even if we augment the PPP model by other variables, the augmented model remains unreliable, as we are going to see later when we discuss the state of exchange rate economics.

The Balassa-Samuelson Hypothesis

PPP can be augmented by introducing the Balassa–Samuelson hypothesis (also called the productivity bias hypothesis), originally due to Balassa (1964) who was sceptical of the validity of PPP as a theory that explains the determination of the equilibrium exchange rate. He suggested that the growth process tends to change relative prices in a way that introduces systematic bias between the actual values of exchange rates and their PPP values. This hypothesis consists of the following propositions: (i) while developed countries have a higher level of (labour) productivity than developing countries, the difference is greater for traded than for non-traded goods; (ii) although wages tend to be equalized in the traded and non-traded goods sectors in each country, they do not tend to be equal across these sectors internationally; (iii) wages are higher in developed countries than in developing countries; (iv) prices are positively related to wages but negatively related to productivity; and (v) while the prices of traded goods tend to be equalized across countries, prices of non-traded goods do not.

Given these propositions, the ratio of non-traded goods prices to traded goods prices tends to be higher in developed countries than in developing countries. Consequently, the PPP-consistent exchange rate calculated from price levels, inclusive of consumer services, tends to underestimate the true equilibrium value of the currency of the developed country. This implies that the currency of the developed country with the higher level of productivity will appreciate relative to what is implied by PPP. In this case, the exchange rate does not only depend on relative inflation rates but also on relative productivity (or income per capita). One consequence of these conditions is that the relative price of non-traded goods rises as income per capita rises. This explains why goods are cheaper in China than in the US and why the modified Big Mac index correctly indicates that the yuan is not undervalued against the dollar.

The Empirical Validity of PPP

PPP in its various forms is supported by the available empirical evidence only over a very long period of time (decades) or under hyperinflation, as was evident during the German hyperinflation of the 1920s. Neither of these conditions are relevant to the current debate. Some claims have been made about the failure of PPP in the recent floating period being a "US dollar phenomenon" and that the validity of PPP is affected by government intervention and announcements concerning exchange rate policies. There is also the claim that PPP seems to perform better when wholesale prices rather than consumer prices are used. In general, however, the evidence is not robust and can only be supportive when dodgy econometric techniques are used to test the theory.

It is often claimed that studies employing the "most sophisticated techniques" have documented more evidence for PPP than those based on conventional techniques. The so-called sophisticated techniques include the Johansen (1988) test, which is the biggest scandal in modern econometrics, and the Bayesian variance ratio test due to Sims (1988). These dodgy tests always produce favourable evidence, no matter how the test is run, and the procedure can be manipulated in several ways to produce the desired results (Moosa, 2011b). The fact of the matter is that PPP tells us that the exchange rate is determined by prices only – this cannot be valid, except under the conditions referred to earlier (hyperinflation and the very long run). It is for this reason that models of exchange rate determination have been developed to explain exchange rates in terms of more than one variable, but even these models have not performed well.

A simple stylized fact that runs against the validity of PPP is the high correlation observed between nominal and the corresponding real exchange rates. If PPP held precisely, the exchange rate would adjust to changes in prices in such a way as to keep the real exchange rate stable. But this is not the case, as we can see in Figure 4.7, which shows the nominal and real effective exchange rates of the dollar since 1980. High correlation results from the absence of adjustment of the nominal exchange rate to prices. Since the nominal exchange rate is more volatile than prices, the real exchange rate becomes as volatile as the nominal rate and follows it closely.

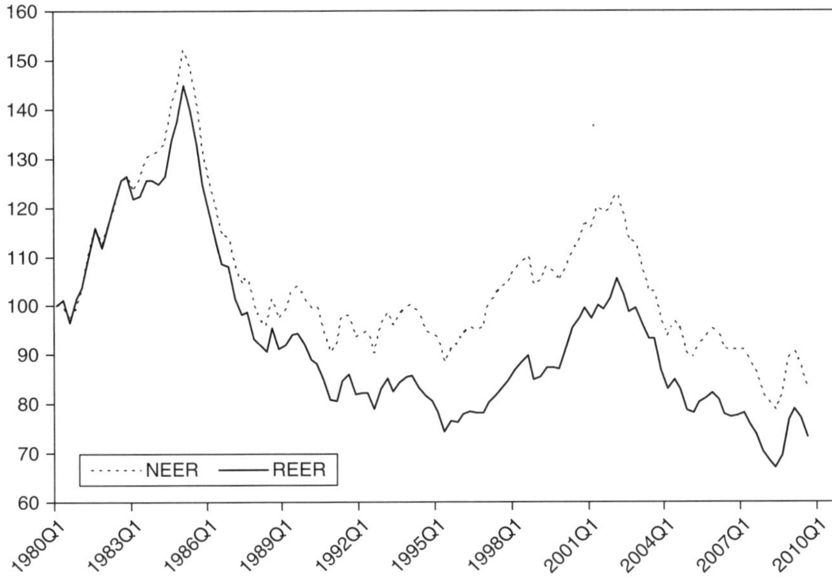

Figure 4.7 The nominal (NEER) and real (REER) effective exchange rates of the US dollar

THE CONCEPT OF THE EQUILIBRIUM EXCHANGE RATE

So far we have implicitly defined the equilibrium exchange rate as that equating common currency prices of identical goods (according to the LOP) or those equating common currency prices of identical baskets of goods (PPP). In this section we discuss other concepts of the equilibrium exchange rate that have been used to show that the yuan is undervalued against the dollar. All of these concepts are too abstract to be useful for any practical purpose. To start with, no one seems to know precisely what "equilibrium" means with reference to the exchange rate. Driver and Westaway (2004) make this point clear by arguing that "when thinking about the meaning of equilibrium it quickly becomes apparent that it is a difficult concept to pin down". The debate over what constitutes equilibrium involves issues as diverse as its existence, uniqueness, optimality, determination, evolution over time, and indeed if it is even valid to talk about disequilibrium. Hence Driver and Westaway express the view that equilibrium means "different things to different people and this is no less true in the context of exchange rates than it is for any other field in economics". A related proposition is that since the exchange rate is determined continuously in the foreign exchange market by the supply of and demand for currencies, the exchange rate will always be at its equilibrium value. Thus we have the concept of the market equilibrium exchange rate, the rate that balances the demand for and supply of the underlying currency in the absence of official intervention. This is a nice theoretical notion that has no place in the real world.

With respect to the equilibrium exchange rate, distinction is made among short-run equilibrium, medium-run equilibrium and long-run equilibrium (Driver and Westaway, 2004). Different equilibrium exchange rate concepts are typically specified in very general terms – no attempt has been made to specify the relevant fundamentals. Since there is more than one definition of equilibrium, the choice between the available approaches must be judged relative to the question of interest. However, there are different ways to measure the equilibrium exchange rate for any given time horizon or underlying question. Before considering these approaches, it may be useful to provide some guidelines for why attempts to measure the equilibrium exchange rate for a given time horizon may give different answers.

Driver and Westaway (2004) make it clear that the literature on exchange rate misalignment is vague about the measure of exchange rate, whether it is nominal or real and whether it is bilateral or effective. If it is the real exchange rate, a question arises as to the choice of the price indices used to convert the nominal exchange rate into the corresponding real rate. For some, the obvious measure of the exchange rate is the nominal bilateral exchange rate, which is the rate involved in the current debate. However, most theories of equilibrium exchange rates emphasize the real effective exchange rate by using different definitions of the relevant price indices used to convert the nominal rate into a real rate. Associated with any given real exchange rate equilibrium is an infinite number of combinations of nominal exchange rates and relative price levels.

The literature says nothing about how the effective rate is measured: whether it should be based on simple trade shares as weights, allow for third-party effects, or whether weights should take into account the distribution of overseas investment holdings. The domestic and foreign price levels themselves can be defined in a number of ways. The choice of the price index matters because real exchange rates measured by using different price indices can move in very different ways. For example Marsh and Tokarick (1994) discuss five indicators of competitiveness: real exchange rates based on consumer price indices, export unit values in manufacturing, normalized unit labour costs in manufacturing, the relative price of traded to non-traded goods, and the ratio of normalized unit labour costs to value-added deflators in manufacturing. Since each indicator of competitiveness has its own shortcomings, no one indicator provides an unambiguous assessment of competitiveness. The empirical analysis of Marsh and Tokarick (1994) shows that none of the indicators works well uniformly across countries.

This point has been by *The Economist* (2010c). While the Americans complain that the Chinese currency is undervalued, it is not clear to which rate they refer. The yuan appreciated by 24 per cent in nominal terms between 2005 and 2010, but calculations by *The Economist* show that the currency strengthened by 50 per cent in real terms during the same period. This estimate is based on the argument that the consumer price index is not the appropriate index to be used to calculate the real exchange rate because the CPI contains the prices of non-traded goods and services. Instead it is suggested that a better measure of competitiveness is the unit labour cost. The problem here is that there are no official statistics on China's unit labour cost, so *The Economist*'s calculations are based on the value-added in industry and the wage bill of urban factories.

BEER, FEER AND ALL THAT

Various concepts of the "equilibrium exchange rate" are used for the purpose of measuring exchange rate misalignment: these concepts (measures) give various results. The problem is that it could be by design that the equilibrium exchange rate is defined in such a way as to produce an undervalued yuan. In this section we examine the various measures of the equilibrium exchange rate that have been used in the literature.

The Behavioural Equilibrium Exchange Rate

The behavioural equilibrium exchange rate (BEER) is the most popular concept. The underlying approach is statistical whereby the real exchange rate is related to fundamentals in a single equation without any underlying theory. A long list of variables appear as determinants of the real exchange rate, including net foreign assets, terms of trade, ratio of total trade to GDP, ratio of consumption to GDP, productivity, interest rates, ratio of outstanding domestic government debt to foreign government debt, both as a percentage of GDP, ratio of the unit value of exports to the unit value of imports, the relative price of traded to non-traded goods, and so on and so forth. One reason why this concept (BEER) is popular is that it is easy to implement as the analysis does not impose any particular functional form or link from economic theory. Instead the links are essentially data determined – hence it is a black box.

The equilibrium rate is typically calculated by using dubious econometric techniques such as the Johansen test, which is notorious for giving the results you wish for (for example, Moosa, 2011b). Clark and MacDonald (1999) use the Johansen test to find two cointegrating vectors in each case, one reflecting real interest rate differentials and the other the remaining variables in the system. The problem is that no one really knows what cointegrating vectors are: structural equations, reduced-form equations or a combination of both (Wickens, 1996). It has also been observed that whenever a long list of potential explanatory variables is available, data mining becomes rather tantalizing. A common procedure would be to "torture" the data until the desirable results are obtained. For China bashers, the desirable results are those showing the largest possible extent of yuan undervaluation.

The Fundamental Equilibrium Exchange Rate

The fundamental equilibrium exchange rate (FEER) is defined as "an exchange rate that is expected to be indefinitely sustainable on the basis of existing policies" (Cline and Williamson, 2009). This rate, which is supposed to define medium-term equilibrium, is expected to generate a current account surplus or deficit that matches the country's underlying capital flow over the cycle, assuming that the country is pursuing policies aimed at achieving internal balance as well as it can and that it is not restricting trade for reasons pertaining to the balance of payments.

FEER is associated with a simultaneous adjustment of the internal balance and external balance to equilibrium. The internal balance is defined as a stage when actual GDP is equal to potential GDP, so that it is consistent with the non-accelerating inflation rate of unemployment (NAIRU). Put differently, internal balance is reached when the economy functions at full capacity accompanied by low inflation. The external balance is a situation characterized by a sustainable current account position financed through long-term capital flows and ensuring external debt.

The problems associated with the estimation of FEER are plentiful. It is less difficult to estimate BEER because the emphasis in the BEER approach is on modelling the behaviour of the real exchange rate, which means that BEER-type calculations do not require fundamentals to be at their equilibrium levels. Then there are the problems associated with determining potential GDP. The simplest statistical method to do this is to use the Hodrick–Prescott filter, which decomposes actual GDP figures into a trend and a cyclical component (Hodrick and Prescott, 1997). Other detrending or decomposition methods give different results. Furthermore, there is no general approach to compute the sustainable position of the current account. Chen (2007) points out that the results of estimating FEER are very sensitive to the modification of parameters when a certain hypothesis changes, particularly for developing countries. Moreover, some of the variables used to estimate FEER may not, in reality, have an influence on the real exchange rate, or cannot be verified because of the unavailability of data in some countries.

The Permanent Equilibrium Exchange Rate

The permanent equilibrium exchange rate (PEER) can be obtained by decomposing the actual real exchange rate into permanent and transitory components, such that the permanent component is taken to be the equilibrium rate. PEER can be derived directly from the BEER estimates by separating out the factors underlying BEER into their permanent and transitory components. An alternative would be to estimate BEER in the normal way and then to replace the actual levels of fundamentals with estimates of their trend levels. Despite the different estimation technique used in its derivation, PEER is comparable with FEER – in other words they are just as bad as each other in being unreliable for any policy decision.

The Natural Real Equilibrium Exchange Rate

The natural real equilibrium exchange rate (NATREX) is the equilibrium exchange rate produced by domestic economic fundamentals. The concept is similar to FEER, except that equilibrium is medium- and long-term. The difference between NATREX and FEER is in the external balance, where the current account is modelled as the difference between saving and investment. Stein (1994) defines NATREX as "the rate that would prevail if speculative and cyclical factors could be removed while unemployment is at its natural rate". It is defined alternatively as the real exchange rate that is consistent with portfolio balance, so that the domestic real interest rate is equal to the world real interest rate. This implies that NATREX should be interpreted as a long-run equilibrium concept.

The Desired Equilibrium Real Exchange Rate

The desired equilibrium real exchange rate (DEER) is related to FEER – the only difference is that in the case of DEER, the internal and external balance positions are defined in terms of desired, rather than sustainable, policy objectives. The difference between the two concepts lies in the difference between "optimal" and "desired".

The Intermediate-Term Model-Based Equilibrium Exchange Rate

The intermediate-term model-based equilibrium exchange rate (ITMEER) is associated with equilibrium that is assumed to be a function of relative current accounts (as a percentage of GDP), relative unemployment, relative net foreign assets to GDP, and the ratio of wholesale to consumer prices. The approach involves the use of the actual levels of these variables rather than either their levels relative to equilibrium or the equilibrium levels themselves. Unless the equilibrium associated with these variables is constant, their actual levels will be an imperfect proxy for disequilibrium. Unlike most of the alternative approaches to the direct estimation of the equilibrium exchange rate described earlier, this framework is not conducive to the use of cointegration analysis. The emphasis is on forecasting nominal bilateral rather than real exchange rate movements.

PITFALLS IN EXCHANGE RATE ECONOMICS

Explaining the behaviour of the real effective exchange rate and measuring its "appropriate" level must be a horrendous job, given that exchange rate economics does not provide a satisfactory model to explain and predict the nominal exchange rate between two currencies. It has long been established that any of the macroeconomic models of the exchange rate that relate the behaviour of the exchange rate to economic fundamentals cannot outperform, in terms of predictive power, the random walk model (for example, Meese and Rogoff, 1983). The meaning of this is simple: if for any reason you need a forecast for the exchange rate prevailing next month, you will be better off assuming that the exchange rate will not change (that is, using a random walk forecast) than using a formal exchange rate model to generate this forecast. This proposition is valid at least when predictive power is measured in terms of the statistical criteria of the mean square error and its variants that emphasize the magnitude of the forecasting error.

The fact of the matter is that exchange rates are too volatile to be explained in terms of macroeconomic variables such as growth rates, inflation and the balance of payments as in the standard models. Exchange rates typically exhibit movements that can be described as bubbles followed by crashes. This simply means that exchange rates exhibit sustained upward movements for a long period of time in a bubble-like movement, then they crash by losing all of the previous gains over a short (or shorter) period of time. Take, for example, the nominal effective exchange rate of the US dollar shown in Figure 4.8 where two episodes of bubbles and

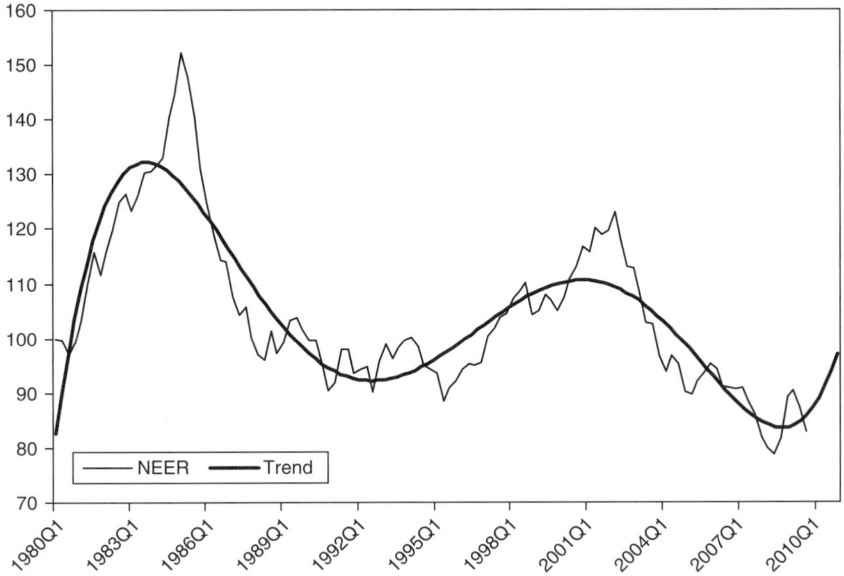

Figure 4.8 Bubbles and crashes in the US dollar's nominal effective exchange rate

crashes can be observed. In the third quarter of 1980, the exchange rate stood at 97.7, but by the first quarter of 1985 it had peaked at 152.3. That bubble prevailed for 18 quarters. It took 12 quarters for the exchange rate to go down to 96.9 in the first quarter of 1988. In the second episode it took 27 quarters for the exchange rate to rise from 88.5 to 123 (between the second quarter of 1995 and the first quarter of 2002), then it took 21 quarters to go back to 88.5 in the first quarter of 2007.

An even better illustration of a bubble and crash can be observed in the movement of the exchange rate of the Australian dollar (measured as an index), which is displayed in Figure 4.9. It took the exchange rate four months to lose what it had gained in the previous five years and two months. The crash was actually more dramatic than what is displayed in the graph, because it masks daily movements. It took the Australian dollar the time between 4 January 2005 and 15 July 2008 to rise from 0.7668 to its peak of 0.9802. By 10 October 2008 the Australian dollar had fallen to 0.6529, a spectacular crash that no model and no forecaster could have predicted. During the first 10 days of October 2008, the exchange rate registered eight and nine-sigma events in two separate days, as it dropped by a percentage that is nine standard deviations away from the mean value. It is interesting to note that the probability of a four-sigma (four-standard deviation)

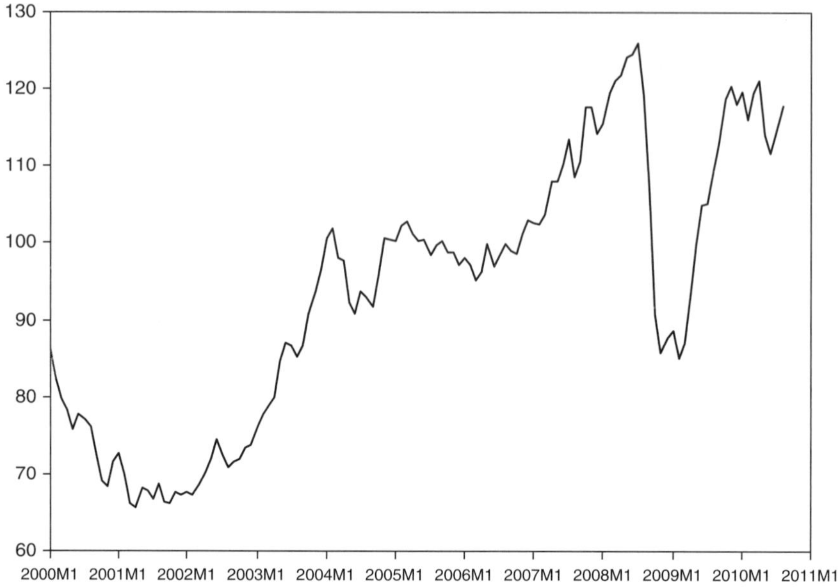

Figure 4.9 The bubble and great crash of the Australian dollar

event on any one day is 0.00317 per cent, which means that it is expected to occur once every 31 560 days. A ten-sigma event occurs with a probability of 7.62×10^{-22} per cent: it is expected to occur once every 5.2×10^{20} years.

It is not only bubbles and crashes that cannot be explained by conventional models of exchange rate determination. These models are also incapable of explaining volatility clustering whereby periods of tranquillity and turbulence alternate in an unpredictable manner. For the exchange rate to be explained in terms of macroeconomic variables, volatility clustering must be observed in at least some of them, which is not the case. In general conventional exchange rate determination models are inconsistent with the observed behaviour of exchange rates, for example, that volatility is the rule rather than the exception.

The problem with exchange rate determination models, apart from the fact that they are not supported by the available empirical evidence, is the very theoretical foundations of these (neoclassical) models – it is these foundations that explain empirical failure. To be more specific, the problem of these models lies in the rational representative agent postulate, which has dominated neoclassical economics since the start of the so-called "rational expectations revolution". This "revolution" has fallen out of favour because it could not survive its encounter with reality in financial markets. The unrealistic assumptions underlying exchange rate models include the following: (i) the representative agent is assumed to maximize utility continuously in an intertemporal framework; (ii) the forecasts made by this agent are rational, in the sense that they are based on the collection and processing of all available information, including information embedded in the structure of the model – hence, no systematic forecasting errors are made; and (iii) the market is efficient, in the sense that exchange rates reflect all available information about the determining fundamental variables. The global financial crisis has demonstrated at a great cost that these assumptions are not valid. If a satisfactory model is unavailable to explain the nominal bilateral exchange rate, what hope have we to explain the real effective exchange rate?

A MIXED BAG OF ESTIMATES

The empirical results of the work conducted by economists since the controversy of the Chinese currency surfaced (and even before that) provide, as expected, mixed evidence on the extent of the misalignment of the yuan/dollar exchange rate. The differences are qualitative (undervaluation versus overvaluation), as well as quantitative (the extent of undervaluation in particular). The results are highly sensitive to a number of factors including the underlying assumptions, sample period, definitions, the methods used to calculate the equilibrium exchange rate, and so on. It is invariably the case that economists who are ideologically motivated (typically anti-Chinese) choose the methods, definitions and sample periods that give them results supporting their beliefs.

Cline and Williamson (2009) provide estimates of fundamental exchange rates (and hence estimates of misalignment) for a number of countries. They reach the conclusion that "the only large countries that display large imbalances and therefore systemic threats are the United States and China". The systemic threat argument is the same argument used by bankers to rip off taxpayers by claiming the too-big-to-fail status – both use the same language of fear. Their results show that the Chinese currency needs 21.4 per cent appreciation to restore equilibrium. They also suggest that other undervalued currencies are those of Malaysia (18 per cent), Taiwan (13.8 per cent), Switzerland (12.7 per cent), Sweden (12.6 per cent), and Singapore (10.6 per cent). The updates reported in Cline and Williamson (2010a, 2010b, 2011) show slight differences, as the yuan appears to be undervalued against the dollar by 19.7 and 22.2 per cent in 2010 and 2011, respectively. This is convenient as there is a case for maintaining the anti-Chinese rhetoric.

The estimates of Cline and Williamson (2009) are interesting because: (i) undervaluation of the currencies of China, Malaysia, Singapore and Taiwan are smaller than what is indicated by the conventional Big Mac index; and (ii) they show that the currencies of Switzerland and Sweden are undervalued, while the Big Mac index shows that they are massively overvalued. This is not meant to imply that the Big Mac index is right and the estimates of Cline and Williamson are wrong. However, one would expect the Swiss and Swedish currencies to be overvalued following the rapid depreciation of the dollar against major currencies as a result of quantitative easing. Intuitively at least, the Big Mac estimates of the misalignment of the currencies of Switzerland and Sweden make more sense than those of Cline and Williamson.

The whole exercise, however, seems to target China as the culprit although the undervaluation of the yuan is not significantly different from, for example, that of Malaysia (no one has told Malaysia to revalue its currency). Still Cline and Williamson (2009) cast doubt on the sufficiency of the hitherto appreciation of the yuan, arguing that it may not be adequate to "reduce the projected surplus [of China] so sharply as to largely eliminate the need for further appreciation in order to reach the target current account levels". What is "clear" for them is that "after the highly appropriate effective appreciation, it is important that China changes its peg from the dollar to a basket to stabilize the effective rate". By the way, Cline and Williamson are associated with the Peterson Institute for International Economics, which holds very hawkish anti-Chinese views.

Another affiliate of the Peterson Institute, Nicholas Lardy, refers to work done by the International Monetary Fund, stating vaguely that "on this metric China's current exchange rate is far from equilibrium" (Lardy, 2005). In a speech delivered in Beijing, John Williamson referred to estimates prepared by his colleagues at the Peterson Institute (Williamson, 2003). He referred to the work of Goldstein and Lardy (2003), suggesting that a revaluation of 15 to 25 per cent was needed. He also referred to the figure chosen by his boss (Fred Bergsten, the director of the Peterson Institute), which is the top half of this range (20 to 25 per cent). The same Fred Bergsten revised his estimates of the undervaluation in 2010 to put it at 25 per cent on a trade-weighted basis and about 40 per cent against the dollar (Bergsten, 2010a).

Goldstein (2004) found the yuan to be undervalued by about 15 to 25 per cent by using two methods to measure the equilibrium exchange rate of yuan: the "underlying balance approach" and an approach based on "adjustment of global payments imbalances". Frankel (2004) used a modified purchasing power parity model to conclude that the yuan was undervalued by approximately 35 per cent in 2000. In contrast, Wang

(2004) found that it is difficult to arrive at any firm and robust conclusion about the equilibrium exchange rate of the yuan, using a variety of existing techniques. And while the PPP-based model of the OECD puts the undervaluation of the yuan at 70 per cent, some studies find the yuan to be slightly undervalued or even overvalued (Thin, 2010). By using the methodology of the current account gap, Wang (2004) found either a small undervaluation or even an overvaluation.

In a study of the effect of de-pegging of the yuan on China's international competitiveness, Sinnakkannu and Nassir (2006) argue that the yuan was slightly undervalued (−1.06 per cent) prior to the July 2005 revaluation and slightly overvalued (0.77 per cent) afterwards. Fu (2009) concludes that as a result of the reform of 2005, "the RMB exchange rate has almost come to its equilibrium value". Another study found the yuan's nominal exchange rate misalignment (presumably meaning undervaluation) to be less than 3 per cent over the period 1994–2006 (Zhang, 2008). Funke and Rahn (2004) used the concepts of BEER and FEER to conclude that "while the renminbi is somewhat undervalued against the dollar, the misalignment is not nearly as exaggerated as many popular claims".

Cheung et al. (2008) found that the estimated misalignment of the yuan detected in their previous study disappeared completely when they examined a new data set. They argue that "this finding highlights the fact that statistical uncertainty is something that needs to be taken seriously in policy debates". After conducting various robustness checks, they concluded that "although the point estimates indicate the RMB is undervalued in almost all samples, in almost no case is the deviation statistically significant". These findings highlight the great degree of uncertainty surrounding the empirical estimates of equilibrium real exchange rates, thereby underscoring the difficulty in accurately assessing the degree of yuan undervaluation.

Dunaway et al. (2006) demonstrate that "equilibrium real exchange rate estimates obtained from the various approaches and models commonly used in the literature exhibit substantial variations in response to small perturbations in model specifications, explanatory variable definitions, and time periods". They make it clear that "because of the methodological and empirical difficulties involved in establishing the equilibrium exchange rate for a currency and/or estimating the deviation of the actual real exchange rate from its equilibrium level, it is not surprising that researchers have come up with a wide range of estimates". Furthermore, they point out that "this has been particularly so in the case of attempts to estimate the equilibrium exchange rate for China's currency". By using a simple model explaining the real effective exchange rate of the yuan in terms of productivity and net foreign assets, they found that the estimate of undervaluation could be reduced by up to 37.9 percentage points just by introducing simple changes, such as replacing the ratio of net foreign assets to GDP with the ratio of net foreign assets to exports. Remember that there is no theoretical or intuitive rationale to prefer one of these variables over another. When another model was estimated for a sample of 11 countries they found that "randomly dropping one country from the 11-country panel changes the estimates of the deviation of the actual real exchange rate from its predicted equilibrium level by 6–43 percentage points relative to the baseline estimates".

Chen (2007) used the BEER model to estimate the equilibrium real effective exchange rate of the yuan against the currencies of China's 13 biggest partners over the period 1994–2006. He used as fundamentals the relative price of non-traded to traded goods, net foreign assets position, terms of trade and commercial policy (using the degree of openness as a proxy). His findings show that the equilibrium exchange rate exhibited a steady rise during the period 1994–9, followed by a steady fall afterwards. While the results show that the yuan was undervalued during most of the sample period, this misalignment has a trend to become smaller and smaller. He concluded that in the after-reform period, a small degree of overvaluation replaced this undervaluation. The results reveal that the yuan was undervalued during most of the sample period but the degree of misalignment is very small (the biggest undervaluation is just 3.94 per cent).

In a study of exchange rate misalignment in India and China, Cheng and Orden (2005) adopt the so-called "reduced-form real equilibrium approach" whereby the real exchange rate is determined by a set of economic fundamentals comprising (i) domestic supply-side factors, such as productivity growth in the tradable goods sector relative to the non-tradable goods sector;(ii) fiscal policy indicators, such as the fiscal deficit; (iii) the international economic environment, including capital inflows, external transfers and terms of trade; and (iv) commercial policy such as trade liberalization in terms of a reduction in import tariffs and export subsidies. In comparison to the Indian rupee, the actual real exchange rate movements of the Chinese yuan during the post-reform era were in general characterized by undervaluation. The predicted degree of undervaluation during the period 1999–2002 averaged about 20 per cent. The problem with these results is that they are based on the dubious Johansen test as applied to a "stir-fry" specification.

The results are all over the place, ranging from 70 per cent undervaluation to some overvaluation. Some economists tend to give the impression that their results are impeccable, representing the truth, the whole truth and nothing but the truth. But even some of those who believe that China is an economic villain cast doubt on the soundness of the estimates of misalignment. Williamson (2003) admits that "none of us has a satisfactory macroeconometric model at our disposal to back up our estimates or guesses". It is refreshing that he uses the word "guesses", because the estimates are no more than guesses even though the authors hide behind sophisticated econometrics and advanced economic theory. Krugman (2010a) agrees with the proposition that no one knows the fair value of the yuan. Evidence on the misalignment of the yuan/dollar exchange rate is a mixed bag and highly unreliable. Liu (2005a) argues that "since the yuan is not a freely convertible currency, there is no market basis to judge if the yuan is undervalued or overvalued".

Cheung et al. (2008) argue that "while the empirical results thus far point to the difficulty in establishing the claim that RMB is significantly undervalued, it is imperative to recognize that these results do not constitute evidence of no undervaluation". They further argue that "the statistical evidence is so weak that we cannot reject a wide range of hypotheses", which means that "the empirical relationship is very imprecisely estimated" and that "the empirical models and data are not sharp enough to allow a definite statistical conclusion". They also argue that "the drastic changes in the estimated degrees of misalignment highlight the uncertainty that is attendant on the data we use in these sorts of analyses". Diversity in the results is highly conducive to "cherry picking" by those who want to confirm a preconceived belief.

UNDERVALUATION JUDGED BY SOME INDICATORS

Some economists and observers believe that there is no need for a formal model to realize that the yuan is undervalued. Williamson (2003) argues that the Chinese currency is undervalued on the basis of more than one indicator. He claims that "one can often get a rough idea of whether an exchange rate is overvalued, in fundamental equilibrium, or undervalued by a cursory examination of a country's macroeconomic situation". Specifically he suggests that "if a country's economy is overheating at the same time that it has a bigger current account surplus (or a smaller current account deficit) than is needed to maintain a sustainable balance of payments position for the foreseeable future, then its currency is undervalued" and that "if the economy is underemployed and it is losing reserves because of a current account deficit larger than can be financed by sustainable capital inflows, then its currency is overvalued".

For these economists, there is no need to calculate the equilibrium exchange rate to realize that the yuan is undervalued. Undervaluation of the yuan is a "reality" indicated by China's massive trade surplus, its enormous foreign exchange reserves, and foreign exchange market intervention. In this section we evaluate these alleged indicators of the yuan.

The Trade Surplus as Indicator of Undervaluation

Goldstein and Lardy (2008) point out that

> any methodology that defines the equilibrium exchange rate for the renminbi as the real effective exchange rate that would produce balance in China's global current account position, or in its basic balance, or in its overall balance-of-payments position, yields the qualitative conclusion that the renminbi is significantly undervalued and probably by an increasing margin over time.

What Goldstein and Lardy are saying is that a country that has some surplus in the balance of payments must have an undervalued currency.

The argument that China has an undervalued currency because it has a surplus means that there is some sort of causation running from the trade balance to the exchange rate or at least that an undervalued currency and a surplus go together because they are determined jointly. However, those who argue that the yuan is undervalued make this argument because it is undervaluation that causes the Chinese surplus (America's deficit). Some economists reject this association, arguing that "it is wrong to define the yuan's value by the size of the current account surplus". A 2008 report of the Conference Board, an American business research organization, argued that "although an undervalued currency contributes to China's trade surplus, it is not a primary cause of it and has very little to do with the bilateral United States–China trade deficit" (*The Economist*, 2008a).

Roubini (2007) is one of the economists arguing that China's surplus is indicative of exchange rate misalignment, that is, yuan undervaluation. For Roubini, therefore, the yuan is undervalued because China has a massive trade surplus. Likewise Lardy (2005), who argues that "by most metrics China's currency remains undervalued", refers to China's current account surplus increasing sharply from $17 billion or 1.5 per cent of GDP in 2001 to $46 billion or 3.2 per cent of GDP in 2003 and to the trade surplus of $32 billion in 2004 compared with a surplus of about $25.5 billion in 2003. Chen (2007) points out that "the hot debate" about the appropriate level of the exchange rate of the yuan and the need for having it revalued and/or for China to adopt a floating exchange rate regime are principally based on "the growing size of the

Chinese current account surplus from the end of 90s". Mussa (2007) is confident that the yuan is undervalued because China's current account balance, despite the explosive growth, "establishes – beyond any reasonable doubt – that the exchange rate of the Chinese yuan is substantially undervalued and is being kept in this position by Chinese government policies that powerfully resist, and are intended to resist, significant appreciation of the yuan". It is not clear at all how some circumstantial evidence, such as the occurrence of a current account surplus, establishes anything, let alone an undervalued currency, "beyond reasonable doubt".

So let us look at the facts and figures. Thin (2010) dismisses the alleged connection between the trade balance position and exchange rate misalignment by arguing that the Indian currency is undervalued by 164 per cent, which means that it should command a massive surplus, but India is currently a deficit country. Fatas (2010) regards as tautology the proposition that "every time we see a current account imbalance we conclude that it is because exchange rates are not right". The counter argument is that a country that has a balanced budget and a surplus of domestic saving over domestic investment, or a country that produces more than it consumes, must have a current account surplus, irrespective of the exchange rate. On the other hand, a country that has a budget deficit and a shortage of saving or a country that spends more than it produces, will have a current account deficit. These are accounting identities that must hold by construction – they are not theories or testable hypotheses.

The big picture can be gleaned from Figure 4.10, which shows the trade balance with the US versus misalignment against the dollar for 42 countries. China (number 7) has the biggest surplus with the US and an undervalued currency according to the Big Mac index (the original version). If the proposition that a deficit is associated with currency undervaluation is valid, then countries with which the US has a deficit must have an undervalued currency and vice versa. But this is not always the case. In 22 cases out of 42 this is true, but in the other 20 cases it is not true. There are countries with overvalued currencies and surplus with the US (such as Canada, Costa Rica, Colombia, Denmark, Sweden, Norway, the Eurozone and Israel) and countries with undervalued currencies and deficit with the US (Argentina, Chile, Egypt, Peru, Hong Kong, Latvia, Lithuania, Poland, Singapore, UAE and the Ukraine). Uruguay's exchange rate is not misaligned, yet Uruguay has a deficit with the US.

It is true that China accounts for a large portion of the total US trade deficit, as shown in Figure 4.11, but if we measure the surplus relative to the size of the economy (GDP), it does not appear to be that big,

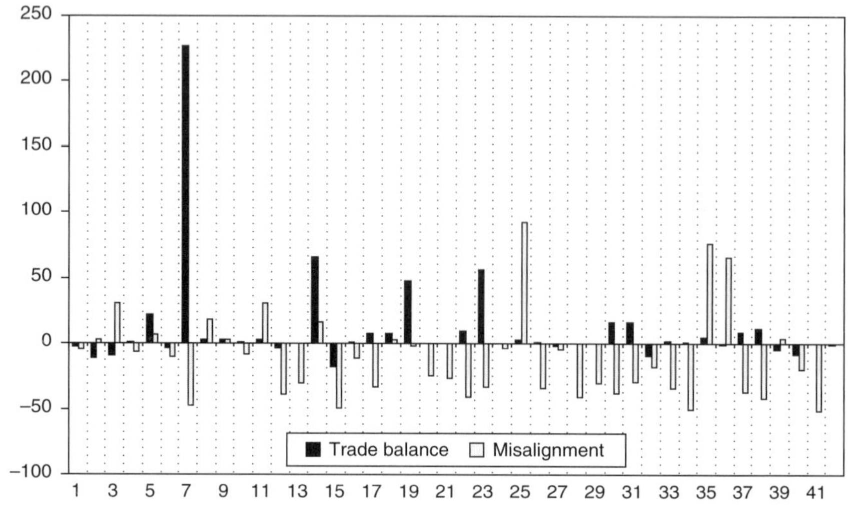

Notes: 1: Argentina; 2: Australia; 3: Brazil; 4: UK; 5: Canada; 6: Chile; 7: China; 8: Colombia; 9: Costa Rica; 10: Czech Republic; 11: Denmark; 12: Egypt; 13: Estonia; 14: Eurozone; 15: Hong Kong; 16: Hungary; 17: Indonesia; 18: Israel; 19: Japan; 20: Latvia; 21: Lithuania; 22: Malaysia; 23: Mexico; 24: New Zealand; 25: Norway; 26: Pakistan; 27: Peru; 28: Philippines; 29: Poland; 30: Russia; 31: Saudi Arabia; 32: Singapore; 33: South Africa; 34: Sri Lanka; 35: Sweden; 36: Switzerland; 37: Taiwan; 38: Thailand; 39: Turkey; 40: UAE; 41: Ukraine; 42: Uruguay

Figure 4.10 Trade balance with the US versus misalignment

as in Figure 4.12. China's surplus with the US is 3.95 per cent of its GDP. This ratio is higher for Israel (4), Malaysia (4.56) and Mexico (5.58). In any case a surplus with one trading partner does not prove that a country's exchange rate is unfair. Even China's total surplus is not that big when measured relative to GDP. In Figure 4.13 China is at the bottom of the list of countries ranked on the basis of the current account to GDP ratio. For China this ratio is 3.37, which is lower than that for Thailand (3.76), Germany (5.97), Singapore (12.99) and Norway (19.95).

Reserve Holdings as Indicator of Currency Undervaluation

China is accused of having an undervalued currency because it holds massive reserves. Roubini (2007) believes that reserves are indicative of China's exchange rate misalignment and Chen (2007) refers to the proliferation of China's foreign exchange reserves. Buiter and Rahbari (2011) argue that "the strongest support for a long-lasting major undervaluation

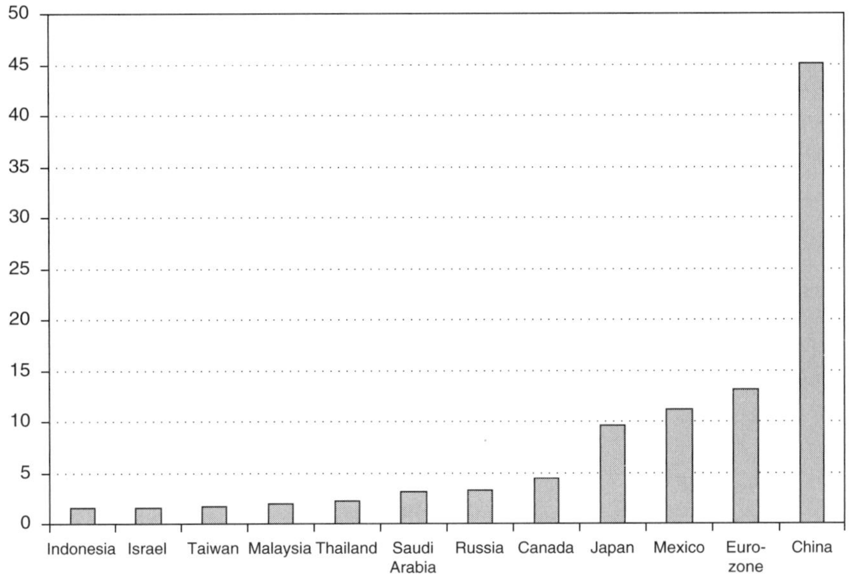

Figure 4.11 Surplus with the US as a percentage of total US deficit

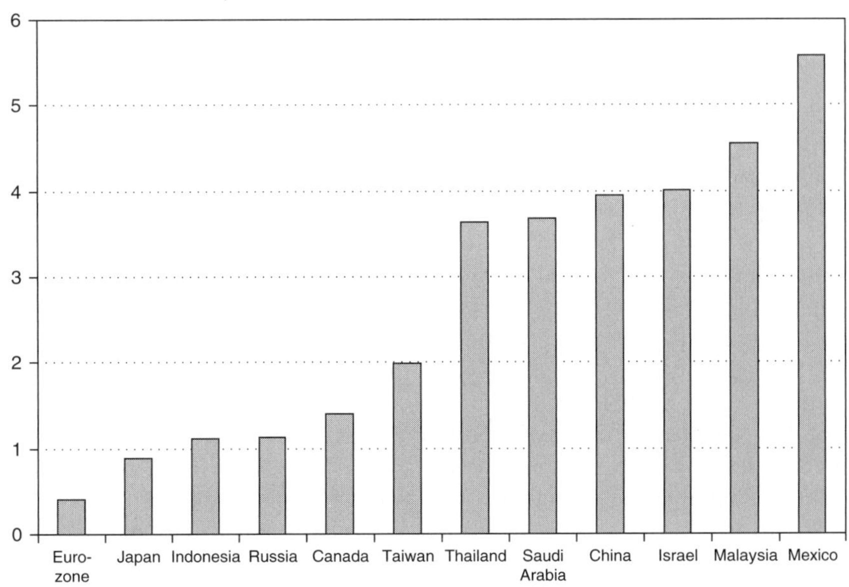

Figure 4.12 Surplus with the US as a percentage of GDP

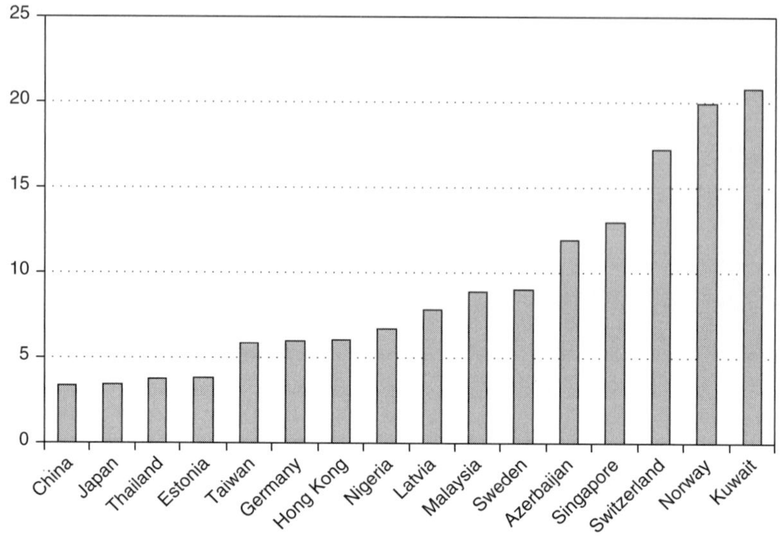

Figure 4.13 Current account as a percentage of GDP

of the Renminbi, however, is surely the accumulation of foreign exchange reserves by the Chinese authorities".

China accumulates reserves because it has a current account surplus and because of the capital flows anticipating revaluation of the yuan caused by the American pressure on China to revalue its currency. Therefore it does not make any sense as to why the Americans are complaining about China accumulating reserves. The US is, in a way, the cause and beneficiary of Chinese reserve accumulation. In any case, there is no visible relation between the size of exchange rate misalignment and reserves, as can be seen in Figure 4.14. In the cases of Brazil, the Eurozone and Switzerland, an overvalued currency is associated with big reserves, while Japan has massive reserves although its currency is not overvalued. Figure 4.15 shows that there is no relation between the misalignment of the yuan (measured by the Big Mac index) and the year-to-year change in reserves, both of which are measured as indices. And China's reserve holdings are not that big if they are measured relative to the size of the economy (Figure 4.16). The ratio of China's reserves to GDP is 4.6 per cent, which falls behind Thailand (5.1), Singapore (10.2) and Hong Kong (11.7).

Investors choose to invest in foreign securities when they believe that the rate of return on the investment is higher than the rate of return on a comparable (in terms of risk, for example) domestic investment. The expected rate of change in the exchange rate, together with the nominal

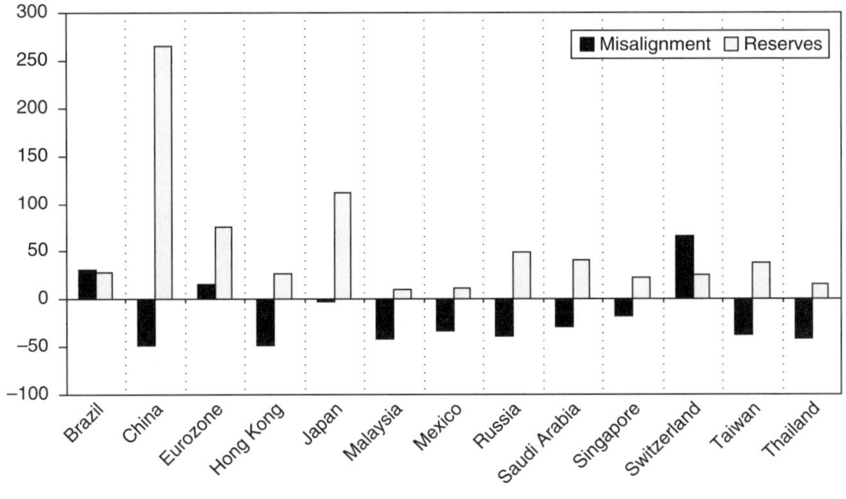

Figure 4.14 Reserves versus exchange rate misalignment

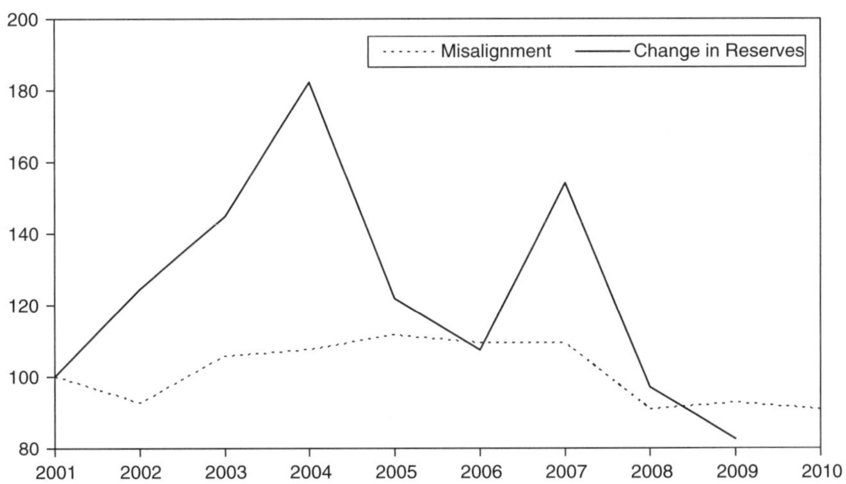

Figure 4.15 Misalignment of yuan/dollar rate versus percentage change in reserves (2001=100)

return in foreign currency terms (interest or dividends plus capital gains), determine the expected rate of return on a foreign security. If a currency is expected to appreciate, the expected rate of return on investment in securities denominated in that currency will be higher, attracting capital flows.

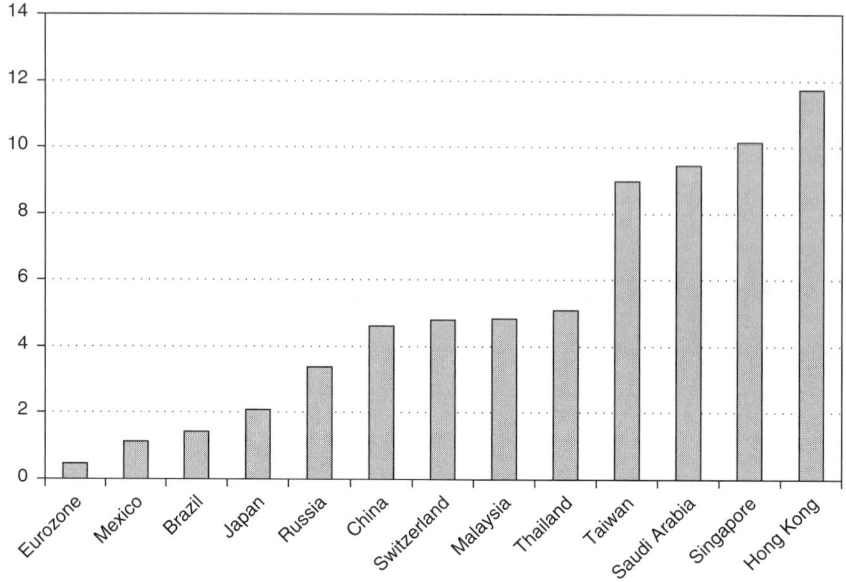

Figure 4.16 Reserves as a percentage of GDP

Thus, a country's financial account will improve if that country's currency is expected to appreciate. This is indeed one reason why China is accumulating foreign exchange reserves, which some attribute mainly to the trade surplus.

Intervention as Indicators of Undervaluation

Krugman (2010a) uses some flawed reasoning to indict China by arguing that "the right way to judge is not the value of the reminbi but rather the scale of currency intervention China must effect to keep its peg in place". Bergsten (2010a) points out that the Chinese authorities buy about $1 billion daily to avoid appreciation of the yuan. So, the more a country intervenes, the more its exchange rate is misaligned (in one direction or another). For this proposition to be valid in the case of China, intervention must: (i) target the level of the exchange rate; (ii) be effective; and (iii) involve the buying of the dollar, targeting the bilateral exchange rate.

Starting with the first condition, there are other reasons for foreign exchange market intervention apart from targeting the level of the exchange rate. These include the desire to (i) slow the rate of change of the exchange rate; (ii) dampen exchange rate volatility (in some cases to satisfy an inflation target); (iii) supply liquidity to the foreign exchange market;

and (iv) influence the level of reserves. And even if intervention targets the level of the exchange rate, this may not be related to the desire to maintain competitiveness but rather to control inflation. Some countries control inflation by using the exchange rate as a nominal anchor for monetary policy. For example, the adoption of Argentina's currency board and of Brazil's quasi-fixed exchange rate regime in the early 1990s put an end to very high inflation in these economies.

In the case of China, a report of the Bank for International Settlements (BIS) (2005) argues that "the use of the exchange rate as a nominal anchor has declined, but the issue remains important for China as it considers approaches to liberalizing its exchange rate regime". Other countries (for example, Chile, Israel and Singapore) have controlled inflation by using an exchange rate path (announced or unannounced) as an indirect or operational target to control inflation, or in support of monetary policy. Another reason for targeting the level of the exchange rate is to prevent crises. If there are significant currency mismatches in the economy so that foreign currency liabilities are not fully backed by foreign currency assets or earnings, domestic currency depreciation can adversely affect the financial position of financial institutions or firms that resort to foreign currency financing. A sufficiently large depreciation could weaken the financial sector or even trigger a financial crisis under these conditions.

But then there are other objectives behind intervention. For example, the BIS report makes it clear that, unlike in most industrial countries, the central banks of many emerging countries consider reserve accumulation a legitimate and important goal of official intervention. Following the currency crises in Asia, Argentina, Brazil, Mexico, Russia and Turkey, "many central banks have come to regard high foreign exchange reserves as a key buffer against external vulnerabilities and debt sustainability problems".

The second condition pertains to the effectiveness of intervention. Anecdotal evidence shows that intervention is ineffective unless it reinforces an already established market trend. Recall the bitter experience of the Bank of England in 1992 and that of the central bank of Thailand in 1997 when they tried to defend their currencies against the market forces unleashed by speculators who took massive short positions on the pound and baht, respectively. The two central banks ended up losing all of their reserves without making any dent in the downward paths of the exchange rates of the two currencies. Recall also that concerted central bank intervention failed to stem the appreciation of the dollar in the first half of the 1980s until the trend changed in 1985 as a result of a shift in market sentiment. In August 2011, the Bank of Japan tried to drive down the yen against the dollar but the attempt failed because of the downgrading of the US credit rating by Standard and Poor's.

The BIS report gives reasons why developed countries no longer engage actively in intervention. To start with, intervention can be effective (at least beyond the very short term) only if it is seen as foreshadowing interest rate or other policy adjustments. The report adds that "without a durable and independent impact on the nominal exchange rate, intervention is seen as having no lasting power to influence the real exchange rate and thus competitive conditions for the tradable sector". A second reason is that large-scale intervention can undermine the stance of monetary policy. A third reason is that private financial markets have adequate capacity to absorb and manage shocks, which means that there is no need to "guide" the exchange rate – hence intervention against market forces cannot be successful.

Some economists claim that while unilateral intervention is ineffective, coordinated intervention does work. For example, Stephen Jen, Morgan Stanley's chief currency economist, claims that joint interventions by the G7 have had a "near perfect record" in turning currencies around" (*The Economist*, 2008b). He gives as examples the Plaza Accord of 1985 to stop the dollar rising, the Louvre Accord of 1987 to halt the dollar's slide, the joint intervention by the US and Japan to put an end to dollar depreciation against the yen in 1995 and to support the yen in 1998, and the G7 action to support the euro in 2000. This enthusiasm for the success of coordinated intervention is subdued as Jen expresses the view that "often intervention did not succeed immediately but, with the exception of the Louvre Accord, later proved to be turning-points". The fact of the matter is that coordinated intervention is not necessarily effective but, as *The Economist* (2008b) puts it, "in the correct circumstances, it is a powerful signalling device for private-sector capital flows". This brings us back to the earlier assertion: intervention, unilateral or coordinated, does not work if it opposes market pressure. There are more question marks hovering over the effectiveness of intervention. For example, a widely held view is that intervention fails if the central bank does not sterilize the operation by selling or buying domestic securities. In other words if a central bank is trying to prevent its currency from appreciation by buying foreign currencies, it must allow its purchases of foreign exchange to reduce the domestic money supply. Another proposition is that intervention cannot be successful unless it is supplemented by changes in interest rates.

Not even coordinated intervention works if it opposes market forces. It is claimed that China has for a long time succeeded in sterilizing foreign exchange inflows (printing yuan to buy incoming dollars and then selling bonds to banks to absorb excess liquidity). While at one time this operation was profitable, as the return on dollar reserves was higher than the rate on the yuan bonds, falling interest rates in the US and rising Chinese rates have changed the situation. It remains true, however, that sterilization or no sterilization, coordinated or otherwise, if the market dictates yuan appreciation, $1 billion a day of intervention cannot prevent that from happening. This is because this amount is 1/40th the daily trading of the yuan against the dollar, which according to the Bank for International Settlements (2010) is ranked 17th, representing 1 per cent of total trading. Some would say that China can succeed because of its capital controls, but we know that in the age of derivatives and financial engineering capital controls can be easily circumvented.

Just like the empirical evidence on exchange rate misalignment, the empirical evidence on the effectiveness of intervention is mixed. Where foreign exchange intervention has been found to be effective, the magnitudes differ substantially across studies. The problem stems not only from differences in the data and methodology employed, but also from difficulties in defining "successful" intervention. In particular, much disagreement exists about the size and persistence of measured effects on the level and volatility of the exchange rate that constitutes success. This is partly a reflection of the absence of a reliable model of exchange rate determination that can be used to proxy the exchange rate path followed in the absence of intervention. Moreover, the objective of central bank intervention can change between intervention episodes so that the true success criteria may be time-dependent. Empirical studies on the effectiveness of intervention in emerging market countries are plagued by severe data limitations and frequent structural breaks.

Neely (2000) identifies a problem with the effectiveness of intervention, which is the use of changes in international reserves as a proxy for the size of intervention. He concludes that "it is difficult to say whether changes in reserves are an adequate proxy for intervention". Goldstein and Lardy (2008) share this position in such a way as to condemn China by arguing that "increases in holdings of foreign exchange reserves are downward-biased estimates of official intervention in the foreign exchange market", meaning that the scale of Chinese intervention is bigger than what it appears to be. Bordo and Schwartz (1991) reviewed the conduct and scale of official intervention by monetary authorities in the US, Japan and Germany in the aftermath of the Plaza Agreement, concluding that "relative to trading volume and the stock of internationally traded assets denominated in foreign currencies, intervention is small scale and sporadic, hence at best limited to transitory effects". Furthermore, they argue that intervention does not appear to reduce the volatility of daily exchange rates.

The third condition, targeting the dollar exchange rate, is referred to in the BIS report, which raises a question as to how far the bilateral exchange rate (for example, vis-à-vis the dollar) is targeted, rather than the effective exchange rate or the bilateral exchange rate against other currencies. The report gives reasons why attention may have shifted to other exchange rates; one of these reasons is the creation of the euro, which brought forth a large single currency trading area, but it is not clear to what extent this has been reflected in exchange rate targets or foreign reserve portfolios outside Europe. The roles played by China and Japan in Asian trade are also important. For example, the growing production networks between China and the rest of Asia suggest that these countries need to pay increasing attention to their exchange rates relative to each other's currencies, rather than focusing exclusively on the US dollar. Also, the fact that Korea (for example) competes directly with Japan in third markets (including the Chinese market) can reasonably motivate the assignment of a greater weight to won/yen fluctuations as opposed to won/dollar fluctuations. This is particularly relevant during periods when the yen weakens against the dollar.

The case is much more intuitive than this. If the yuan is undervalued then market forces should dictate appreciation. Allegedly the Chinese are preventing this appreciation via intervention to buy the dollar. Buying the dollar may be motivated more by the desire to accumulate reserves than to target the level of the exchange rate. Then if market forces dictate appreciation, even the massive Chinese reserves cannot match the power of the market. Intervention in the foreign exchange market cannot be taken to imply exchange rate misalignment.

CONCLUSION

The first argument put forward by those claiming that China is the cause of the US trade deficit, that the yuan is undervalued, is not supported by empirical evidence. No one really knows whether the yuan is undervalued or overvalued because no one knows where the exchange rate should be. Even the most enthusiastic China bashers, such as Paul Krugman, admit that no one knows the yuan's fair value.

For a long time, *The Economist* magazine maintained that the yuan was undervalued against the dollar because that is what its Big Mac index showed. Not any more: the modified Big Mac index suggested by *The Economist* recently shows that the yuan is not undervalued. The underlying argument is ludicrous because we should expect nothing other than that Big Macs are cheaper in China than in America. This is exactly what the modified Big Mac index shows after adjusting the original index to reflect differences in GDP per capita. The results derived from PPP are also unreliable because it has been established that PPP is valid only under hyperinflation or over a very long period of time. The "more sophisticated" approaches to the estimation of the real effective exchange rate provide the means whereby the results can be manipulated to arrive at the desired conclusion.

Last, but not least, there is no foundation whatsoever for the propositions that undervaluation of the yuan can be judged merely by looking at some indicators, such as the trade balance itself, foreign exchange market intervention and the accumulation of reserves. In short, those who are out to prove that the yuan is undervalued are motivated by ideology as opposed to a quest for the truth.

5. The cause and cure: simple numerical illustrations

INTRODUCTION

In this chapter simple numerical illustrations are used to validate the proposition that, unlike what China bashers believe, revaluation of the yuan will not eliminate or even reduce the US trade deficit with China. This is because a number of inhibiting factors and unsatisfied conditions disturb or prevent the effect of exchange rate adjustment from being transmitted to the trade balance (for example, Moosa, 2011a). In these illustrations, revaluation of the yuan necessarily means devaluation (or depreciation) of the dollar, and the US trade deficit with China is equivalent to China's surplus with the US. The illustrations can be presented from either a Chinese or a US perspective, but we will predominantly consider the situation from a Chinese perspective (not that it matters, anyway). In this case we consider the question regarding whether or not a revaluation of the Chinese currency against the dollar eliminates or reduces the Chinese surplus with the US, which is equivalent to the question of whether or not depreciation of the dollar will eliminate or reduce the US deficit with China. The starting point in this exercise is to explain how the trade balance (or current account) is related to the foreign exchange market where the exchange rate is determined.

For the purpose of the following discussion, the term "exchange rate adjustment" is used to refer to both revaluation and devaluation (or both appreciation and depreciation), while the term "foreign exchange" is used to refer to either currencies, depending on which perspective we use (Chinese or American). Initially it is assumed that Chinese exports to the US are invoiced in yuan terms. In reality, however, Chinese exports to the US are invoiced in dollar terms, that is, Chinese goods sold to the US are priced in dollars. We will return to this point later to demonstrate that this practice reduces the effectiveness of exchange rate adjustment.

THE TRADE DEFICIT AS EXCESS DEMAND FOR FOREIGN EXCHANGE

The relation between the balance of payments and the foreign exchange market arises because transactions involving trade and capital flows (which are recorded on the balance of payments) give rise to demand for and supply of currencies. Transactions in the market for goods and services (such as imports and exports) give rise to the demand for (buying) and supply of (selling) foreign exchange, respectively. Americans buy the yuan to pay for Chinese goods, whereas the Chinese buy the dollar to pay for US goods. In the language of supply and demand, the demand for yuan (supply of dollar) comes from Americans wishing to buy Chinese goods, whereas the supply of yuan (demand for dollar) comes from the Chinese wishing to buy American goods. Transactions in financial markets (which are recorded on the financial or capital account of the balance of payments) also lead to demand for and supply of foreign exchange. The sale of domestic securities and purchase of foreign securities give rise to demand for foreign exchange (supply of the domestic currency). Conversely, the purchase of domestic securities and sale of foreign securities give rise to demand for the domestic currency (supply of foreign exchange). The following discussion is restricted to the trade balance (the balance of the exports and imports of goods) although the arguments are valid for any part of the balance of payments.

In an ideal world the relation between the trade balance and the foreign exchange market is not difficult to understand. For each transaction on the foreign exchange market related to the buying and selling of goods across borders, there is a corresponding entry on the trade balance. A deficit in the trade balance corresponds to excess demand for foreign exchange, while a surplus implies excess supply of foreign exchange. The demand for foreign exchange is equivalent to the amount a country spends on imported foreign goods (import expenditure). The supply of foreign exchange is equivalent to the amount foreigners spend on exported domestic goods (export revenue). When export revenue is less than import expenditure there is excess demand for foreign exchange, hence a deficit in the trade balance. Import expenditure depends on the quantity and price (in domestic currency terms) of imports, whereas export revenue depends on the quantity and price (in foreign currency terms) of exports.

The proposition that the trade balance is affected by changes in the exchange rate is simple and rather intuitive. Changes in the exchange rate affect the domestic currency price of imports and consequently the demand for imports and import expenditure. Export revenue also changes in response to changes in the exchange rate via consequent changes in the foreign currency price of exports. Depreciation or devaluation of the domestic currency raises the domestic currency price of imports and reduces the foreign currency price of exports. The demand for imports falls while the demand for exports rises, hence the difference between export revenue and import expenditure rises and the trade balance improves. Appreciation or revaluation of the domestic currency works the other way round. This sounds a logical line of reasoning, which supports the argument that revaluation of the yuan will eventually eliminate the US trade deficit with China. However, this sequence of events occurs only when a number of conditions and assumptions are satisfied, which is unlikely to happen in practice. The following simple analysis illustrates these conditions and assumptions.

REVALUATION OF THE YUAN: HOW IS IT SUPPOSED TO WORK?

Consider a simple example in which the initial situation involves China exporting one product to the US valued at CNY15 per unit, which gives a US price of $2.31 at the initial exchange rate (CNY/$) of 6.50. At this price the US demand for the Chinese product is 200 units, which means that China's export revenue (US import expenditure) is $461.54. At the same time, China imports 20 units of the US product valued at $15 or CNY97.50 at the initial exchange rate. At this price, China's import expenditure is $300. At the initial exchange rate, therefore, China's trade surplus with the US is $161.54.

Consider now what happens if China revalues its currency, such that the exchange rate becomes 6.00. The change in the exchange rate does not affect the yuan price of exports or the dollar price of imports. What will be affected directly are the dollar price of Chinese exports, which rises to $2.50, and the yuan price of imports, which falls to CNY90. Because exports are now more expensive while imports are cheaper, the demand for exports declines while the demand for imports rises. But by how much will demand rise and fall? This depends on the elasticity of demand, which is a measure of the responsiveness of the quantity demanded to changes in the price. If demand is not responsive at all to changes in the price (the elasticitiy of demand is zero) the quantities of exports and imports will not change and revaluation will not achieve the underlying objective of trade balance adjustment.

Let us assume that the elasticity of demand is 1, which means that as the price rises (falls) by x per cent, the quantity demanded will fall (rise) by x per cent. On the exports side, the US dollar price rises by 8.33 per

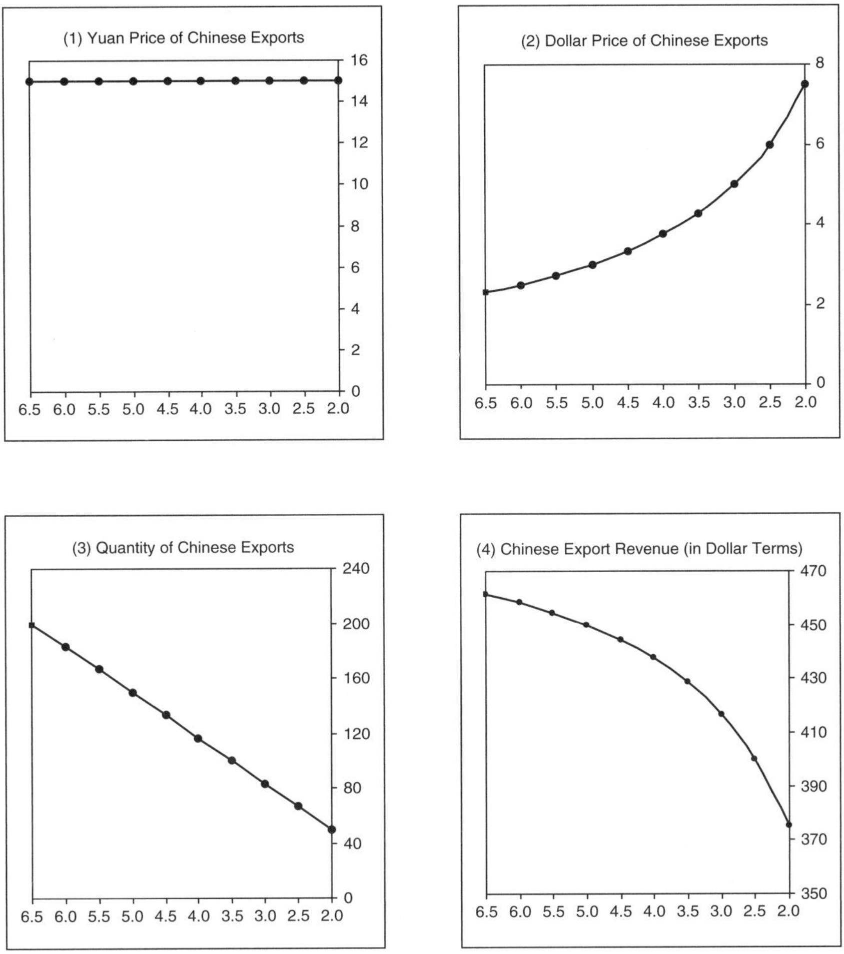

Figure 5.1 The effect of revaluation on the exports side (elasticity = 1)

cent, which causes a fall in the quantity of exports by the same percentage to 183.33. Hence, China's export revenue falls to $458.33. On the imports side, the yuan price of imports declines by 7.69 per cent, causing a rise in the demand for imports by 7.69 per cent to 21.54, which means that Chinese import expenditure rises to $323.08. As a result of these changes, the Chinese surplus with the US drops to $135.26.

In this example, further revaluation of the yuan will bring about further reductions in the Chinese surplus with the US as we can see in Figures 5.1 and 5.2 (note that the scale on the horizontal axis is reversed to show

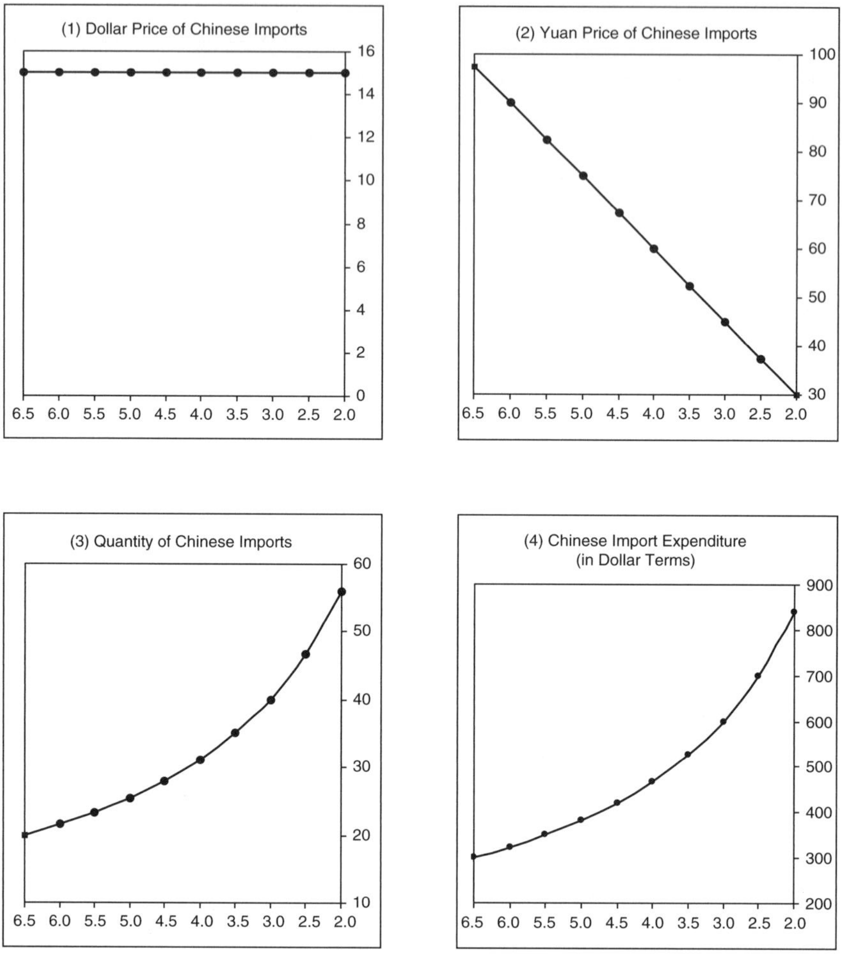

Figure 5.2 The effect of revaluation on the imports side (elasticity = 1)

the effect of a fall in the exchange rate, that is, revaluation of the yuan). Figure 5.1 illustrates what happens on the exports side. As the exchange rate drops from 6.5 to 2 (as the yuan becomes stronger), nothing happens to the yuan price of Chinese goods, but the dollar price of these goods (exports) rises (Chinese goods become more expensive for Americans). As a result, the quantity of Chinese exports declines, and the overall result is a decline in the dollar value of Chinese export revenue. Figure 5.2 shows what happens on the imports side. Like the yuan price of Chinese exports, the dollar price of Chinese imports is unaffected by changes in the exchange rate. However, the yuan price of Chinese imports declines, making American goods more attractive for the Chinese. As a result the quantity of imports rises and so does Chinese import expenditure. The combined effect of rising import expenditure and falling export revenue results in a shrinkage of the Chinese surplus with the US. This sequence of events occurs only because certain assumptions underpin these calculations. In the remainder of this chapter we consider these assumptions and see what happens when they are relaxed.

THE ELASTICITIES ASSUMPTION

We reached the conclusion that revaluation does work only because we assumed that the elasticity of demand for imports and exports is 1. Let us see what happens when the elasticity is 0.5, as illustrated in Figures 5.3 and 5.4. Starting from the same initial conditions as in the previous case, revaluation of the yuan from 6.5 to 6 causes a 4.17 per cent decline in the demand for exports and a 3.85 per cent increase in the demand for imports. Export revenue actually rises to \$479.17, while import expenditure rises to \$311.54. The reason why export revenue rises in this case is inelastic demand, that is, the quantity demanded does not respond strongly (or responds less than proportionately) to price changes. The rise in the price resulting from revaluation more than offsets the decline in quantity, which boosts export revenue. If the exchange rate goes down to 2, the surplus will be \$263.56.

Figure 5.5 shows what happens as the exchange rate rises under four assumptions for the values of the elasticity of demand for exports and imports. When elasticity is 1, the Chinese trade surplus falls as the exchange rate declines. At an exchange rate of around 4.25 (revaluation of some 34 per cent) the Chinese surplus will be eliminated completely. If the rate goes down further to 2, China will have a deficit with the US of \$465. When the elasticity of demand for exports and imports is 0.2, revaluation of the yuan leads to a bigger trade surplus for China. If, on the other hand, demand is highly elastic (say, elasticity is 1.5), trade balance correction happens more quickly, requiring only 19 per cent revaluation to 5.25 to eliminate the Chinese surplus.

The outcome of yuan revaluation, therefore, depends on the elasticities of demand for exports and imports. The importance of elasticities can be illustrated by examining how the value of elasticity affects the extent of currency revaluation required to eliminate the Chinese surplus in our hypothetical example. Starting from an initial exchange rate of 6.5 and assuming that the elasticity of demand for exports is unchanged at 0.5,

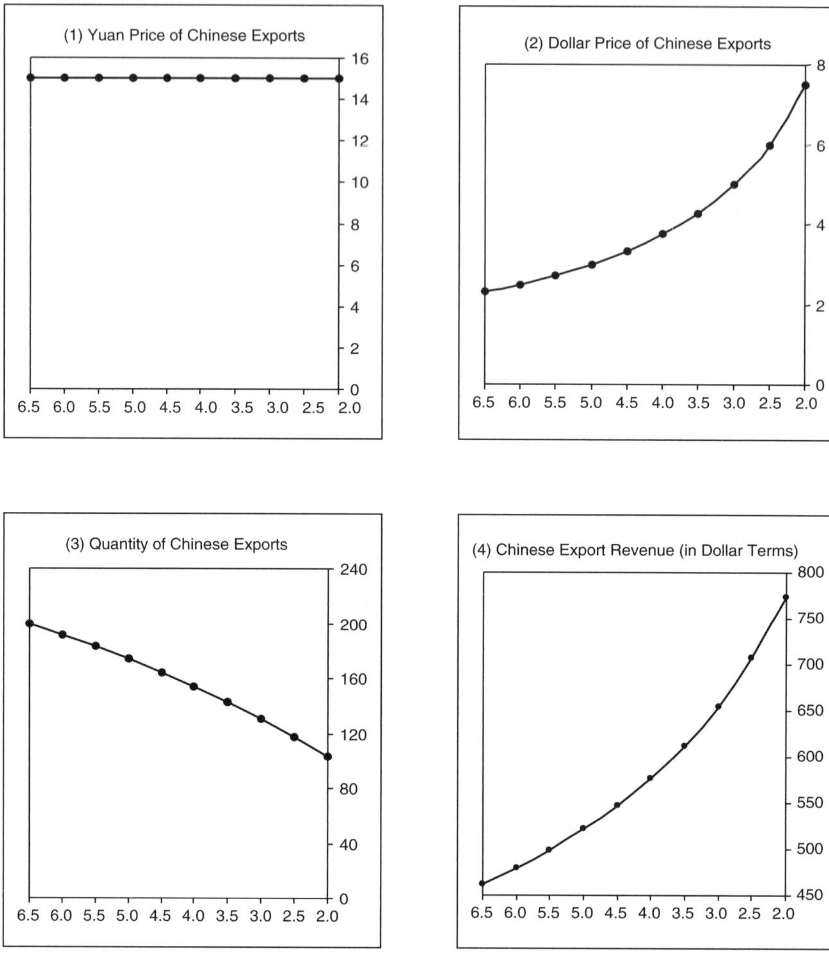

Figure 5.3 The effect of revaluation on the exports side (elasticity = 0.5)

we calculate the revaluation required to eliminate the surplus at various values of the elasticity of demand, starting from an initial value of 0.5. In this case the exchange rate must decline from 6.5 to 2.87 to eliminate the surplus. If the elasticity of demand for imports is 0.6, the exchange rate must fall to 2.93. In general, the higher the value of the elasticity of demand for imports, for a given value of the elasticity of demand for exports, the smaller the revaluation needed to eliminate the Chinese surplus, as shown in Figure 5.6. However, the elasticity of demand for imports is more crucial for the revaluation required to eliminate the surplus.

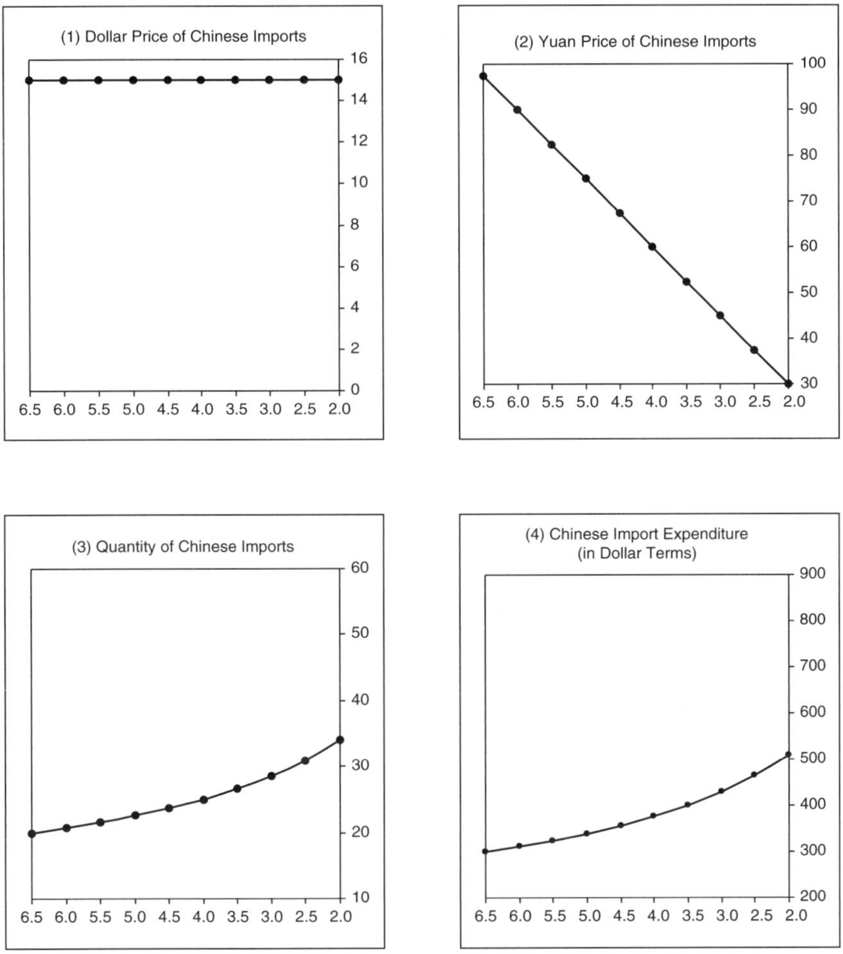

Figure 5.4 The effect of revaluation on the imports side (elasticity = 0.5)

So, when we relax the assumption that the demand for exports and imports is elastic and assume instead that demand is inelastic, revaluation does not work. In practice, therefore, the effectiveness of revaluation depends, among other things, on the elasticities of demand for imports and exports. But this is not all. Even if demand is elastic, revaluation will be effective only if supply is also elastic. If the increase in the Chinese demand for American goods resulting from revaluation cannot be accommodated by an increase in supply, revaluation will not work. Supply may not be elastic if, for example, restrictions are imposed on the exports of

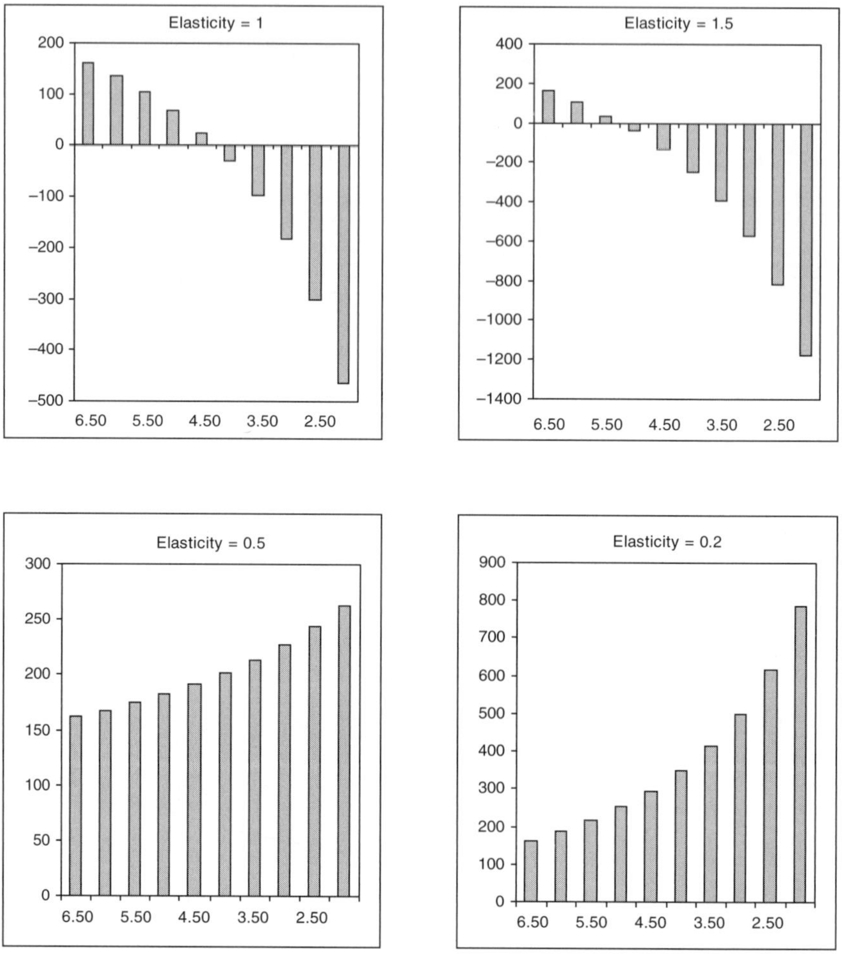

Figure 5.5 *China's trade balance following revaluation under four elasticity assumptions*

"sensitive" goods to China or if the US has no capacity in the production of cheap labour-intensive goods. The effect of inelastic supply is illustrated in Figure 5.7 in which the demand for exports is assumed to be elastic. Starting from a surplus of \$162, revaluation of the yuan will produce a deficit of \$465 when the exchange rate declines to 2. This happens only because of the assumption of elastic supply, that is, the US can meet the increase in Chinese demand for its goods as they become cheaper.

Consider now what happens when the supply of US exports to China

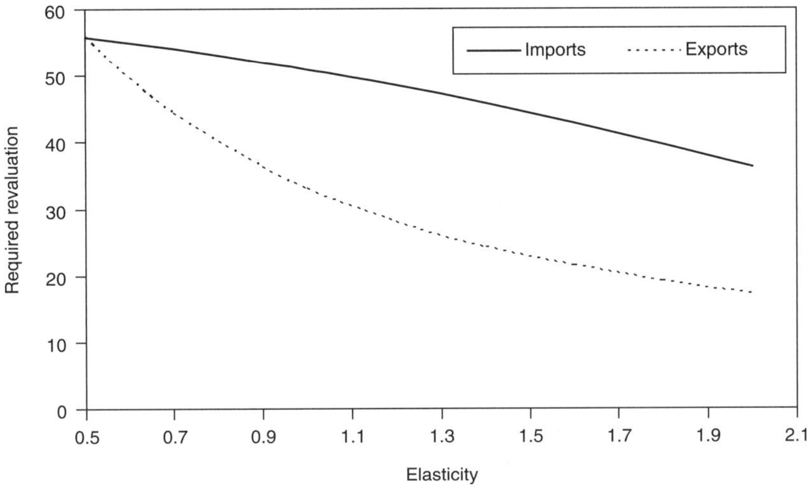

Figure 5.6 *Revaluation required to eliminate the Chinese surplus for various values of the elasticity of demand*

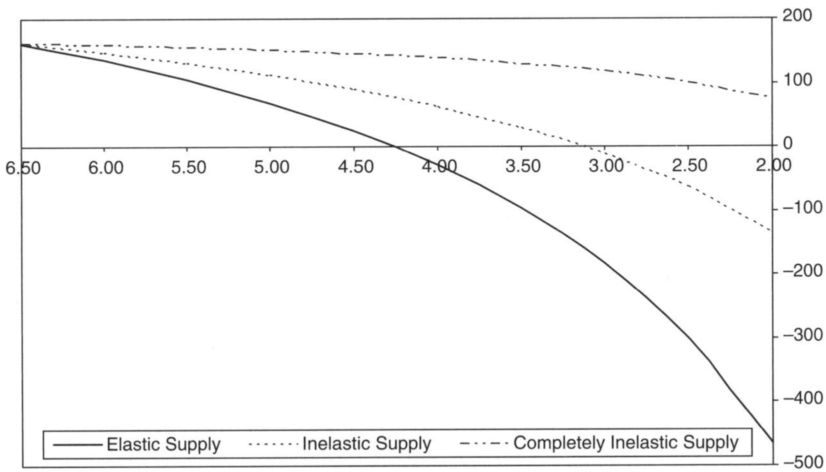

Figure 5.7 *The effect of yuan revaluation when the supply of US exports is elastic and inelastic*

is inelastic, in the sense that US exporters can only meet 50 per cent of the increase in Chinese demand. The surplus becomes a deficit of $135 at the exchange rate of 2, which means that revaluation is less effective in this case. In the extreme case where the supply of US exports is completely inelastic (in the sense that US exporters cannot meet any of the increase in the Chinese demand for US exports) the surplus will be reduced but not eliminated. In this case there is no change in the quantity of Chinese imports from the US, which means that no change occurs in Chinese import expenditure.

TIME AND THE J-CURVE EFFECT

One of the factors that determine elasticities is time, because demand is more elastic in the long run (no economist would, however, tell you how long the long run is or how short the short run is). Because demand is inelastic in the short run, the immediate effect of devaluation of the domestic currency (or revaluation of the foreign currency) would be deterioration in the trade balance. Consider the case, using our hypothetical data, of a one-off revaluation of the yuan from 6.5 to 5, and assume that elasticities increase with the passage of time, starting with a value of 0.4 for both exports and imports. Immediately after the revaluation of the yuan, the Chinese surplus increases from $161.5 to $200.3. With the passage of time, as elasticities increase, the surplus starts to decline until it is eliminated after nine periods of time, as shown in Figure 5.8. If revaluation is smaller, it will take longer for the surplus to be eliminated. For example, if the yuan is revalued from 6.5 to 6, it will take almost 28 periods to eliminate the surplus.

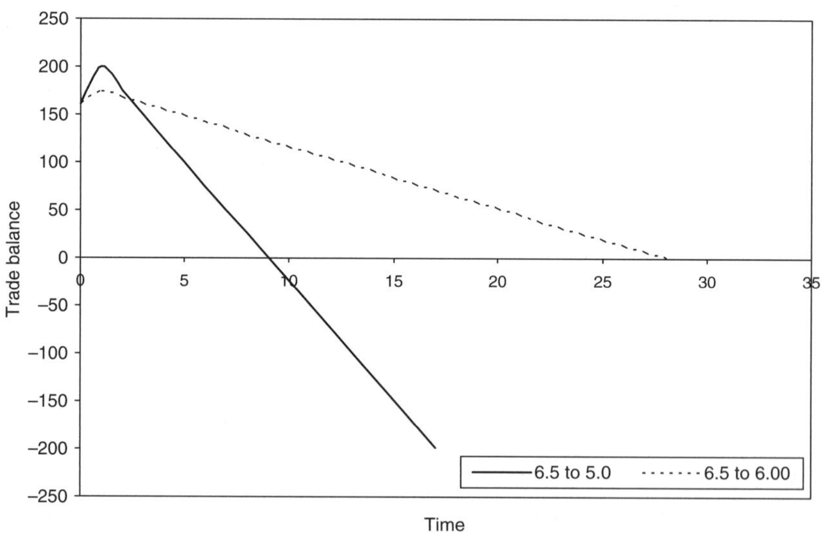

Figure 5.8 The time required to eliminate the Chinese surplus

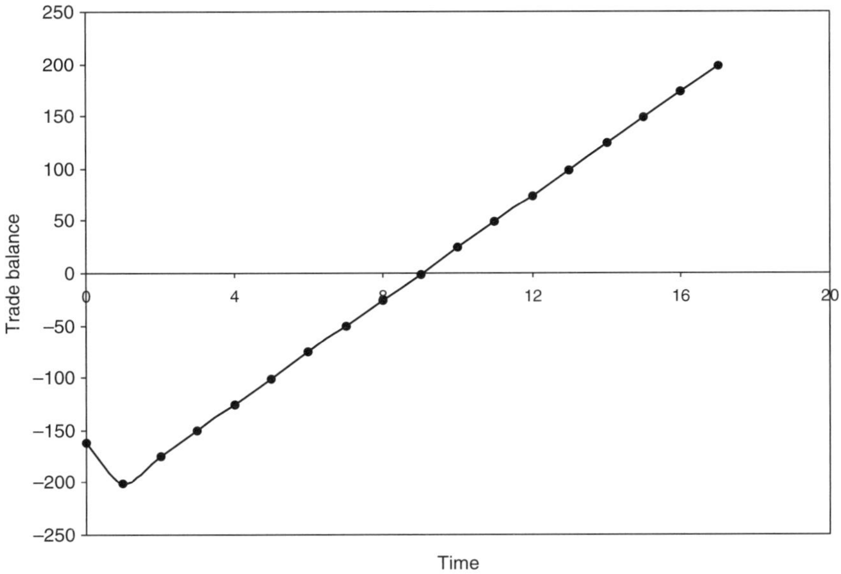

Figure 5.9 The J-curve effect

The reason why this process is called the J-curve effect becomes obvious if we plot the US deficit, which is the negative of the Chinese surplus. The time path of the US deficit looks like the letter J, as shown in Figure 5.9. We will come back to the J-curve effect and provide some explanations for the phenomenon in Chapter 6. It will be demonstrated that the J-curve is not the only phenomenon that we observe in practice in conjunction with the time path of the trade balance following an exchange rate adjustment.

THE EFFECT OF EXCHANGE RATE PASS-THROUGH AND THE CURRENCY OF INVOICING

So far in this simple analysis we have assumed that (i) a change in the exchange rate is transmitted in full to the foreign currency price of exports and the domestic currency price of imports; and (ii) the currency of invoicing is that of the exporter. More specifically, we have assumed that a 10 per cent revaluation of the yuan leads to a 10 per cent rise in the dollar price of Chinese exports and a 10 per cent decline in the yuan price of imports from the US. In the jargon of international economics we have assumed a full pass-through effect when the Chinese use the yuan as the currency of

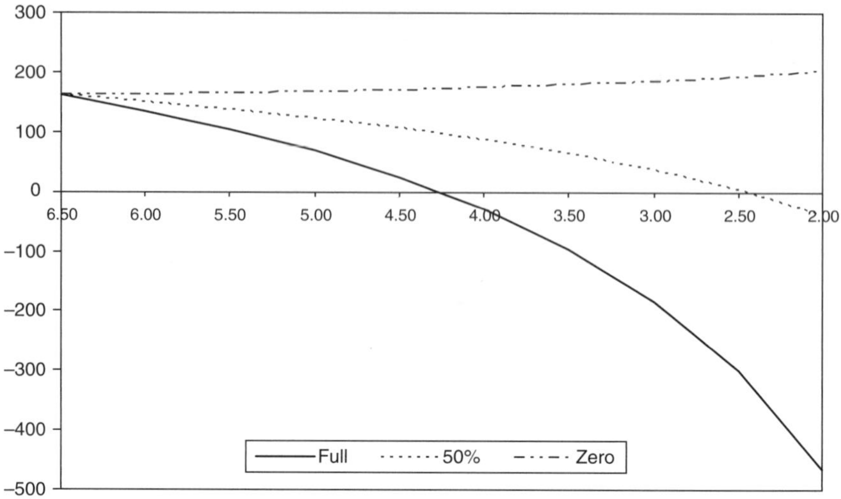

Figure 5.10 The effect of exchange rate pass-through

invoicing. A less than full pass-through of the effect of yuan revaluation would occur when Chinese exporters deliberately reduce the yuan price of their exports to offset, partially or completely, the rise in the dollar price resulting from the revaluation of the yuan. On the imports side, a less than full pass-through (of exchange rate to the price of imports) would arise if American exporters to China decide to reduce the US dollar price to offset, partially or completely, the effect of yuan revaluation on the yuan price of Chinese imports from the US.

Full versus Partial Pass-Through

Consider the example portrayed in Figure 5.10, which shows what happens to the Chinese trade surplus with the US as the exchange rate falls from 6.5 to 2 under three scenarios: (i) a full pass-through, (ii) a 50 per cent pass-through, and (iii) a zero pass-through. We also assume that the pass-through occurs on the exports side and imports side, that is, the Chinese reduce the yuan price of exports to the US to offset the increase in the dollar price as a result of revaluation, and the Americans reduce the dollar price of Chinese imports from the US to offset the effect of the rising yuan price. We also assume that the elasticities of demand for exports and imports are equal to 1. When there is a full pass-through effect, the Chinese do not adjust the yuan price of exports to the US, while the Americans do not adjust the dollar price of Chinese imports from the US. Under these conditions revaluation of the yuan is effective: a surplus of $161 at an exchange rate of 6.5 turns into a deficit of $465 at an exchange rate of 2.

Consider now what happens when there is a 50 per cent pass-through, that is, only half of the change in the exchange rate is transmitted to the yuan price of Chinese exports to the US and the dollar price of Chinese imports from the US. When the exchange rate goes down from 6.5 to 6, the Chinese reduce the yuan price of exports to the US from 15 to 14.42, while the Americans reduce the dollar price of Chinese imports also from 15 to 14.42. As a result, the Chinese surplus declines from the initial level of $161 to $150, a smaller reduction than under a complete pass-through. As the exchange rate goes to 2, the Chinese will have a small deficit of $37. Under zero pass-through, as the exchange rate goes from 6.5 to 6, the yuan price of Chinese exports to the US and the dollar price of Chinese imports from the US decline from 15 to 13.85 – consequently the Chinese surplus rises slightly to $163. At an exchange rate of 2 the Chinese surplus is up at $203.

Mark-ups, Distribution Costs and Profit Margins

Incomplete pass-through may result even if there is no deliberate action by exporters to adjust their prices. So far, we have assumed that the dollar price of Chinese goods is a direct translation of the yuan price at the current exchange rate. In practice, however, this is not so because American importers of Chinese goods will add extra dollar-denominated charges to cover the costs of transport, storage, insurance and, of course, to earn profit. Since these mark-ups are dollar-denominated, they will not be affected by revaluation of the yuan. In the case of China, there are also mark-ups added by the Hong Kong intermediaries who deal with Chinese exports to the US via Hong Kong.

The effect of mark-ups in various shapes and forms is illustrated in Figure 5.11, which shows what happens to the Chinese surplus with the US as a result of yuan revaluation under three scenarios: (i) zero mark-ups, (ii) 10 per cent mark-ups, and (iii) 20 per cent mark-ups. Revaluation is most effective under the first scenario as a surplus of $161 at an exchange rate of 6.5 becomes a deficit of $465 at an exchange rate of 2, hence a decline by 388 per cent. Under the second scenario of a 10 per cent mark-up, a surplus of $230 becomes a deficit of $395, a decline by 271 per cent. And when the mark-up is 20 per cent, a surplus of $762 declines by 81 per cent to $147. Hence the higher the mark-ups, the weaker will be the effect of yuan revaluation.

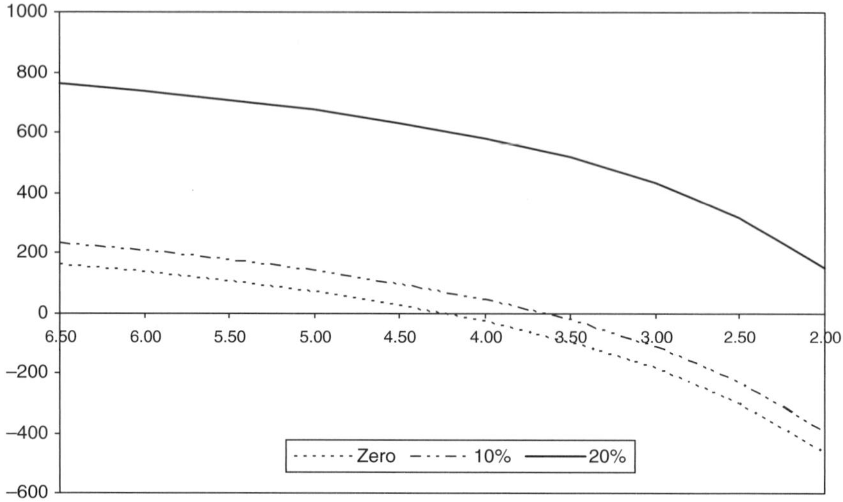

Figure 5.11 The effect of mark-ups

The Currency of Invoicing

Consider now the effect of the currency of invoicing. When the Australian dollar depreciated significantly in 2001, consumers in Australia did not feel any noticeable change in the prices of imported goods because, according to some market sources, Australian imports are predominantly denominated in Australian dollars from the source (this is actually what Microsoft does in dealing with Australian importers). Thus, the cost of the depreciation of the Australian dollar was borne by foreign manufacturers. If the currency of invoicing is that of the importer (that is, if China invoices its exports in dollar terms) revaluation of the yuan will be weaker because it will only affect the imports side, that is, it will affect the yuan price of Chinese imports but not the dollar price of exports. If also US importers invoice the Chinese in yuan terms, revaluation of the yuan will be totally ineffective.

Consider Figure 5.12, which shows what happens when (i) the Chinese use the yuan as the currency of invoicing, (ii) the Chinese use the dollar as the currency of invoicing, and (iii) the Chinese use the dollar while the Americans use the yuan as the currency of invoicing. Under scenario (i), when the currency of invoicing is that of the exporter, revaluation is effective. Under scenario (ii), the use by the Chinese of the dollar as the currency of invoicing reduces the effectiveness of revaluation. If both countries use the other country's currency as the currency of invoicing as under scenario

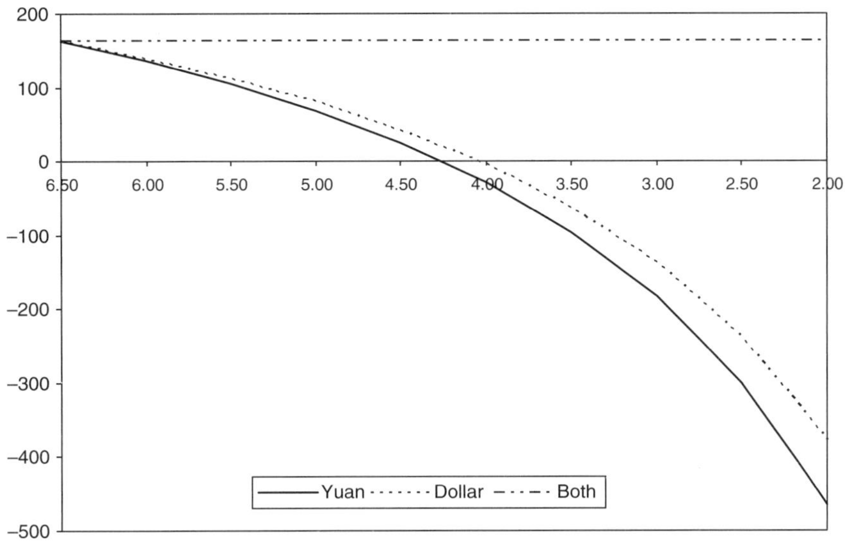

Figure 5.12 The effect of the currency of invoicing

(iii), revaluation of the yuan will be totally ineffective. In this case revaluation will not affect the dollar price of Chinese exports or the yuan price of imports, hence there is no change in either export revenue or import expenditure, and the Chinese surplus with the US remains unchanged.

THE EFFECT OF GROWTH, INFLATION AND TRADE RESTRICTIONS

For exchange rate adjustment to be effective, there must be no offsetting effects of other factors that affect the trade balance. We cannot predict the change in one factor (the exchange rate) on the trade balance by assuming that other factors stay unchanged. In reality, this cannot be done because the *ceteris paribus* condition does not hold. This is a heroic assumption used by economists to imply that all other things (apart from the factor under consideration) stay unchanged.

The Effect of Growth and Inflation

One of the factors affecting the trade balance is economic growth. It is plausible to postulate that imports are positively related to domestic income whereas exports are not, since the latter depend on foreign income.

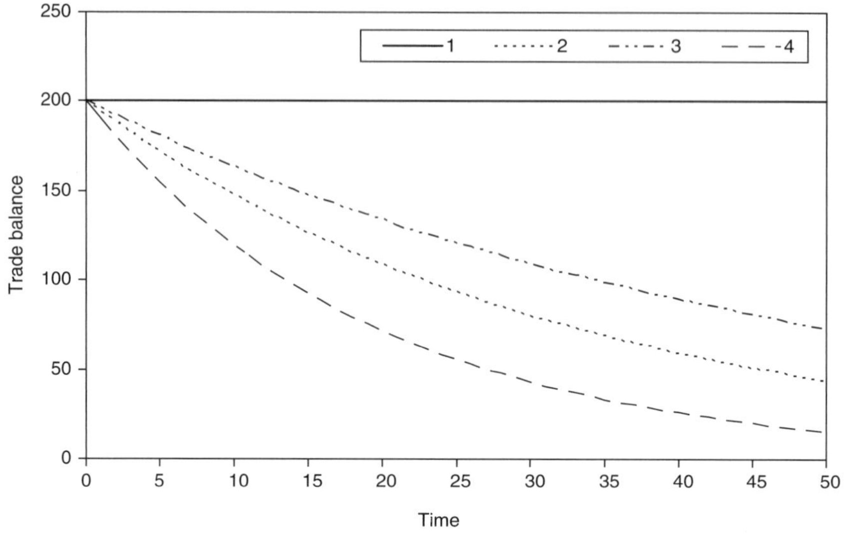

Notes:
Scenario 1: baseline where Chinese surplus is stable over time
Scenario 2: Chinese growth causes 3 per cent reduction in surplus each time period
Scenario 3: Chinese exports decline by 2 per cent each time period
Scenario 4: China experiences the combined effect of faster growth and higher inflation

Figure 5.13 The effect of growth and inflation over time under four scenarios

Thus, if a country has a higher growth rate than those of its trading partners, its demand for goods and services (including imported goods and services) will rise faster than the demand of its trading partners for its goods and services. Assuming that other factors are unchanged, it follows that the country with the higher growth rate will experience deterioration in its trade balance. So why is it that countries like Japan, Singapore and China have simultaneously experienced rapid growth and a trade surplus? The answer is simple: the trade balance is determined by the combined effect of a variety of factors, not just by economic growth.

Another determining factor is inflation. A country that has a higher inflation rate than its trading partners suffers from deterioration in the trade balance. This is because inflation erodes the competitive position of the economy by making domestic goods more expensive and hence less competitive in foreign markets. Thus while growth affects the quantity of imports, inflation affects the price of exports.

Figure 5.13 illustrates the effect of growth and inflation over time,

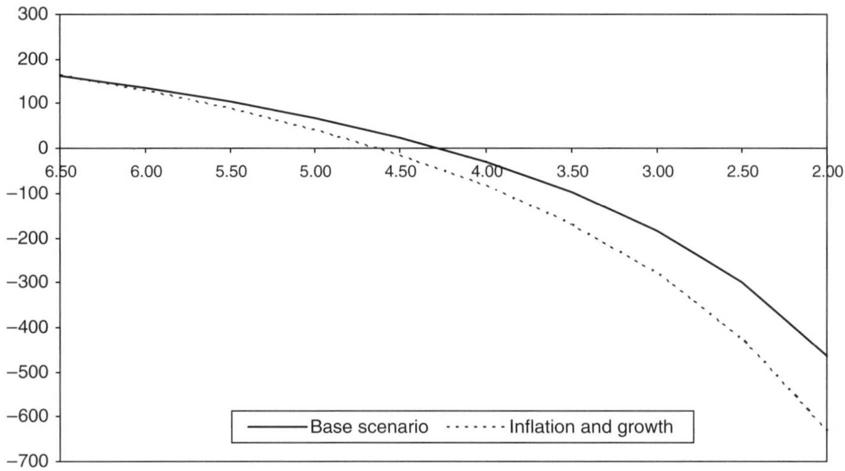

Figure 5.14 The effect of growth and inflation on the effectiveness of revaluation

starting from a Chinese surplus of \$200 at time 0. Consider what happens over 50 time periods under four scenarios: (i) the baseline scenario (scenario 1) in which the Chinese surplus is stable over time as growth and inflation in China are similar to those in the rest of the world; (ii) scenario 2 in which Chinese growth causes a 3 per cent reduction in the surplus each time period (as a result of growth in imports); (iii) scenario 3 in which Chinese exports decline by 2 per cent each time period (as a result of higher export prices); and (iv) scenario 4 in which China experiences the combined effect of faster growth and higher inflation. Starting from a Chinese surplus of \$200, nothing changes under scenario 1. Under scenarios 2, 3 and 4, the surplus declines to \$43.6, \$72.8 and \$15.4, respectively. Figure 5.14 demonstrates that the effectiveness of revaluation can be enhanced by the effect of growth and inflation (when China has higher growth and inflation rates than the rest of the world). As the exchange rate declines from 6.5 to 2, China's surplus becomes a deficit of \$465 without the effect of growth and inflation (base scenario) and a deficit of \$634 with the effect of growth and inflation.

In this example we have assumed that exchange rate adjustment works, which can only be the case if all of the conditions described earlier are satisfied. The objective is merely to show the effect of growth and inflation. Since China has both faster growth and higher inflation, these forces should bring about a reduction in the Chinese surplus over time, irrespective of the exchange rate. Unlike in the case of exchange rate adjustment,

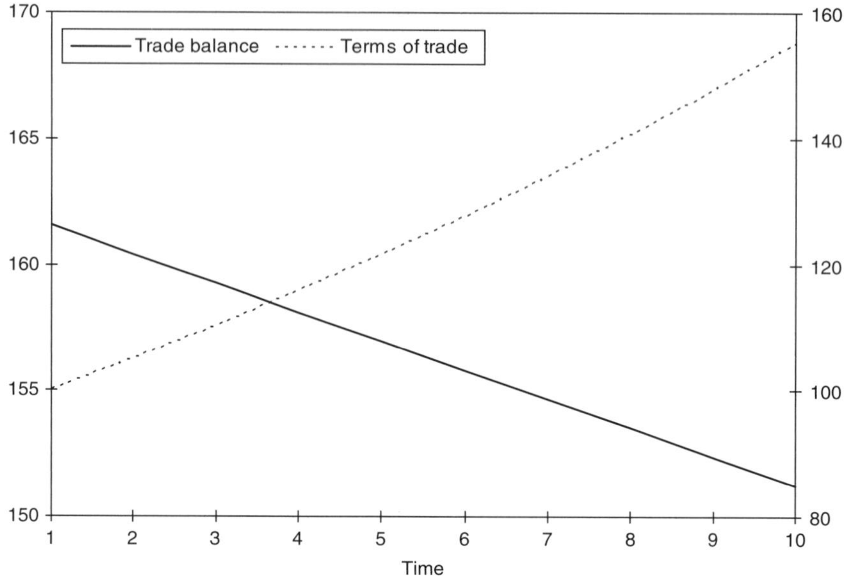

Figure 5.15 The trade balance and terms of trade (elasticity = 1)

the logic behind the effects of growth and inflation on the trade balance is straightforward.

The Terms of Trade

Inflation affects another factor that is believed to affect the trade balance, which is the terms of trade. The terms of trade represent a measure of export prices relative to import prices – the ratio of export prices to import prices. As export prices rise relative to import prices, the terms of trade improve, and vice versa. However, the effect of changes in the terms of trade on the trade balance depends on the elasticities of demand for exports and imports.

In Figure 5.15 we consider what happens as the price of Chinese exports rises by 5 per cent each period, without any change in the exchange rate or the price of imports, implying an improvement in the terms of trade. If we assume that the demand for exports is elastic, export revenue declines, leading to a deteriorating trade balance. Hence when the elasticity of demand for exports is high, the terms of trade and trade balance move in opposite directions. In Figure 5.16, the demand for exports is inelastic, hence a rise in the price of exports leads to a rise in export revenue and

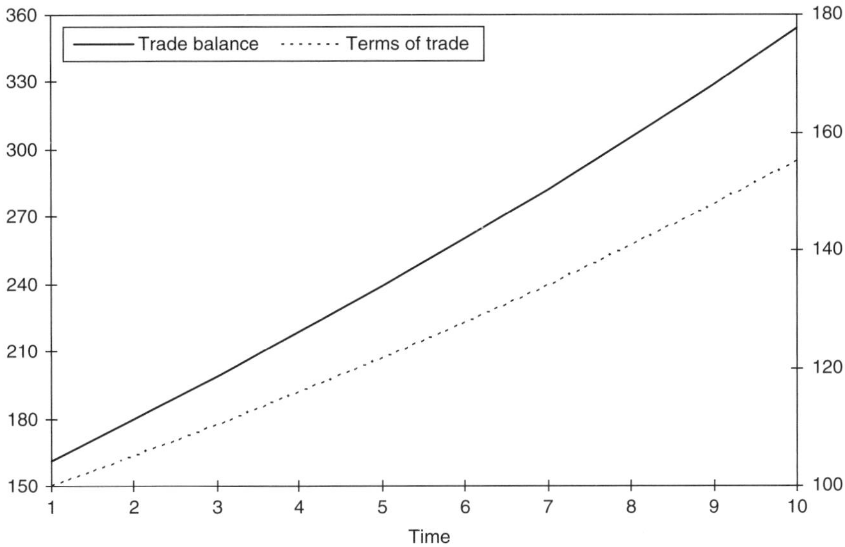

Figure 5.16 The trade balance and terms of trade (elasticity = 0.2)

consequently an improvement in the trade balance. When demand for exports is inelastic, the terms of trade and trade balance move in the same direction. The same reasoning applies when there is a change in import prices.

The Effect of Trade Restrictions

Consider now what happens if the US imposes trade restrictions on China. These can be of two kinds: tariffs and quotas. Tariffs are taxes on imports, which is what the US is threatening China with, whereas quotas are quantitative restrictions on imports. Assuming that China does not respond by imposing its own tariffs and quotas on imports from the US, the effects of these restrictions are illustrated in Figure 5.17, starting with a Chinese trade surplus of $200. The effect of a one-off tariff is to reduce exports by 10 per cent, hence the Chinese surplus shrinks to $140. The quota reduces Chinese exports to the US by 10 per cent from the level that would be obtained otherwise each time period. With the passage of time the deficit is eliminated. But this is easier said than done: the demand for cheap Chinese products in the US is so big that Americans cannot impose a quota, given the unavailability of suitable (American) substitutes. Figure 5.18 shows that revaluation

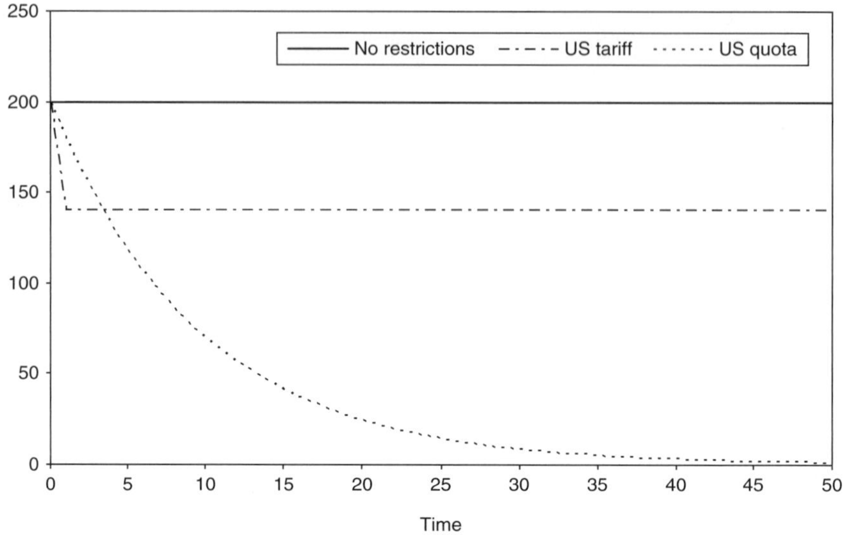

Figure 5.17 The effect of tariffs and quotas

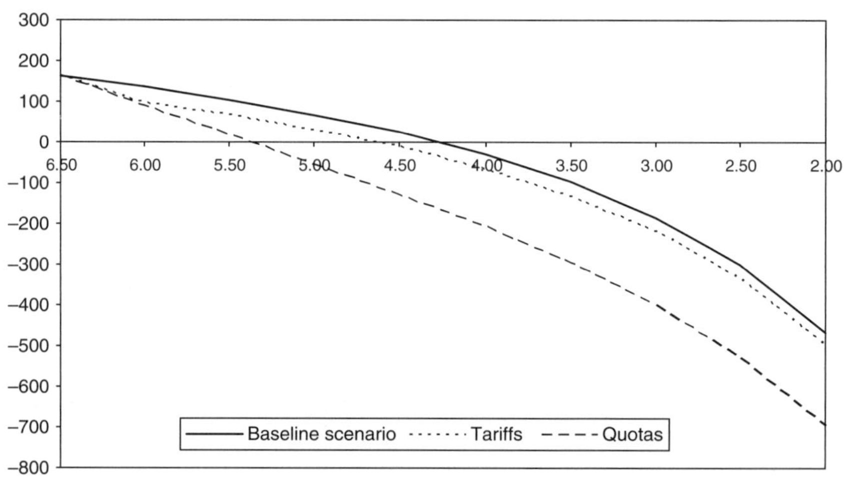

Figure 5.18 The effect of revaluation with US tariffs and quotas

of the yuan can be made more effective by imposing trade restrictions. All this of course is unlikely to work in practice because China will impose its own restrictions on US exports. A trade war will simply benefit no one.

CONCLUDING REMARKS

In theory, exchange rate adjustment can be used to implement an expenditure switching policy that diverts spending from foreign goods to domestic goods, leading to improvement in the trade balance. The underlying mechanism is that changes in the exchange rate affect the foreign currency price of exports and the domestic currency price of imports, forcing changes in the volumes of exports and imports and hence in the trade balance (via changes in export revenue and import expenditure).

While it sounds nice and easy, even in theory this process works only if several conditions are met: (i) the demand for imports and exports is sufficiently elastic; (ii) the supply of exports and imports is sufficiently elastic; (iii) there is a full exchange rate pass-through effect; (iv) the currency of invoicing is that of the exporter; (v) there is an absence of offsetting effects from other factors that affect the trade balance; and (vi) the imposition of trade restrictions by one country is not matched by changes in the other factors that determine the trade balance such as the growth, inflation and the terms of trade. This is a formidable list of conditions that must be satisfied for exchange rate adjustment to have any effect on the trade balance. In Chapter 6, we will examine all of these conditions using actual data for a number of countries. We will then explain why exchange rate adjustment does not work and why the stylized facts do not show any connection between the exchange rate and the trade balance.

6. The effect of exchange rate adjustment on the trade balance

THE STYLIZED FACTS

The stylized facts described in this chapter pertain to movements in the exchange rate, trade balance and trade volumes. To start with, a large number of historical episodes show that the trade balance does not improve following domestic currency devaluation or depreciation. One such episode that is frequently referred to is the significant deterioration of the US trade balance in 1972 despite the 1971 devaluation of the dollar following the collapse of the Bretton Woods system. In this section we examine the facts and figures about how the exchange rate is related to the trade balance. The analysis is based on data (covering several countries) extracted from the *International Financial Statistics* of the International Monetary Fund.

The Bilateral Figures

Consider first Figure 6.1, which shows the US trade deficit with China (dotted line) and the yuan/dollar nominal exchange rate since June 1993. A trend is superimposed on the trade balance to emphasize the observation of a long-term tendency for the deficit to widen, irrespective of the exchange rate. The most striking observation is that during the period up to July 2005, when the exchange rate was fixed, the deficit widened continuously while exhibiting some sort of a seasonal pattern (the almost regular ups and downs). The widening of the US trade deficit with China while the exchange rate was fixed is typically explained in terms of the undervaluation of the yuan, in the sense that the exchange rate was at such a high level that it made the US uncompetitive against China. However, common sense tells us that if two variables are indeed causally related, we should expect no change in one variable if the other variable does not change. The laws of physics, for example, tell us that the volume of gas depends on temperature and the pressure exerted on the gas. If temperature is held constant, the volume of gas is inversely proportional to pressure, in the sense that it shrinks as pressure intensifies. If pressure is kept unchanged,

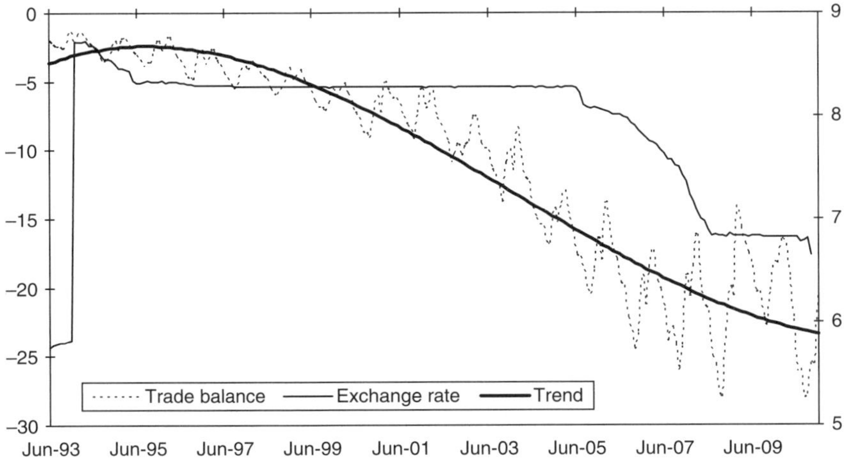

Figure 6.1 The US trade deficit with China (with a trend) and the nominal exchange rate

nothing happens to the volume of gas – it stops shrinking. If the US deficit with China is caused by the exchange rate, then starting from an initial position, the deficit should be maintained at a constant level if there is no change in the exchange rate. This means that this kind of behaviour tells us that the deficit must be caused by something else, perhaps aliens from distant galaxies, but not the exchange rate.

As if this observation is not damaging enough for the claims of those blaming China for the US trade deficit, consider what happened next – more specifically, during the period July 2005 to August 2008 – when the yuan appreciated by some 21 per cent against the dollar. This did not change the behaviour of the deficit at all, although it should have narrowed. When the exchange rate was fixed again, during the period July 2008 to June 2010, the trade deficit shrank. What seems to be some sort of improvement in the trade balance towards the end of the period was caused by the effect of the Great Recession on imports following the global financial crisis.

Let us sum up. Initially, the US trade deficit with China widened without any change in the exchange rate. This behaviour did not change as the deficit continued to blow up despite the appreciation of the yuan against the dollar. Then the balance improved while the exchange rate was fixed again. No relation whatsoever appears to be holding between the exchange rate and the trade balance, at least in this case. Some pundits might say that it is not the nominal exchange rate, but rather the real exchange rate, that matters. This observation is counter-factual, because the yuan has appreciated more in real terms than in nominal terms (*The Economist*, 2010c). Actually, because inflation in China is currently higher than that in the US, inflation will over time produce the real appreciation that the US is demanding, even without a change in the nominal exchange rate.

On the other hand, the income effect is quite conspicuous as the recession associated with the global financial crisis reduced imports, leading to an improvement in the trade balance. It is strange that those who can only see China as the culprit attribute the 2009 improvement in the trade balance to the exchange rate when it is more straightforward to attribute it to the income effect. For example, Cline (2010a) attributes the improvement to the delayed effect following the protracted appreciation of the yuan against the dollar since 2005. Cline describes as a "myth" the observation that the yuan/dollar exchange rate does not affect the US–China trade balance, arguing that it is a typical misinterpretation of the observation that during the period 2005–8 the trade deficit widened as the yuan strengthened. This misinterpretation, he claims, "results from failure to recognize the lagged effect of the exchange rate in driving trade". It is a rather strange coincidence that the effect of the exchange rate only materialized during the Great Recession. Cline's argument is obviously an ideologically-driven distortion backed by flawed economic analysis.

The Multilateral Figures

Let us now see if actual data for China and seven other countries display any relation between the nominal effective exchange rate and the trade balance. This is illustrated in Figure 6.2 for Australia, Canada, China, Japan, Korea, Malaysia, Singapore and the UK. We will consider the US figures at a later stage when we discuss the J-curve effect. No consistent relation is observable between the trade balance and the exchange rate for any of these countries. The relation is expected to be negative if domestic currency depreciation leads to an improvement in the trade balance, but the relation is strongly positive in the cases of Australia, Japan and Singapore, meaning that (on average) the trade balance improved whenever the domestic currency appreciated.

There are certainly episodes in which the trade balance improved when the domestic currency depreciated. For example, consider Australia during the period 1982–7, when a 37 per cent depreciation of the Australian dollar was associated with a turnaround of the trade balance from a deficit of $2714 million to a surplus of $492 million. Between 1989 and 2001, the currency depreciated by 27 per cent while the trade balance improved from a deficit of $3350 million to a surplus of $1737 million. But between 2002 and 2010, the currency appreciated by 36 per cent while the trade balance improved from a deficit of $5514 million to a surplus of $18 180 million. Notice the use of the phrase "associated with" to indicate that these numbers do not reflect a causal relation, because no one knows whether causation runs from the exchange rate to the trade balance, or vice versa. There is also the effect of other factors playing a role behind the scenes displayed by Figure 6.2. For example, it is believed that the Australian trade balance is affected mostly by the terms of trade (and hence commodity prices).

Now consider the case of China. Between 1983 and 1995, the Chinese currency depreciated in effective terms by 75 per cent while the trade balance improved by a factor of nine. Was that caused by the depreciation of the currency? The answer is "no", because between 1995 and 2009 the currency appreciated by 32 per cent while the trade surplus rose by a factor of 14. For those who claim that the exchange rate is the cause and cure for the US deficit with China, the stylized facts show that this is not the case. The relation between the two variables is ambiguous at best, and we cannot conclude anything about the causal effect while ignoring other, perhaps more important factors such as the terms of trade and the income effect.

It is interesting to observe what happened in 2010 as the world economy recovered from the Great Recession. Australia is a particularly interesting case, because while the Australian dollar soared in value, Australia's persistent trade deficit turned into a surplus, thanks partly to the rapid Chinese growth that boosted Australia's commodity exports. While Canada also had a strong currency, its trade deficit worsened, but not because of currency appreciation. Canada's deficit deteriorated because of declining exports to the US, its major trading partner. Japan and Korea had appreciating currencies and rising trade surpluses. The UK had a worsening trade deficit although the pound was stable in effective terms in 2010. There is nothing whatsoever in these stylized facts to show that the exchange rate bears any causal relation to the trade deficit.

Trade Volumes

Exchange rate changes are portrayed as affecting the trade balance through their effect on the volumes of exports and imports via changes in the foreign currency price of exports and the domestic currency price of imports. This channel of causation was explained in Chapter 5 with the help of numerical examples. Let us see what the stylized facts tell us about these propositions, using data from Australia, Canada, Japan and Singapore. Figure 6.3 displays the movement of the exchange rate relative to export and import volumes over the period 1982–2010. What we

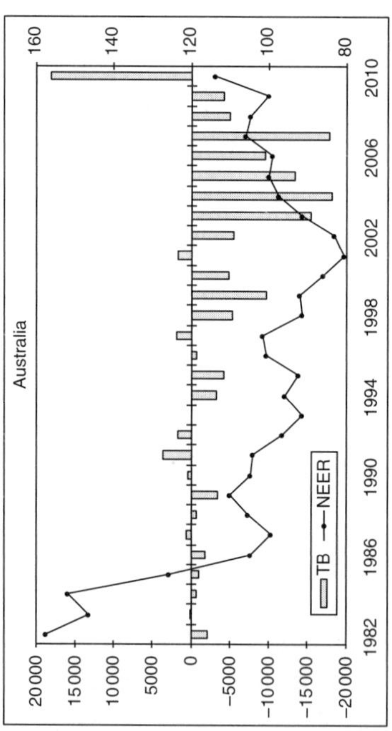
Australia
TB
NEER
20 000
15 000
10 000
5000
0
−5000
−10 000
−15 000
−20 000
160
140
120
100
80
1982
1986
1990
1994
1998
2002
2006
2010

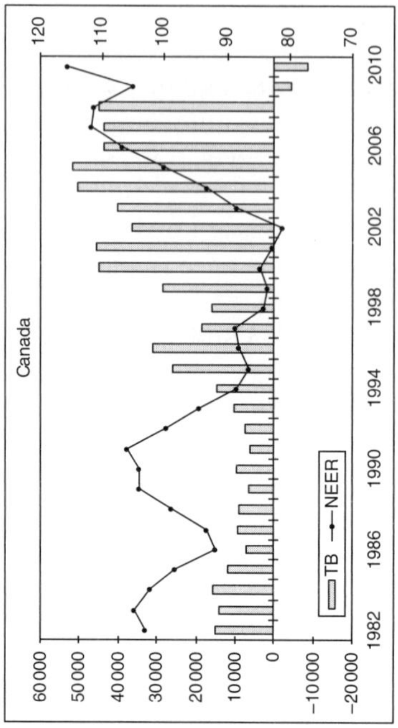
Canada
TB
NEER
60 000
50 000
40 000
30 000
20 000
10 000
0
−10 000
−20 000
120
110
100
90
80
70
1982
1986
1990
1994
1998
2002
2006
2010

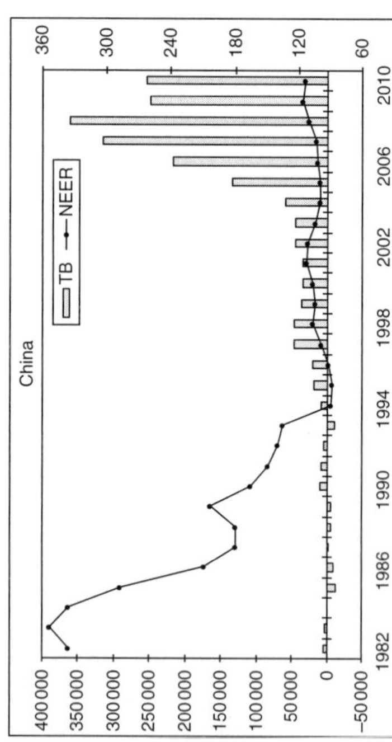
China
TB
NEER
400 000
350 000
300 000
250 000
200 000
150 000
100 000
50 000
0
−50 000
360
300
240
180
120
60
1982
1986
1990
1994
1998
2002
2006
2010

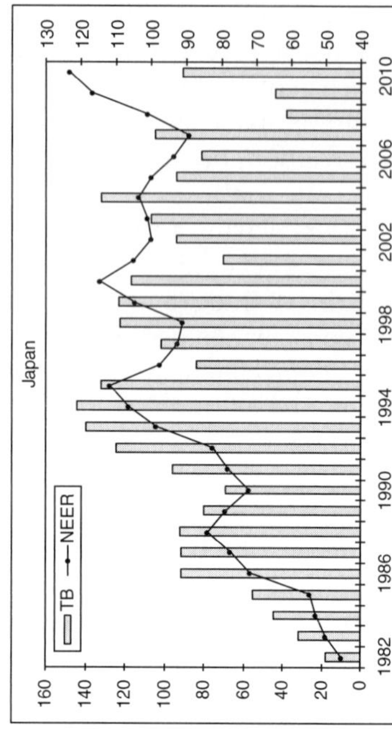
Japan
TB
NEER
160
140
120
100
80
60
40
20
0
130
120
110
100
90
80
70
60
50
40
1982
1986
1990
1994
1998
2002
2006
2010

Figure 6.2 The nominal effective exchange rate (NEER) and trade balance (TB)

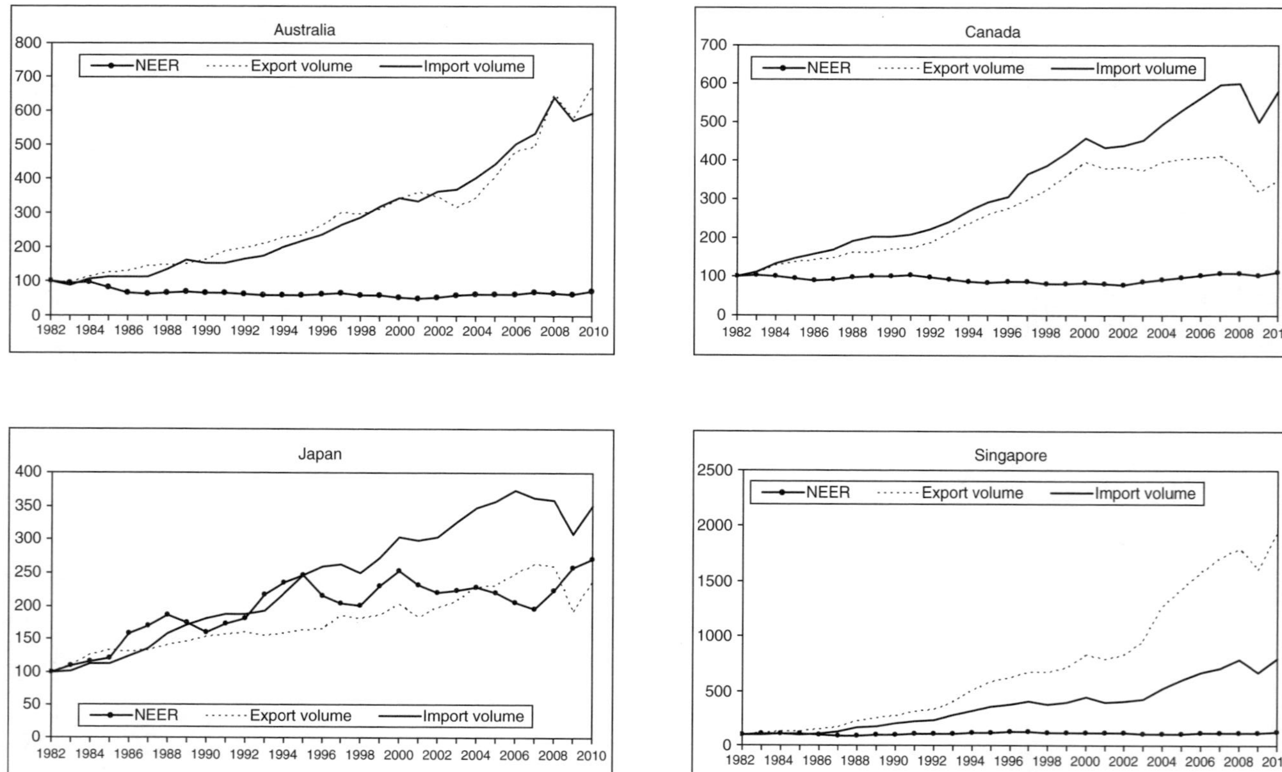

Figure 6.3 The nominal effective exchange rate and trade volumes

can see immediately and conspicuously is that volumes of exports and imports fell across the board in 2009, not because of changes in exchange rates but because of the income effect resulting from the Great Recession (when people lose their jobs they spend less on goods and services, including imported goods and services). In all cases export and import volumes move in the same manner, which means that they must be determined by the same factors that do not include the exchange rate. These factors include economic and population growth.

Depreciation of the domestic currency is supposed to produce a higher export volume and a lower import volume. These changes are to be seen nowhere. Take Australia, for example. During the period 1982–93, the Australian dollar depreciated at an average annual rate of 4.8 per cent. During the same period export volume rose by 7 per cent and import volume by 5 per cent. During the period 1997–2001, the currency depreciated at an annual rate of 6 per cent but that was associated with a 4.7 per cent rise in export volume and a 5.9 per cent rise in import volume. We know very well that Australian exports are primarily commodities that have nothing to do with the exchange rate, which means that the depreciation of the currency was not the reason for the rise in export volume. As for the import volume, it is determined mainly by economic growth, and if the currency of invoicing is the Australian dollar, which is predominant for Australian importing firms, the exchange rate becomes completely irrelevant to the determination of import volume.

It is again interesting to observe what happened in 2010 as the world economy recovered from the Great Recession. In all cases, both export and import volumes rose, irrespective of what happened to the exchange rate. The significant dip of 2009 was followed by a significant rise in 2010, simply because of the growth effect. In a study of the British trade balance following the recent depreciation of the pound, Alloway (2009) concluded that "while the exchange rate will be an important launching pad for UK exporters, the prospects for trade critically depend on global demand". She points out that "on our estimates global demand is nearly five times as important as the currency in driving export volumes". It is interesting to compare the cases of Australia and Canada as exhibited in Figure 6.3. Export volume rose much faster than the import volume in the case of Australia, but not in the case of Canada. The difference in the two cases is that the rapid growth of the Chinese economy propelled Australia's exports, while the sluggish recovery of the US economy did not provide adequate boost to Canada's exports.

It may be claimed that Figure 6.3 obscures the relation between trade volumes and the exchange rate because of the dominance of strong upward trends in trade volumes. Exchange rates do not exhibit strong trends, hence the effect would be more conspicuous if we look at what happens year on year. If also the exchange rate affects trade volumes with a time lag (a delayed effect of, say, two years) we should examine the relation between the percentage changes in trade volumes in one year and the percentage change in the exchange rate two years earlier. This is shown in Figure 6.4 for the same four countries as in Figure 6.3. What we can observe immediately is that changes in import and export volumes move together and that they are more strongly correlated than either of them with changes in the exchange rate (particularly in the cases of Canada and Singapore). If export and import volumes move in the same direction, they cannot be related to the exchange rate because they are supposed to move in opposite directions (domestic currency depreciation boosts exports and curtails imports). Even if there is any effect for the exchange rate on trade volumes, it is dominated by other factors that make export and import volumes move in tandem.

Exchange rate adjustment does not automatically lead to changes in the trade balance, even if there is a genuinely strong causal link between these two variables. Liu (2004) argues that "the logic of revaluing the yuan, or any other currency, as a means of balancing trade is flawed" because "exchange rate moves affect the price of both import and export, but their impact on trade balance may only result in changes in the volume of trade rather than the monetary value of trade". In other words, changes in the volumes of exports and imports do not necessarily imply that the difference between export revenue and import expenditure will rise.

THE ELASTICITIES APPROACH

The elasticities approach to the balance of payments is a description of the response of the trade balance (or current account) to changes in the exchange rate. The generic literature is about the effect of the devaluation of the domestic currency on the domestic trade balance, which is equivalent in our case to the effect of the revaluation of the yuan on the US trade deficit. As we saw in Chapter 5, for exchange rate adjustment to have an effect on the trade balance, the demand for exports and imports must be sufficiently elastic. The Marshall–Lerner condition tells us that "sufficiently elastic" means that the sum of the elasticities of demand for imports and exports must be greater than 1 (Marshall, 1923; Lerner, 1944). If elasticities are sufficiently high to satisfy the Marshall–Lerner condition, domestic currency devaluation or depreciation leads to a fall in the demand for imports and a rise in the demand for exports, and consequently to improvement in the trade balance.

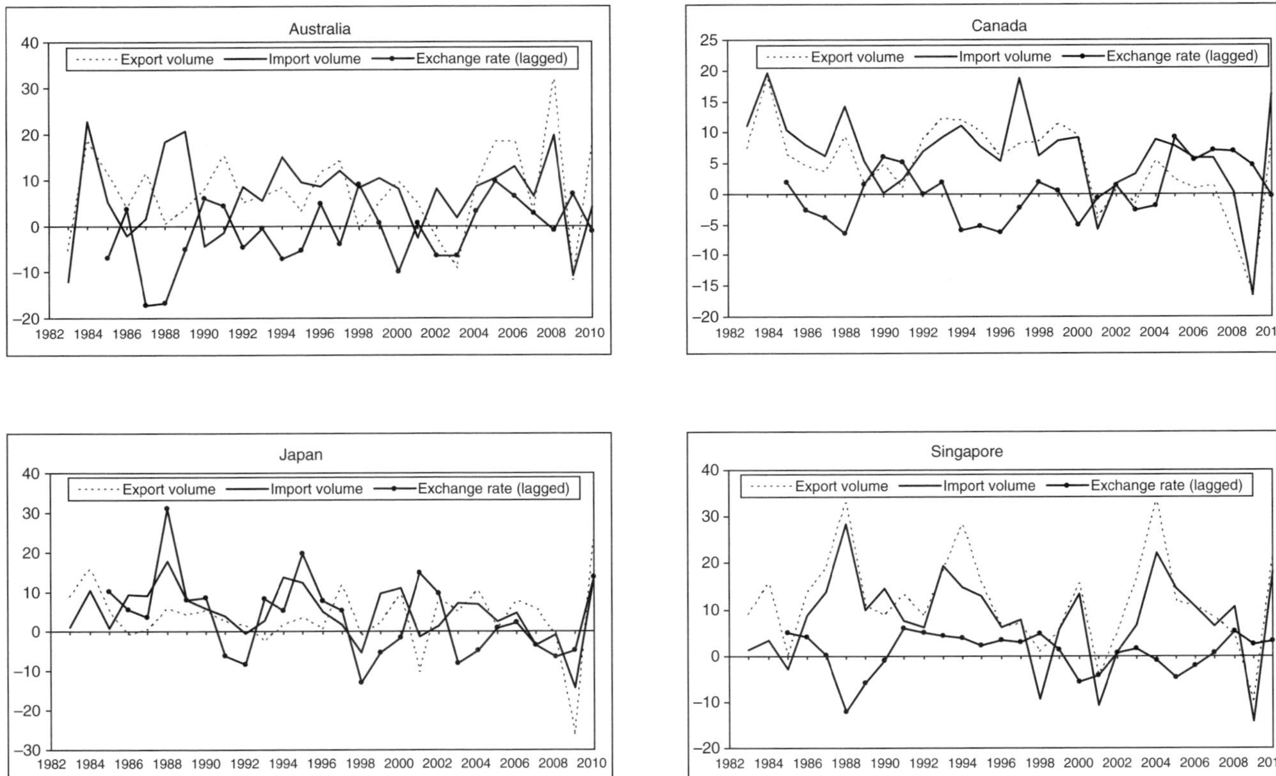

Figure 6.4 *Percentage changes in trade volumes and the nominal effective exchange rate (lagged two years)*

Given that elasticities determine the effectiveness or otherwise of exchange rate adjustment in correcting trade imbalance, a question arises as to what determines whether demand is elastic or inelastic. One of the determining factors of elasticity is the degree of the necessity of the underlying product. The demand for more necessary goods (such as food and fuel) is less elastic than the demand for less essential goods (such as first-class air travel and diamond rings). Another factor is the availability of close substitutes. The demand for a product that has no close substitutes (such as petrol) is less elastic than the demand for another product with a wide range of close substitutes (such as a particular brand of bottled water). Yet another factor is the price of the product, because demand is less elastic when the price is low and also when consumers spend a small portion of their incomes on that product (such as salt).

Applying these principles to the Chinese demand for American goods (Chinese imports) and the American demand for Chinese goods (Chinese exports), we come to the conclusion that the US demand for Chinese goods is inelastic while the Chinese demand for US goods is elastic. It is unlikely that the Chinese will buy American textiles and footwear as a result of the revaluation of the yuan because they will still be cheaper in China and other Asian countries and because the American textile and footwear industries have all but disappeared. The demand for Chinese products is inelastic because they are cheap, and because there is no suitable American substitute as the American production of low-tech, labour-intensive manufactured goods has become a thing of the past. Although Cline (2010a) describes as a "myth" the proposition that the US no longer manufactures anything imported from China, he admits that "this characterization reasonably applies to some products such as footwear, television sets, toys, and sporting goods". Although the Chinese demand for US high-tech goods is inelastic, purchases may be prohibited by the US government, in which case revaluation of the yuan will not affect US exports of these goods to China.

The problem with the elasticities approach is that it is based on the assumption that exchange rate adjustment affects the prices (and hence volumes) of exports and imports but nothing else. Furthermore, some conditions must be satisfied for this process to work. For example, the fulfilment of the Marshall–Lerner condition cannot produce improvement in the trade balance unless there are unemployed resources to absorb excess demand for domestic output. Thus if resources were fully employed, the excess demand for domestic output resulting from exchange rate adjustment would drive the real exchange rate back to its initial level via a proportional rise in domestic prices. This is not to say that revaluation of the yuan will not work because the US does not have under-utilized productive capacity and unemployed resources, when in fact it does have significant spare capacity in the aftermath of the Great Recession. However, this is still one of the conditions that must be satisfied for the process to work. But then, the US does not have adequate capacity (or has no capacity at all) in the production of some goods that are currently imported from China (footwear and textiles, to name just two).

We must also bear in mind that the elasticities approach as described here ignores the elasticities of supply of exports and imports, in the sense that supply is assumed to be perfectly elastic; that is, any increase in the demand for exports or imports can be met adequately by expansion in domestic and foreign production, respectively. Thus the effect of exchange rate adjustment on the trade balance depends on four rather than two elasticities. With respect to footwear and textiles, for example, the US supply is completely inelastic. People seem to forget the fact that China exports to the US goods that are different from the goods and services exported by the US to China.

THE J-CURVE EFFECT

The concept of the J-curve effect was first introduced by Magee (1973) to explain why the US trade balance deteriorated from a surplus of $2.2 billion in 1970 to a deficit of $2.7 billion in 1971 and continued to deteriorate to $6.8 billion in 1972 despite the devaluation of the dollar in 1971. In the current debate the J-curve effect provides a convenient explanation for why appreciation of the yuan has not affected the US trade deficit with China. Those advocating the idea that the Chinese should revalue their currency would argue that exchange rate adjustment takes time to work, which means that if it does not appear to be working this is only because it needs more time.

The J-curve effect is the tendency of the trade balance to deteriorate following the depreciation or devaluation of the domestic currency. This happens because immediately after devaluation, exports become more expensive and imports cheaper but – because elasticities are low in the short run – volumes will not be affected. As elasticities rise in the long run, volume will be affected and the trade balance starts to improve. The reverse J-curve effect happens when the domestic currency appreciates or is revalued; in this case, the trade balance (surplus) improves before it starts to deteriorate. Rose and Yellen (1989) list the conditions required for the J-curve effect to materialize as follows: (i) a short-run inelastic response of import volume to import prices; (ii) a short-run elastic response of import prices to the exchange rate; and (iii) a sluggish response of export value to the exchange rate.

Needless to say, we do not know how long the long run is or how short the short run is. Arguably, this is an empirical issue in the sense that the length of time it takes the trade balance to reverse its direction following exchange rate adjustment depends on the circumstances and differs from one episode to another. Not knowing how long it takes the effect to materialize brings with it the risk that, irrespective of the time lapsing between exchange rate adjustment and the non-materialization of the hoped-for improvement in the trade balance, China bashers would insist that improvement is coming, hence their preaching of patience. This reminds me of the manager of a weak football team that took part in the 1982 World Cup tournament in Spain, who insisted that his team (against all odds) would reach the final. When that team was knocked out of the tournament in the first round, the manager made a heroic remark by declaring to journalists: "we will win the World Cup even if we have to wait one million years". By analogy, those believing that revaluation of the yuan will bring about improvement in the US trade balance may claim that improvement will come even if we have to wait one million years. For them, this is a safe bet because they will not be around one million years from now, which means that no one will say to them "you were wrong".

Several reasons have been put forward to rationalize the existence of the J-curve effect. This phenomenon may emanate from the fact that at the time the exchange rate changes, goods already in transit and under contract have been purchased, and the completion of those transactions dominates short-term changes in the trade balance. Therefore the trade balance deteriorates first, but with the passage of time (during which the elasticities have a chance to change) it begins to improve. This is why the J-curve effect tends to emerge in the period during which contracts already in force in specified currencies dominate trade balance transactions. Over time, however, post-devaluation contracts start to dominate, and the pass-through of devaluation begins to materialize. Also, it is argued that expansion in exports and contraction in imports occur only after substantial lags. Five different lags are involved in the process: (i) recognition of the changed situation following exchange rate adjustment; (ii) the decision to change real variables (volumes); (iii) delivery time; (iv) replacement of inventories and materials; and (v) production time. Magee (1973) concentrated on three adjustment lags: (i) contracts signed prior to devaluation; (ii) the pass-through effect; and (iii) the quantity adjustment period.

Let us consider the stylized facts for the US, using quarterly data on the trade balance and exchange rate during the period 1973–2010. In Figure 6.5, which displays the two variables, four big swings in the exchange rate can be observed immediately. Between the third quarter of 1980 and the first quarter of 1985, the dollar appreciated by 60 per cent, yet the trade deficit hardly moved (remaining at about $23 billion). Between the first

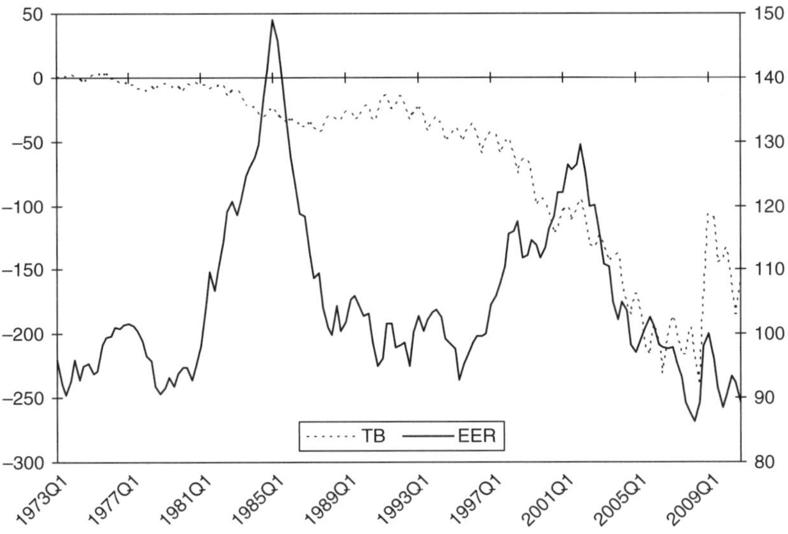

Figure 6.5 US trade balance (TB) and the effective exchange rate (EER)

quarter of 1985 and the second quarter of 1988, the dollar depreciated by 33 per cent, but the trade deficit rose to $30 billion. Between the second quarter of 1995 and the first quarter of 2002, the dollar appreciated by 22 per cent while the trade deficit rose from $45 billion to $98 billion. But then between the first quarter of 2002 and the second quarter of 2008, the dollar depreciated by 33 per cent, yet the trade deficit increased significantly to $220 billion. Swings in the exchange rate are too wild to explain the US trade balance, which has been moving further and further into the red.

Now, try to detect the J-curve effect in Figure 6.6, which shows the trade balance with a superimposed (moving average) trend. Some sort of J-curve effect can be observed during the period between the first quarter of 1985 and the third quarter of 1992. While a J-curve effect is supposed to be preceded by a depreciation of the domestic currency, the US dollar actually appreciated by 26 per cent on that occasion. Between the fourth quarter of 2005 and the third quarter of 2007 the dollar depreciated by 9 per cent and that was followed by some sort of J-curve effect between the third quarter of 2007 and the first quarter of 2009. Observing a graph like this is like observing the "mumbo-jumbo" charts used by technical analysts to make money in the stock market. They tell you that you should buy because there is a "head and shoulders" formation, and sell because there is an "inverse head and shoulders" formation. In Figure 6.6 we can also observe an L-curve effect, a V-curve effect and an inverted V-curve effect, not that

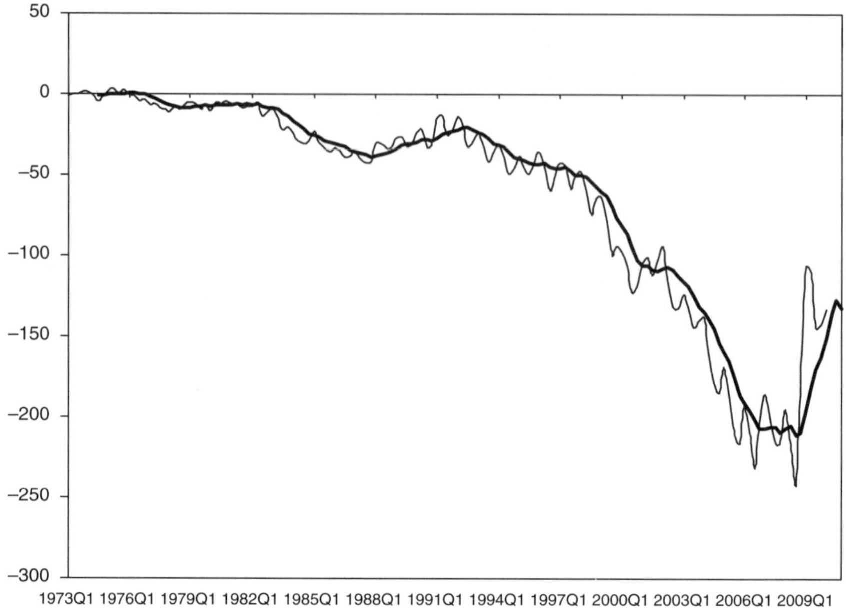

Figure 6.6 US trade balance with a trend

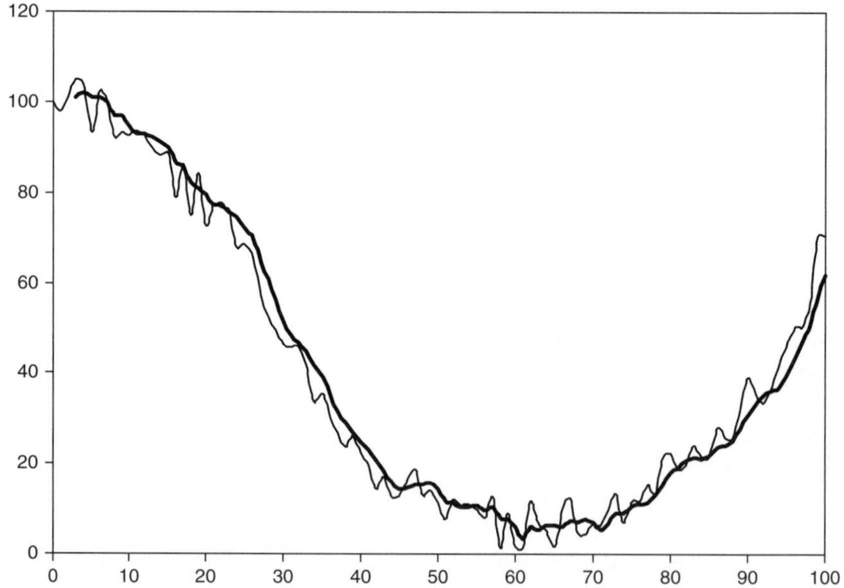

Figure 6.7 J-curve, V-curve and L-curve effects in random numbers

these formations mean or imply anything. Figure 6.7 displays computer-generated random numbers with a superimposed moving average trend. We can observe J-curve, V-curve and L-curve effects. These movements have nothing to do with the exchange rate or any causal variable.

ALTERNATIVES TO THE ELASTICITIES APPROACH

The elasticities approach to the balance of payments is based on the assumption that devaluation of the domestic currency affects the prices (hence volumes) of exports and imports, and nothing else. However, devaluation (assuming that it works) also exerts an expansionary effect on the economy by boosting exports. Therefore, it is not price changes alone, but also income changes, that determine the effect of devaluation on the trade balance. It has long been recognized that while the Marshallian partial equilibrium analysis of supply and demand is a useful tool for analysing the factors determining the price and output for a single good, its extension to the analysis of the effects of devaluation on imports and exports as a whole is questionable. Partial equilibrium analysis refers to the determination of market prices and quantities using the supply and demand analysis of Alfred Marshall, which is typically found in introductory microeconomics textbooks. In this sense, the elasticities approach represents partial analysis because it does not take into account the effect of devaluation on income. The complexity of the relations that govern demand and supply conditions in international trade means that the elasticities approach ignores the effect of changes in other variables (such as income) that may offset the price effects of devaluation.

The Absorption Approach

A better explanation for the effect of devaluation on the trade balance is provided by the absorption or the aggregate spending approach, where "absorption" means spending by domestic residents on goods and services. This approach, first suggested by Alexander (1952), takes into account the effects of changes in both prices and income following a devaluation of the domestic currency. Strictly speaking, this analysis applies to the current account of the balance of payments. Since the trade balance constitutes the bulk of the current account, and since we are mostly concerned with the trade balance, we refer to the trade balance rather than the current account.

The analysis is based on the national income identity, showing that total income (or output) is equal to consumption (spending by households on goods and services) plus investment (spending by firms on plant, equipment, structures and inventory) plus government expenditure (spending by the government). This means that the total output of the economy is bought by households, firms and the government while foreigners purchase the part of national output represented by exports. Since absorption is the sum of spending by households, firms and the government, it follows that total output is equal to absorption plus net exports (the trade balance). The trade balance, therefore, is the difference between output and absorption. If output exceeds absorption, the trade balance is in surplus, while if output is below absorption, it is in deficit. In other words, if a country spends more than what it produces it will have a trade deficit. Notice that if output exceeds absorption, the foreign sector contributes to national income, whereas if output falls short of absorption, the foreign sector is a drag on the domestic economy. This is actually a good explanation for the US deficit, as spending beyond its own means has been a widely accepted characterization of the US economy.

Devaluation of the domestic currency leads to two effects on the absorption of goods and services. First, it leads to an increase in real income, which boosts consumption (a component of absorption) proportionately to the increase in income. Second, devaluation has a direct effect on absorption. Thus we have (i) devaluation affects income; (ii) a change in income affects absorption; and (iii) devaluation affects absorption directly at any given level of income. In order to analyse the effect of devaluation, one has to take into consideration the entire economic structure of the devaluing country and of the rest of the world. The elasticities approach is a "partial" approach because it only looks at a subset of the entire economy.

Like the price effect, for the income effect of devaluation to materialize some conditions must be met, the first of which is the availability of unemployed resources in the devaluing country. The effect of devaluation on income depends on two other factors: (i) the degree to which a higher level of output is likely to materialize without an extensive rise in prices in the devaluing country, and (ii) the degree to which the rest of the world can absorb the increase in exports associated with the decline in the foreign price of exports resulting from devaluation. The analysis is not as straightforward as some observers make it out to be. What we are dealing with here is a complex system whose parts move simultaneously without "central control".

The net effect of devaluation on the trade balance (resulting from the price and income effects) depends not only on the total amount of additional production induced in the devaluing country, but also on the difference between the total amount of production and the induced increase in consumption. Under conditions of unemployment, devaluation produces a positive effect on the trade balance only if the increase in absorption is smaller than the increase in income, provided that the Marshall–Lerner condition is satisfied. The point to be made here is that even if the Marshall–Lerner condition is satisfied, devaluation may not be effective. Those who believe that revaluation of the yuan will reduce the US deficit with China only consider the price effect of exchange rate adjustment, hence they are very selective with respect to theory. Given that Americans have a high propensity to consume imported goods, if exchange rate adjustment is to affect income it is likely that the income effect will more than offset the price effect, producing no improvement in the trade balance.

To reiterate, if devaluation of the domestic currency boosts exports it will also boost imports via the income effect, consequently reducing the extent of the rise in net exports resulting from devaluation. The satisfaction of the Marshall–Lerner condition is not a sufficient condition for devaluation to have a favourable effect on the trade balance. Whether or not devaluation leads to an improvement in the trade balance depends on absorption, not on the Marshall–Lerner condition. Moreover, whether or not devaluation has a favourable effect on the trade balance depends on whether or not the economy's resources are underemployed. If resources are fully employed, a rise in absorption following devaluation leads to a proportional rise in domestic prices, eventually offsetting the effects of devaluation on exports by making them more expensive.

The Macroeconomic Identity

Let us look at the matter differently, in terms of the macroeconomic identity showing that the trade balance (or current account) is equal to the sum of the budget deficit (the difference between tax revenue and government spending) and the saving–investment balance (the difference between saving, or the flow of funds available for borrowing, and investment, which is the amount firms wish to spend on plant, equipment, structures and inventory). If the saving–investment balance is unchanged, the trade balance will change proportionately with the budget position. If the budget is in deficit, the trade balance will also be in deficit, thus we have the twin deficit phenomenon, which has become an established characteristic of the US economy since the early 1980s (except for three years in the late 1990s when the budget was in surplus). If there is no change in the budget position, a rise in consumption (a fall in saving) will exacerbate the trade deficit problem. A large budget deficit, a low saving rate and a high level of consumption cause (or at least they are associated with) a trade deficit, which is the situation in the US at present. While the logic of this argument is based on the national income accounting identity, some causal links are also conspicuous. For example, a high level of consumption means a high level of imports and a deteriorating trade balance. We will return to the issue of the twin deficit in Chapter 7.

In a study of the size and determinants of the US–China trade balance, a Chinese version of the macroeconomic identity is used by Feenstra et al. (1998) to demonstrate that the major cause of China's trade surplus is its high household saving rate. For this purpose, the Chinese economy is divided into three sectors, each with a saving–investment balance: (i) the private sector; (ii) state-owned enterprises; and (iii) the government. If the sum of the saving–investment balances of the state-owned enterprises and the government is taken to be equivalent to the budget deficit/surplus in the conventional macroeconomic identity, it turns out that the trade deficit is equal to the sum of the saving–investment balances of the three sectors. Thus, it is argued that "the primary determinants of the overall trade balance are macroeconomic and structural in nature, and they work through saving and investment behavior". The high saving rate in China is attributed to "China's demographic profile, the absence of social insurance for the bulk of the population, and the post-1978 appearance of investment-motivated saving in response to the scarcity of formal financial intermediation to finance the investment of the non-state sector". Feenstra et al. (1998) explain the widening of the US–China bilateral trade deficit in recent years in terms of: (i) macroeconomic forces in the US and China moving in opposite directions, causing their respective overall trade balances to move in opposite directions; and (ii) the accelerated relocation of production of US imports from East Asia to China.

In this framework Feenstra et al. (1998) envisage that revaluation of the yuan would reduce the US deficit "by lowering the private saving rate because the rise in the purchasing power of domestic wealth would reduce the amount needed to be saved in order to make the required purchase" and because "investment spending could also increase because the decline in the price of imported capital goods would allow more investment projects to be implemented sooner". The flaw in this argument is the implicit assumption that the Chinese save only to buy foreign goods, which is not the case. However, Feenstra et al. (1998) correctly attribute the widening deficit to developments on both sides: the opposite movements of macroeconomic forces in the two countries, reinforced by demographic trends and by China's reforms. To a first approximation, the widening bilateral trade deficit reflects a slowdown of saving in the US (that has been pulling in foreign resources to finance capital formation) and the surge in investment-motivated saving in China (which is necessary to compensate for the low level of financial intermediation available to the increasingly liberalized non-state sector).

The Saving–Investment Balance

It is because of the saving–investment balance that some economists dismiss the exchange rate as an important variable when it comes to trade balance adjustment. For example, Al-Eyd et al. (2005) argue that "the emergence of a sustained deficit does not automatically necessitate a fall in the exchange rate, and a fall in the exchange rate may not correct such a deficit". Even Bergsten (2009), who is rather hawkish on China and one of the most pronounced callers for China to revalue the yuan, admits that "the only healthy way to reduce the United States' external deficits to a sustainable level is to raise the rate of national saving by several percentage points", which "could be achieved by a combination of increased private saving and a reduced federal budget deficit".

Furthermore, distinction may be made between the deficits caused by exchange rate movements, which are likely to be temporary, and those that either emerge for long-term structural reasons or result from structural imbalances in the economy, such that a structural deficit may be attributed to low domestic saving or high domestic government borrowing. Hence Al-Eyd et al. (2005) argue that "all these factors have influenced the increase in the US deficit in the past decade, and it is difficult to see how a correction to the deficit can occur without one of the domestic drivers changing in some way". From 2001, a fall in US national savings and a reduction in the inflows of foreign savings have accompanied falling levels of investment and rising consumption, which means that the large and growing deficits of recent years are a direct result of the drop in the level of national saving. The change in national saving is a consequence of the increase in the federal budget deficit, or in government borrowing.

Since the trade balance is equivalent to net exports, the prescription for reducing a deficit centres on increasing exports and/or reducing imports via expenditure switching policies. If we look at the prescription in terms of the macroeconomic identity, we reach the conclusion that reducing the deficit requires measures that boost domestic saving and reduce domestic borrowing, including borrowing by the government.

THE EMPIRICAL EVIDENCE

In this section we examine the empirical evidence on two issues discussed in this chapter: (i) the effect of exchange rate adjustment on the trade balance, and (ii) the J-curve effect.

The Effect of Exchange Rate Adjustment on the Trade Balance

There is mixed evidence on the effect of exchange rate adjustment on the trade balance, as revealed by an often-cited survey study conducted by Bahmani-Oskooee and Ratha (2004). The 37 studies surveyed produced mixed conclusions, including the following: (i) the long-run impact of devaluation on the trade balance is favourable, (ii) devaluation improves the balance of payments but not the trade balance; and (iii) there is a causal link between the nominal and real exchange rates and export volume, but not between the nominal and real rates and imports.

Rose (1990) examined the impact of the exchange rate on the trade balance for 30 developing countries and found that "a depreciation of the real exchange rate is not strongly associated with a significant improvement in the trade balance". Chinn (2004) estimated import and export equations over a period spanning the so-called "new economy boom" of the 1990s and the subsequent recession and dollar depreciation. His results indicate a low responsiveness of imports to exchange rate changes and that a combination of low price elasticity of imports and the size of the trade deficit means that any reduction in the trade deficit will necessarily be accompanied by large exchange rate and income adjustments. Agbola (2004) suggests that devaluation does not improve the trade balance of Ghana in the long run. These are only a few examples from an extensive literature, just to demonstrate that a causal relation between the exchange rate and trade balance should not be taken for granted.

Evidence on the Chinese trade balance is available in a number of empirical studies. In a study conducted by Cheung et al. (2009) on the relation between China's current account and exchange rate, they find that Chinese trade flows respond to the trade-weighted exchange rate, but "the relationship is not always precisely estimated". In addition, the direction of the effects is sometimes different from what is expected a priori. For instance, Chinese imports may rise in response to yuan depreciation, although Chinese exports appear to respond to yuan depreciation in the expected manner. As far as China's trade with the US is concerned, they find that "the China–US trade balance should respond to real exchange rate and relative income movements in the anticipated manner", but they point out that "in neither the case of multilateral nor bilateral trade flows should one expect quantitatively large effects arising from exchange rate changes". They further point out that "these results are not informative with regard to the question of how a change in the RMB/USD exchange rate would affect the overall US trade deficit". They also stress that considerable uncertainty surrounds the estimates of the responsiveness of trade flows to movements in exchange rates. Hence they cast a big shadow of doubt on the effectiveness of exchange rate adjustment as a tool that can be used to correct the US–China trade imbalances.

The available evidence indicates that factors other than the exchange rate affect the trade balance more strongly. Cline (2005) developed a current account model in which exports depend on the exchange rate (with a lag) and foreign GDP growth, whereas imports depend on the exchange rate and domestic GDP growth (transfer payments as well as income receipts and payments on foreign assets and liabilities are taken into account). Based on this model he derives results showing that a 10 per cent effective depreciation of the dollar reduces the current account deficit by 1.4 per cent of GDP after three years and by about 1.6 per cent after five years. Specific simulations also indicate that about 80 per cent of the change is the product of a reduction in the deficit on goods and services, with the remainder reflecting changes in payments on international assets and liabilities. Given that the US has a GDP of about $14.5 trillion, Cline concludes that a change of 1.5 per cent in four years would amount to a $218 billion reduction in the current account and a $175 billion decline in the trade balance (80 per cent of the total change in the current account). In other words, a 1 per cent effective depreciation of the dollar translates to a reduction of about $22 billion in the current account deficit, with the great bulk occurring in the balance of trade in goods and services.

In another study, Cline (2010b) demonstrates that China's current account responds to its exchange rate, and that the US–China bilateral trade balance responds to China's exchange rate as well. Specifically, he shows that a 10 per cent rise in the value of the yuan leads to an improvement in the US trade balance by an amount ranging from $22 billion to $63 billion. Cline and Williamson's (2010a) calculations show that the effective exchange rate of the yuan needs to rise by about 15 per cent in order for China to reduce its current account surplus from the 2015 level of 8 per cent of GDP projected by the IMF to a benchmark of only 3 per cent of GDP. In all of this, what is emphasized is the time lag involved in the process. In his 2005 study, Cline provides statistical evidence that "US trade responds with approximately equal weights to the exchange rate in each of the two prior years, rather than the current year". Cline (2010b) shows that the trade balance can be explained in terms of the previous year's exchange rate as well as that of the year before – hence there is a lagged effect. He concludes that the rise of the renminbi during 2006–8 "played an important role in the decline of the imbalance in 2009–10". This is a rather strange claim, given that the US deficit with China reached a new record in 2010 even though the yuan has resumed its appreciation.

It is amazing that the studies conducted by scholars associated with the Peterson Institute typically produce results that are so precise and, of course, supportive of the anti-Chinese stance of the Institute. Naturally, there is no explanation as to why these results are inconsistent with the stylized facts and with the well-rationalized proposition that exchange rate adjustment has no bearing on the trade balance because of the inhibiting factors such as using the dollar as the currency of invoicing. Moosa (2011c) presents empirical results showing that the yuan/dollar exchange rate does not have any effect on the US–China trade balance.

The J-Curve Effect

In a survey of the literature on the J-curve effect, Bahmani-Oskooee and Ratha (2004) conclude that "while there are reasons to believe that the J-curve phenomenon characterizes the short-run dynamics, there are also reasons why it may not" and that "the empirical evidence has been rather mixed, or inconclusive". It turns out that the J-curve may be no more than an aberration. Some authors found evidence for the N-curve, M-curve, I-curve, L-curve, S-curve, inverse J-curve and delayed J-curve. Some of the conclusions reached by the studies surveyed by Bahmani-Oskoowee and Ratha are the following: (i) there may or may not be a J-curve; (ii) there is evidence for the inverse J-curve; (iii) there is no evidence for the J-curve or delayed J-curve; (iv) there is no support for the J-curve; (v) the evidence supports the J-curve in some cases; (vi) the results support a new definition of the J-curve in 11 out of 18 cases; (vii) there is evidence for the delayed J-curve; (viii) there is evidence for the J-curve, N-curve, M-curve and I-curve; (ix) there is evidence for the S-curve; (x) there is no specific short-run pattern supporting the J-curve phenomenon; (xi) there is evidence for the J-curve in two out of five cases; and (xii) there are significant differences in the duration and extent of the J-curve effect across countries. In a more recent survey of the literature on the J-curve and S-curve conducted by Bahmani-Oskooee and Hegerty (2010), the results are all over the place: the J-curve is present; the J-curve is not present; it is present for some countries but not for others; there is a J-curve for Japan only; there is a J-curve for all except Japan; 41 out of 60 cases have an S-curve; and so on and so forth. So, what are we supposed to believe? Definitely not that there is a predictable pattern of behaviour of the trade balance following a change in the exchange rate.

Bahmani-Oskooee and Alse (1994) found a mixed bag of results when they tested for the J-curve effect for 19 developed and 22 less developed countries. They found evidence for the J-curve effect in Costa Rica, Ireland, the Netherlands and Turkey, but not for other countries. It is not clear what special characteristics these countries have to exhibit a J-curve effect, while other countries do not. It is not that easy to envisage that

Ireland and the Netherlands have something in common with Turkey and Costa Rica. Another study of the Turkish trade balance has been carried out by Yazici (2006) who tested the J-curve hypothesis using data on the Turkish agricultural sector over the period from 1986:1 to 1998:3. The results of this study indicate that, following devaluation, the agricultural trade balance initially improves, then worsens and then improves again (S-curve). Another important finding is that devaluation worsens the trade balance of the agricultural sector in the long run, a result that is inconsistent with the earlier findings for the Turkish economy as a whole.

Meade (1988) examined the outcome of a continuous decline in the dollar's exchange rate at 10 per cent per annum, but only found the negative J-curve effect to be small and that it is soon overcome. Thus, she did not support the then dominant view that negative J-curve effect explains the persistence of the US trade deficit. Rose and Yellen (1989) found no evidence for the J-curve effect in 25 years of American bilateral and aggregate data. As they put it, "the hypothesis of a J-curve can be rejected robustly with American data". They defend their results by arguing that the studies that found support for the J-curve have problems that they (Rose and Yellen) tackled.

Moffett (1989) examined the trade balance of the US over the period 1967:1 to 1987:4 and found that the response did not resemble a J-curve. Rose (1990) found similar results for the trade balances of a number of developing countries. In a study of Canadian data over the period 1981:1 to 2005:12, Georgopoulos (2008) concluded that "the J-curve does not exist". This study is critical of the underlying literature because it overlooks two crucial points: the degree to which exporters pass through exchange rate movements into local currency prices and the degree to which trade volumes respond to the exchange rate. These are two of the factors that impede not only the emergence of a J-curve effect but any effect of the exchange rate on the trade balance, irrespective of whether a J-curve, S-curve, L-curve or V-curve emerges.

CONCLUDING REMARKS

The stylized facts, as well as the results of empirical studies, show that the relation between the trade balance and the exchange rate is rather weak to the extent that it is unlikely that expenditure switching policies implemented via changes in the exchange rate are likely to affect the trade balance or current account. There is also little evidence for the J-curve effect – in other words it is unlikely that exchange rate adjustment produces a delayed impact in the desired direction on the trade balance. The discussion presented in this chapter suggests that the trade balance position is more readily explainable in terms of the macroeconomic identity and the absorption approach to the balance of payments, which bring in the role of the income effect, the saving–investment balance and the budget position.

In Chapter 7 we elaborate on the roles of the saving–investment balance and the budget position when we discuss the twin deficit phenomenon. We will also consider the effects of factors that hinder the working of exchange rate adjustment, including the pass-through effect, the currency of invoicing and local currency mark-ups, as well as the effect of other determinants of the trade balance. It will be demonstrated that the relation between the exchange rate and trade balance is not straightforward but rather ambiguous.

7. Why revaluation of the yuan will not work

INTRODUCTION

The controversy over the US trade deficit with China has become ideological and has turned ugly. In particular there is a heated debate about whether or not revaluation of the yuan will work, in the sense that it will eliminate or at least reduce the US trade deficit with China. For example, a Nobel Prize winner, Joseph Stiglitz, thinks that revaluation will not work but another Nobel Prize winner, Paul Krugman, says that it will. Robert Mundell, a Nobel Prize winner himself, agrees with Stiglitz by arguing that "there's no evidence that exchange rates correspond with trade balances" and that "the US arguments in this regard are intellectually weak" (Dukes, 2005).

Fatas (2010) casts a big shadow of doubt on Krugman's argument that trade imbalances cannot be corrected without an exchange rate change, as he (Krugman) "almost implies that current account imbalances are always the result of exchange rate misalignments", which is such an extreme position. Fatas argues that while the current account may react to changes in the exchange rate, changes in saving and investment (which is what matters for the current account) are driven by many other factors.

Krugman's argument is that an increase in Chinese consumption will not reduce China's current account surplus unless this consumption translates into imports, and for this to happen "we need a relative price change". Fatas puts forward the view that "the Chinese will have to get used to consume more, Americans will need to understand that they need to save more and this will be the main factor that will drive the current account adjustment". Although this argument does not put the blame totally on China, asking or telling the Chinese to consume more does not sound right. What is obvious is that a brilliant international economist, Krugman, has chosen (for not-so-obvious reasons) to forget about economic theory, empirical evidence, stylized facts and simple intuition so as to take part in a witch-hunt against China. Franks (2010) says the following in response to Krugman's argument: "Economic textbooks say that if a currency rises, its exports become more expensive to customers in other countries, while a weaker currency makes exports less expensive. In a vacuum that makes sense, but reality shows that this simplified concept is false."

The naive view is that the trade balance improves following domestic currency depreciation because imports become relatively more expensive, leading to a reduction in the purchase of foreign goods (imports), while exports become more attractive for foreigners as they are relatively cheaper. This view, however, overlooks all of the conditions required for this process to work smoothly and the changes in other factors that may sabotage it. Goldberg and Tille (2006) put it succinctly as follows:

> A number of things must happen before exchange rate changes lead to trade balance adjustments. First, the exchange rate change must lead to changes in the border prices of goods imported by the destination market. Next, the change in border prices must lead to a change in the price of goods charged to consumers. Finally, the consumer must react to the relative price of import goods, substituting away from imports if they have become more expensive, or increasing demand for imports if they have become relatively cheap. If the exporters adjust their own profit margins to insulate foreign prices from exchange rate fluctuations, nominal trade balance implications arise purely due to revenue effects of exchange rates on existing quantities of goods traded.

Goldberg and Tille, therefore, refer to the complications and conditions that impede the working of exchange rate adjustment. All of these factors will be examined throughout this chapter.

THE TWIN DEFICIT PHENOMENON

The term "twin deficit" was coined in the early 1980s as the Reagan administration embarked on a programme of tax cuts, leading to a significant increase in the budget deficit. At the same time the trade balance moved into sizeable deficit as the US economy grew faster than those of major trading partners. Likewise, the re-emergence of the twin deficit in the first decade of the twenty-first century came in the aftermath of increased government spending and the Bush tax cuts. The phenomenon, therefore, implies the simultaneous occurrence of a budget deficit and a trade (or a current account) deficit.

While the twin deficit phenomenon is based on an accounting identity that also involves the saving–investment balance, some causal links between the two balances can be detected, and they have indeed been suggested. For example, a high level of government spending may involve spending on imports, thus leading to a widening of the trade deficit.

Another example is that tax cuts (which cause a budget deficit) encourage consumption spending, including spending on imports, with implications for the trade deficit.

A more elaborate causal link between the two deficits is provided by Labonte and Makinen (2005) who describe the process as follows. An increase in the budget deficit puts upward pressure on interest rates, particularly when the saving rate is low. Foreigners rush to buy the now high-yielding domestic assets and consequently the domestic currency. As a result the domestic currency appreciates, making exports more expensive and imports cheaper. The outcome will be a widening of the trade deficit. The problem with this cause and effect process is that it requires conditions to hold so that the exchange rate can influence the trade balance – this is the very issue that we are talking about here.

Controversy over the Twin Deficit

A number of economists are extremely dubious when it comes to the twin deficit phenomenon while others have been supportive of it. For example, Jackson (2003) states sarcastically that "the twin deficit fallacy seems to be the economic equivalent of the ghost who walks". He gives examples of Norway having one of the largest current account deficits while having one of the biggest budget surpluses among OECD countries, and Italy, which has the largest budget deficit among OECD countries while its current account is virtually in balance.

Bernanke (2005) casts doubt on "any presumed causal relationship between the budget deficit and trade deficit", arguing against the notion that the two deficits necessarily move in lockstep or that the budget deficit fully explains the trade deficit. However, he does not deny that the budget deficit may act to exacerbate and contribute to a widening trade deficit. A number of scholars have urged the US government to recognize the role of US fiscal policy in widening the trade deficit. For example, Chinn (2005) asserts that "reducing the rate of government spending and raising tax revenues should be at the top of the country's economic agenda". In a testimony before the US Senate, Cline (2007) argued that "fiscal policy is directly relevant because government saving is part of national saving" and that "fiscal policy is the only instrument that can be effectively employed to increase national savings hence reduce the trade deficit". This is why Thompson (2008) argues that "[at least] a reduction of the federal budget deficit follows a complementary path towards the ultimate goal of reducing the trade deficit". The sceptics seem to forget the *ceteris paribus* condition or as Labonte and Makinen (2005) put it: "there are other forces besides the federal budget deficit that can influence the US trade deficit".

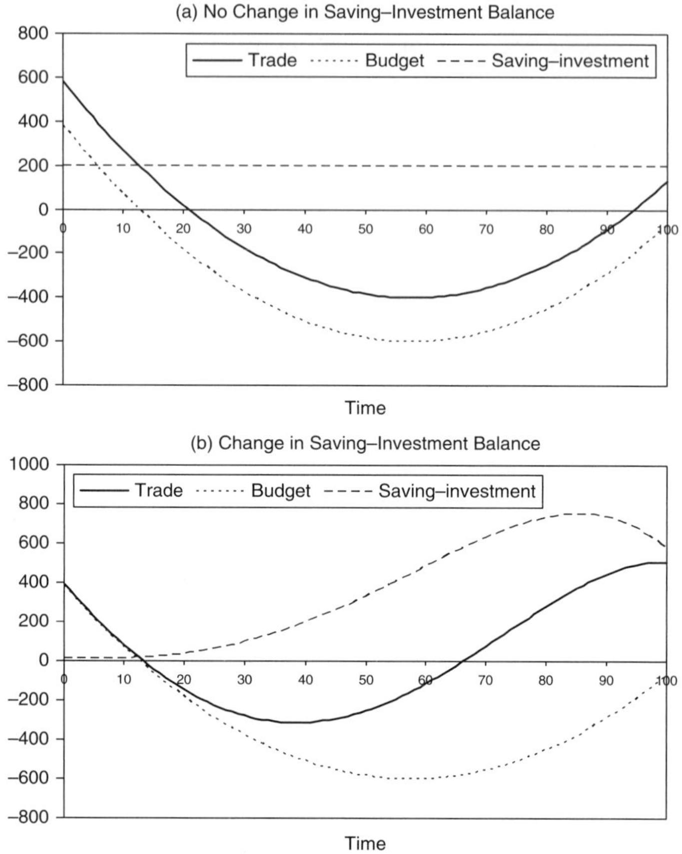

Figure 7.1 The twin deficit under two conditions

The Role of the Saving–Investment Balance

Bearing in mind the identity that the trade deficit is equal to the budget deficit plus the saving–investment balance, it becomes rather intuitive that a budget deficit may or may not be associated with a trade deficit, depending on movements in the saving–investment balance. A country with a high level of saving is capable of financing the budget deficit by borrowing locally rather than internationally, in which case government borrowing does not have consequences for the external account. It is because of the role played by the saving–investment balance that some countries have a trade deficit and a budget surplus, or vice versa.

Figure 7.1 shows a theoretical example of how the two deficits may

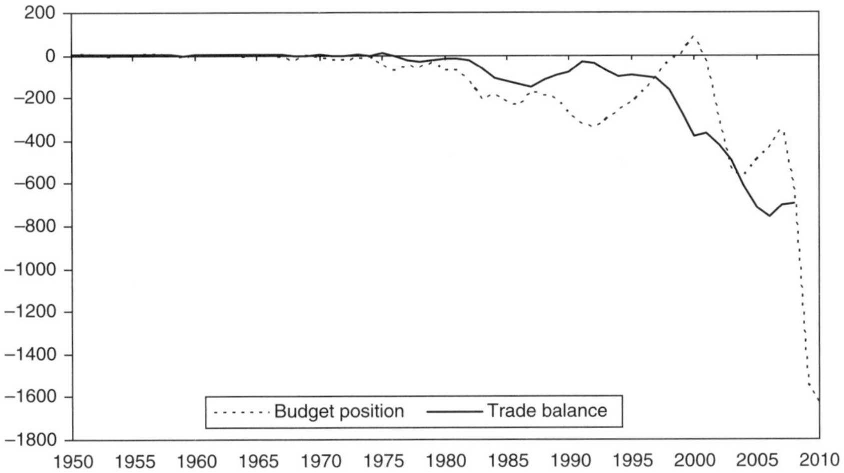

Figure 7.2 US budget and trade deficits (1950–2009)

move in the same direction or in opposite directions. When there is no change in the saving–investment balance, as in Figure 7.1(a), the budget position and trade account move together, exhibiting a one-to-one relation – that is, a dollar increase in the trade deficit (surplus) is associated with a dollar increase in the budget deficit (surplus). In Figure 7.1(b) the saving–investment balance fluctuates, which eliminates the one-to-one relation between the budget position and trade account, to the extent that they could move in opposite directions. Figure 7.2 shows the US budget position and trade balance since 1950. The two positions do not move according to a straightforward one-to-one relation because of variation in the saving–investment balance. We can see that while there has been a tendency for both deficits to grow, there are occasions when they moved in opposite directions. Nothing is unusual about Norway and Italy having a deficit on one side and a surplus on the other.

The US Experience

It is a well accepted casual observation (or stylized fact) that "the twin-deficit hypothesis accurately captures the US experience in the 1980s and the first years of the new century" (Bartolini and Lahiri, 2006). Some would also argue that the twin deficit hypothesis worked well in the 1980s and the first decade of the twenty-first century but not in the 1990s when a current account deficit co-existed with a budget surplus. Referring to those who believe in the twin deficit phenomenon, Jackson (2003) argues that "these

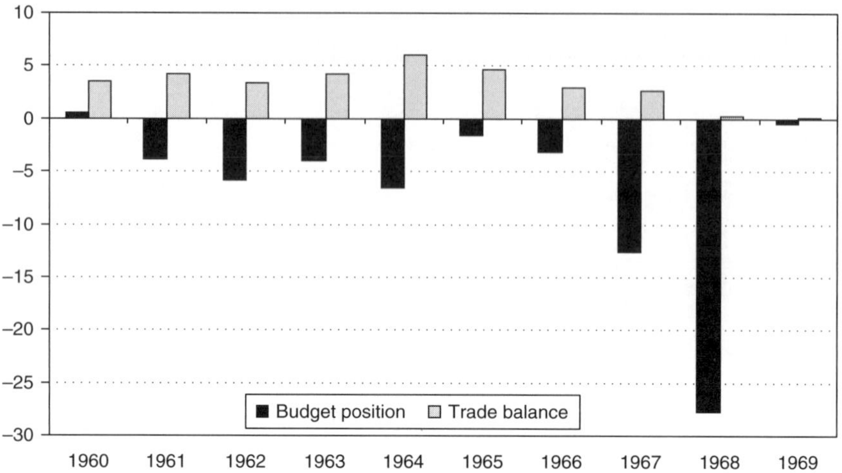

Figure 7.3 US budget and trade deficits (1960–69)

people overlook the fact that in the 1960s America also ran a domestic surplus while simultaneously running a balance of payments deficit". But this observation is not substantiated by the actual data displayed in Figure 7.2. To see clearly what happened in the 1960s, the figures for the period 1960–69 are magnified, as in Figure 7.3. We can see that the only year in the 1960s in which the US had a budget surplus was 1960 ($0.5 billion), and in that year there was a surplus in the trade balance. Thereafter the US had a budget deficit in every year of the 1960s (the figures were obtained from the 2010 *Economic Report of the President*).

The twin deficit phenomenon was more conspicuous in the 1980s than at any other time. In Figure 7.4 the two deficits as a percentage of GDP are plotted over the period 1981–9. It is clear that the two deficits moved together, both reaching their peaks (or rather troughs) in 1986 before improving all the way through to 1989. But the story was different in the second half of the 1990s. As the budget turned from a deficit of 2 per cent of GDP in 1995 to a surplus of 1.2 per cent in 2000, the trade deficit rose over the same period from 0.9 per cent to 3.9 per cent of GDP (Figure 7.5). The difference in the behaviour may be explained in terms of rising investment in the expansion of the 1990s, compared to the expansion of the 1980s, as shown in Figure 7.6. Improvement in the budget deficit was offset by a falling saving–investment balance. Labonte and Makinen (2005) explain the difference between the two episodes in terms of what caused the upward pressure on interest rates. In the 1980s pressure came from the rise in the budget deficit, while in the

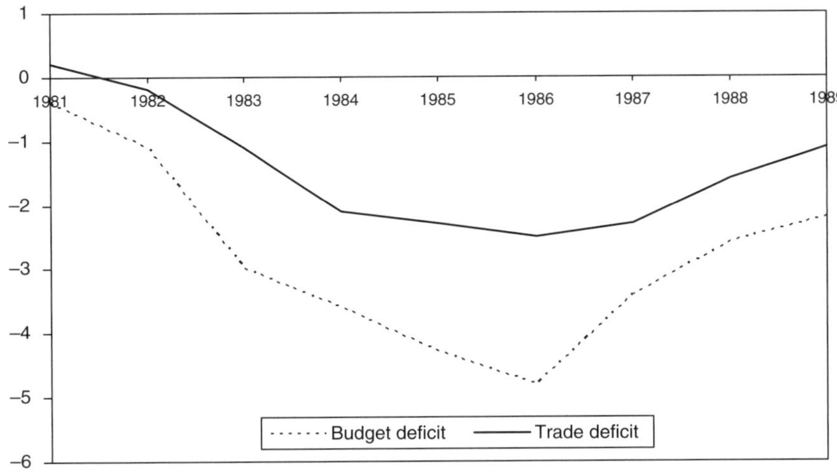

Figure 7.4 US budget deficit and trade deficit as a percentage of GDP (1981–9)

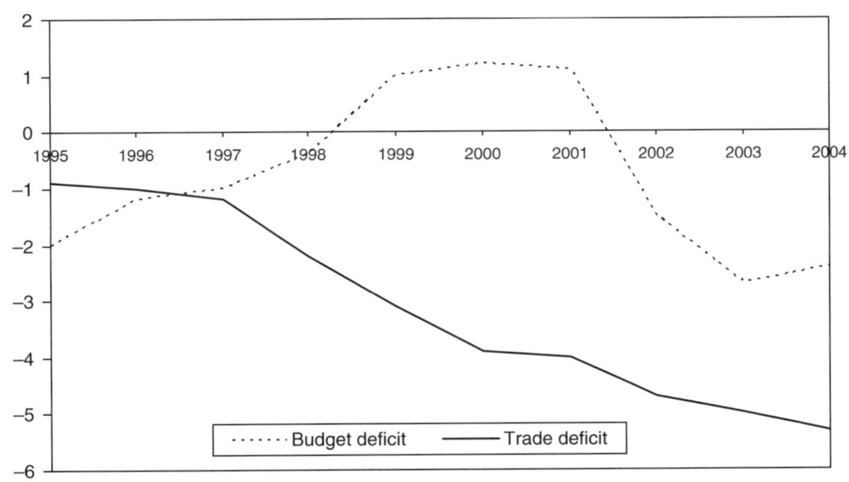

Figure 7.5 US budget deficit and trade deficit as a percentage of GDP (1994–2004)

1990s it came from higher productivity and the profitability of private investment.

Although theory indicates that the budget deficit and the current account deficit should move together, Figure 7.2 shows that they followed

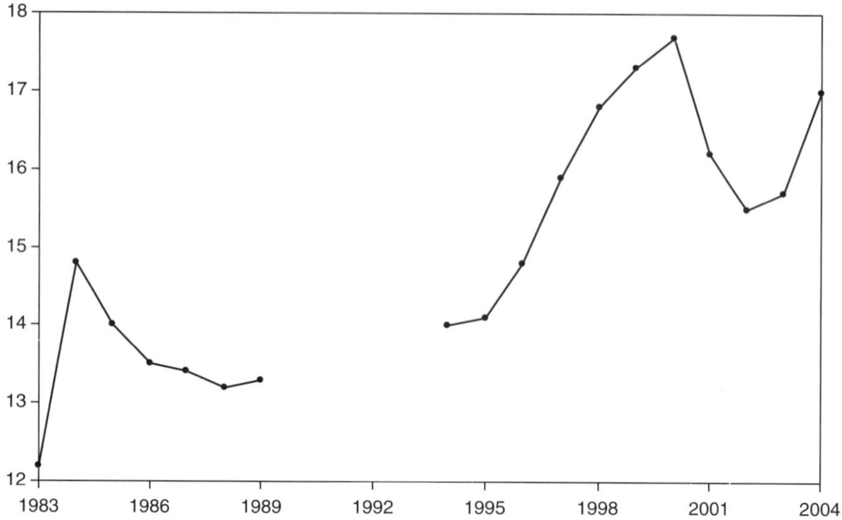

Figure 7.6 Real gross domestic investment as a percentage of GDP

quite divergent paths from 1987 to 2001. One possible explanation for this divergence is related to the impact of output fluctuations on budget and current account deficits (Cavallo, 2005a). Suppose, for example, that the economy enjoys a surge in productivity that prompts an expansion in economic activity. To reap the opportunities of higher productivity, private investment goes up. As investment expenditure typically reacts more strongly to the business cycle than private saving does, the current account balance deteriorates. At the same time, output expansion generates both an increase in tax revenue and a decline in government spending, due (for example) to a decline in unemployment benefits. Therefore the budget balance improves.

Irrespective of the theoretical explanations of the link between the budget and trade positions, the two deficits are related by an accounting identity that must hold by construction. Those who believe that the two deficits do not necessarily coincide, and take this to provide evidence against the twin deficit phenomenon, overlook the role played by the saving–investment balance. The accounting identity involves complex interactions that may produce two deficits, two surpluses, a surplus and a deficit, or a deficit and a surplus. What is important for the current debate is that the twin deficit phenomenon provides logical reasoning for why low saving, high consumption and high government spending can be translated into a trade deficit.

THE PASS-THROUGH EFFECT AND PRICING TO MARKET

As we saw in Chapter 5, full or high exchange rate pass-through is necessary for exchange rate adjustment to affect the trade balance. The rationale for the proposition that exchange rate adjustment can be used to correct a trade deficit is that a change in the exchange rate affects proportionately the domestic currency price of imports and the foreign currency price of exports, implying a full pass-through effect. This process, which is a pivotal argument in the current debate, is typically taken for granted in textbook expositions, but it is unlikely to materialize in practice, as we typically observe a less than full pass-through effect that has been declining over time. Sekine (2006) argues that one of the effects of the decline in exchange rate pass-through is that it weakens the effectiveness of expenditure switching policies.

The pass-through effect is the extent to which changes in exchange rates affect the foreign currency price of exports and domestic currency price of imports. A full pass-through effect means, for example, that a 10 per cent appreciation of the domestic currency should lead to a 10 per cent increase in the foreign currency price of exports and a 10 per cent decline in the domestic currency price of imports. If this is not the case then we have a partial pass-through effect. If there is no change in the foreign currency price of exports and/or the domestic currency price of imports, this would imply a zero pass-through effect, in which case exchange rate adjustment will be totally ineffective. And if the foreign currency price of exports becomes even lower following appreciation of the domestic currency (the domestic currency price of imports becomes even higher), we have a situation of negative pass-through.

Partial and negative pass-through effects have been repeatedly observed. Two conditions are required to be met for a full pass-though: (i) constant mark-ups of price over cost, and (ii) constant marginal cost, that is, the cost of expanding production from the current level is constant. Neither of these conditions is likely to be satisfied in practice as exporters often change mark-ups of prices over cost, depending on market conditions, and the marginal cost of production is likely to change because of economies or diseconomies of scale and scope.

Consider the following real-life example of partial and negative pass-through (Goldberg and Knetter, 1997). On 5 January 1994 the dollar was worth 113 yen, but by 19 April 1995 it was worth 80 yen. In 1994 a Toyota Celica made in Japan sold in the US for $16968 but in 1995 it was worth $17285, a price increase of just 2 per cent. During the same period the retail price of a large screen SONY Trinitron fell by 15 per cent. These events motivated research on exchange rate pass-through in an attempt to answer the following questions:

- Why was there so little change in the US dollar price of imports of Japanese goods to the US?
- Was the response simply delayed?
- Did Japanese exporters perceive the exchange rate change to be only temporary?
- Does incomplete pass-through imply that Japanese exporters reduced their profit margins on exports to the US?

The most likely explanation for what happened on that occasion was that Japanese manufacturers reduced the yen price of their products to offset the effect of the appreciation of the yen. The partial pass-through in the case of Toyota resulted from Toyota reducing the yen price of their exports to the US so that the dollar price would rise by less than the percentage appreciation of the yen. The negative pass-through in the case of the television set is that SONY reduced the yen price of their exports to the US by more than the percentage appreciation of the yen, resulting in a lower dollar price than the pre-appreciation level. Companies do that all the time, either across the board (that is, for all destination countries) or selectively, in which case we have on our hands a phenomenon called "pricing to market".

Pricing to Market

Pricing to market is not necessarily associated with changes in exchange rates. As we saw in Chapter 4, *The Economist* magazine practises pricing to market by charging lower prices in poor countries. Neither is it true that any change in the domestic price of the product in reaction to exchange rate changes is associated with pricing to market. In general, however, partial pass-through results from a deliberate action by exporters to reduce the domestic currency price of their products to offset the effect of domestic currency appreciation on the foreign currency price of exports. What happens in this case is that exporters absorb currency movements in their profit margins. Reduction of profit margins by Chinese firms to preserve market share has been observed in practice (*The Economist*, 2010f). Pricing to market and any other action taken to offset the increase in the foreign currency price of exports acts to limit the pass-through from exchange rate changes to prices, which undermines the effectiveness of the expenditure switching effect of exchange rate adjustment. As long as there is less than a full pass-through effect, expenditure switching policies implemented through changes in the exchange rate will not be effective in terms of correcting a trade imbalance.

The Role of Local Mark-ups

One reason why a partial pass-through effect is more likely to be observed in practice revolves around local mark-ups. Goldberg and Tille (2006) point out that "import price sensitivity to exchange rates is not identical to consumption price sensitivity" because "after goods arrive at the docks of importing countries, other local services and costs are incurred before the goods reach consumers". These local costs arise from distribution services, including expenditure on wholesalers, retailers, transport, as well as on finance and insurance services. The effect of the costs of distribution services is to insulate partially retail prices in the destination country from exchange rate movements. In other words mark-ups drive a wedge between retail prices in the destination country, which are equivalent to consumption prices, and import prices (also called border prices), which are foreign currency prices converted at the current exchange rate into local currency. Hence the consumption or retail price of a product is the import price plus local mark-ups expressed in local currency terms.

It has been estimated that the costs associated with local distribution services are, on average, 32 to 50 per cent of the total cost of goods across OECD countries (Campa and Goldberg, 2005). These figures imply that the consumption prices of imported goods may exhibit one-third to half of the sensitivity to exchange rates of import prices at the border. In addition, adjustments of distribution margins can absorb some of the remaining exchange rate-induced price changes. Overall, the pass-through of exchange rates into the consumption prices of imported goods could be less than half of the pass-through into the border prices of those same goods. Goldberg and Knetter (1997) identify increased foreign outsourcing as yet another reason for incomplete pass-through.

THE CURRENCY OF INVOICING

Expenditure switching policies based on exchange rate adjustment fail completely if the currency of the importer is used on both sides as the currency of invoicing. If Chinese firms use the dollar for invoicing their exports to the US, the effect (if any) of the revaluation of the yuan will be limited to imports. If also American exporters use the yuan as the currency of invoicing, there will be no change in either the dollar price of Chinese exports to the US or the yuan price of imports from the US. In general, if exporters set prices in their own currencies – the so-called "producer currency pricing" strategy – exchange rate movements are transmitted to consumer prices. This is not the case if exporters set prices in the currency of their customers' currencies – the so-called "local currency pricing" strategy. In this case, the relative price of domestic and imported goods is not affected by changes in exchange rates.

Goldberg and Tille (2006) argue that the pass-through effect is important for US trade in particular because of the international role of the dollar. They point out that the use of the dollar as the currency of invoicing in international trade transactions is consistent with the evidence indicating low pass-through of exchange rate movements into the import prices of the US and the higher pass-through into the import prices of other countries. A consequence of this status of the US dollar is that "the trade balance effects of exchange rate depreciation can be dramatically different for the United States compared with other countries". Under these conditions depreciation of the dollar is expected to lead to little change in US demand for imports (because the dollar price of imports will not be affected by changes in exchange rates) but the price of US exports will decline in foreign currency terms. Goldberg and Tille conclude that "the special international role of the dollar and the related low degree of exchange rate pass-through into US import prices will lead the trade balance response to be primarily through increased quantities of US exports". They attribute the use of the dollar as the currency of invoicing to: (i) the share of the US market as a destination for world production; (ii) the size of dollar bloc countries outside the US; (iii) the importance of global trade in commodities and homogeneous goods relative to total trade; and (iv) transaction costs that provide an incentive for using the dollar rather than the euro as the currency of invoicing.

Chinese exporting firms (or most of them) do not use the yuan as the currency of invoicing. Rather they mainly use the dollar, and recently, following the appreciation of the dollar against the yuan, they started using other currencies such as the euro. For example, Yi (2008) argues that "the fact that the US dollar is the world's vehicle currency for most international transactions, the majority of China's exports are denominated in the dollar". Bernard (2008) points out that using the dollar as the currency of invoicing by Chinese firms may "help explain why the People's Bank of China is reluctant to allow the RMB to undergo a rapid appreciation against the dollar". Betts and Devereux (2000) conclude that the prices of many goods are set in the local currency of the buyer, which implies that real exchange rate movements are driven primarily by fluctuations in the nominal exchange rate.

Goldberg and Tille (2006) point out that "international trade transactions between other countries and the United States are primarily invoiced in US dollars" and that "more than 99 per cent of US exports and 92 per cent of US imports were invoiced in dollars in early 2003". They find that those countries using their own currencies on part of their sales to the US are the UK, Japan and some euro area countries. For Asian countries on the exports side, they have Japan at 48 per cent, Korea at 83 per cent, Malaysia at 90 per cent and Thailand at 84 per cent. Although China is not mentioned by Goldberg and Tille, it is likely that the percentage of dollar-invoiced exports is comparable to that of Malaysia and Korea.

OTHER DETERMINANTS OF THE TRADE BALANCE

While those who accuse China of wrong-doing with respect to the US trade deficit envisage that the trade balance is determined only or primarily by the exchange rate, economic theory tells us otherwise in the sense that other factors may be more important with respect to the effect they have on the trade balance. We have already seen how the trade balance (or current account) may be taken to be a reflection of the saving–investment gap or the budget deficit. There are, however, factors that determine the trade balance directly (via a causal link) by affecting the prices and/or volumes of exports and imports. Since the trade balance is the difference between export revenue and import expenditure, which are determined by the prices and quantities of exports and imports, any factor that affects the prices of exports and imports is likely to affect the trade balance as well. Exchange rate adjustment may not work because these other factors may offset the effects resulting from changes in the exchange rate. For example, an increase in imports propelled by economic growth could overwhelm any effect the exchange rate may have on the trade balance in the opposite direction.

Even if exchange rate adjustment were critical for the trade balance, the effectiveness of devaluation requires no offsetting effects of other factors that also affect the trade balance. *The Economist* (2011h) makes this point by stating that "movements in nominal exchange rates often do not achieve the desired adjustment in real rates because they may be offset by changes in domestic prices". We cannot predict the change in one factor (the exchange rate) on the trade balance by assuming that other factors stay unchanged. In reality, this cannot be done because the *ceteris paribus* condition does not hold.

We have seen from the numerical illustrations presented in Chapter 5 that growth, inflation and trade restrictions affect the trade balance. Figure 7.7 displays import and export prices of Australia and Canada

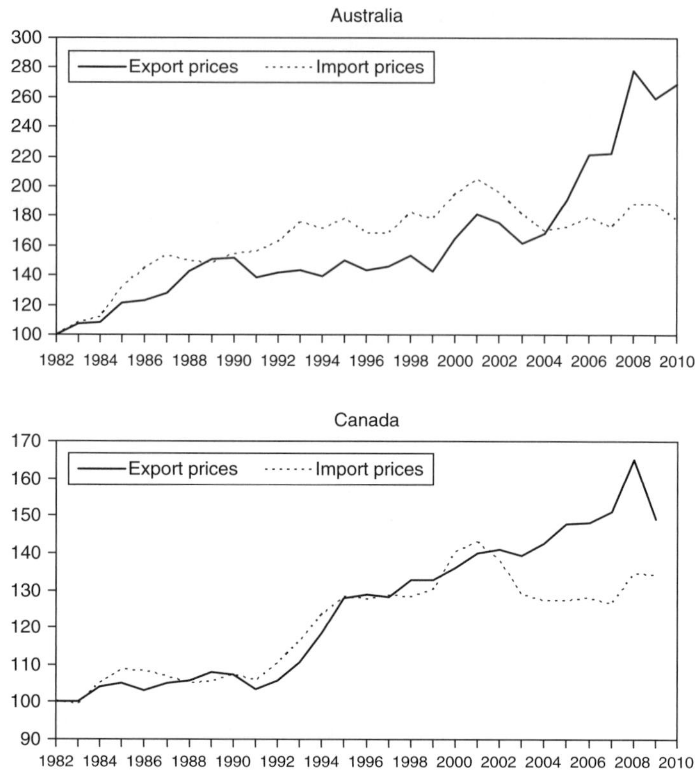

Figure 7.7 Import and export prices for Australia and Canada

over the period 1982–2010. We can observe that export and import prices move together because they are determined by growth and inflation, and this is why they tend to rise over time. We can also observe clear cyclical variation in export and import prices. In 2009 there was a more significant drop in export prices than import prices for both countries, which can be readily explained in terms of the effect of the Great Recession that affected commodity prices. As a result of the recovery in 2010, Australian export prices rose, but import prices declined.

Trade Restrictions

Trade restrictions (tariffs and quotas) affect the volumes and prices of exports and imports directly – they lie at the heart of protectionism and trade war. In fact one reason for imposing trade restrictions is the desire to protect the trade balance. The effect of trade restrictions is to reduce imports and hence produce an improvement in the trade balance – unless other countries retaliate by imposing similar restrictions, reducing the home country's exports. If such a trade war escalates, the effect will be to reduce the volume of international trade, depriving countries of its benefits.

Terms of Trade

An alternative view on the "cause and cure" has been put forward by Liu (2010) who attributes the US trade deficit with China to disparity in wages and (consequently) the terms of trade. He attributes disparity in wages to the "politically induced restriction on cross-border mobility of labour", which is the reason why "globalized trade has been primarily driven by cross-border wage arbitrage". Liu (2005b) argues that a nominal wage gap (between the US and China) of 35 to 1 (or 9 to 1 on a PPP basis) is due to what he calls "unbalanced terms of trade" and that "until wage parity is attained, free trade will continue to be driven by cross-border wage arbitrage in favour of China". Thus Liu's explanation of the US trade deficit with China is rather intuitive. China has cheap labour, which makes the price of exports low, while the US has expensive labour, which makes the price of Chinese imports from the US expensive. Hence the terms of trade (the ratio of export prices to import prices) are conducive to China having a trade surplus with the US.

What Liu means by "cross-border wage arbitrage" is that since American enterprises face expensive labour in the US and cheap labour in China, they choose to locate their enterprises in China via foreign direct investment. Hence, unless wage disparity disappears, unbalanced terms of trade will persist and so will the trade deficit. For Liu, the most effective way to correct trade imbalance is to change the terms of trade, which can be accomplished, *inter alia*, by regulating cross-border wage arbitrage (thus raising Chinese wages) and by a more effective Chinese environmental protection regulation.

The numerical examples presented in Chapter 5 show that the trade balance is negatively correlated with the terms of trade when the elasticity of demand for exports and imports is high, while positive correlation would be the case when demand is inelastic. Consider deterioration in the terms of trade resulting from a rise in import prices without any change in export prices. Export revenue should not be affected while import expenditure may rise or fall, depending on whether the demand for imports is inelastic or elastic, respectively. Consider now an improvement in the terms of trade resulting from a rise in export prices while import prices are unchanged. In this case, import expenditure is unaffected while export revenue may rise or fall depending on whether the demand for exports is

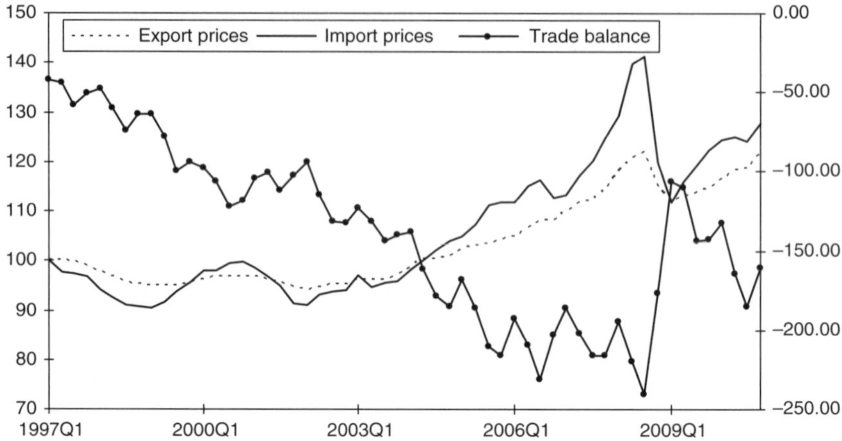

Figure 7.8 US export prices, import prices and trade balance

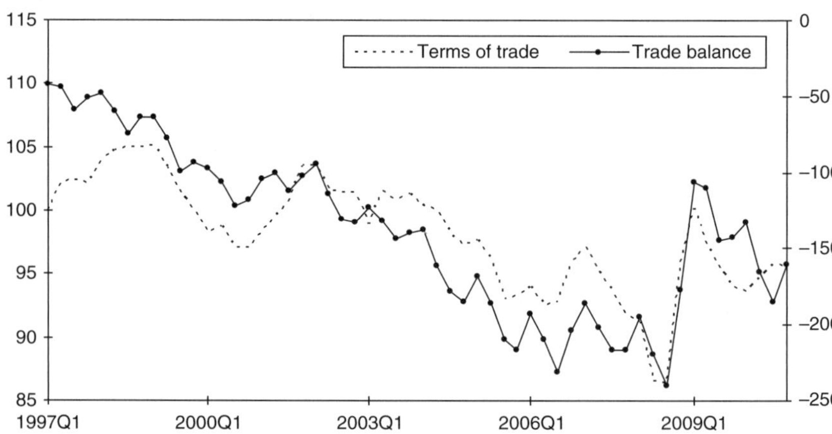

Figure 7.9 US terms of trade and trade balance

inelastic or elastic, respectively. Thus the trade balance may improve or deteriorate, depending on whether the demand for exports is inelastic or elastic, respectively. In short, the terms of trade and trade balance move in the same direction if the demand for exports and/or imports is inelastic, and vice versa.

Let us look at the stylized facts using data for the US over the period between the first quarter of 1997 and the fourth quarter of 2009, as displayed in Figure 7.8 and Figure 7.9. In Figure 7.8 we can see that import prices rose with some cyclical variation in the early part of the period, while the trade balance was deteriorating. We can also see that import prices rose and fell more sharply than export prices. Figure 7.9 exhibits very strong positive association between the terms of trade and the trade balance, thus the trade balance deteriorated as the terms of trade deteriorated. The only explanation for this kind of behaviour is that the demand for imports is inelastic. As import prices rise, import expenditure rises because of inelastic demand, leading to a deterioration in the trade balance while the terms of trade are also deteriorating. These observations tell us that the exchange rate plays no part in the close association between the trade balance and the terms of trade and that the configuration of elasticities is unlikely to make exchange rate adjustment effective in reducing the US deficit.

The patterns for other countries (Canada, Japan, Korea and Singapore) are different, as shown in Figure 7.10. For Canada and Japan, the trade balance moves positively with the terms of trade, which is similar to the case for the US. In the cases of Korea and Singapore, the trade balance and terms of trade move in opposite directions, particularly so in the case of Singapore. This difference in the behaviour of the trade balance in relation to the terms of trade can be rationalized in terms of the elasticity explanation presented earlier for the positive association between the terms of trade and trade balance in the US. The implications for the current debate are alarming: even if the US terms of trade against China improved (for example, because of a rise in Chinese wages relative to US wages) the US trade deficit with China would not disappear.

THE EMPIRICAL EVIDENCE

In this section we present some of the available empirical evidence on issues discussed in this chapter. Specifically the results of some empirical studies are presented: those pertaining to the twin deficit, exchange rate pass-through, the currency of invoicing and other determinants of the trade balance.

The Twin Deficit

Unlike the evidence on the effect of exchange rate adjustment and the J-curve effect, there is substantial evidence that supports the twin deficit phenomenon. Those studies that found no support for the phenomenon explain the divergence between the two balances in terms of other factors, pertaining primarily to the saving–investment balance. Some studies dismiss the twin deficit phenomenon just because the relation between the

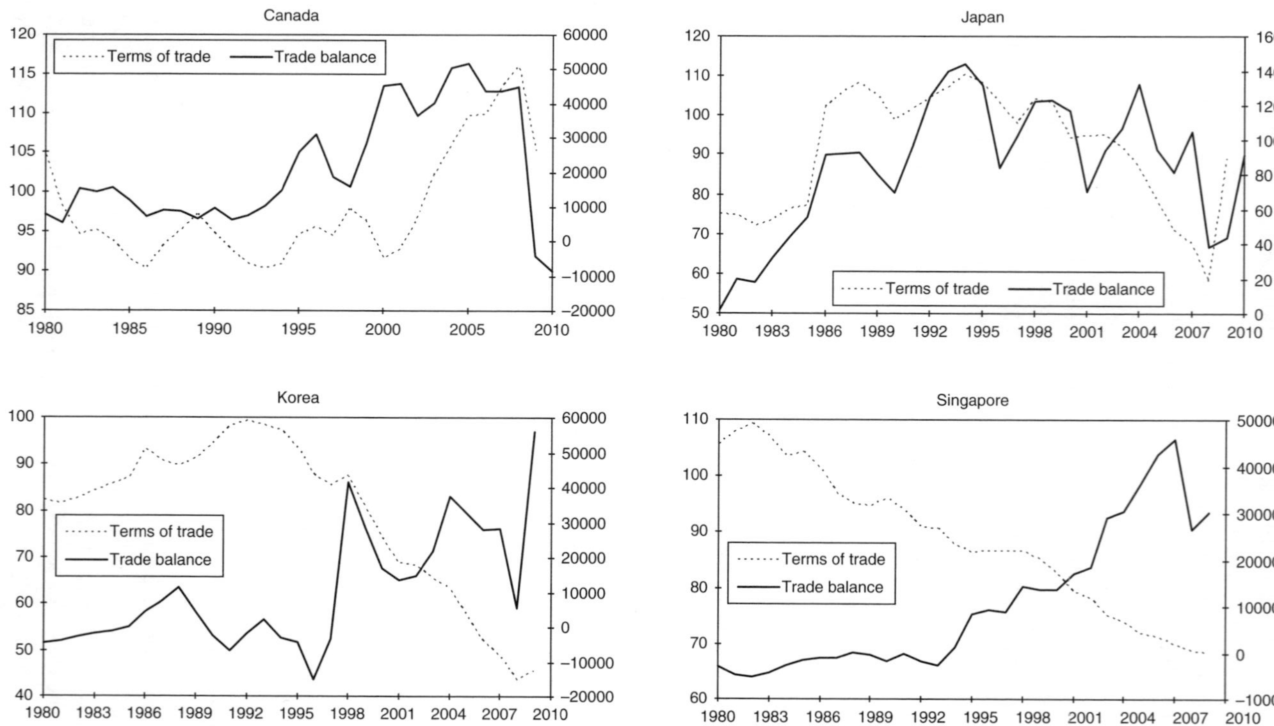

Figure 7.10 Terms of trade and the trade balance

budget deficit and trade deficit does not always hold without controlling for other factors, thus reaching the wrong conclusion by invoking the *ceteris paribus* condition. For industrial countries in general, Ito (2009) found that a one percentage point increase in the budget balance raises the current account balance by 0.10–0.49 percentage points.

Baxter (1995) examined the reaction of a model economy to two deficit-spending fiscal policies: (i) an increase in government expenditure that is not matched by higher tax revenues; and (ii) a decrease in labour and capital tax rates that is not matched by reduced expenditure. The results of this study reveal that, under both policies, the budget deficit rises to about 1 per cent of GDP in the short run, but it dies out gradually over the long run. The results also show that, following an increase in the budget deficit, the current account balance deteriorates by about 0.5 per cent of GDP. It must be made clear here that a one-to-one relation between the two deficits cannot be obtained unless the saving–investment balance stays unchanged, as explained earlier with the help of Figure 7.1.

Kim and Roubini (2004) conducted an empirical study of the effect of the budget deficit on the current account by accounting for the effect of output fluctuations (the business cycle). They found that output fluctuations explain most of the divergence between the budget balance and the current account at horizons of one to two years. After controlling for the effects of the business cycle on the budget and current account balances and isolating variations in the budget balance that are independent of output fluctuations, they found that an increase in the budget deficit has a positive impact on the current account in the short run, regardless of whether the deficit arises from a higher level of spending or lower taxes. This finding is explained in terms of the resulting increase in private saving and the reduction in domestic investment. Kim and Roubini found that higher private saving and lower domestic investment are more than adequate to offset the decline in government saving in the short run and contribute to the current account improvement. Their study, therefore, provides evidence for the potential role of private saving as a "cause and cure".

Another study explored the process whereby the trade balance responds to an increase in the budget deficit that arises from either higher government spending or reduced labour tax rates (Erceg et al., 2005). The results of this study reveal that the budget deficit, irrespective of its origin, has a far more modest effect than what was found by Baxter (1995). In particular, they found that a deficit-financed increase in government spending corresponding to 1 per cent of GDP induces the trade balance to decline by about 0.15 per cent of GDP, while a persistent cut in labour tax rates that produces a decline in tax receipts equivalent to 1 per cent of GDP induces a trade balance deterioration of about 0.12 per cent of GDP. The modest effect on the trade balance is explained in terms of domestic currency appreciation resulting from higher interest rates, which makes domestic goods relatively more expensive than imported goods. However, Cavallo (2005a) argues against this line of reasoning by suggesting that "a considerable share of international trade in goods and services between the United States and the rest of the world tends to be relatively insensitive to exchange rate fluctuations, at least in the short run".

Cavallo (2005b) draws attention to the composition of government current spending, particularly, the wage costs of government employees (for example, general public service, national defence, public order and safety, health, education, and so on). She finds that an increase in government spending on these labour services corresponding to 1 per cent of GDP produces deterioration in the current account balance of barely 0.05 per cent of GDP. This result is explained as follows: an increase in this component of government spending is accommodated by an increase in the number of hours that people work, rather than deterioration in the current account. The conclusion is that a budget deficit generated by an increase in spending on non-traded labour services has a substantially smaller impact on the current account than one generated by an increase in spending on tradable goods.

The results of Bartolini and Lahiri (2006) are highly supportive of the twin deficit in a large group of countries. They examine consumption behaviour in relation to fiscal balances, both of which are measured as shares of GDP, while controlling for changes in other fiscal variables (government consumption and public debt) and in other variables traditionally associated with consumption behaviour (income growth and population growth). On the basis of their results, they reach the conclusion that each dollar rise in the fiscal deficit is associated with an average rise in private consumption of 33 to 37 cents. For the US the results show that a dollar increase in the budget deficit leads to a rise of 23 cents in private consumption. They also found that each dollar increase in the fiscal deficit is typically associated with a decline in national saving of 33 to 37 cents and that each dollar rise in the fiscal deficit is associated on average with a 30 cent decline in the current account. They conclude that changes in national saving are reflected almost one-for-one by changes in the current account. It is important to emphasize the accurate use of the phrase "associated with" rather than "is caused by". Irrespective of the existence or otherwise of a causal relation between the budget and trade deficits, the accounting identity linking the two deficits tells us clearly that a change in one of them should be associated with a change in the other.

Exchange Rate Pass-Through

Since the mid-1980s, evidence has been accumulating to indicate limited pass-through from exchange rate movements to import prices. Marston (1990) estimated an average degree of exchange rate pass-through for industrialized countries of about 50 per cent. In a series of subsequent papers, Knetter (1989, 1993) and Gagnon and Knetter (1995) found pass-through estimates at even lower levels. In their review of the literature on goods prices and exchange rates, including exchange rate pass-through and pricing to market, Goldberg and Knetter (1997) concluded that the domestic currency prices of foreign goods do not respond fully to changes in exchange rates. They summarize their findings by stating that "the local currency prices of foreign products do not respond fully to exchange rates" and that "while the response varies by industry, a price response equal to one-half the exchange rate change would be near the middle of the distribution of estimated responses for shipment to the US". They attribute a significant portion of the "muted price response" to destination-specific changes in mark-ups on exports. This simply means incomplete exchange rate pass-through that depends on the destination market.

By reviewing several studies, Goldberg and Tille (2006) conclude that the US is typically found to have low exchange rate pass-through into import prices, with estimates ranging from 25 to 40 per cent (for example, Olivei, 2002; Campa and Goldberg, 2005; Marazzi et al., 2005). Kreinin (1997) estimated pass-through to US import prices to be only 50 per cent, compared to 60 per cent for Germany, 70 per cent for Japan and 90 per cent for Canada. In a study covering 23 OECD countries, Campa and Goldberg (2005) revealed the presence of partial pass-through in the short run. In a study of the car industry, Gagnon and Knetter (1995) found that Japanese car exports offset approximately 70 per cent of the effect of exchange rate changes on buyers' prices through mark-up adjustment. Another study of the effect of changes in exchange rates on Japanese export prices found incomplete pass-through as a transitory consequence of export pricing in currencies other than the yen (Kikuchi and Sumner, 2002).

Sekine (2006) estimated first and second stage exchange rate pass-through of six major industrial countries where the first stage effect runs from the exchange rate to import prices, whereas the second stage effect runs from import prices to consumer prices. He found that both stages of the pass-through effect have declined over time for all of the countries considered. Devereux and Yetman (2008) suggest that a low pass-through can be attributed to the slow adjustment of prices.

In the particular case of China, a study conducted by the Hong Kong

Monetary Authority of the pricing behaviour of Chinese firms shows that "there is incomplete pass-through of exchange rate changes to export prices" and that "about half of the exchange rate changes are reflected in domestic price adjustments" (Li et al., 2009). The study concludes that Chinese firms "adjust the mark-up in order to stabilize the prices in destination markets", which is another way of saying that they try to insulate, at least partially, the foreign currency price of exports from changes in exchange rates. The results of this study imply that "the price adjustment of exports in real terms has been well short of the nominal exchange rate changes, which will be one force limiting the effectiveness of the exchange-rate policy in influencing export growth" (and therefore the effectiveness of expenditure switching policies through exchange rate adjustment). It has been found that China's exports to the US and US exports to China going via Hong Kong are subject to a mark-up estimated to be between 22.4 per cent and 29.8 per cent (Feenstra et al., 1998).

In another study of the Chinese case, Ma and Zhang (2008) explore the impact of the yuan appreciation on the prices of exports to the Eurozone and on the adjustment of the Sino–Euro trade surplus. The empirical results of this study indicate that "the pass-through elasticities of different sections vary from each other", that "the exchange rate movements induce substantial change in export prices denominated in RMB", and that "the appreciation of RMB doesn't depress the exports of SITC6 and SITC7, which account for more than half of China's export value to Euro Area". Hence, they conclude that "the appreciation of RMB has limited effect on the adjustment of trade imbalances".

The Currency of Invoicing

Page (1981) presents direct evidence for the proposition that many export goods for a number of industrialized countries are invoiced in the local currency of the buyer rather than in the currency of the seller. For example Japanese firms invoice as much as 62 per cent of all exports in dollars. The empirical research conducted by Grassman (1973) and Page (1977) shows that trade between two advanced countries tends to be invoiced in the exporter's currency, whereas trade between advanced and developing countries is generally invoiced in the advanced country's currency. Studies of Chinese firms show that they predominantly use the dollar as the currency of invoicing (for example, Bernard, 2008).

Ou (2005) found no support for causality between the real effective exchange rate and Chinese exports, pointing out that "the variation of real effective exchange rate can't explain the variation of domestic enterprises' exports effectively either in the short or the long run". The emphasis on the exports side is most likely due to the issue of the currency of invoicing, as the use by Chinese firms of the dollar renders the exchange rate totally irrelevant to the trade balance.

Other Determinants of the Trade Balance

The Bahmani-Oskooee and Ratha (2004) survey of the studies dealing with the effect of the exchange rate on the trade balance shows that a variety of potential determinants of the trade balance, apart from the exchange rate, have been used. These determinants include domestic real income, foreign real income, the relative price of exports, growth rate, ratio of base money to output, ratio of government consumption to output, world income, money supply, world base money, import prices, import volumes, export prices, export volumes, terms of trade, the general price level, consumption, investment, and volume of world trade. While the results are all over the place, the evidence invariably shows that a number of factors are more important than the exchange rate as determinants of the trade balance.

The list of potential determinants of the trade balance derived from the Bahmani-Oskooee and Ratha (2004) survey is not exhaustive. Fratzscher et al. (2007) examine the role of asset prices in comparison to other factors, in particular exchange rates, as a driver of the US trade balance. They found that equity market shocks and housing price shocks account for up to 30 per cent of the movements of the US trade balance at a horizon of 20 quarters. By contrast, they found that shocks to the real exchange rate have been less relevant, explaining about 9 per cent and exerting a more temporary effect on the trade balance. Their findings suggest that large exchange rate movements may not necessarily be a key element of an adjustment of today's large current account imbalances and that relative global asset price changes could be a potent source of adjustment.

Miles (1979) tried to explain the trade balance as a percentage of GDP in terms of the exchange rate, growth rate, money supply and government spending. He found that devaluation of the domestic currency leads to an improvement in the capital account rather than the trade balance. He suggested that devaluation causes a mere portfolio adjustment, resulting in a surplus in the capital account. Falk (2008) investigates the determinants of the trade balance using panel data for 32 industrialized and emerging economies for the period 1990–2007. His results show that the trade balance as a percentage of GDP is positively related to real foreign GDP per capita and negatively related to real domestic GDP per capita. While he found some evidence suggesting that domestic currency depreciation leads to improvement in the trade balance for countries with a negative trade balance and/ or a large positive net foreign direct investment position, the trade balance is much less sensitive to movements in the real effective exchange rate. In a study of the determinants of the Malaysian trade balance, Duasa (2007) found that the trade balance is affected by the money supply and income, but not by the exchange rate. Liew et al. (2003) demonstrate that the trade balances of the ASEAN-5, including Malaysia, is affected by the money supply rather than the exchange rate, thus suggesting that the role of the exchange rate in the trade balance has been exaggerated.

Zhuang et al. (2007) examined the determinants of the US trade balance in agricultural products, concluding that per capita income "appears to be the most important determinant of US trade balance in consumer-oriented products". Specifically, the study shows that a 1 per cent increase of US consumer income, all other things being equal, would reduce US export share by 1.151 per cent. This indicates that as domestic per capita income rises, the imports of consumer-oriented goods grow faster than exports. The results also show that a 1 per cent increase of foreign per capita income, all other things being equal, would lead to an increase of 0.409 per cent of the export share. In other words, the study explains, "as per capita income increases in foreign countries, their imports of consumer-oriented products from the United States will grow faster than their exports". As far as the exchange rate is concerned, the study concludes that a 1 per cent appreciation of the US dollar would lead to a decrease of 0.098 per cent in the export share of the US. Another determinant of the trade balance was found to be foreign direct investment (FDI). A 1 per cent increase of FDI inflows from the US to foreign countries reduces the US export share by 0.139 per cent, suggesting that "FDI and exports of consumer-oriented products have a substitute relationship". Foreign market openness is also found to have a positive impact on the US trade balance, although the magnitude of the effect is small. The results suggest that an increase in per capita income and trade liberalization in foreign countries would improve the US trade balance.

AN AMBIGUOUS RELATION

Another reason why revaluation of the yuan will not work is the lack of a precise causal relation running from the exchange rate to the trade balance. The exchange rate–trade balance nexus does not constitute a mechanical or physical system where the push of a button or a change in the cause produces a predictable outcome. Rather, the nexus constitutes an ambiguous relation that does not produce a predictable outcome. This is why it is strange that China bashers are confident that revaluation of the yuan will eliminate or reduce the US trade deficit.

The proposition that devaluation of the domestic currency leads to an improvement in the trade balance is described by Copeland (2005) as being "not strictly wrong, but certainly incomplete and usually misleading". The process rests on the assumption of a unidirectional causal relation running from the exchange rate to the trade balance, but economic theory also tells us that the relation could be running from the trade balance to the exchange rate. We often hear, particularly from financial media reports, that a particular currency depreciated on a certain occasion because of the announcement of a big trade deficit, in which case currency depreciation is a consequence, not a cause, of the trade balance deterioration. It is also interesting to note that when changes in the exchange rate are postulated to affect the trade balance, the relation is inverse, that is, a weaker currency leads to improvement in the trade balance. However, when it is envisaged that the trade balance affects the exchange rate, the relation is positive in the sense that improvement in the trade balance leads to currency appreciation. Surely, there is no reliable way of discerning which way the cause and effect relation goes. Economists use the so-called causality testing to discern this process but it is often the case that testing reveals causality in both directions. Like many of the tools used by economists for quantitative analysis, causality testing is unreliable and the results are highly sensitive to how the model is specified (Moosa, 2011b). Then "causality" in economics does not really mean causality in the commonly understood meaning of the word; rather, it means "temporal ordering" (which comes first, time wise). In this sense something causes something else if the something occurs before the something else.

Further complications arise because the relation between the exchange rate and trade balance could be direct or indirect. For example, if for the sake of argument we assume that changes in exchange rates affect trade flows, domestic currency appreciation reduces inflation (by reducing the domestic currency price of imports) and depresses growth (by adversely affecting exports). Both of these effects have implications for the trade balance, but the kind of effect is indirect. The relation between the trade balance and the exchange rate is not straightforward, but is rather complex. This gives rise to an alternative view that the exchange rate and the trade balance are determined jointly and that they are affected by a similar set of factors. For example, in the Mundell–Fleming model, a fiscal expansion under a floating exchange rate causes domestic currency appreciation, an increase in income, a higher real interest rate (as long as capital is imperfectly mobile) and a deterioration in the current account. This implies the absence of direct causation running from the exchange rate to the trade balance, or vice versa. In the same model, a monetary expansion causes depreciation of the domestic currency, a rise in income, a fall in interest rates (when capital is not completely mobile), and an improvement in the current account (see, for example, Copeland, 2005).

The monetary model of exchange rates, popularized in the 1970s following the move to floating exchange rates, tells us that under fixed exchange rates the consequence of a once-and-for-all devaluation of the domestic currency is a temporary improvement in competitiveness and improvement in the trade balance. However, the ensuing inflation (arising from a higher level of reserves) erodes the competitive advantage over time, until the country finds itself back where it started from. The portfolio balance model predicts that currency appreciation is associated with a current account surplus, while currency depreciation is associated with a current account deficit. Copeland (2005) stresses that "this is not a genuine relationship of cause and effect" and that "the current account imbalance is itself a consequence of a disturbance, the adjustment process which requires a long-run change in the volume of foreign currency assets in the economy".

Other economists have made remarks to point out ambiguity in the relation between the trade balance or current account and the exchange rate. For example, Larrain (2003) presents a model showing that "exchange rates determine the current account, and the current account in turn determines exchange rates". Greenwood (1984) examined the relation among the trade balance, balance of payments, relative price of non-traded goods and the real exchange rate, reaching the conclusion that "the relation between these variables is theoretically ambiguous".

It is not the case that causation runs from the exchange rate to the trade balance and that the working of this relation is not impeded or distorted by other movements in the economy. It is far from certain that devaluation of the domestic currency produces a necessarily favourable effect on the trade balance. Ambiguity of the relation between the two variables is yet another reason for being sceptical about the possibility that revaluation of the yuan will solve America's external deficit problem.

8. The morality and legality of Chinese policies

THE CASE OF CHINA VERSUS THE REST OF THE WORLD: WHAT THE PROSECUTOR SAYS

The list of accusations against China is vast and it is not confined to its exchange rate policy. China is accused of choosing an improper exchange rate regime, currency manipulation, refusal to revalue an undervalued currency, excessive accumulation of reserves, too much saving and too little consumption, violation of the IMF and WTO rules, causing global imbalances, hurting the world economy by adopting a policy of export-led growth, causing the global financial crisis, pushing up oil prices, buying the corporate world aggressively, and undermining US security. Even more accusations could be found, but this list is adequately comprehensive and bad enough. If convicted, China would be labelled a villain that is pursuing anti-rest-of-the-world policies.

Both the media and academic literature report these accusations on a regular basis. For example, Ensinger (2010) argues strongly that "the US must be more forceful in tackling China's currency manipulation, export controls, discriminatory domestic procurement policies and trade-distorting subsidies". More specifically, he accuses China of (i) promoting industrial policies that manipulate trade rules to benefit domestic firms to the detriment of American and other foreign competitors; (ii) failure to live up to its commitment to transition away from a state-directed economy to a more market-based approach; (iii) using a "slew of trade distorting practices" to ensure that the economic relationship with the US is far from balanced; (iv) ensuring that it holds a surplus with the US through the manipulation of its currency; (v) restricting the export of rare earth metals, which are vital to the production of a whole host of alternative energy products and components; (vi) protecting domestic industries through an increasingly restrictive investment regime and export restrictions; and (vii) adopting a restrictive investment regime that encourages the transfer of crucial technology and the outsourcing of production. In conclusion, he argues that "if China's unfair trade practices are not addressed, China will continue to gain ground on the US economically, meanwhile the US will continue to accumulate debt and cede ground to China in other areas". Likewise, Goldstein and Lardy (2009) recommend that China "disavow any strategy of competitive undervaluation of the yuan that might be aimed at dealing with reduced global demand for Chinese exports". They call for a rejection of export promotion measures, even if such steps are technically consistent with China's WTO obligations. On hearing these accusations, one can only wonder if China has ever done anything right towards the US and the rest of the world.

But it is not about China and the US only. Goldstein (2004) presents a comprehensive list of the alleged victims of China's exchange rate policy, arguing that China is hurting the "international community", comprising the US, Europe, Japan and emerging Asia (naturally, Africa and the Middle East do not belong to the international community). For the US, China is blamed for a jobless recovery, the rapid decline in manufacturing employment and (of course) the bilateral trade deficit. For the Eurozone, China is criticized for the anaemic growth performance, low interest rates and strong currency. Japan, according to Goldstein, was (or is) complaining about weak economic growth, deflation and the challenge posed by China to Japan's leadership in Asia. Emerging Asian countries criticize China for not having a clearer picture of how to respond to the challenge posed by China's low labour costs and the skill-upgrading of China's exports. One can only wonder if there is any mishap anywhere that China is not responsible for. It is heartening, however, to see that Goldstein admits that the criticism of China is a "reflection of scapegoating, policy failure, and lack of strategic planning outside China". Still he describes China's exchange rate policy as "seriously flawed given its current macroeconomic circumstances and its longer-term policy objectives".

In this chapter we analyse these allegations and argue that none of them is valid and that China's policies are neither illegal nor immoral. It is suggested here that the choice of exchange rate regime is a sovereign right that is compatible with current IMF rules and that currency manipulation is a requirement for the preservation of a fixed exchange rate regime, which leads to the accumulation of reserves. In general it is argued that China is pursuing policies that are suitable to its stage of development and that countries typically adopt economic policies deemed suitable for their domestic economic conditions (which naturally change over time). The allegation that China is hurting the world economy should actually be replaced by gratitude that China has kept the lid on world inflation by producing cheap manufactured goods, thus contributing to the so-called "great moderation".

EXCHANGE RATE REGIME CHOICE

Exchange rate regime choice is governed by the international monetary system in operation at the time and by the relevant country's own circumstances. Some international monetary systems do not give countries a choice of regime; for example, countries were required to be on fixed and fixed but adjustable exchange rates under the gold standard and the Bretton Woods system, respectively. In this case, a country may choose not to join the system (for example, most countries were not on the gold standard when it was in operation) or it may just choose to ignore the rules, which is exactly what Canada did in the 1950s when the country experimented with floating exchange rates while under the Bretton Woods system. Under the present system, countries have a choice of adopting their preferred exchange rate regime. Article IV of the revised IMF Articles allows countries to "tie their currencies to any external anchor with the sole exception of gold" – meaning fixed exchange rates. The rules specifically allow a member country to maintain the value of its currency "in terms of the special drawing right or another denominator, other than gold". The rules also allow cooperative arrangements (such as the European Monetary Union) and "other exchange arrangements of a member's choice". The same Article specifies that a country should endeavour to direct its economic and financial policies "with due regard to its circumstances". Under the present system, countries can shift from one exchange rate regime to another, provided that they inform the IMF of the regime change. However, there have been scores of cases where countries adopt a particular exchange rate regime and report another.

A History of China's Exchange Rate Regimes

Ilzetzki et al. (2008) have documented the historical developments of exchange rate regimes for almost every country in the world. According to their study China followed managed floating between June 1969 and December 1973, crawling band around the dollar from January 1974 to February 1981, managed floating from March 1981 to July 1992, crawling band against the dollar from August 1992 to January 1994 and a dollar peg from January 1994 until the present time. If we consider Figure 8.1, we observe the following, notwithstanding the fact that it is not possible to tell what the exchange rate regime is just by looking at a graph of the exchange rate over time. However, it is clear that China was on a system of fixed exchange rates during the period 1957–71, with the yuan pegged to the dollar at the rate of 2.46. That was perfectly in

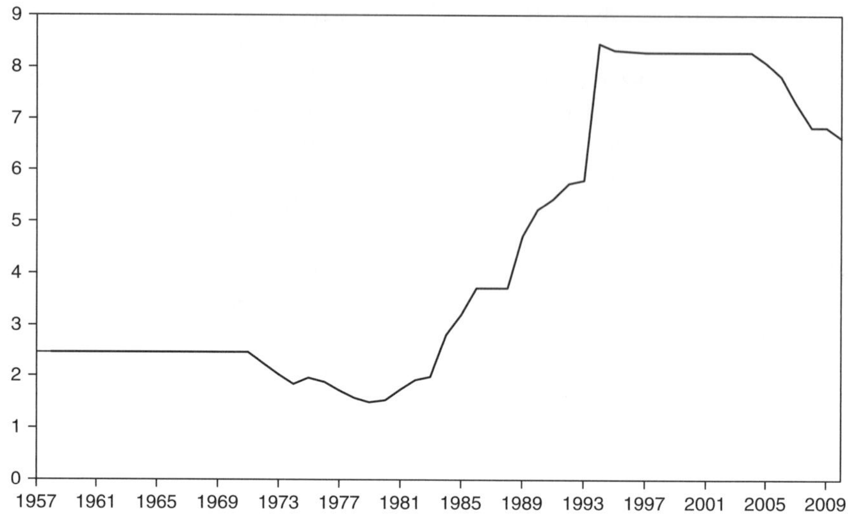

Figure 8.1 The yuan/dollar exchange rate (1957–2010)

line with the Bretton Woods system in operation at that time. During the period 1971–9 the yuan appreciated against the dollar to 1.50, which was due to the weakness of the dollar at that time, so it could have been a system of crawling band against the dollar. At that rate the Chinese could have felt that the yuan was extremely overvalued, and so the currency was allowed to depreciate against the dollar when the latter was becoming strong. This kind of behaviour is not compatible with a crawling band unless the crawling band was constructed around different higher central rates. It could also be compatible with managed floating.

A fixed peg to the dollar was introduced in 1997 at around 8.28, so the yuan was definitely devalued by a deliberate policy action against the dollar. That system remained in operation until July 2005, when the Chinese revalued the currency and declared a move to a basket peg. What in fact happened was that the Chinese moved to a crawling peg against the dollar whereby the yuan is allowed to appreciate gradually while introducing some uncertainty to curb speculation (Moosa, 2008b; Moosa et al., 2009). That policy was interrupted briefly by the global financial crisis, but there was nothing illegal about it as it is (and was) well within the IMF rules. Figures 8.2 and 8.3 display the movements of the yuan against the yen and pound over the period 1957–2010, which reflect the movements of the yuan against the dollar.

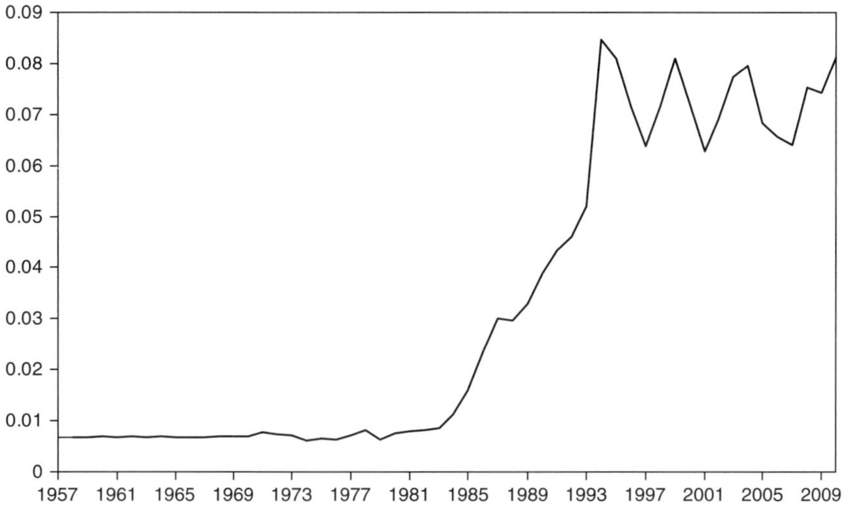

Figure 8.2 The yuan/yen exchange rate (1957–2010)

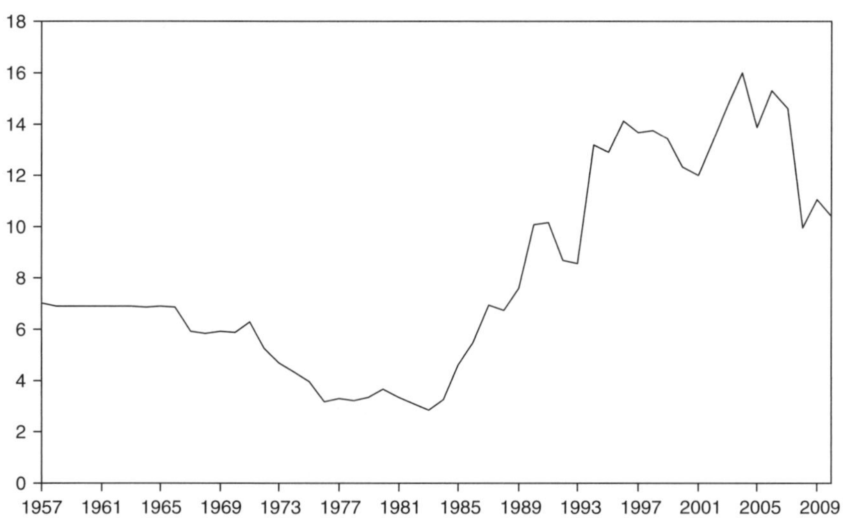

Figure 8.3 The yuan/pound exchange rate (1957–2010)

Denying China the Right to Choose

China bashers deny China the right to choose its exchange rate regime under the current international rules. For example, Mussa (2007) describes as a "logical absurdity" the proposition of unilateral sovereign authority to determine a country's exchange rate because the exchange rate involves two currencies and hence two countries. What is absurd is in fact Mussa's argument, because a country can, if it chooses, fix its exchange rate against the currency of another country. To preserve a system like this, the fixed rate must be defended against market forces, which may or may not succeed. In the 1970s the East Germans had an exchange rate of 1:1 against the Deutsche mark while the West Germans had an exchange rate of 4:1. The East Germans imposed their exchange rate by requiring visitors crossing the border from West Berlin to East Berlin to convert a certain amount at their rate. That did not prevent the smuggling of East German marks from the West to the East at the West's exchange rate. Neither country told the other that it indulged in exchange rate malpractice or that it had no right to fix the exchange rate at a particular level. Countries that adopt a dual exchange rate system use two rates against another currency, and that is quite legitimate. Mussa's incomprehensibly flawed and rather naive argument provides every reason not to take seriously his proposition that China is violating IMF rules.

Williamson (2003) puts forward an equally bizarre idea by arguing that "exchange rates are inherently the business of more than one country", which means that "a small country can expect that the rest of the world will allow it to choose its exchange rate without too much interference, but large countries have to recognize that their partners have a legitimate interest in what they choose because their choice influences those partners' effective exchange rates". He suggests that "China should operate its foreign exchange market with wider margins and should change its peg from the US dollar to a basket of the three major currencies" and that "it should be more willing to contemplate changes in the value of the peg, while keeping each individual change in the peg small so as to avoid creating strong speculative pressures". One can only wonder whether these arguments are based on legal principles or sound economics. Neither, probably. From a legal point of view, there is nothing in the IMF rules that says that exchange rate regime choice depends on country size. From an economic point of view, Williamson does not present any argument as to why the move from a dollar peg to a basket peg is good for China and the rest of the world. Indeed if the arguments for and against flexible exchange rates are applied to the case of China we will find, on the balance of the pros and cons, that China is better off with fixed exchange rates. We will return to this point later.

Palley (2005) denies China the right to choose its exchange rate regime, although he is humble enough to say that "no one is calling for China to float its currency now" (actually there is a consensus among China bashers that a floating currency is a must). He only suggests that China switches from a dollar peg to a basket peg. Likewise, McNally (2010) suggests that China should "once and for all remove the lack of transparency and aura of manipulation surrounding the yuan's exchange rate management" and that "China should move to a floating rate based on market forces with a reference to a basket of currencies". He calls this a "win–win proposition" – how and why, is unclear. McNally overlooks or is unaware of the fact that even the lack of transparency is allowed as a country may choose to peg its currency to a basket with undisclosed components; transparency is counter-productive in this case because it encourages arbitrage or speculation against the currency.

Robert Mundell stridently defends the Chinese exchange rate policy of pegging the yuan to the US dollar, arguing that he had always supported a fixed rate policy "for the same reasons I supported the euro and am now supporting a world currency" (Dukes, 2005). He actually advised China to keep its exchange rate fixed as long as the dollar is stable and presented 12 reasons why revaluing the renminbi would be a bad idea for China, Asia and the world, including the assertion that a possible move to float the yuan "would delay the convertibility of the Chinese currency, cut down on the inflow of foreign direct investment, reduce economic growth greatly, aggravate the non-performing loans situation in Chinese banks, hurt the profitability of Chinese enterprises, increase the unemployment rate, add more deflation distress in rural sectors and reward speculators, all of which would add to instability in China and Asia and hurt the worldwide economy". Likewise, John Nash (perhaps thinking in terms of game theory) defends exchange rate stability "because stable currencies lead to economic certainty and soundness" (Dukes, 2005).

Disputing the Choice of Fixed Rates

Lardy (2005) disputes the Chinese reasoning for choosing fixed exchange rates on the basis of the need for stability by presenting two arguments: (i) given the volatility of the dollar against major currencies, the yuan would be volatile on a trade-weighted basis (Figure 8.4); and (ii) the Chinese have made many major adjustments in the (nominal) exchange rate of the yuan since 1978, when economic reform began. These arguments do not make sense. Countries that use a single-currency peg realize that their trade-weighted rates (and even the bilateral exchange rates against other currencies) will be volatile, but the very idea of a single currency peg is

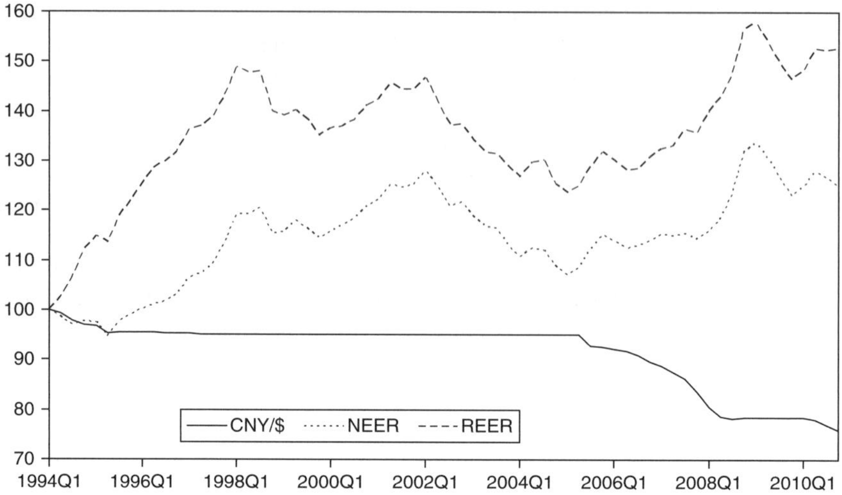

Figure 8.4 Nominal and real exchange rates of the yuan

motivated by the desire to maintain the stability of the bilateral exchange rate against a specific currency. As to the frequency and timing of changing a fixed but adjustable exchange rate, this is dictated by the prevailing economic conditions and the judgement of the monetary authorities of the underlying country. What Lardy chooses not to understand is that the Chinese are concerned that a premature end to the peg would bring about financial instability (destabilizing capital flows), bearing in mind what happened in Japan as a result of the significant appreciation of the yen in the period following the Plaza Accord of 1985. When Japan was a star performer in the 1960s, the yen was pegged at 360 to the dollar. That period witnessed significant growth in output, productivity and wages. All that changed after the US put pressure on Japan to maintain a strong currency (Xiao, 2010).

Furthermore, a stable exchange rate between the dollar and yuan may be in the interests of both countries, given the potential for cross-border investment. Pegging the yuan to the dollar has been an important element of the stabilization policies pursued since China opened up to the rest of the world. This is because a dollar peg provides a monetary anchor for price stability by linking domestic monetary policy to the inflation rate of a large, non-inflationary economy, which, according to Obstfeld (2006), has been an important benefit of dollar pegging for China. In the meantime China is allowing its currency to appreciate against the dollar, but only gradually. Shengjun (2010) argues that "all the signs indicate that the central bank [of China] will ensure that the currency appreciates gradually, say by between 2 per cent and 5 per cent a year". In the long run, the yuan is likely to be an international currency when it becomes fully convertible once the Chinese economy has undergone full transformation into a market economy. At that time, floating will make a lot of sense.

Fixed versus Flexible Exchange Rates

Recall the arguments for and against flexible exchange rates listed in Chapter 2. The first argument for flexible rates is that they are conducive to a smooth balance of payments adjustment because they move continuously in reaction to disequilibria. In theory, yes, but in practice this has not happened, perhaps because a system of purely flexible exchange rates does not exist. The fear of floating does not only provide an incentive to declare floating and practise pegging but also to interfere with the working of market forces so that a worldwide system of floating exchange rates in its purest form does not exist. Likewise, flexible exchange rates have not led to the achievement of free international trade or policy independence. The global financial crisis has demonstrated that countries with flexible exchange rates were not in a better position to cope with the crisis than those with fixed rates – perhaps the opposite is true. Therefore, there is nothing much for China to gain by adopting flexible exchange rates.

On the other hand, the arguments against flexible exchange rates sound more valid. That they cause uncertainty and inhibit international trade is a matter that is supported by empirical evidence and by the very existence of the European Monetary Union. Furthermore, flexible exchange rates are not suitable for countries that do not have sophisticated financial systems, and China is such a country. The argument that flexible exchange rates are inflationary and unstable makes them unappealing to China, which is currently experiencing rampant inflation. Harbaugh (2004) argues that exchange rate stability has made investment by domestic and foreign firms less risky and has reduced pressure on domestic prices. Exchange rate volatility is likely to affect FDI inflows and may cause financial distress in the absence of tools that can be used to deal with foreign exchange risk. Irwin (2011a) points out that the most frequently drawn lesson from the 1930s was that fixed exchange rates were necessary to provide monetary stability and avoid chaotic exchange rate movements. Nurkse (1944) warned that floating exchange rates would be destabilizing and would seriously disrupt international trade.

Liu (2005a) makes a very interesting point concerning the US position on exchange rates. He writes:

> When the dollar was rising, as it did in the 1980s, the US, to protect its export trade, hailed the stabilizing wisdom of fixed exchange rates. When the dollar falls, as it has been in recent years, the US, to deflect the blame of its trade deficit, attacks fixed exchange rates as currency manipulation, as it targets China's currency now which has been pegged to the dollar for a decade, since the dollar was lower.

Inconsistent and time-varying positions on various issues have been characteristic of US policy towards the rest of the world. It is not only about fixed or flexible exchange rates – recall the positions on free trade and Saddam Hussein.

China's Right to Choose

It is not clear why China bashers refuse to acknowledge the fact that countries have the right to choose their exchange rate regimes and defend them, if they can, against market forces. Wyplosz (2010) correctly argues that "the nominal rate is in the hands of the Chinese authorities, who have opted for a fixed exchange rate regime", which "is perfectly compatible with IMF principles". On balance, there is more for China in fixed than in flexible exchange rates.

It is not up to Goldstein, Lardy, Mundell or the author of this book to tell China which exchange rate regime it should adopt. They can make suggestions, but China has the privilege of accepting or rejecting the advice. Mundell puts it succinctly by saying: "regardless, China is in the best position to decide" (Dukes, 2005). If America has the right to tell China which exchange rate regime is best, China should have the right to call on the US to abandon floating and peg the dollar to the yuan, because this serves the interests of China.

CURRENCY MANIPULATION

China is accused of currency manipulation just because it is exercising a legitimate right to adopt a fixed exchange rate regime and defend it via intervention in the foreign exchange market and by other means. From time to time, the US Treasury issues a list of "currency manipulators", countries that satisfy certain criteria. The list, of course, does not include the US despite intentional efforts to keep the dollar weak via quantitative easing.

The criteria used by the US Treasury to identify the "bad guys" are spelt out by Bivens and Scott (2006) who argue that "a serious reading of all evidence on the matter [currency manipulation] clearly shows that China has exceeded all well-established limits that have been used to determine currency manipulation in the past". They use three criteria to identify currency manipulators: (i) a high and rising bilateral trade surplus with the US; (ii) a high and rising global current account surplus; and (iii) a high and rising accumulation of international reserves. Since China satisfies all of these criteria, they suggest that "every available indicator demonstrates that China is manipulating the value of its currency with the intent of spurring the growth of its trade surpluses". This currency manipulation, they argue, "has had damaging effects on some sectors of the US economy and has been a primary contributor to the enormous run-up in the American trade and current account deficits".

In Chapter 4 strong arguments were presented against the propositions that the trade balance position and accumulation of international reserves are indicative of exchange rate misalignment. These arguments render as invalid the indicators used by Bivens and Scott (2006) to identify currency manipulators. One question remains: why is the use of quantitative easing not an indicator of currency manipulation, particularly for a country (the US) that claims to adopt free floating and has full faith in the power of the market? Buiter and Rahbari (2011) argue that it is

> controversial to call for an appreciation of the Reminbi when at the same time the US monetary authorities are engaged in a market-mediated downward manipulation of the external value of the US dollar through the pursuit of a monetary policy that is more expansionary than the average of the monetary policies pursued by its trading partners.

One wonders how China bashers would respond to this legitimate question.

Wyplosz (2010) suggests that calling what China is doing "manipulation" is "not just outside any legal norm, it would also concern the tens of other countries that also peg their currencies to the dollar – and (why not?) those that maintain fixed exchange rates vis-à-vis currencies like the euro". Even some of those who think that China is doing something wrong do not accuse China of currency manipulation. For example, Spruk (2010a) argues that "it would be foolish to mark China as currency manipulator and an ultimate source of US trade deficit and manufacturing loss". Zakaria (2010) is against the currency manipulation issue, making the interesting remark that "the US imports more than it exports from 90 countries around the world", which is not due to "currency manipulation by those countries" but rather "a result of fundamental choices we [Americans] have made as a country to favour consumption over investment and manufacturing". He alternatively argues that what has made China "the key manufacturing base of the world" are factors like "low wages, superb infrastructure, hospitality to business, compliant unions and a hard-working labor force" – not currency manipulation. Persaud (2010) argues that "for the average American voter familiar with floating currencies, the whole idea of a fixed exchange rate smells of manipulation, but in fact it is easier to manipulate a floating exchange rate than a fixed one".

Accusing China of currency manipulation is preposterous and indicative of extreme naivety. Of course China manipulates its currency because it has chosen to adopt a system of fixed exchange rates, which is allowed by international rules. Until 1971, the Bretton Woods Agreement of 1944 required all countries to have fixed but adjustable exchange rates while floating was outlawed. That did not prevent some countries, such as Canada, from experimenting with floating exchange rates. What is important here is that it was a requirement for all countries to "manipulate" their currencies to be compliant with the agreement. In 1971 the US dismantled the Bretton Woods system by abolishing the convertibility of the dollar into gold. After a period of turmoil (during which countries did what they thought was best for their economies), the Jamaica Accord of 1976 gave countries the freedom to choose from an exchange rate arrangement menu ranging from the very fixed to the very flexible regimes. China has chosen to use a fixed exchange rate regime, which requires "manipulation", that is, maintaining the regime via intervention and other means. Unless there is a new international agreement that outlaws fixed exchange rates, no one should complain about China's "manipulation" of the exchange rate.

A fact that US Treasury officials choose to overlook is that China has some sort of fixed but adjustable exchange rate, which makes it a policy instrument. They instead claim that the US dollar exchange rate is determined in a free market, hence it cannot be manipulated. Buiter and Rahbari (2011) argue that "this line of reasoning contains a serious flaw" because the weakening of the US exchange rate "has been all-but-inevitable consequence of US interest rate cuts or quantitative easing not reciprocated to the same degree abroad". They add that "whether one calls it 'manipulation' or not is a matter of rhetoric rather than positive economics". It is therefore strange that, according to Mussa (2007), manipulation can be conducted through "excess intervention in exchange markets or through the imposition of capital controls" (but not through quantitative easing, of course). So, the use of capital controls is a violation of Article IV of the IMF, which is rather strange because it means that capital account liberalization is a commitment on every country's part. This kind of nonsense presumably disappeared after the carnage inflicted by the Asian financial crisis, which prompted the victim countries that had followed the IMF (do-as-I-say) advice to resort back to capital controls in the late 1990s. Mussa himself admits that "because this concept of exchange rate manipulation is potentially so broad, virtually all countries could be considered to be 'manipulating' their exchange rate almost all the time". They all do it, it seems, but only China has a bad intent, or so it sounds!

THE ACCUMULATION OF RESERVES

A related charge to that of currency manipulation is the accumulation of international reserves. The reasoning goes as follows: China manipulates its currency by intervention in the foreign exchange market, which requires buying dollar-denominated securities. It is not clear at all what is wrong with this, which makes the most natural response to these claims to be "so what?". To start with, China has the right to accumulate reserves to defend its currency against a speculative attack (is that not what the Bank of England tried to do and failed in 1992?). Foreign exchange reserves are important indicators of ability to repay foreign debt and to determine sovereign credit ratings and the country's risk status.

Reserves could be seen as collateral that helps attract foreign investors, and this is why countries tolerate low returns or losses on reserve holdings, given the growth and development benefits. However, holding reserves does not go without costs. Fluctuations in the foreign exchange market result in gains and losses in the purchasing power of reserves. For example, depreciation of the US dollar results in a loss of wealth for China. In addition to fluctuations in exchange rates, the purchasing power of the reserves is eroded by inflation. It is up to China to strike a balance between the costs and benefits of holding reserves,

The situation is really strange: the Americans complain about the Chinese accumulating reserves, but they also complain that the Chinese may not want to hold US Treasuries as reserves or may even dump their holdings. For example, Ahearne et al. (2007) suggest as a solution to the global imbalances problem that "China needs to curb its accumulation of foreign exchange reserves". Cooper (2009) entertains the proposition that China could threaten US national security with its extensive dollar holdings, which can be used as a "weapon" (of mass destruction?) to destabilize the US financial system. He is, however, prompt in answering this question in the negative although he does not rule out the possibility of "transitory turbulence in particular markets". Gagnon and Hufbauer (2011) put forward the proposition that the US should impose a withholding tax on the interest paid to China as a holder of Treasury bonds. The idea is that China will be discouraged from buying US government bonds, implying that it will not intervene in the foreign exchange market, which will eliminate exchange rate misalignment and the US trade deficit. Until that happens, if it happens, how would the US finance its deficit without borrowing from China? This is indeed a strange way to avoid a trade war, which is what they claim. For the US to do that, it is the perfect example of, as the expression goes, shooting oneself in the foot.

Johnson (2010) argues that China holds large reserves because it intervenes to buy dollars in order to hold down the value of its currency. The first part of the statement is valid but the second part should read: "in order to preserve the adopted exchange rate regime in accordance with the current international rules". Johnson (who characteristically is fair and balanced, but not on this occasion) is wrong in suggesting that "foreign-exchange market intervention on this scale is a breach of China's international commitments (as a member of the International Monetary Fund) and constitutes a form of unfair trade practice". There is indeed neither a violation of international commitments nor an unfair trade practice. Thompson (2008) argues that if China does not intervene in the foreign exchange market the US will be deprived of the capital inflows that are needed to finance the current account deficit.

However, Johnson (2010) feels that apprehension about the risk of China reducing its purchases of US government securities is overblown. Foreign exchange market intervention leads to the accumulation of foreign assets, which means that China would buy some foreign assets other than US government bonds. Johnson considers four scenarios, none of which is detrimental to the US. If the Chinese buy other dollar-denominated assets issued by American entities, this would push down spreads on those assets relative to Treasuries, which would directly help private American borrowers. If they buy dollar-denominated assets issued by non-American entities, this will still reduce spreads more broadly and help American borrowers. If they buy dollar equities, this would help the stock market, household balance sheets and firms' access to funding (as well as helping to shift the US economy from debt to more equity financing, which would be a desirable move in any case). And if they buy non-dollar assets, given that the Fed will keep interest rates near to zero, this will push down the value of the American dollar and help boost America's economic growth.

Referring to Tim Geithner's repeated talk about currency manipulation, Merk (2009) argues that "talking about manipulation is helpful only if one's intent is to impress a local and insult a foreign audience". He even claims that "the US is doing its share to try to manipulate the dollar, albeit with mixed results". But then there are those who go as far as to argue that Chinese currency manipulation should be subject to the same kinds of criticism that are levelled at its military build-up and human rights abuses (for example, Goldstein, 2006). The fact remains that it is reasonable for the US to print money to keep the dollar weak, but illegal (even criminal) for China to preserve its exchange rate regime by intervening in the foreign exchange market. This view is "fair and balanced" *à la* Fox TV.

REFUSAL TO REVALUE THE YUAN

Those calling on China to float the yuan, or to introduce more flexibility in the exchange rate want a measure like this to be preceded by a big revaluation of the yuan. For example, Williamson (2003) refers to a "first step revaluation" before moving away from a dollar peg, while Roubini (2007) thinks that "China should allow its currency to appreciate significantly and move to a regime of more flexible exchange rates". This accusation has also been expressed as "competitive devaluation" or what Geithner calls "competitive non-appreciation" (*The Economist*, 2010a). Johnson (2010) argues that "it is in the interests of both the United States and global economic prosperity that China allows its currency to appreciate".

To start with, China revalued its currency in July 2005 and has been allowing it to appreciate gradually since then. This behaviour is not consistent with "competitive devaluation" or "competitive non-appreciation". It is more than that; what China bashers want is a big revaluation to be introduced immediately, which does not make much sense. If the exchange rate is allowed to be determined by the market, then the market should put the exchange rate at the "right level", in which case there is no need for a big revaluation.

The argument for a big revaluation is motivated by the belief that the yuan is still undervalued and that this undervaluation is hurting not only the US but also China itself and the world economy at large. Dunaway (2010) blames China for the slow recovery of the world economy since the global financial crisis because the yuan is undervalued against major currencies. Likewise, Bivens and Scott (2006) claim that "Chinese currency policies affect more than just bilateral trade between China and the United States". The yuan–dollar peg, they argue, affects third-party (China/European Union) trade relations as well because depreciation of the dollar against other currencies means depreciation of the yuan against other currencies. They also argue that "there is a cost to developing nations from the Chinese currency peg" and that "by pursuing mercantilist exchange rate policies, China has robbed market share from smaller developing countries and forced many into managing their own exchange rates with the goal of matching China's competitive position". Refusal to revalue the currency, they say, "is one of the primary impediments to resolving global trade imbalances that threaten both individual and the global economies".

Incidentally, accusing China of adopting mercantilist policies does not sound right according to Liu (2005c) who believes that "in a world of fiat currencies not backed by gold, mercantilism cannot exist by definition", hence "any nation that incurs export trade surpluses denominated in a foreign fiat currency is engaged in reverse mercantilism, i.e. shipping real wealth overseas for paper". He goes on to say that

> it is outrageously preposterous for the US, a country of recurring trade deficits denominated in fiat dollars, to accuse its exporting trade-surplus partners of practicing mercantilism when the US trade deficit is essentially an undisguised abuse of unearned privilege of inexhaustible national purchasing power in the form of dollar hegemony.

The argument that China's exchange rate policy is hurting other countries overlooks the fact that the appreciation of the yuan against the dollar since July 2005 has not been translated into appreciation against other currencies because of the weakness of the dollar against other currencies as a result of quantitative easing. This is not to say that appreciation of the yuan against other currencies is a prescription for the cure of anaemic growth in other countries. And even if the yuan is undervalued against other currencies, some countries (most notably Germany) are doing rather well in their trade with China. In the case of Germany, it is simply because the Germans can compete with the Chinese on a non-price basis (for example, the high quality of German cars makes them competitive). Using the same flawed line of reasoning, China could actually blame the US for the slow recovery of other countries by keeping interest rates extremely low and the dollar too weak.

Williamson (2003) presents arguments against the reasons suggested by China for resisting revaluation. He responds to the argument that China's current account surplus has recently diminished by saying that although the surplus has fallen, it is still a surplus rather than the deficit that is appropriate for a country in China's situation. He responds to the argument that a revaluation would threaten Chinese growth by suggesting that growth does not depend solely on demand and that supply limitations are constraining Chinese growth. If a current account deficit implies that a country is living beyond its means, it is not clear how a deficit is appropriate for China.

Goldstein and Lardy (2009) argue that refusal to revalue the yuan will sustain its undervaluation, which causes the following problems: (i) distortion of domestic investment decisions; (ii) undermining of government efforts to transition to more consumption-driven growth; (iii) retention of investment and human resources in the lowest value-added industries, thus impeding the growth and expansion of both services and industries that China seeks to develop; (iv) failure to resist protectionism; (v) attraction of growing criticism of what are deemed to be beggar-thy-neighbour policies; and (vi) the perpetuation of the undervaluation of the currency by large-scale intervention in the foreign exchange market will need to be accompanied by continued sterilization of the resulting increases in the money supply. Notwithstanding the fact that these claims are no more than rhetoric, the underlying assumption is that the yuan is still undervalued. If it is not so, then a big revaluation will make it overvalued, which is what China is worried about.

Goldstein and Lardy (2009) put forward a "three-stage approach" that would "permit China to continue to reduce the undervaluation of the renminbi as well as its very large global current account surplus while keeping a lid on domestic social pressures". The three stages are: (i) abandoning competitive devaluation as a mechanism to deal with reduced external demand; (ii) allowing the yuan to appreciate sufficiently rapidly while reducing intervention in the foreign exchange market; and (iii) reducing intervention even while dropping the daily fluctuation limit, so that the yuan would essentially be floating. They do not, however, explain how this would benefit China (particularly "keeping a lid on social pressures"), so that the Chinese authorities may be enticed to buy the proposal. It is not clear what "abandoning competitive devaluation" means when China has been allowing the yuan to appreciate since July 2005.

China has been reluctant to allow massive currency appreciation (or a big one-off revaluation) because it is wary of the fear of overvalued currency. Japan experienced a long period of stagnation after the 1985 Plaza Accord whereby a substantial appreciation of the yen was engineered. Chinese officials have repeatedly declared that reforms to re-balance the Chinese economy away from its current dependence on exports are well underway and that the yuan is being allowed to appreciate gradually (which no one can question). Chinese Premier Wen Jiabao warned that if China is forced to revalue its currency too fast, there will be social unrest, bankruptcy for export-dependent companies and "disaster for the world" (Beattie et al., 2010). Robert Mundell argues that a rash revaluation might see the yuan appreciate in the short run, but in the long run it will go in the opposite direction. He also warns that currency instability would bring great uncertainty to Sino–US trade (Dukes, 2005).

Apart from the economic arguments against forcing China to revalue its currency and change the exchange rate regime, Thompson (2008) points out that by forcing China to do something like that, the US runs the risk of "solidifying its position as a coercive hegemon". At a time when it is perceived and resented as a bully, Thompson argues that the US cannot afford to "increase resentment by coercing China to pursue an economic agenda that is counter to its own autonomous policy goals".

HIGH SAVING/LOW CONSUMPTION

China is accused of hurting the world economy because the Chinese save too much and consume too little. Ma and Yi (2010) argue that "China's very high savings rate is many things to many people – a source of global imbalances for some economists, a sign of financial repression for others, a potent source of growth and a nest egg to make up for the absence of social security for the mass of the Chinese people". For others a high saving rate is not necessarily good because "it may reflect a lack of social insurance – or it may reflect poor firm governance" (Fernando, 2010). For the sake of the rest of the world, therefore, the Chinese government must force its citizens to spend more and save less. Of course those who call on China to be a more consumption-oriented economy claim that this would be good for the Chinese economy. Instead of tackling the US trade deficit by taking measures to reduce excessive spending and encourage saving in the US, the Chinese are expected to be profligate to eliminate the US deficit. Then the Chinese are actually spending more, but not on American goods, which would not solve the US–China deficit problem. Demand from China for high-quality German manufactured goods (such as luxury cars) was one factor that propelled the German economy in the second half of 2010.

Those who think this way forget the fact that China is still a developing economy that needs a lot of growth. They do not realize that the high saving rate is rooted in Chinese history and culture. For example, Kapoor (2010), who describes Chinese consumers as "notorious savers", attributes Chinese saving habits to the "Confucian values of thrift and frugality". She also identifies, as three key factors, young demographics, big expenses (such as weddings) and medical and post-retirement costs. We know from macroeconomics that growth is propelled by investment (hence the need for saving) and that there is no such thing as consumption-based growth. Thompson (2008) makes this point clear by arguing that "it is investment, and not consumption, that is generally thought to provide the foundation for sustained economic growth". As a developing country, China is not alone in having a high saving rate as this is a phenomenon that is typically observed in emerging countries. *The Economist* (2010b) highlights the importance of saving, stating that "emerging economies, as a group, still save more than they invest, which explains why global imbalances – notably the controversial surplus in China and deficit in America – remain so big". It is noteworthy that Kapoor's description of Chinese consumers as "notorious savers" is an insult to Chinese generosity.

The Chinese justifiably indulge in precautionary saving "due to the need to provide for healthcare, basic education and retirement, given the lack of sufficient public provision of these services" (Cappiello and Ferrucci,

2008). Xiao (2010) argues that "it is no secret that even high- and middle-income Chinese parents need to save for many years or decades to pay for their children's expensive overseas education". In any case, these are domestic issues on which China has the last say in accordance with its national economic interests.

Several studies have been conducted to explain the high saving rate in China. The following explanations have been suggested.

The Lack of a Social Safety Net

Feenstra et al. (1998) argue that the absence of pensions and medical insurance for most of the Chinese population necessitates a higher saving rate to prepare for retirement and health emergencies. Chamon and Prasad (2010) refer to the rising private burden of expenditure on housing, education and health care. Likewise, Pettis (2009) argues that the absence of a social safety net makes it necessary for Chinese households to self-insure, which means that "they save on average much more than they need on average to cover these costs". Roubini (2011) points out that "the Chinese save a lot because their social-security benefits are puny – a paltry $150 per citizen over a lifetime after retirement – and they need savings for old age". Another aspect of the safety net identified by Roubini (2011) is that there is little of a social safety net in China now that the "iron rice bowl" system of cradle-to-grave public services has broken down – meaning that there is a need for a buffer of precautionary savings.

Social Policy and Demographic Factors

Wei and Zhang (2011) suggest that sex selection in China has led to intense competition for brides, consequently saving rates have shot up as families strive to boost the odds of marriage for their sons. The study postulates that the strict 30-plus-year-old one-child-per-family plan is the primary driver of the high saving rate. This factor, coupled with a cultural preference for male offspring, has led to a significant imbalance between the number of male and female children in China, creating incentives for men and parents with sons to boost savings in order to have a competitive edge in the marriage market. Their estimates show that about half of the increase in the saving rate over the last 25 years can be attributed to rising sex ratio imbalance. They also point out that even those not competing in the marriage market must compete to buy housing and make other significant purchases, pushing up the saving rate for all households.

The one-child policy has an impact on the demographics of the Chinese population with implications for the saving rate. Feenstra et al. (1998)

argue that the one-child policy has reduced the number of dependent children, enabling the parents to save more, and that a large proportion of China's labour force is now in the phase of the lifecycle to begin saving seriously in anticipation for retirement. Pettis (2009) refers to the declining dependency ratios, particularly via a decline in the number of young people, which means that a much larger share of the population is of working age today compared to 30 years ago. As China's working population grows faster than its total population, Chinese production has grown faster than Chinese consumption, which implies an increasing saving rate.

Roubini (2011) talks about the demographic consequences of the one-child policy, arguing that they have increased the need for savings for old age. The old social-security model of China – children taking care of old parents – is breaking down because of urbanization and the weight of the burden, with one child often having to take care of two parents and four grandparents. Modigliani and Cao (2004) use the life cycle hypothesis (LCH) to explain what they call the "Chinese saving puzzle". They suggest that the explanation is provided by the LCH, which emphasizes income growth and the demographic structure of the economy while disregarding per capita income. They suggest that the move towards a market economy in the late 1970s boosted growth, while the one-child policy changed the demographics.

Investment-Motivated Saving and Financial Underdevelopment

Feenstra et al. (1998) argue that because the state banks do not channel much of the private savings to private investors, the only way to start a business in China is to accumulate savings, which is a feasible option because the threshold size for the average Chinese enterprise is small. They link this phenomenon to the current account by pointing out that "the failure of the domestic banks to match the available private saving flow with desired private investment creates the twin phenomena of a high private saving rate and a persistent current account surplus". The desire to invest is also emphasized by Woo (2005) who argues that it is an important reason why the rural sector has increased its savings rate. Chamon and Prasad (2010) explain the rise of China's saving rate in terms of financial underdevelopment as reflected in constraints on borrowing against future income and low return on financial assets.

Financial underdevelopment also has implications for the saving rate via the channel of consumption (as opposed to investment). Pettis (2009) argues that "without easy availability of consumer credit, households who want to borrow to purchase big-ticket items have little choice but to save today for a future purchase". Harbaugh (2004) considers two aspects of financial underdevelopment, the first of which is that of undeveloped insurance markets. When incomes are uncertain, consumers are interested in saving to smooth their consumption, not just over predictable variations in income, but over unpredictable variations as well. The second is liquidity constraints. If credit markets are undeveloped, the life cycle pattern of dissaving in youth, saving in middle-age, and dissaving in retirement might not be realized. In particular, younger consumers might not be able to go into debt for education, housing and other expensive items, but rather have to accumulate the necessary funds first. As a result even young people might be substantial savers.

Uncertainty about the Future

A common view is that the rise in the saving rate reflects uncertainty about the future that many state-owned enterprise (SOE) workers feel in the face of widespread privatization of loss-making SOEs. Woo (2005) disputes the validity of this explanation, describing it as "grossly incomplete" because there has also been a rise in the rural saving rate even though rural residents have little to fear about the loss of jobs in the state-owned enterprise sector because none of them are employed there.

He and Cao (2007) argue that the widely adopted view of precautionary saving, which is regarded as the top reason for maintaining a high saving rate in China, is misleading because this conclusion is drawn from the household survey data. Based on flow of funds data, they show that the household saving rate has declined dramatically since the mid-1990s. They attribute the high national saving rate to the increasing shares of both government and corporate disposable income.

Undervalued Currency, Low Interest Rates and Rapid Growth

Pettis (2009) suggests the peculiar explanation that countries with artificially low exchange rates (that is, undervalued currencies) tend to have high saving rates, perhaps because one consequence of an undervalued currency is lower real wages. This proposition requires that the Chinese spend their incomes mostly on imported goods, which is not the case. He also argues that low interest rates create higher saving rates in countries like China, which he explains in terms of portfolio effects and income effects. The explanations that he presents are, however, unconvincing. He suggests that when per capita wealth grows very rapidly, it may take a while for people to change their consumption behaviour, so growth in consumption lags growth in wealth; the difference between the two is the rising saving rate. Roubini (2011) makes a similar point by arguing that the Chinese policy of an undervalued currency and low cost of capital for public firms (and thus low return on household savings) has implied a massive transfer of income from households (that thus cannot spend much) to SOEs (that thus over-invest).

Harbaugh (2004) also talks about rapid growth, referring to subsistence consumption. A simple reason why savings initially increase in rapid growth economies is that poor people are too poor to save. Only when incomes rise above subsistence levels is there any surplus that can be stored for future consumption. Another simple but powerful explanation for the connection between growth and saving is that as incomes rise, consumers have a choice of whether or not to adjust their consumption upwards, and they might be reluctant to do so if they fear the prospects of having to readjust their consumption downwards later on. Yet another explanation for high savings in rapid growth economies arises from the desire of consumers to maintain their consumption levels relative to other consumers. Rising incomes would appear to induce excessive consumption via a "demonstration effect" as consumers attempt to "keep up with the Joneses".

The Role of State-Owned Enterprises

Roubini (2011) makes the interesting observation that while "the average citizen in China doesn't save more than one in Hong Kong, Singapore, or East Asia", the big difference is that "a whopping 25 percent of savings in China is in the form of the retained earnings of the corporate sector, mostly state-owned enterprises (SOEs)". These enterprises do not distribute dividends but rather accumulate retained earnings that are channelled into more investment in productive capacity. Hence Roubini (2011) recommends the privatization of the SOEs or massively taxing their profits and transferring that income to households, otherwise "savings will remain too high, consumption too low, and investment excessive". Of course we all know that privatization has been the means whereby good quality public assets are sold to wealthy individuals and multinational corporations. If the Russian experience is anything to go by, the Chinese should justifiably say "thanks, but no thanks". Roubini would be wiser to propose the taxing of US financial institutions and use the proceeds to look after the 50 million or so Americans who live below the poverty line.

Policy Implications

Harbaugh (2004) discusses the implications of a high saving rate for the Chinese economy, arguing that "China's high saving rate is widely recognized as one of the determining factors in China's successful transition from a planned, low-income economy to a market-based, middle-income economy". First, the availability of savings has played an early role in China's successful transition by allowing the country to maintain rapid investment growth throughout the reform period. It is for this reason that "China was able to avoid the collapse in investment witnessed by Eastern Europe and Russia". Second, because rapid growth generates high savings, China has been able to enjoy a virtuous cycle of high savings leading to high growth, and vice versa. Third, the high saving rate has allowed China to reduce the need for international debt and to accumulate large foreign exchange reserves, thereby reducing the risk of financial crises. Furthermore, China's high saving rate has helped domestic financial stability. Despite the high rates of non-performing loans, banks have been able to avoid a crisis in part because of the increasing inflows of new savings. Harbaugh (2004) argues that "while it can be argued that high saving rates have encouraged tolerance of bad banking practices, reforming a socialist banking system cannot be done rapidly and high savings rates have given China the opportunity to gradually reduce the non-performing loan problem".

Zhu and Kotz (2010) put forward some suggestions to enable the Chinese government to reduce saving and boost consumption. They argue for: (i) reducing income inequality; (ii) nationalizing or re-nationalizing private and foreign firms; and (iii) enforcing stricter regulation in labour markets. They also suggest that reducing the saving rate and boosting consumption require an improvement in the welfare system, the decommercialization of health and education and the provision of housing on a much less profit-oriented basis. While these arguments make a lot of sense, it is unlikely that free marketeers (and most China bashers are free marketeers) will find these proposals appealing. They simply believe in income inequality as natural, reject nationalization and regulation, and view profit maximization as the means whereby markets allocate resources efficiently.

EXPORT-LED GROWTH

China is blamed for hurting the world by depending on exports, which is rather strange. Exports represent one side of a transaction that can be completed only if another country is willing to import (it takes two to tango). Take, for example, the argument put forward by Roubini (2011) who suggests that

> the traditional Chinese model of economic growth required the US and a few other countries to be consumers of first and last resort, spending more than their income and running ever-larger trade deficits – so that China could be the producer of first and last resort, spending less than its income and building ever-larger trade surpluses.

Roubini, therefore, is blaming China for the fact that the Americans spend too much and have been living beyond their means. He further argues that China's growth model is "now challenged, if not altogether broken, because the excessive accumulation of private and public debt and deficit by the US has forced a painful deleveraging: the over-indebted US consumer needs to spend and consume less, import less, and save more to reduce debt". Well, if the Americans decide to consume less and save more that is good for them, but it is nothing to do with China. Roubini advises China to "radically change its broken growth model in the direction of reduced exports, investment and savings, and increased consumption". In other words, Roubini advises the Chinese to follow the American example and live beyond their means, borrow and over-indulge in consumption.

The same argument is put forward by Goldstein and Lardy (2009) who suggest that China should reduce excessive reliance on investment and external demand to sustain economic growth and rely instead on services and domestic demand. It is not clear what "reliance on services" means. Does it mean that China should again follow the American example, abandoning manufacturing industry and shifting to services? They cannot be serious. It is rather ludicrous to claim that the Chinese model of growing by exporting is broken while the American model of leveraged over-indulgence is the way forward. Where will we (citizens of the world) be if China abandons manufacturing industry?

Spruk (2010b) argues that China's export-led growth model has tremendously affected the macroeconomic performance of developing nations. He makes the same recommendation: "without shifting the major engine of growth from export-boosting exchange rate undervaluation to consumption-based growth, Chinese economy will no longer be able to sustain high productivity growth rates". This argument and similar ones do not only involve flawed economic reasoning, they also ignore history – thus they are hypocritical. Britain and America have not grown and developed to what they are now by depending on the consumption of services (recall the discussion in Chapter 3). Japan and Korea have become what they are now by depending on export-led growth. Harbaugh (2004) argues that the promotion of exports has allowed China to move rapidly into new industries that might not otherwise have developed.

Vistesen (2010) does not see anything wrong with export-propelled growth; rather, he thinks it is the way forward for the US. His argument is as follows: "we are all rapidly ageing and soon will hit the threshold where we effectively become dependent on external demand in order to achieve economic growth, pay pensions, build roads etc.". In addition to the demographics, Vistesen argues, "the US economy has over-spent and over-borrowed to the extent that the amount of private sector and public sector leverage implies that [the two sectors] are simply tapped out". Hence, he argues, "we cannot rely on the US consumer anymore" and that "the US economy now needs to export more than she imports in order to turn the boat around".

One reason why it is felt that Chinese growth policy is harmful is that it requires currency manipulation. China, therefore, has been growing fast only because it has an artificially weak currency that makes Chinese exports cheap, hence the export-led growth. This is nothing short of travesty. Xin and Liu (2011) list a large number of factors that have buoyed Chinese economic growth, including the following: reduction in trade barriers, low wages and available supplies of unskilled labour, low cost of communication and transport, flows of foreign direct investment, the large-scale potential of the Chinese domestic market, the opening up to world markets, better policies, and cultural factors.

No one disputes the proposition that China cannot sustain double digit growth for ever, particularly by depending on exports. And no one would argue against the proposition put forward by Zhu and Kotz (2010) that "China's growth trajectory poses a number of serious problems including environmental destruction, rising inequality, a high degree of exploitation of the migrant labour force, and weak oversight of product safety" and that put forward by Scott (2008) that "China engages in extensive suppression of labor rights". But change will come naturally and gradually, and change will come from abroad as much as it comes from within China; remember the decision to import less from China (hence reduce Chinese exports) belongs to foreign consumers, not to the Chinese government. Zhu and Kotz (2010) argue that "China's rapid growth was initially based on its domestic market, specifically rising consumption by households and government".

VIOLATION OF WTO RULES

It has been suggested that China's exchange rate policy is as much a violation of the WTO rules as the Chinese violation of intellectual property rights (for example, Palley, 2005). The underlying reasoning is that an undervalued currency works as an import tax and export subsidy. Ahn

(2010) argues that for China to be violating the WTO rules as enshrined in the Agreement on Subsidies and Countervailing Duties (SCM Agreement), several conditions must be met (in practice they are not met). Staiger and Sykes (2009) dispute the idea of equivalence between the alleged currency undervaluation and import tax/export subsidy because "currency devaluation does not alter export volumes, and in the short run, its effects depend on firms' invoicing decisions". Hence they advise policy makers to take care before turning to trade sanctions as a remedy. However, politicians seem to love the idea of equivalence to which they attribute the loss of US manufacturing jobs. As a result, various proposals for action against China have been put forward in the US Congress over the past few years.

Politicians have been insisting that the Treasury Department should refer the matter to the IMF and require the US trade representative to bring a formal complaint to the WTO so that China's alleged currency undervaluation is treated as a source of dumping or countervailable subsidies that would permit the imposition of anti-dumping or countervailing duties on Chinese imports. The problem, of course, is that of translating the magnitude of exchange rate misalignment into equivalent import tariffs and export subsidies that could then be evaluated under the rules of the WTO. Matto and Subramanian (2008) suggest that the WTO should be enforced to "discipline cases of significant undervaluation that are clearly attributable to government action", rationalizing this suggestion in terms of the trade consequences of undervaluation (the import tariff and export subsidy argument). Likewise, Bergsten (2007) suggests that the US should file a WTO case against China's currency intervention as an exchange rate subsidy and/or as a violation of the WTO rules. Well, does this mean that the US should be disciplined by hurting Australian retailers as a result of deliberate action to keep the dollar weak through quantitative easing?

Staiger and Sykes (2009) offer three reasons for caution with respect to this issue: (i) exchange rate adjustment does not necessarily imply real trade effects; (ii) the claim that undervaluation is equivalent to a tariff or subsidy is not by itself sufficient to establish a case for WTO- or WTO-consistent action; and (iii) estimates of exchange rate misalignment are not reliable for the quantification of WTO-relevant effects. They argue that "one simply cannot make a leap from equilibrium exchange rate models, which may suggest that China's currency is undervalued by some percentage, to the proposition that China's policies are the real economic equivalent of an illegal import tariff increase and an illegal export subsidy in that same percentage".

It is not claimed here that China does not violate WTO rules – it does as almost every other member of the WTO. Between 2001 (when China joined the WTO) and 2005, China was a party to two of the 93 trade disputes that were taken to the WTO. In the period 2005–10 China was involved in 26 out of the 84 cases filed with the WTO (*The Economist*, 20011i). In 2009 China was accused of restricting the exports of certain industrial raw materials, which China defended on the grounds of its desire to conserve the limited supplies and to protect the environment from the pollution resulting from their extraction. China may be in violation of the WTO rules in this case, but so were all of the countries that banned some food exports in 2008 when food prices soared. This, of course, is totally different from accusing China of violating WTO rules because its currency is allegedly undervalued.

The possibility that China may be violating WTO rules in other ways, such as intellectual property rights, is a different matter that we are not concerned with here. While it may be legitimate to complain about Chinese pirating of DVDs and CDs, about restrictions on the sale of foreign films and music in China, and about Chinese environmental standards, suggesting that the alleged undervaluation of the yuan is a deliberate policy that is tantamount to subsidies is way off the mark. If anything, threats of tariff imposition by the US against China is a clear violation of WTO rules. McKinnon (2007) refers to the March 2005 bill designed to impose tariffs, arguing that signing that bill into a law "would have been an egregious violation of America's WTO commitments".

CHINA AS A (OR THE) CAUSE OF THE GLOBAL FINANCIAL CRISIS

In January 2011 the Financial Crisis Inquiry Commission (2011) submitted its report on the causes of the global financial crisis. The report listed ten reasons for the crisis, the most important three being: (i) the availability of easy credit made possible by the surpluses of developing countries (meaning China); (ii) the US housing bubble; and (iii) the increasing occurrence of subprime mortgages in the US. Commenting on the report, Hitt (2011) reaches the sarcastic conclusion: "yes, folks, it's all China's fault", by arguing that cause (i) is a necessary condition for causes (ii) and (iii), which leaves cause (i) as the "uber-origin of the current global economic crisis".

Suominen (2011) surveys the views on the role of global imbalances in the global financial crisis, which she divides into three categories. First, there are those who regard the imbalances as a "sideshow", even as an "innocent bystander", blaming financial regulation and supervision and moral hazard (DeLong, 2008; Dooley and Garber, 2009; Backus and Cooley, 2010; Whelan, 2010; Truman, 2010; Greenspan, 2010a). Taylor

(2008) posits the crisis originated in the Federal Reserve's loose monetary policy. Bibow (2008) points to the post-9/11 expansionary monetary and fiscal policies as the trigger for the global boom. The second category are those who believe that imbalances were the "leading cause of the crisis" because they resulted in a low cost of financing (for example, Portes, 2009). Most analysts, who comprise the third category, view the imbalances as "a more or less central contributor to the crisis". The reasoning is as follows: imbalances relaxed credit constraints and perpetuated low US real interest rates that, in turn, caused borrowing and the housing bubble (Sester, 2008; Paulson, 2008; Wolf, 2008; Bini-Smaghi, 2008; Bernanke, 2008; Caballero et al., 2008; Dunaway, 2009; Obstfeld and Rogoff, 2009; IMF, 2009; Caballero and Krishnamurthy, 2009; Blanchard and Milesi-Ferretti, 2009; Roubini, 2009; Kohn, 2010).

There is some question hovering over where to put Bergsten (2010b) who insists that "the higher imbalances themselves could sow the seeds of a new financial crisis just as they helped sow the seeds of the last crisis" because "such huge inflows of foreign [Chinese] capital would keep US financial markets excessively liquid, hold interest rates down, promote underpricing of risk, and thus again generate irresponsible lending and borrowing". So, the Chinese are accused of making the Americans irresponsible borrowers and American banks irresponsible lenders. Is not this the ultimate scapegoating?

If it were not for China, it seems, the global financial crisis would not have happened because China is responsible for the greed and incompetence of the Wall Street wizards, the deregulation of the US financial system, and the great inventions of financial engineers with the blessing of Nobel Prize winning Chicago economists. After all, it is China that relaxed credit constraints and ran US monetary policy in the run-up to the global financial crisis. Johnson and Kwak (2009) put it sarcastically as follows:

> According to this story, the global financial crisis was caused by hardworking Chinese factory workers who committed the sin of over-saving, which created a glut of money that needed to be invested . . . This beast from the East, seeking higher yields than it could find in Treasury bonds, flooded into the housing market, pushing down interest rates and pushing up housing prices, and creating a bubble that finally collapsed, with the results we all know.

Johnson and Kwak (2009) argue that "the time is here for our nation to actually do something about the recent financial crisis – that is, do something to prevent it from happening again", but instead "many people are finding it easier to pass the buck than to, say, regulate the financial sector effectively".

CHINA AS THE CAUSE FOR HIGHER OIL PRICES

Typically, China is accused of being responsible for high and rising oil prices because of insatiable appetite for oil as its economy grows in double digits. There is nothing illegal or immoral about this. It has been recognized that oil prices behave like financial prices because they are determined primarily in the futures market by traders who are not interested in the physical commodity. Thus the high volatility of oil prices cannot be explained in terms of the smooth growth of the Chinese economy but rather in terms of the portfolio behaviour of those trading crude oil futures contracts. Incredibly, even this channel of causation is taken to implicate China in a conspiracy to raise oil prices and hurt the world economy, as if China itself is not part of the world economy and as if it is to the benefit of China to pay more for its oil imports. It would take a big suspension of disbelief to swallow the underlying reasoning whereby China is accused of quantitative easing.

Schaefer (2009) quotes Philip Treick, Managing Partner of Thermopolis Partners, as saying that "a large part of the reason oil and copper have been strong is because [*sic*] the Chinese have re-pegged their currency, the Yuan, to the dollar, since July 2008", referring to the temporary suspension of the gradual appreciation of the yuan since July 2005. Schaefer explains the process as follows:

> In order to maintain that peg – which means forcing the Yuan down – the Chinese must print Yuan out of thin air to buy US dollars. This increases their money supply. To offset that, they then need to sell Yuan via debt – create an obligation that is an offset to that new increase in money supply . . . This has had the effect of flooding the Chinese banking system with capital, which has gone into new lending by banks, the stock market . . . and hard assets like oil, driving up growth and prices in an otherwise contracting global economy.

This argument is littered with flaws. To start with, maintaining the peg does not require forcing the yuan down – China has not forced the yuan down since July 2005. Second, China does not need to print yuan to buy the dollar because dollar flows come from exports (Chinese firms use the dollar predominantly as the currency of invoicing exports). Third, those speculating on oil prices are not interested in the "hard asset", which presumably means the physical commodity. While oil prices are determined predominantly in the futures markets, there is no evidence whatsoever to indicate that the major players in the oil futures markets are Chinese or speculators financed by Chinese capital.

What is really naive about Schaefer's analysis is that it attributes the rise and fall of oil prices during the period 2007–9 to the change in Chinese

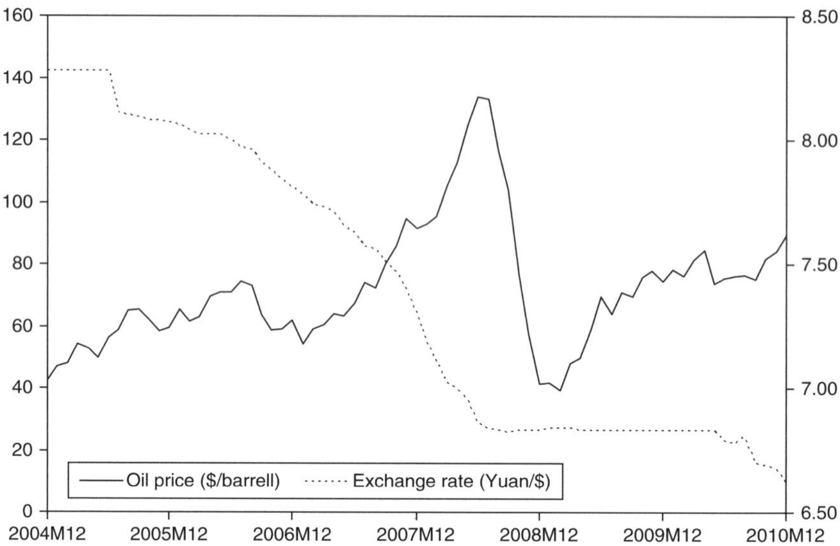

Figure 8.5 The yuan/dollar exchange rate and oil prices ($/barrel)

exchange rate policy. Specifically, Schaefer points out that when the Chinese do not allow the yuan to appreciate, oil prices rise, and when they allow it to appreciate, oil prices fall or at least they do not rise. To verify his view, he uses a chart showing oil prices and the yuan/dollar exchange rate, not realizing that the chart tells exactly the opposite story. Figure 8.5 is an updated version of his chart, showing the yuan/dollar exchange rate and the price of the WTI oil over the period December 2004 to December 2010. Between June 2005 and September 2008, the Chinese allowed the yuan to appreciate, but at the same time the price of oil rose by over 84 per cent. Between September 2008 and May 2010 the exchange rate was fixed, so oil prices should have risen according to Schaefer's analysis – instead the price of oil declined by 29 per cent. Then, between May 2010 and December 2010, the Chinese authorities resumed the policy of allowing a gradual appreciation of the yuan. Contrary to what Schaefer predicted, the price of oil rose 20 per cent.

Schaefer's "theory" is dead wrong, voodoo economics at best. There is simply no connection between the yuan/dollar exchange rate and the price of oil. The rise and fall of oil prices before and during the global financial crisis was caused by the building up of long positions on futures contracts followed by massive unwinding of these positions because of increased risk aversion and the need for liquidity when the crisis struck. The most recent rise in oil prices came in response to the resumption of the building of long positions on oil futures and to a lesser extent the fragile economic recovery. The movement of the exchange rate is determined by the Chinese authorities and has nothing to do with oil prices.

CHINA IS BUYING UP THE CORPORATE WORLD

In 2010 Chinese state-owned firms accounted for 10 per cent of cross-border deals by value as they bid for a wide variety of firms in all corners of the world. This trend has given rise to opposition from those who believe that capitalists should not allow communists to buy their companies (*The Economist*, 2010g). Australia and Canada are creating hurdles for Chinese firms, particularly when a deal involves the resources sector, although these two countries have traditionally been open markets for takeovers. The Americans feel that Chinese aggressive buying of companies in the high-tech sector may even threaten American national security.

While the general feeling is that the Chinese are buying foreign companies so that the Communists can control the world, the fact of the matter is that going global is motivated by the usual factors: the desire to acquire raw materials and technical know-how and to gain access to foreign markets. This is exactly what the theory of foreign direct investment tells us, and China is no different. *The Economist* (2010g) suggests many reasons why this concern is over-blown and unjustifiable. To start with, Chinese firms are not capable of posing any threat because they are only starting to feel their way in other countries. As far as natural resources are concerned, China is not controlling supply to the extent that it can manipulate markets. Even if Chinese companies run the foreign firms they buy for politics, not profit, this would not matter "so long as other firms could satisfy consumers' needs". The fear of cheap Chinese capital is thought to be exaggerated because "America and Europe could use the money" and "the danger that cheap Chinese capital might undermine rivals can be better dealt with by beefing up competition law than by keeping investment out". *The Economist* (2010g) believes that Chinese foreign direct investment could bring several benefits to the rest of the world, including: (i) injecting new energy and capital into flagging companies; (ii) hiring local managers and investing in local research; and (iii) aligning Chinese interests with those of the rest of the world. The fear of corporate China is therefore unfounded.

Take the following example, reported by *The Economist* (2010h). A small town in Queensland, Australia, has a population of 400 but it is expected that this town will be transformed significantly, thanks mainly to an A$7.5 billion investment by the Metallurgical Corporation of China, a state-owned firm. The investment is aimed at building Australia's biggest coal mine and a 490 km railway to carry the coal to the coast on its way to China. It is thanks to China that Australia hardly felt the effect of the global financial crisis and the Great Recession. This is because the Chinese economy can grow even when the US economy slides into recession.

It is interesting to examine two responses to the piece in which *The Economist* (2010g) defended Chinese buying of the corporate world. In a letter to the editor published in the issue of 27 November, Peter Navarro of the University of California-Irvine, wrote: "China will buy foreign companies around the world for two purposes: strip them of their technology and acquire their marketing and distribution channels, for the broader goal of improving the competitive advantage of their national champions" (it is unclear what he meant by "national champions"). On the other hand, another letter justified what China is doing on the grounds that all other big powers have done the same, arguing that "nation states use the tools at their disposal to protect and advance their interest; China is no exception". As examples the author of that letter mentions Britain and other European countries that extracted value from North America, China and India, and the US that extracted value from the Philippines and a score of other countries without going through the formalities of colonial control.

CHINA AS A THREAT TO AMERICAN SECURITY

China is seen as a threat to American security in that it is a "nasty authoritarian regime with a rapidly modernizing army far larger than its defensive needs require". *The Economist* (2005) quotes a Pentagon review declaring that while China does not face a direct threat from another nation, it continues to invest heavily in its military and that China's military modernization could pose a credible threat to the region (look who's talking!). A flurry of books and articles with provocative titles such as *China: The Gathering Threat* and *How we would Fight China* can only add fuel to the fire. *The Economist* (2005) correctly argues that "as China sees it, America's current Sinophobia is beginning to rival its preoccupation with terrorism".

It is absolutely valid to suggest that China today is different from the Soviet Union and the nineteenth-century European powers. China is not seeking to export its ideology, neither does it have ambitions to acquire colonies. According to *The Economist* (2010i) "superpowers can coexist peacefully when the rising superpower believes that it can rise unhindered and the incumbent power believes that the way it runs the world is not fundamentally threatened". In June 2003, the Bush administration decided that China's expanding role on the world stage required more consideration. A decision was taken to hold an annual forum to discuss issues surrounding China, inviting the UK, Canada, New Zealand, Japan and Australia to participate – Australia wisely declined the invitation for fear of losing a lot by alienating China. Liu (2005a) argues that

> it is pathetic that US Secretary of Defense Donald H. Rumsfeld tries to persuade the world that China's military budget, which is less than one tenth of that of the US, is a threat to Asia, even when he is forced to acknowledge that Chinese military modernization is mostly focused on defending its coastal territories, not on force projection for distant conflicts, as is US military doctrine.

There is nothing in China's modern history to indicate its willingness to bomb another country back to the stone age as a pre-emptive strike – this cannot be said about the US.

The threat to American security is also linked to the Chinese buying of the corporate world. In June 2005, China tried to buy Unocal, an American oil firm. According to *The Economist* (2005), "security hawks were horrified that such a strategic asset might fall into potentially hostile hands". When the House of Representatives voted 398 to 15 to urge a presidential review of the bid, China decided to withdraw. It remains to say that Unocal accounts for no more than 1 per cent of America's oil consumption.

CHINA, THE GREAT MODERATION AND THE WORLD ECONOMY

It is arguable that we should be grateful to China for being the manufacturing power house of the world, particularly in low-tech consumer goods. China has indeed contributed to the so-called "great moderation" before the financial engineers of Wall Street made it a thing of the past.

The great moderation was a period of an unusually high degree of macroeconomic stability, with steady growth and low and stable inflation in most of the advanced economies. Bean (2009) provides three explanations for the great moderation. Explanation 2 is that changes in the structure of the economy could have meant that similar sized shocks had smaller macroeconomic effects. Explanation 3 is that better macroeconomic policies, including improved policy frameworks, had moved economies closer to the "eponymous Taylor frontier", which traces out the lowest achievable inflation volatility for a given volatility of the output gap. However, explanation 1 is about the role of China. This is what Bean said:

> First, it could just have been a happy accident, if this was a period characterised by unusually small, or a benign sequence of, shocks. In particular, access to a cheap source of manufactured goods as a result of the rapid development of China and other emerging market economies created a terms of trade gain for the advanced countries and a beneficial "tailwind", which only mutated into a "headwind" towards the end of the period as rapid global growth put upward pressure on oil and other commodity prices.

Likewise, Blanchard et al. (2010) argue that "improvements in inventory management and good luck in the form of rapid productivity growth and the trade integration of China and India likely played some role". Referring to the great moderation, *The Economist* (2009b) argues that "the addition of these two great nations [India and China] to the international financial system was a supply shock that put downward pressure on inflation rates".

Those who blame China for the problems facing the world economy and accuse the Chinese of economic wrong-doing should instead be grateful for the contribution to the great moderation, often claimed to be a product of global capitalism. China did not do this by following the Washington Consensus blindly. Rodrik (2004) argues that "China reformed its incentives in a two-track manner by grafting a market system on top of a central planning system, rather than abandoning the latter altogether".

China is important for the world economy not only as a producer of manufactured goods but also as a consumer. *The Economist* (2010h) makes this clear by arguing that "it is hard to exaggerate the Chinese economy's far-reaching impact on the world, from small towns to big markets". The numbers tell us that in 2009 China accounted for 46 per cent of the world's consumption of coal, and the same goes for zinc and aluminium. During the same time China consumed more steel than the EU, the US and Japan put together. But it is not only about the consumption of raw materials. China buys more cars than the US and more mobile phones than the rest of the world. In the first quarter of 2010, Audi sold more cars in China than in Germany. China is the biggest export market for a number of countries including Brazil, South Africa, Japan and Australia. The fact that the US has nothing much to sell to China is not China's problem, it is America's problem. Cappiello and Ferrucci (2008) argue that "following years of rapid expansion, China has become one of the world's largest economies, a key global exporter and an important trading partner for many developed and developing economies."

A CONCLUDING REMARK

Policy change in China will come, but only gradually. It is up to the Chinese to determine when to introduce changes to domestic economic policy. Frankel and Wei (2007) correctly argue that "everything we know about Chinese government officials, from their history of economic reforms to their own words, points to policy change that is gradual". Even the much wished-for appreciation of the yuan will materialize, if not by changes in the nominal exchange rate, then through inflation. It remains to say that the best way to make China a foe is to treat it as one.

9. The US trade deficit as an American problem: leveraged over-indulgence

INTRODUCTION

Historians attribute the collapse of the Roman Empire, which once seemed invincible, to three factors: (i) overstretched and overconfident military; (ii) moral deterioration; and (iii) fiscal profligacy. These factors are symptomatic of contemporary America. The US military is overstretched, fighting unnecessary wars here and there, some of which have nothing to do with the "war on terror" and a lot to do with the "war of terror". The fact that the US military is overconfident is symbolized by Donald Rumsfeld's belief, in his heyday, that the invasion of Iraq would be a "walk in the park" and by George W. Bush's infamous statement of "mission accomplished", not to mention the US's catastrophic adventure in Vietnam. Moral deterioration is exemplified by the transfer of money from the average taxpayer to wealthy bankers under the pretext of "too big to fail", Donald Trump's call for free oil from Iraq and the control of the mineral resources of Afghanistan to compensate America for the "liberation" of these two countries, the authorization of torture and kidnapping by George Bush II, the glorification of war, the justification of profiteering by all necessary means, the rationalization as "natural" of extreme income and wealth inequality, contempt towards the rest of the world (symbolized by the do-as-I-say attitude), and the attitude of blaming others for its own problems.

Fiscal profligacy, which is related to the first two factors, means extravagant and wasteful spending – living beyond one's means and sustaining this kind of lifestyle by borrowing from others. Peter Morici, University of Maryland professor and former chief economist in the US International Trade Commission, is quoted as saying explicitly that "the trade deficit indicates Americans live beyond their means" and that "they're not producing the goods they wish to use" (*Business Today*, 2011). Excessive spending and low saving by both the private and pubic sectors necessarily imply a trade deficit – it does not need an economist to figure that out. The potential bankruptcy of the US is acknowledged by the most right-wing commentators of Fox TV.

The proposition that the US trade deficit is an American problem is easy to rationalize. If I spend more that I earn and finance my spending by borrowing, I will have negative saving and a trade deficit, a self-inflicted problem of mine. Likewise the US trade deficit is an American problem that only America can deal with. Johnson and Kwak (2009) make this point in a sarcastic manner by arguing that "it takes two to tango" and that "no one put a gun to the American consumer's head and forced them to buy a new flat-screen TV or to do so by taking out more debt". The Congressional Budget Office identifies "three major changes in the US trade deficit since 1970" (CBO, 2000). These changes can be traced to three primary sources: "a long decline in saving as a share of gross domestic product (GDP) that began in the mid-1950s and accelerated in the 1980s, fluctuations in the business cycle, and relatively attractive investment opportunities in the United States in the 1990s". The CBO attributes the trade balance not to international trade but to "factors affecting international capital flows", which are "largely of domestic origin – a long decline in saving, a prolonged upswing in the business cycle, and perhaps a number of changes in the US economy that have made it a particularly productive place for international investors to put their funds". As a result the US has become a "habitual borrower", a term that is used by Liu (2005b) to describe "a trading partner that runs a recurring trade deficit".

In this chapter and the following one we examine issues pertaining to how excessive spending, low saving and massive debt have created an unsustainable trade deficit. The three factors that led to the collapse of the Roman Empire provide a better explanation for the US trade deficit than the exchange rate.

IS THE TRADE DEFICIT A PROBLEM?

The views differ on whether or not the trade deficit is indeed a problem that we need to be concerned about. Some economists believe that a trade deficit is a drag on economic growth but the justification of this view on the basis of the national income identity is not that convincing (for example, Griswold, 2007). The reasoning goes as follows: since net exports constitute a component of GDP, a trade deficit would reduce GDP as growing imports displace domestic production. This view is rather naive because it ignores the effect of changes in net exports on the domestic components of GDP. For example, the trade deficit could be caused by massive imports of capital goods without which economic growth would be hampered. This is why some economists believe that the trade deficit is not a problem, expressing the view that it is a phenomenon that reflects variation in economic growth. In this sense a trade deficit is good news because it indicates economic expansion: a country that grows faster than its trading partners will have a trade deficit. In a comment on the news that the US trade deficit has reached a new record, Joseph La Vorgna, chief United States economist for Deutsche Bank, is quoted as saying that "the deficit showed an enormous widening, but the numbers actually imply a very healthy economy" (*Business Today*, 2011). Paul O'Neil, George W. Bush's first Treasury secretary, thinks that "it is silly to worry about external imbalances in a global economy where capital flows freely" and that "a current-account deficit was merely the accounting consequence of these capital inflows". (*The Economist*, 2003).

The "deficit is good" argument is supported by Poole (2005) who sees the trade deficit as a virtue of economic strength, which is to be celebrated rather than feared. The trade deficit is good because the corresponding capital account surplus means that the US is a good place to invest. There are, however, two problems with this argument: (i) the US economy is driven by consumption rather than investment; and (ii) capital inflows take the form of purchases of Treasury securities rather than foreign direct investment. Thompson (2008) interprets the nature of capital inflows to imply that "the deficits represent a problem and liability rather than any kind of virtue".

The Anti-Mercantilist and Free Market Arguments

The classical view that the trade deficit is not a problem is based on anti-mercantilist and pro-free market arguments. Motivated by his objection to mercantilism and the objective of achieving a trade surplus, Adam Smith (1776) thought that a trade deficit was not that harmful:

> In the foregoing part of this chapter I have endeavoured to show, even upon the principles of the commercial system, how unnecessary it is to lay extraordinary restraints upon the importation of goods from those countries with which the balance of trade is supposed to be disadvantageous. Nothing, however, can be more absurd than this whole doctrine of the balance of trade, upon which, not only these restraints, but almost all the other regulations of commerce are founded. When two places trade with one another, this [absurd] doctrine supposes that, if the balance be even, neither of them either loses or gains; but if it leans in any degree to one side, that one of them loses and the other gains in proportion to its declension from the exact equilibrium.

Likewise, Milton Friedman contended that some of the concerns of trade deficits are "unfair criticisms in an attempt to push macroeconomic policies favorable to exporting industries" (Friedman and Friedman,

1980). Being the free-marketeer that he was, Friedman believed that a trade deficit was not a problem because it would eventually be corrected by market forces, particularly under a system of flexible exchange rates. He argued that trade deficits were not necessarily important as high exports raise the value of the currency, reducing exports, and vice versa for imports, thus naturally removing trade deficits. This is why Friedman (1953) advocated flexible exchange rates when the world was on fixed exchange rates under the Bretton Woods system. With the benefit of hindsight we know now that the smooth trade balance adjustment mechanism that was envisaged under flexible exchange rates has not materialized. Friedman's line of reasoning is actually confused and unrealistic, as it requires bidirectional causality between the trade balance and the exchange rate. We have already seen that the relation between the two variables is rather obscure and that many factors hinder the transmission of the effect of changes in the exchange rate to the trade balance.

Friedman also justified his view that the trade deficit did not matter by using David Hume's argument against mercantilism. Hume (1742) suggested that England could not gain from exports permanently because hoarding the gold generated from exports would make it more plentiful in England, raising the prices of English goods relative to those of goods from other countries and balancing out trade balances. Friedman's argument was that a piece of currency comes back to the country of origin through multilateral trade, hence the "worst case scenario" of the currency never returning to the country of origin was the best possible outcome in the sense that the country concerned purchased real goods by exchanging them for pieces of cheaply-made currency notes. As Friedman put it, "this would be the same result as if the exporting country burned the dollars it earned, never returning it to market circulation". It is amazing that an economist of the calibre of Milton Friedman did not realize that those "pieces of cheaply-made currency notes" represent a claim on the issuing country's real assets and resources.

Stockman (2010) is very critical of Friedman's notion of "just let the free market set currency exchange rates" and the proposition that "the trade deficits will self-correct". This was, according to Stockman, the advice that persuaded President Nixon in 1971 to "unleash on the world paper dollars no longer redeemable in gold or other fixed monetary reserves". Thus he calls this advice "Friedman's $8 trillion error", referring to the cumulative current account deficit realized by the US since the collapse of the Bretton Woods system in 1971.

The nineteenth-century economist and philosopher Frederic Bastiat expressed the idea that trade deficits were actually a manifestation of profit, rather than a loss. Bastiat (1848) argued that the national trade deficit was an indicator of a successful economy, rather than a failing one. He believed that a successful, growing economy would generate greater trade deficits, and an unsuccessful, shrinking economy would produce lower trade surpluses. This is the same idea expressed by Milton Friedman, motivated mainly by ideology and the proposition that free markets always achieve the best outcome, even if it is a trade deficit.

The View of Warren Buffett

The free-market justification for the acceptance of a trade deficit as "good" or "natural" is not shared by everyone. For example, the successful American businessman and investor, Warren Buffett, believes that "the US trade deficit is a bigger threat to the domestic economy than either the federal budget deficit or consumer debt and could lead to political turmoil" (Buffett, 2006). On another occasion, Buffett (2003a) warned that "America's growing trade deficit is selling the nation out from under us"; that "our trade deficit has greatly worsened, to the point that our country's net worth, so to speak, is now being transferred abroad at an alarming rate"; and that "perpetuating this transfer will lead to major trouble". He further wrote:

> In effect, our country has been behaving like an extraordinarily rich family that possesses an immense farm. In order to consume 4% more than we produce – that's the trade deficit – we have day by day, been both selling pieces of the farm and increasing the mortgage on what we still own . . . We were taught in Economics 101 that countries could not for long sustain large ever-growing trade deficits. At point, so it was claimed, the spree of the consumption-happy nation would be braked by currency-rate adjustment and by unwillingness of creditor countries to accept an endless flow of IOUs from the big spenders. And that's the way it has indeed worked for the rest of the world, as we can see by the abrupt shutoffs of credit that many profligate nations have suffered in recent decades.

Buffett, therefore, puts a very strong view against the proposition that the trade deficit is irrelevant, let alone good. He also suggests that the deficit is indeed an American problem resulting from profligacy.

Three Views from Greg Mankiw

Mankiw (2006b) suggests three views of the trade deficit: an extreme view of "no worries", another extreme view of an impending crisis, and a view somewhere in between. The first of the two extreme views is that the trade deficit is no big deal, which he believes to be similar to the view expressed by Bernanke (2005) who attributes the US trade deficit to the "global saving glut". Bernanke argues that with so much saving in the rest of the world, "it is natural that foreigners would want to invest some of that saving in the United States rather than on their own shores", thus the widening trade gap presents no real problems so long as investment funds keep flowing into the US economy. It seems, however, that this view confuses the cause with the result, postulating that the US must run a trade deficit because it has a capital account surplus, hence the capital account surplus causes the trade deficit. There are two problems with this view: the first is that it blames the US trade deficit on Asians saving too much, whereas the second is that it overlooks the very fact that the deficit is a problem for the very reason that it is financed by borrowing from abroad.

The second of the extreme views is adopted by Krugman (2005) who argues that the trade deficit and the accompanying capital inflows are a problem because they are a "financial crisis waiting to happen". Krugman also argues that "we can run huge deficits for the time being, because foreigners – in particular, foreign governments – are willing to lend us huge sums", adding that "one of these days the easy credit will come to an end, and the United States will have to start paying its way in the world economy". Bergsten (2009) recognizes the substantial risk posed by the external deficit to the US economy because "foreign investors might at some point refuse to finance these deficits on terms compatible with US prosperity" (meaning near-zero interest rates). He suggests that "any sudden stop in lending to the United States would drive the dollar down, push inflation and interest rates up, and perhaps bring on a hard landing for the United States – and the world economy at large". However, he argues that "it is now evident that it can be equally or even more damaging if foreign investors do finance large US deficits for prolonged periods".

Mankiw's "middle-of-the-road" view is that "the trade deficit is not a problem in itself but is a symptom of a problem", identifying the problem as "low national saving". Hence, Mankiw argues that he is "not eager for the trade deficit to disappear, because that would mean that domestic investment would need to fall to the low level of national saving". The problem is that Mankiw's argument, apart from confusing the cause and the result, ignores the causal relation between low saving and the trade deficit. Low saving means excessive consumption, including the consumption of imported goods, which causes the trade deficit. It also implies that domestic investment can only be financed by borrowing from abroad.

Perhaps Good, Perhaps Bad

A trade deficit may be good or bad, depending on the following factors: (i) whether the deficit is temporary (induced by cyclical factors) or a long-run phenomenon caused by structural factors; (ii) whether it is a small or a large fraction of GDP; and (iii) whether the deficit is caused by excessive imports of capital goods or consumer goods. A chronic deficit that comprises a high percentage of GDP and caused by excessive spending on imported consumer goods is not a sign of economic strength and cannot be healthy, as some would argue.

The other issue is that the trade deficit has to be financed somehow. A country may do that by resorting to international reserves, which will be depleted eventually. If that happens there will be exchange rate implications as the currency comes under pressure to depreciate. A country may cover a trade deficit by exporting services, in which case a deficit on the trade balance and a surplus on the service account produce a balanced current account. There are some economies where transfers from nationals working abroad contribute significantly to payments for imports. In poor countries, foreign aid may fill the gap. The deficit may be financed by a surplus on the capital account, which is where the US finds itself today. The problem here is, what happens when foreigners are no longer willing to provide the capital flows required to achieve a capital account surplus for the US? Financing the trade deficit may be problematical, particularly if it persists for a long time. By taking all of these considerations into account, one has to reach the inevitable conclusion that the US trade deficit is indeed a problem.

EXCESSIVE PUBLIC DEBT

The US public debt is a measure of the obligations of the US government as represented by the Treasury. It consists of two components: (i) the outstanding Treasury securities held by institutions and individuals outside the US government; and (ii) inter-governmental holdings representing the obligations of the federal government for specified programmes such as social security and Medicare. At the end of April 2011, the US public debt stood at $14.2 trillion. In March 2003, at the start of the invasion of Iraq, the debt was at $6.5 trillion. Between 2005 and 2008 it increased at an average rate of $2.27 billion per day, only to grow faster in the aftermath of the global financial crisis because of the bailout of failing financial institutions.

The Debt Figures

Figure 9.1 shows the size of public debt in billions of dollars and as a percentage of GDP during the period 1910–2010 over ten-year intervals

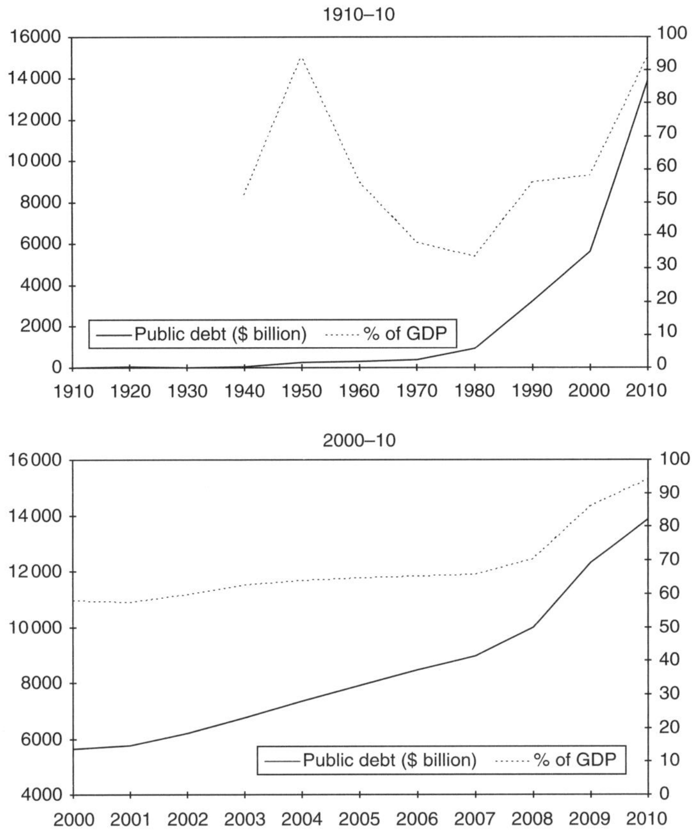

Figure 9.1 Total public debt ($ billion and as a percentage of GDP)

and the period 2000–10 on an annual basis. In 1910, public debt stood at $2.6 billion. The financing of World War II and the social programmes introduced by the Roosevelt and Truman administrations in the 1930s and 1940s led to an increase in public debt by a factor of 16, from $16 billion in 1930 to $257 billion in 1950. Subsequently, the growth of public debt closely matched the inflation rate as it tripled in size from $257 billion in 1950 to $909 billion in 1980. The spending spree of President Ronald Reagan (mostly on military programmes but also on the bailout of Continental Illinois under the notorious pretext of "too big to fail") followed by that of another Republican President, George Bush I, caused public debt to quadruple during the period 1980 to 1992, to stand at nearly $3 trillion at the end of the period.

A combination of unnecessary tax cuts and excessive military spending

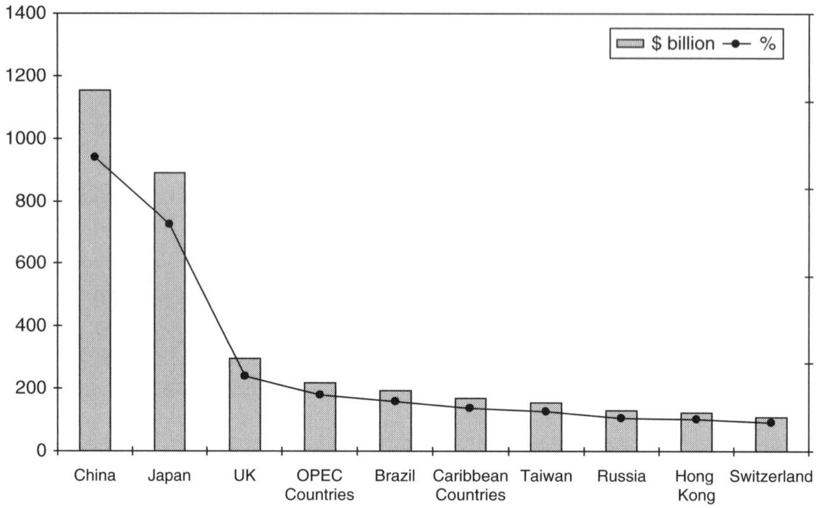

Figure 9.2 Leading foreign owners of Treasury securities (February 2011)

by the administration of George Bush II took public debt from $5.8 trillion in 2001 to about $10 trillion in 2008. Under the Obama administration public debt grew bigger because of the generous schemes to bail out financial institutions and the Great Recession that followed the global financial crisis. By the end of 2010 public debt stood at $13.9 billion or 94 per cent of GDP. The Congressional Budget Office predicted that public debt would rise from 70.2 per cent of GDP in 2008 to 100.6 per cent in 2012 (CBO, 2011). The CBO (2010) attributes the rapid growth of public debt in recent years to the budget deficits preceding the Great Recession and the global financial crisis, warning that the ratio of public debt to GDP will increase if "current policies remain in place".

For some observers what is even more alarming is that an increasing portion of US public debt is held by foreigners. As of January 2011 foreigners owned $4.45 trillion of US debt, about 32 per cent of the total public debt and 47 per cent of the debt held by the public (Treasury securities). Figure 9.2 shows that about 60 per cent of the holdings by foreigners (just over $2 trillion) belong to China and Japan. Other countries with significant holdings are (surprisingly) the UK, OPEC countries, Brazil, Caribbean countries, Taiwan, Russia, Hong Kong and Switzerland. Friedman (2008) argues that increasing dependence on foreign sources of funding will render the US less able to act independently. He quotes the old saying "he who has the gold makes the rules" and suggests that "we

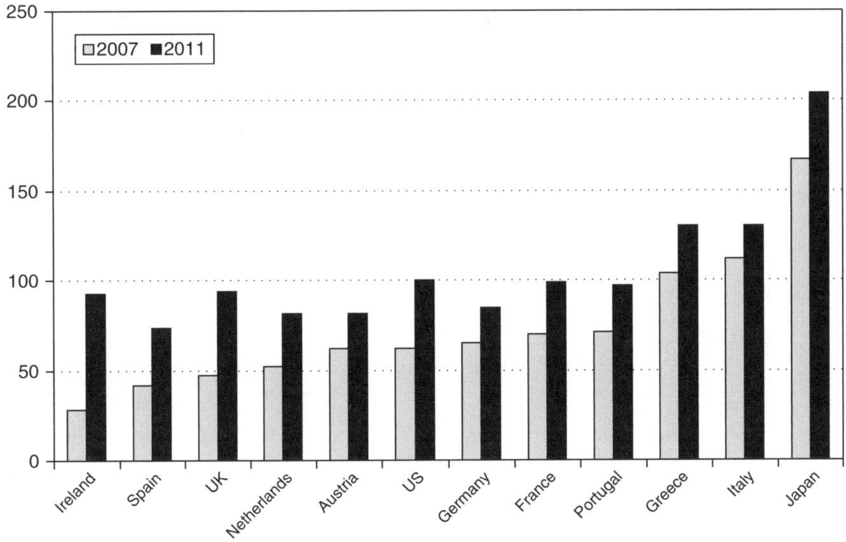

Figure 9.3 Public debt as a percentage of GDP

[the US] no longer have as much gold, and until we get some, we will have to pay more heed to the rules of those who lend us theirs". Buffett (2003a) argues that foreign ownership of public debt is no less than the transfer of the country's net worth to foreigners. Unlike domestic debt holders, foreign lenders are concerned about the exchange rate factor, which makes the US more vulnerable to the sentiment of foreign providers of credit.

Compared with other countries, the US has a lower public debt to GDP ratio than Greece, Italy and Japan, as shown in Figure 9.3, but there are differences. Given the low saving rate in the US (and the privileged position of being the issuer of the dollar, some sort of an international legal tender), foreigners command a bigger portion of public debt than in the cases of other countries, with all of the ramifications of foreign ownership of debt. Unlike other countries that have sizeable public debt, the US has high non-bank corporate debt, high mortgage debt, high financial institutions debt, high unfunded Medicare liability, high unfunded social security liability, high external debt and a serious deterioration in the net international investment position (foreign assets net of foreign liabilities). Figure 9.4 shows the alarming rate at which US indebtedness has been rising (both in dollar terms and as a percentage of GDP), including that of the non-financial business, financial business, debt to the rest of the world and the net foreign asset position. In any case, Stockman (2010) argues that "the US public debt – if honestly reckoned to include municipal bonds and

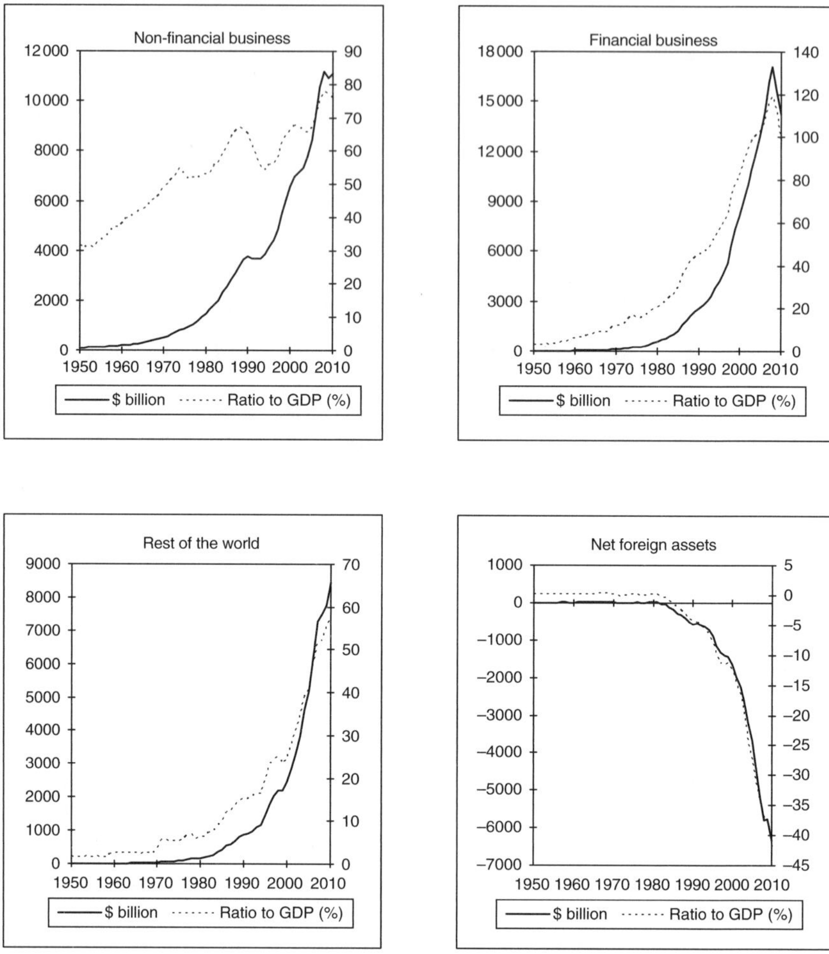

Figure 9.4 *Measures of US indebtedness ($ billion and as a percentage of GDP)*

the $7 trillion of new deficits baked into the cake through 2015 – will soon reach $18 trillion", which is "a Greece-scale 120 per cent of gross domestic product, and fairly screams out for austerity and sacrifice".

Other countries that have big public debt do not have massive indebtedness across the board. Japan, for example, has a significantly higher public debt (relative to GDP) than the US but other sectors of the economy are not heavily indebted, while the high saving rate of the private sector means that the deficit can be financed from internal sources. And while countries like Greece, Spain, Italy and even the UK are trying to do something about their finances by taking painful austerity measures and requesting bailouts, it is still "business as usual" thinking in the US. After all, George W. Bush thought that he could fight wars, fly to Mars and cut taxes for the rich at the same time. This line of thinking is still alive and kicking.

Is Excessive Debt Harmful?

The question is whether or not excessive debt is harmful. A moderate level of debt that is used to finance productive projects is useful but excessive debt can be rather harmful, particularly if it is used to finance unproductive activity, such as military spending. Consider the following effects of excessive public debt, which have been identified by the Congressional Budget Office (CBO, 2010):

- A growing portion of private savings would be used to finance the acquisition of government securities rather than used to finance investment in productive capital goods and job creation ventures. This would have adverse effects on growth and employment. Some observers have warned that this leads to boosting non-job-creating growth in some government activities at the expense of the productive sectors of the economy (for example, Friedman, 2002).
- Rising public debt results in higher interest rates and competition between the public sector and private sector for loanable funds. The outcome is a crowding out of productive private sector investment, which adversely affects growth and employment.
- High interest rates represent high borrowing costs for the US. They also reduce the value of existing Treasury bonds, inflicting capital losses on the holders of these bonds.
- A high level of public debt would undermine the role of the dollar as a reserve currency, which would deprive the US of a privilege that it has been enjoying since the end of World War II. This privilege enables the US to earn the seignorage resulting from issuing the dollar as the most internationally accepted currency.
- A high level of debt triggers demand by borrowers for a higher risk premium, thus it becomes more expensive for the US to borrow.
- A high level of debt may also trigger a downgrading of the credit rating of the country, thus increasing funding costs. In early August 2011, Standard and Poor's downgraded the US credit rating despite (or perhaps because of) a last minute agreement on raising the federal debt ceiling to avoid default. The rationale for S&P was that the deal did not represent a long-term solution to the debt problem

– actually, raising the debt ceiling implies that more debt will be accumulated (Moosa, 2011d).

- If higher marginal tax rates were used to cover rising interest costs, savings would be reduced and work would be discouraged.
- Rising interest costs force reductions in important government programmes.
- If the government chooses to finance interest payments and other spending by creating (printing) money, that will boost inflation with adverse effects on the economy.
- Restrictions on the ability of policy makers to use fiscal policy to respond to economic challenges.
- Excessive debt forces the government to borrow more on a short-term basis, as opposed to a long-term basis, to finance payments for maturing securities.
- A growing level of debt boosts the probability of a sudden fiscal crisis during which investors lose confidence in the ability of the government to manage its budget, thus it becomes difficult to borrow at affordable rates. This is exactly what has happened to Greece.

A study of the Bank for International Settlements also warns of the hazards of accumulating debt (Cecchetti et al., 2010). The study identifies three serious consequences of excessive public debt. The first is that investors demand a higher risk premium for holding the bonds issued by heavily indebted countries. The second is that a higher level of public debt implies that a significant amount of resources is allocated to debt service, which will eventually require high taxes. The third is that a high debt burden is likely to reduce the size and effectiveness of fiscal response to an adverse shock. *The Economist* (2010j) goes as far as to describe public debt as a "Ponzi scheme that requires an ever-growing population to assume the burden – unless some *deus ex machina*, such as a technological breakthrough, can boost growth".

The Danger Level of Debt

A question that often arises concerns the "danger" level of debt. Reinhart and Rogoff (2009) argue that the danger level is 90 per cent of GDP. In a testimony to the US Senate, Reinhart (2010) made the following points:

> Our main finding is that across both advanced countries and emerging markets, high debt/GDP levels (90 per cent and above) are associated with notably lower growth outcomes. Above 90 per cent, median growth rates fall one per cent, and average growth falls considerably more. In addition, for emerging markets,

> there appears to be a more stringent threshold for total external debt/GDP; when external debt reaches 60 per cent of GDP, annual growth declines by about two per cent and for higher levels, growth rates are roughly cut in half. Seldom do countries simply 'grow' their way out of deep debt burdens.

This characterization of the danger level of debt is not accepted by economists across the board. For example, Krugman (2010b) disputes the existence of a solid debt threshold or danger level, arguing that "low growth causes high debt rather than the other way around". He also points out that this has been the case in Europe, Japan and the US. In the US the only period of debt over 90 per cent of GDP was after World War II when "real GDP was falling, not because of debt problems, but because wartime mobilization was winding down and Rosie the Riveter was becoming a suburban housewife". Bernanke (2010) also disputes the presence of a debt threshold. He writes:

> Neither experience nor economic theory clearly indicates the threshold at which government debt begins to endanger prosperity and economic stability. But given the significant costs and risks associated with a rapidly rising federal debt, our nation should soon put in place a credible plan for reducing deficits to sustainable levels over time.

The CBO (2010) makes the same point by referring to the financial crises of Argentina, Ireland and Greece, suggesting that "the crisis occurred at different levels of government debt to GDP, showing that the tipping point for a crisis does not depend solely on the debt to GDP ratio". The CBO suggests other important factors such as the long-term budget outlook, near-term borrowing needs and the health of the economy.

The Situation is Alarming

Irrespective of the existence or otherwise of a debt threshold, the US debt situation is alarming. Some observers argue that the situation is not serious because the debt to GDP ratio is lower than that of Japan and other developed countries, nominal long-term interest rates are low, the dollar is the world's reserve currency and because China, Japan and other countries still like US Treasuries. Kotlikoff (2006) responds to these remarks by saying that official debt does not reflect fiscal fundamentals, implying that they are weak, because "federal discretionary spending and medical expenditures are exploding". He also argues:

> The United States has a history of defaulting on its official debt via inflation . . . the government has cut taxes well below the bone . . . countries holding

US bonds can sell them in a nanosecond . . . the financial markets have a long history of mispricing securities, financial implosion is just round the corner.

Kotlikoff also argues that the extent of the dire fiscal situation in the US is not measured by the public debt to GDP ratio but in terms of the fiscal gap. In 2006, David Walker, the then head of the Government Accountability Office (an arm of Congress that audits and evaluates the performance of the US government), warned that "if the United States government conducts its business as usual over the next few decades, a national debt that is already $8.5 trillion could reach $46 trillion or more, adjusted for inflation." He added that "a hole that big could paralyze the US economy . . ., just the interest payments on debt that big would be as much as all the taxes the government collects today" (CBS News, 2006). Penner (2010) argues that "the budget deficit is on a ruinous path and getting off the path involves far more significant policy changes than the American people are used to". The situation is indeed alarming.

THE BUDGET DEFICIT: EXCESSIVE PUBLIC SPENDING

The budget deficit is related to public debt because debt arises from government borrowing to finance the deficit. Figure 9.5 displays the cumulative

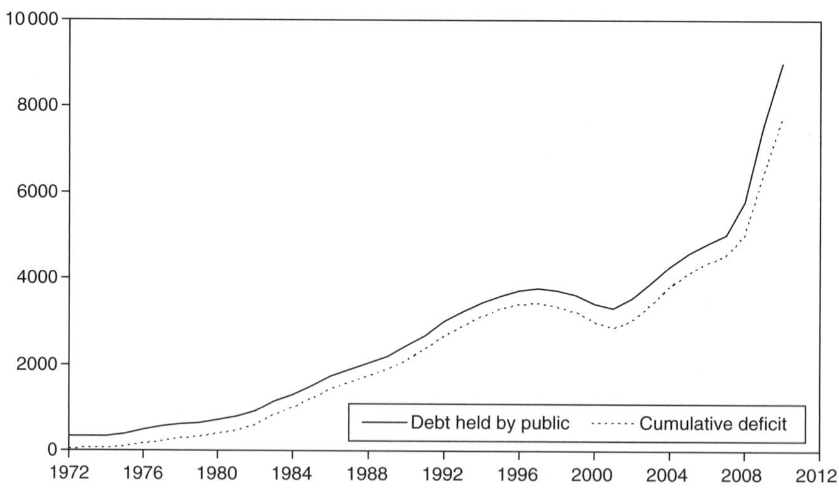

Figure 9.5 The cumulative budget deficit and debt held by the public ($ billion)

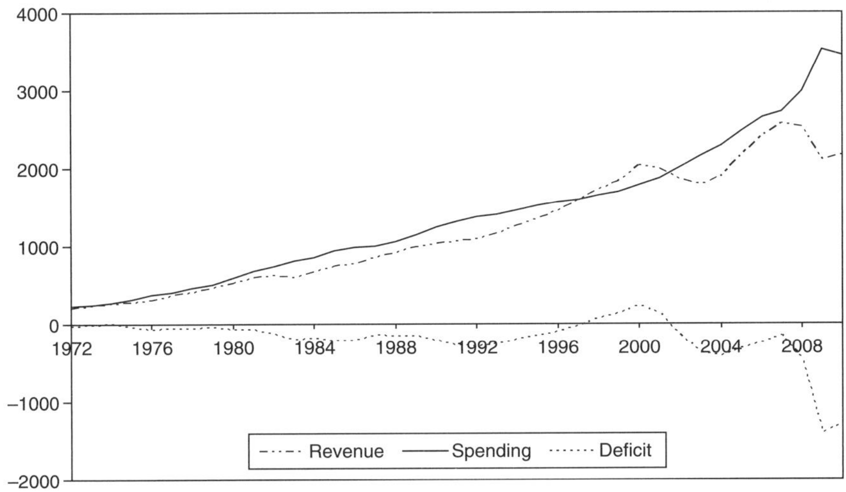

Figure 9.6 Revenue, spending and deficit ($ billion)

budget deficit (measured as a positive number) and the debt held by the public over the period 1972–2010. We can see that while the cumulative deficit and debt move together, they are not exactly equal, the difference being attributable to at least two factors: (i) the social security surplus, which reduces the "off-budget" deficit often reported in the media; and (ii) non-budgeted spending, such as the spending associated with the Iraq and Afghanistan wars. This difference is represented by the gap between debt and the cumulative budget deficit.

Figure 9.6 displays the US government revenue, spending and the difference between them, which is the deficit (or surplus), over the period 1972–2010. Deficits were recorded every year except for the years 1998–2001 when surpluses were recorded as a result of rapid economic growth, which boosted tax revenue, and deliberate spending cutting actions by the Clinton administration. The blow-up of the deficit since then has been due to slow growth or recession, expansion of military spending and the bailout of failed financial institutions in the aftermath of the global financial crisis. The improvement in 2010 resulted from lower spending compared with the massive spending of 2009. It is likely, however, that the deficit will keep on expanding. The Congressional Budget Office warns that "unless policymakers restrain the growth of spending, increase revenues significantly as a share of GDP, or adopt some combination of those two approaches, growing budget deficits will cause debt to rise to unsupportable levels" (CBO, 2010).

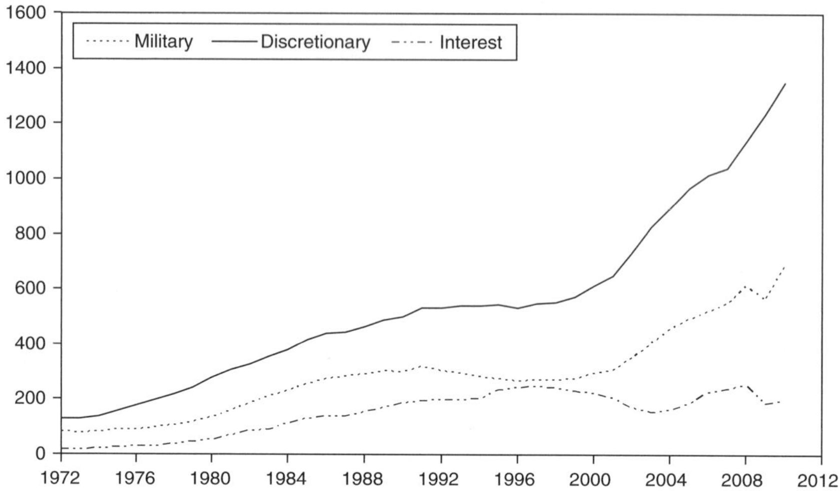

Figure 9.7 Military spending, interest payments and total discretionary spending ($ billion)

Classification of Spending

Spending is classified into discretionary and mandatory. Discretionary spending, which has to be funded through annual appropriation legislation, includes military spending, interest payments on public debt, and everything else (including education, transport, agriculture, housing, space and science, natural resources and the payment of salaries to keep government functioning). Mandatory spending does not require annual Congressional approval because the US government is legally committed under current law to payments for programmes such as Medicare (the federal health programme for the elderly), Medicaid (the federal-state health programme for the poor) and social security (pensions). Figure 9.7 shows the growth of military spending, interest payments and total discretionary spending during the period 1972–2010, over which total discretionary spending grew at an average annual compound rate of 6.4 per cent, interest payments at 6.9 per cent and military spending at 5.6 per cent. Figure 9.8 shows that in 2010 mandatory spending was about 60 per cent of total spending; about one third of that went to cover social security payments. Discretionary spending was just over 40 per cent of total spending.

Figure 9.9 shows the composition of discretionary spending: just over half was claimed by the military, 15 per cent went to interest payments and everything else took 34 per cent. Because of the increase in public debt

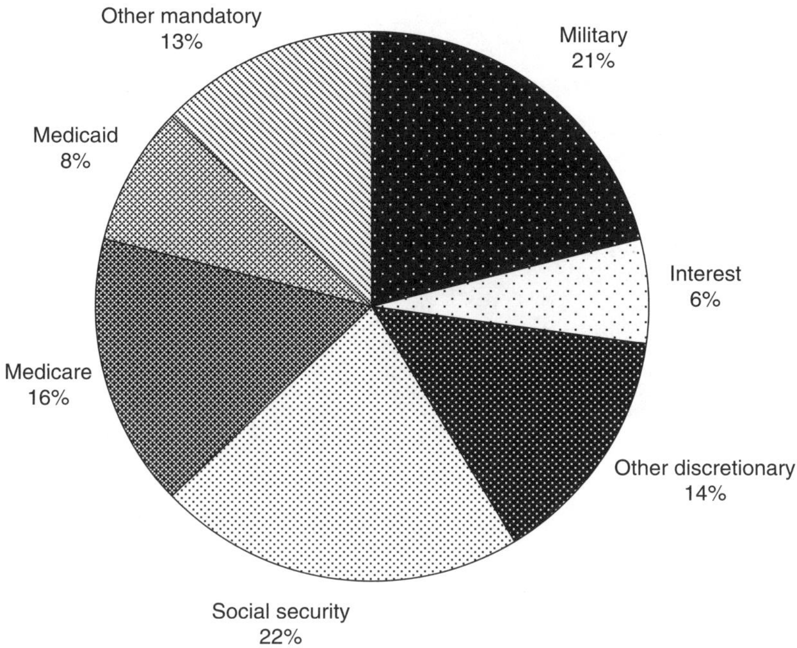

Figure 9.8 The distribution of mandatory and discretionary spending (2010)

owned by foreigners, nearly 50 per cent of interest payments are made to foreigners. Interest expenses are projected to grow dramatically as debt grows and as interest rates rise from very low current levels to more typical historical levels. The CBO (2010) predicts that nearly half of the debt increases over the period 2009–19 will be due to interest payments.

The Debate over Military Spending

The massive military spending has been the subject of a heated debate. It has been suggested that the fuel bill of the US Airforce is worth more than what is spent on the State Department, including all of the US embassies abroad (a measure of the use of military action as opposed to diplomacy in US foreign relations). While the accuracy of this claim cannot be confirmed, a large number of observers believe that the massive increase in military spending is unjustifiable. Hartung (2007) criticized the military spending spree of George Bush II, arguing that it "comes at a time when America's main enemy is not a rival superpower like the Soviet Union, but

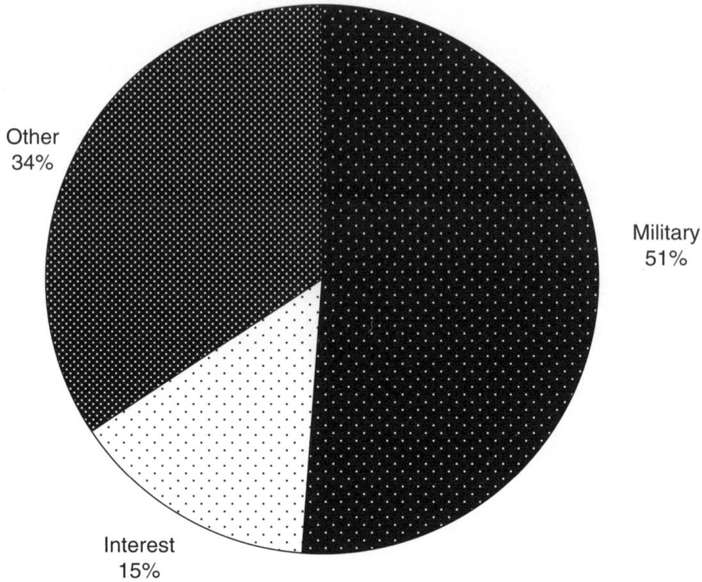

Figure 9.9 The distribution of discretionary spending

a network of terrorist groups armed primarily with explosives, shoulder-fired missiles, and AK-47s". He also points out that "even if one accepts the 'need' to fight a war like the current US occupation of Iraq, there are tens of billions of dollars in the administration's budget proposal that will never be used in that conflict". These include requests for systems like the F-22 fighter ($4.6 billion), the V-22 Osprey ($2.6 billion), the CVN-21 aircraft carrier ($3.1 billion), the SSN-774 Virginia attack submarine ($2.7 billion), the Trident D-5 submarine-launched ballistic missile ($1.2 billion) and ballistic missile defence ($10.8 billion). Hartung describes these items as "weapons that are unnecessary, unworkable, or both". In an editorial, *The Economist* (2011j) urged the US government to scrap the F-35 fighter project which is expected to have a life-time cost of $1 trillion.

Hossein-Zadeh (2007) describes the George Bush II administration's escalation of war and military spending as a "boon for Pentagon contractors", arguing that these profiteers of war and militarism have also played a critical role in creating the necessary conditions for war profiteering, that is, "instigating the escalation of the recent wars of choice and the concomitant boom of military spending". Specifically he describes giant arms manufacturers such as Lockheed Martin, Boeing, and Northrop Grumman as "the main beneficiaries of the Pentagon's spending bonanza". Reporting on some of the effects of this policy, Shane and Nixon (2007) suggested that "without a public debate or formal policy decision, contractors have become a virtual fourth branch of government". They attributed the explosive increase in spending on contractors to a "philosophy that encourages outsourcing of almost everything government does". It should be pointed out that the Pentagon's contractors not only include the likes of Boeing and Lockheed (the arms manufacturers) but also companies like Blackwater, for the provision of mercenaries (officially called security people) in Iraq, and KBR, a subsidiary of Dick Cheney's Halliburton that was in charge of providing catering and cleaning services in the Green Zone in Baghdad. It was rumoured that KBR charged the Pentagon $200 for each haircut given to a resident of the Green Zone (naturally, there was no way of verifying the actual number of haircuts rendered by KBR).

Despite the fact that US military spending is enormous in both absolute terms and in relation to total spending and GDP, Higgs (2004) believes that the military budget is bigger than it appears. When President Bush II signed the "Defense Authorization Bill" for fiscal year 2004 on 24 November 2003, the event received considerable attention in the news media because of the sheer size of the budget ($401.3 billion). Bush justified massive military spending in terms of the "war on terror", as he pledged that "we will do whatever it takes to keep our nation strong, to keep the peace, and to keep the American people secure" (and perhaps to keep the Pentagon contractors well fed). Higgs argues that this enormous amount is "only part of the total bill for defense". Specifically he argues that "other lines identify funding that serves defense purposes just as surely as – sometimes even more surely than – the money allocated to the Department of Defense". These items, according to Higgs, include the nuclear weapons activities of the Department of Energy and more or less all of the activities of the Department of Homeland Security (DHS).

Higgs even believes that much of the budget for the State Department and for international assistance programmes ought to be classified under military spending because "the money serves to buy off potential enemies and to reward friendly governments who assist US efforts to abate perceived threats". A great deal of US foreign aid, currently more than $4 billion annually, takes the form of foreign military financing and even funds allocated to economic development may serve military purposes indirectly. Likewise, a big fraction of interest payments represents the cost of military spending financed in the past by borrowing. Higgs' estimates indicate that these items add one third to the military budget, which means that the 2010 figure of $689 billion is more like $896 billion. If a fraction of interest payments is added then, according to his calculations, the figure for 2010 should be $1.17 trillion. Higgs concludes that if we take into account the complexity of the budget document (hence the omitted items) "a well-founded rule of thumb is to take the Pentagon's (always well publicized) basic budget total and double it". You "may overstate the truth", he argues, "but if so, you'll not do so by much".

Liu (2005a) makes a very interesting comment whereby he relates the military budget to the trade deficit. By referring to the 2004 figures, when the trade deficit and the budget deficit were about 6 and 4 per cent of GDP respectively, he argues that "the trading partners of the US are paying for one and a half times of the cost of a military that can someday be used against any one of them for any number of reasons, including trade disputes". This follows from the ability of the US to print dollars and use them to buy goods and services under the umbrella of dollar hegemony. Incidentally, Liu believes that "the dollar is a fiat currency not backed by gold, not backed by US productivity, not backed by US export prowess, but by US military power".

THE BUDGET DEFICIT AS A MAJOR PROBLEM

The US budget deficit has been recognized as a major problem that threatens the long-term prospects of the US economy. In a June 2010 opinion piece in the *Wall Street Journal*, the former chairman of the Federal Reserve, Alan Greenspan, noted that "only politically toxic cuts or rationing of medical care, a marked rise in the eligible age for health and retirement benefits, or significant inflation, can close the deficit" (Greenspan, 2010b). He warned that "if significant reforms are not undertaken, benefits under entitlement programs will exceed government income by over $40 trillion over the next 75 years". Kotlikoff (2006) argued that the US "must eventually choose between bankruptcy, raising taxes, or cutting payouts". In general he points out that "countries can go broke, the United States is going broke, that remaining open to foreign investment can help stave off bankruptcy, but that radical reform of US fiscal institutions is essential to secure the nation's economic future". He offers three policies to eliminate the fiscal gap and avert bankruptcy: (i) a federal retail sales tax; (ii) personalized social security; and (iii) a globally budgeted universal healthcare system.

Kotlikoff (2006) suggests that "the proper way to consider a country's solvency is to examine the life-time fiscal burdens facing current and future generations". If these burdens exceed the resources of these generations or are close to doing so, he argues, "the country's policy will be unsustainable and can constitute or lead to national bankruptcy". A measure of the fiscal burden is the fiscal gap (also called fiscal exposure) – the present value of the difference between future government spending and revenue. The calculations of Gokhale and Smetters (2005) show that the US fiscal gap is $65.9 trillion, which is more than 4.5 times the level of GDP – meaning that even if all discretionary spending were cut, it would not be adequate to solve the problem. Kotlikoff concludes with the sombre note that "our country has only a small window to address our problems before the financial markets will do it for us". Likewise, Walker (2008) argues that "the status quo is not an option", pointing out that "balancing the budget in 2040 could require actions as large as cutting total federal spending by 60 percent or raising federal taxes to two times today's level".

Warnings about the prospects of an uncontrollable budget deficit and the consequences for public debt have become quite common. For example, a report of the Peter Peterson Foundation (2010) states the following: "The US faces a looming fiscal crisis. With escalating deficits, mounting levels of public debt, growing unfunded promises for large individual, entitlement programs, and increasing reliance on foreign lenders, we as US citizens should be very concerned about the deteriorating financial conditions of our nation."

The problem with the US deficit is that it is not just a passing phenomenon; rather it is a structural long-term problem created by addiction to excessive spending and the belief that tax cuts pay for themselves. The Peter Peterson Foundation (2010) describes the situation as follows:

> The deficits for fiscal years 2009 and 2010 are largely attributable to significant declines in revenue due to a recession and weak economy, the cost of the wars in Iraq and Afghanistan, and various government bailouts and stimulus actions. These items do not represent long-term and recurring fiscal challenges. However, even after the economy recovers, the special federal interventions are complete, the wars are over, and unemployment levels are down, deficits and debt are expected to grow at a rapid rate. As a result, the US will find itself in an unsustainable fiscal position in the years to come. If current policies are left unchanged, debt held by the public is projected to spike even further, reaching over 300 percent of GDP in 2040.

According to the Peter Peterson Foundation (2010), a big threat comes from interest payments, which are projected to be "the largest single line item in the federal budget – larger than defense, Medicare or Social Security". It is estimated that by 2040, assuming that the US does not have to pay a risk premium, federal interest costs will account for 14 per cent of the entire US economy. If interest rates rise just two percentage points, interest costs alone could represent about 20 per cent of the economy by 2040. The estimates show that by 2024, historical revenue levels of about 18 per cent of GDP will not cover interest payments, social security,

Medicare and Medicaid. This means the government will need to borrow to pay for other essential programmes such as education, transport and everything else that keeps the economy going. The dismal conclusion of the report of the Peter Peterson Foundation is that:

> If we continue down this path, rising deficit and debt levels will impact our everyday lives by threatening our nation's economic strength (lower investment and growth), our international status (weaker standing in the world and international capital markets), our standard of living (higher interest rates for loans and mortgages, higher unemployment rates, lower wages), and possibly our national security (higher dependency on foreign governments that purchase US debt). Moreover, higher debt levels mean more resources devoted to compounding interest payments on the debt, which increasingly go abroad rather than stay in this country. Thus, we have fewer resources available for domestic investment in research and development, education, infrastructure and other crucial investments that maintain our economic competitiveness.

Yet nothing is being done about the problem. Samuelson (2009) argues that "the president does not want to confront Americans with choices between lower spending and higher taxes". The deficit problem cannot be solved with only spending cuts or higher taxes. Elements of a comprehensive solution may include, according to the Peter Peterson Foundation (2010), the reduction of military spending to pre-war levels, implementation of Department of Defense reforms, reviewing weapons systems, making procurement programmes more efficient, making military compensation and benefits more affordable, and reviewing and eliminating other ineffective programmes. Hence the underlying belief of the authors of the report is that excessive military spending is indeed a big problem that must be solved to get the budget deficit under control. On the tax side, it is suggested that the George Bush II tax cuts should be reconsidered while restructuring consumption tax and simplifying the tax code. Bergsten (2009) suggests that the tax system should be changed by shifting the focus of taxation from income to consumption and that a mandatory saving scheme should be created along the lines of what is used in Australia and Singapore. What is happening, however, is exactly the opposite. America is telling Europe that reducing military spending is wrong, while the Republicans and the pundits of Fox TV think that the way out is tax cuts (preferably for those who earn more than $2 million a year). America is even lecturing Europe on the urgency of dealing with the debt crisis in the European Union. The Germans have made their attitude of "look who's talking" quite clear.

The Economist (2010k) makes a comparison between Europe and the US, by commenting on a report of the IMF declaring that "America's structural deficit and the growth in debt over the medium term are among the worst in the rich world". For example, Germany has passed a balanced budget constitutional amendment, the UK has launched a four-year plan to deal with the deficit and France has raised the pension age. The US, on the other hand, has no taste for austerity measures, which is justified by saying that the economy is not in a good shape for taxes to be raised. It is, however, ideology rather than macroeconomic conditions that motivate US distaste for austerity measures.

TAX CUTS: A CAUSE OR A SOLUTION?

Controversy is currently rampant about the effect of tax cuts (or alternatively not raising taxes), particularly the proposition that tax cuts pay for themselves. Since the late 1970s, some supply-side economists have contended that tax reductions stimulate economic growth to such a degree that tax revenue will rise rather than fall. However, there is little empirical evidence to support this hypothesis. In a study of the Joint Committee on Taxation (2005) that examined the economic effects of reducing marginal tax rates, it is suggested that "growth effects eventually become negative . . . because accumulating federal government debt crowds out private investment". The study concludes that "lowering marginal tax rates is likely to harm the economy over the long run if the tax reductions are deficit financed".

The Evidence

One way to evaluate the proposition that higher tax rates have negative (or positive) effects on economic growth is to examine the relation between tax rates and economic growth over time. If high taxes are bad for the economy, we should expect robust economic growth during periods characterized by low tax rates, and vice versa. This is not the conclusion reached by Aaron et al. (2004) who found that "historical evidence shows no clear correlation between tax rates and economic growth" and that "comparisons across countries confirm that rapid growth has been a feature of both high- and low-tax nations". Allard and Lindert (2006) undertook an extensive examination of economic performance in developed countries since the 1960s, analysing the relation between economic performance and government policy across a wide range of areas, including tax policy, spending policy and regulatory policy in product and labour markets. They also controlled for various economic and demographic factors that could be expected to affect economic performance. Their results show that at levels of taxation at or even significantly above those now seen in the US, increasing the ratio of tax revenue to GDP leads to an improvement in economic performance. They explained this result by noting that the additional revenues raised by higher-tax countries are frequently used to undertake growth-promoting activities like investment in public education, infrastructure and public health.

Mazerov (2010) evaluates proposals to cut state corporate income taxes, arguing that "corporate income tax cuts are unlikely to have a positive impact on a state's rate of economic growth or the pace at which it generates private-sector jobs". On the contrary, he argues that such actions: (i) would produce no net short-term stimulus, due to state balanced-budget requirements; (ii) could lead to a near-term drop in total in-state economic activity because corporations are unlikely to spend the full amount of the tax cut in-state; (iii) would create little or no added incentive for corporate investment in the long run; (iv) could adversely affect long-term growth by leading to cuts in public services; and (v) are not rooted in real-world economic success stories. On the "pay for themselves" proposition, he argues that "the small economic impacts of state corporate tax cuts and the large loss of revenue mean that such cuts do not stimulate enough new taxable economic activity – and thus enough new revenues – to fully offset the revenues lost from the tax cut".

The Congressional Budget Office and the Congressional Research Service have evaluated the effects of cuts in federal corporate taxes and identified the shortcomings of such a mechanism for stimulating economic growth. The CBO (2008) concludes that "a general cut in business tax rates will tend to generate significantly less investment demand for each dollar of [lost] revenue than a cut that applies only to new investment" and that "a cut in corporate rates is also less effective because it does not apply to businesses that are not subject to the corporate tax". Likewise, the CRS concludes that "most evidence does not suggest that business tax cuts would provide significant short-term stimulus" (Gravelle et al., 2009).

The CBO (2005) analysed the macroeconomic effects of a 10 per cent reduction in all federal tax rates on individual income. The estimates show that the output effect ranges from +0.5 to +0.8 per cent over the first five years and from −0.1 per cent to +1.1 per cent over the second five years. The budgetary impact of the economic changes was estimated to offset between 1 per cent and 22 per cent of the revenue loss from the tax cut over the first five years and add as much as 5 per cent to that loss or offset as much as 32 per cent of it over the second five years.

The Bush Tax Cuts

A variety of tax cuts were enacted under President George Bush II between 2001 and 2003 (commonly referred to as the "Bush tax cuts") through the Economic Growth and Tax Relief Reconciliation Act of 2001, and the Jobs and Growth Tax Relief Reconciliation Act of 2003. Kogan (2003) evaluated the claims that the Bush tax cuts of 2001 would boost growth and found "little support for claims made by Administration officials and other proponents of these tax cuts that either the 2001 tax cut or the new 'growth' package would generate substantial improvements in long-term economic growth", that "these tax cuts would have only a small effect on the economy over the long term", and that "the effect is as likely to be negative as positive". On the same issue the CBO (2001) concluded that "the cumulative effects of the new tax law on the economy are uncertain but will probably be small". Likewise, Gale and Potter (2002) found that the effect on long-term economic growth was more likely to be a small negative than a small positive.

Elmendorf and Reifschneider (2002) modelled a tax cut closely resembling the 2001 income tax rate cuts and concluded that "a sustained tax cut reduces output [GDP] in the long run and raises output by less than 50 cents per dollar of tax reduction in the short run". Auerbach (2002) conducted multiple simulations and found that "in the long run, the level of capital and hence output [GDP] has been permanently reduced by the prolonged period of reduced national saving induced by the tax cut [because of the tax cut's effect in swelling budget deficits]".

Kogan (2003) argues that "the proposition that tax cuts can pay for themselves – like most claims of a 'free lunch' – is too good to be true" and that "it does not withstand scrutiny". He goes so far as to argue that "the President's [George Bush II] own Council of Economic Advisers does not believe the tax cuts will come closer to paying for themselves". He compares what happened in the 1980s (a period of tax cuts) with the 1990s (a period of tax hikes) and concludes that income tax revenue grew 13 times faster in the 1990s than in the 1980s.

The *Washington Post* (2007) disputed the claim of George Bush II that "it is also a fact that our tax cuts have fueled robust economic growth and record revenues", arguing that "the claim about fueling record revenue is flat wrong" and that "it is shocking that the president should persist in making such errors". The article refers to work by Gregory Mankiw (who served as the chairman of Mr Bush's Council of Economic Advisers) to test the hypothesis on which Mr Bush's claim is based. Mankiw looked at the extent to which tax cuts stimulate extra growth and the extent to which that growth generates extra tax revenue that offsets the initial loss of revenue from the tax cut. He concluded that:

> even over the long term, once you've allowed all of the extra growth to feed through into extra revenue, cuts in capital taxes juice the economy enough to recoup half of the lost revenue, and cuts in income taxes deliver a boost that recoups 17 per cent of the lost revenue.

The article refers to the work of some Treasury economists who calculated how much extra growth would result from making the Bush tax cuts permanent. They concluded that output would rise by about 0.5 per cent in the first six years and by an additional 0.2 per cent in the long run. Since the US government collects around 18 per cent of GDP in taxes, a 0.7 per cent growth in GDP produces extra tax revenue that is equivalent to 0.13 per cent of GDP. That would offset less than a tenth of the revenue that would be lost because of the tax cuts.

Ruffing and Horney (2010) disagree with the proposition that George W. Bush's policies bear little responsibility for the budget deficit and that the Obama Administration is to blame, arguing that "together with the economic downturn, the Bush tax cuts and the wars in Afghanistan and Iraq explain virtually the entire deficit over the next ten years". They add the following:

> The events and policies that have pushed deficits to these high levels in the near term, however, were largely outside the new Administration's control. If not for the tax cuts enacted during the presidency of George W. Bush that Congress did not pay for, the cost of the wars in Iraq and Afghanistan that were initiated during that period, and the effects of the worst economic slump since the Great Depression (including the cost of steps necessary to combat it), we would not be facing these huge deficits in the near term.

Furthermore, they dispute a report of the Heritage Foundation claiming that tax cuts and other policies initiated by George Bush II are not a significant factor behind the deficits (Reid, 2010). The report attributes the deficit to rapidly growing spending on Medicare, Medicaid, social security and interest payments and dismisses the significance of the weak revenues in general and the 2001 and 2003 tax cuts. They describe the Heritage Foundation's analysis as being "both misguided and seriously misleading". In particular they argue that the analysis ignores the fact that rapidly-rising interest payments result in significant part from the tax cuts and other fiscal policies of the Bush era. Specifically they point out that tax cuts and the wars in Iraq and Afghanistan accounted for over $2.6 trillion of the national debt by 2008, which will add another $7 trillion by 2019, at which time the interest bill will be $450 billion in that year alone.

In 2003, 450 economists, including ten Nobel Prize laureates, signed a statement opposing the Bush tax cuts (available at http://www.epi.org/page/-/old/stmt/2003/statement_signed. pdf). They expressed the view that economic growth had not been sufficient to generate jobs and prevent unemployment from rising, but "the tax cut plan proposed by President Bush is not the answer to these problems". The statement made it clear that "passing these tax cuts will worsen the long-term budget outlook, adding to the nation's projected chronic deficits" and that "this fiscal deterioration will reduce the capacity of the government to finance Social Security and Medicare benefits as well as investments in schools, health, infrastructure, and basic research". Moreover, it was suggested that "the proposed tax cuts will generate further inequalities in after-tax income". Those who signed the statement include Nobel Prize winners George Akerlof, Kenneth Arrow, Lawrence Klein, Daniel McFadden, Franco Modigliani, Robert Solow, Joseph Stiglitz, Paul Samuelson and William Sharpe.

Widespread Opposition to Tax Cuts

Opposition to tax cuts and disputing the proposition that they pay for themselves runs across the board, encompassing academics, business people and government officials. Krugman (2007) argues that "supply side doctrine, which claimed without evidence that tax cuts would pay for themselves, never got any traction in the world of professional economic research, even among conservatives". Roubini (2010) suggests that the Republican Party is "trapped in a belief in voodoo economics, the economic equivalent of creationism". Buffett (2003b) commented on the proposed reduction in taxes on dividends by arguing that "when you listen to tax-cut rhetoric, remember that giving one class of taxpayer a 'break' requires – now or down the line – that an equivalent burden be imposed on other parties". In other words, he said, "if I get a break, someone else pays", which means that "government can't deliver a free lunch to the country as a whole". And former Comptroller General of the United States David Walker stated in January 2009 in a documentary film called *IOUSA* (available at http://www.iousathemovie.com): "you can't have guns, butter and tax cuts" because "the numbers just don't add up". Fukuyama (2008) argues against the idea that tax cuts pay for themselves, pointing out that "the traditional view was correct: if you cut taxes without cutting spending, you end up with a damaging deficit". He refers to some historical stylized facts: "the Reagan tax cuts of the 1980s produced a big deficit; the Clinton tax increases of the 1990s produced a surplus; and the Bush II tax cuts of the early 21st century produced an even larger deficit".

THE BUDGET DEFICIT: A SPENDING PROBLEM OR A REVENUE PROBLEM?

The current debate is about whether the budget deficit represents a spending problem, a revenue problem or both. This issue can be looked upon retrospectively (what caused the deficit) and prospectively (what can be done to reduce the deficit). The conservative Republicans think that it is a spending problem, thus they oppose any tax increases (some of them even advocate tax cuts). Republican Congressman and Speaker of the House, John Boehner, believes that "Washington has a spending problem, not a revenue problem" (Boehner, 2011). These remarks were made at a press conference with Republican leaders on 13 April 2011 in which Boehner declared:

> The American people know that we can't continue to spend money we don't have. And I think the American people also understand that this hurts our economy and hurts job creation in our country . . . You are also aware I have been pushing the president for months to engage in this discussion about our long-term fiscal mess. And I'll just say this: we can't tax the very people that we expect to reinvest in our economy and to create jobs. Washington has a spending problem, not a revenue problem.

Variations on this statement have been made by other Republicans, such as House Majority Leader Eric Cantor, who suggested that "most people understand that Washington doesn't have a revenue problem, it has a spending problem", emphasizing that "we can't raise taxes" (Cantor, 2011).

Of course, it is also wrong to think that the deficit is only a revenue problem. It is both: too much spending and too little tax revenue. Bartlett (2009) argues that without benefit cuts in Medicare and social security, federal taxes would have to increase by 8.1 per cent of GDP now and forever to cover estimated programme shortfalls, while avoiding debt increases. The 30-year historical average tax revenue is 18.4 per cent of GDP, which means that what is required is a substantial increase, relative to historical levels, in tax revenue as a share of GDP. Bartlett also considers mandatory spending such as social security and Medicare. These spending items are sometimes called "entitlements" because people meeting relevant eligibility requirements are legally entitled to benefits, although most pay taxes into these programmes throughout their working lives. The problem is that the US government has been so fiscally imprudent that this money is not really available. Bartlett explains the situation as follows:

> Most Americans believe that the Social Security trust fund contains a pot of money that is sitting somewhere earning interest to pay their benefits when

> they retire. On paper this is true; somewhere in a Treasury Department ledger there are $2.4 trillion worth of assets labeled "Social Security trust fund." The problem is that by law 100% of these "assets" are invested in Treasury securities. Therefore, the trust fund does not have any actual resources with which to pay Social Security benefits. It's as if you wrote an IOU to yourself; no matter how large the IOU is it doesn't increase your net worth.

Krugman (2011a) attributes the disappearance of the budget surplus of the late 1990s to: (i) the Bush tax cuts, which added roughly $2 trillion to the national debt over the last decade; (ii) the wars in Iraq and Afghanistan, which added an additional $1.1 trillion or so; and (iii) the Great Recession, which led both to a collapse in revenue and to a sharp rise in spending on unemployment insurance and other safety-net programmes. He blames the tax cuts and wars on the ideology of George Bush II as he writes:

> President George W. Bush cut taxes in the service of his party's ideology, not in response to a groundswell of popular demand – and the bulk of the cuts went to a small, affluent minority. Similarly, Mr. Bush chose to invade Iraq because that was something he and his advisers wanted to do, not because Americans were clamoring for war against a regime that had nothing to do with 9/11. In fact, it took a highly deceptive sales campaign to get Americans to support the invasion, and even so, voters were never as solidly behind the war as America's political and pundit elite.

Dismal Prospects

By the end of 2011 the prospects for sorting out America's fiscal mess were not promising. The August agreement to raise the debt ceiling did not solve the problem – on the contrary, political wrangling over the issue is indeed indicative that the mess will not be sorted out. The problem, according to *The Economist* (2011k), is that "the vast majority of Republicans, driven by the wilder-eyed members of their party and the cacophony of conservative media, are clinging to the position that not a single cent of the deficit reduction must come from a higher tax take". On 23 June 2011 Eric Cantor, the leader of the Republican majority in the House of Representatives, walked out of a meeting chaired by Vice President Joe Biden in which a suggestion was made to reduce the deficit by introducing $2 trillion spending cuts and raising $400 billion in tax revenue by closing loopholes. Cantor wanted the closing of loopholes to be offset by tax cuts (*The Economist*, 2011m). This attitude is described as "economically illiterate and disgracefully cynical".

With a mentality like this, it is doubtful if America's fiscal mess is going to be sorted out any time soon. The Bank for International Settlements warns that "failure to do so will raise the chance of an unexpected and abrupt rise in government bond yields at medium and long maturities, which would put the nascent economic recovery at risk" (Cecchetti et al., 2010). Likewise, Walker (2008) makes it clear that "the sooner we started, the better".

The August 2011 deal, signed into law by President Obama, involves $917 billion in tax cuts over the next decade in return for a two-stage increase in the debt ceiling of $900 billion. *The Economist* (2011n) argues that in reaching the deal "neither Republicans nor Democrats were forced to slaughter their sacred cows" in the sense that Republicans kept higher taxes off the table, while Democrats did the same with Medicaid, Medicare and social security. Still the agreement was more like a victory for the Republicans and their voodoo economics. The deal also involved the formation of the 12-member United States Congress Joint Select Committee on Deficit Reduction (the so-called "Supercommittee") entrusted to find $1.5 trillion of further deficit reductions (meaning spending cuts). Towards the end of November 2011, the committee announced its failure by not reaching any compromise. *The Economist* (2011v) suggests that "with the deficit-reduction committee's failure, American fiscal policy is drifting in a dangerous direction".

CONCLUDING REMARKS

The events leading to the downgrading of the US credit rating on 5 August 2011 and the whole US macroeconomic situation, including the possibility of yet another recession, point to one miserable state of affairs: too much debt and too little political will to deal with its consequences. The debt ceiling deal did nothing to change this perception (and perhaps reinforced it). *The Economist* (2011p) describes the deal as "flawed on two counts: it enshrines short-term fiscal contraction and fails to reduce the medium-term deficit". Specifically the deal focuses on discretionary spending, which can be changed by future legislation. *The Economist* (2011q) argues that "a more durable deficit reduction means reforming both the tax system and entitlements such as pensions and health care for the elderly".

It was mentioned at the beginning of this chapter that one of the problems of contemporary American politics is the culture of blaming one's own problems on others. On 5 August 2011, China got some reprieve, as US officials directed their anger at Standard and Poor's for downgrading the US credit rating from AAA to AA+. But the decision to downgrade America's credit rating was sound, not poor and untimely as Yang (2011) thinks. The decision was justified on the grounds that the US public debt as a percentage of GDP was rising to unsustainable levels in contrast to the situation in other AAA-rated countries such as the UK and Germany, where plans have been put in place to stabilize the debt-to-GDP ratio. In an article entitled *Looking for Someone to Blame*, *The Economist* (2011r) suggests that the political analysis of Standard and Poor's is "spot on" because "American governance and policymaking are becoming less stable, less effective and less predictable". In another piece, *The Economist* (2011s) suggests that "American politicians are intent, not on improving their country's competitiveness, but on gouging each other's eyes out".

The Republicans, in particular, are motivated by their ideology to think that taxes should not be raised although it has become crystal clear that cutting spending will not solve the deficit, hence the debt, problem. Their argument is that raising taxes on the rich will hurt the economy, because it is the rich who create jobs. When the richest man in America, Warren Buffett, called for higher taxes to be imposed on the rich, the Republicans blasted back at him. Referring to the super-rich, Buffett suggests that "my friends and I have been coddled long enough by a billionaire-friendly Congress" and that "it's time for our government to get serious about shared sacrifice" (Geiger, 2011). With Republicans being in charge, it is difficult to see how this is going to happen. The prospects for sorting out America's fiscal mess are indeed dismal.

10. The US trade deficit as an American problem: saving and economic structure

PRIVATE SAVING, CONSUMPTION AND DEBT

The US trade deficit is an American problem because it is the result of too little saving and too much consumption financed by too much debt. The Congressional Budget Office makes this point quite clear by suggesting that "the US current account deficits of the past two decades were brought on primarily by a long downward trend in domestic saving as a percentage of GDP that began in the mid-1950s and accelerated in the early 1980s" (CBO, 2000). Likewise Kotlikoff (2008) argues that "the decline of the saving rate explains, in large part, why the United States has run a very large current account deficit in recent years".

The current situation in the US has materialized as follows. The decline in the saving rate led to a shortage of funds available for domestic investment, which caused interest rates to rise, attracting capital flows from abroad. As saving declined, consumption increased – this is because saving means consuming less out of current income in the present in order to consume more in the future. Therefore the decision to save now is equivalent to the decision to defer consumption and to store it in the form of an asset. The problems associated with a low saving rate include dependence on foreigners and retrenchment risk in consumer spending. If the saving rate falls too low to be consistent with sound long-run plans, a sudden correction of consumption habits may translate into a substantial reduction in consumption expenditure and therefore aggregate demand. Moreover, saving is important for capital formation and economic growth.

In June 2005, *The Christian Science Monitor* reported that "Americans have stopped saving for a rainy day" and that "they are living paycheck to paycheck, depending on credit cards to get them through emergencies, and hoping that the rising value of their homes will give them a retirement nest egg" (Marks and Scherer, 2005). The article warned that "the nation's paucity of savings is raising alarms from the Federal Reserve to consumer watchdogs, who worry that the nation is counting on foreign savings to maintain a spendthrift lifestyle". It is even suggested that the tax system needs to be changed to encourage saving instead of spending. Nancy Register, of the Consumer Federation of America, is quoted as saying that "in two generations it seems that we've lost the culture and habit of savings" and that "there's so much marketing pressure to spend and buy and have instant gratification".

Likewise, the Federal Reserve former chairman, Alan Greenspan, is quoted as warning that "the low savings rate is impairing the nation's long-term economic prospects" and that "an improved savings rate would provide investment money for businesses, which would create jobs" (Marks and Scherer, 2005). It is strange, therefore, that Bergsten (2010b) makes it sound as if Americans consume excessively because of altruism towards the rest of the world when he argues that "the United States must convince the world that it is unwilling again to become the consumer and borrower of the last resort". This view is rather ludicrous and not worthy of any comment. A more credible view is expressed by Persaud (2010) who refers to a "consumption binge in the US, evidenced by a negative personal saving rate, excessive leverage, historically high unemployment levels and record international deficits".

The Figures

Figure 10.1 shows the personal saving rate (private saving as a percentage of personal disposable income) during the period 1959–2010. We can observe short-term changes, primarily related to stock market activity (the rate drops when the stock market is booming) and the state of the economy (it may fall in a recession as people dig into their savings or rise as they cut back on consumption). The saving rate dropped between 1973 and 1976 because of the recession of the 1970s and again post-1981 because of the recession of the 1980s. Then it fell during the period 1984–6 because of the recovery (thus a higher level of consumption) and stock market boom and rose following the stock market crash of October 1987.

The big rise of the saving rate between 2007 and 2008 was due to the global financial crisis, then it was maintained despite the Great Recession because of the government stimulus spending. However, what is more important for the purpose of our discussion is the long-term decline of the saving rate since 1984. In the earlier period the saving rate rose steadily as consumer credit was not easily available. Since the mid-1980s the availability of easy credit and the widespread use of credit cards caused the secular decline in the saving rate. Figure 10.2 shows the rapid growth in outstanding household debt, which stood at 12.5 trillion at the end of 2010, despite the decline caused by the global financial crisis. Low interest rates and

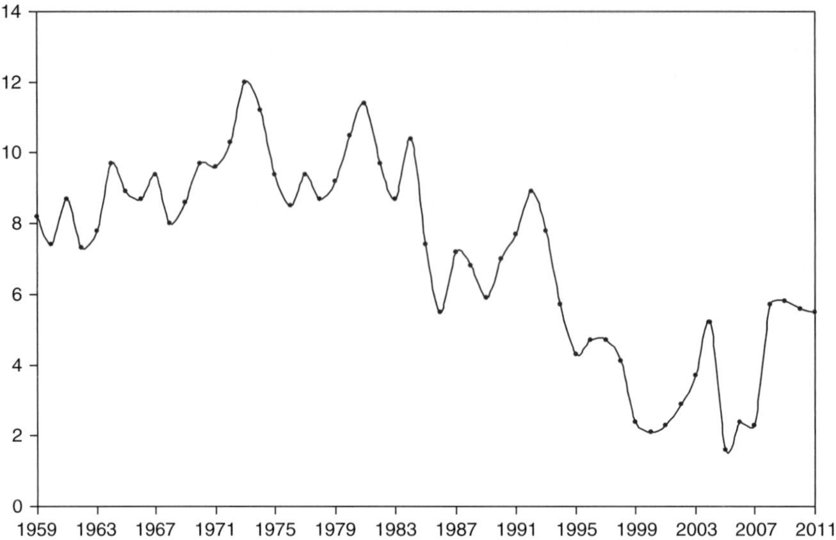

Figure 10.1 The personal saving rate in the US

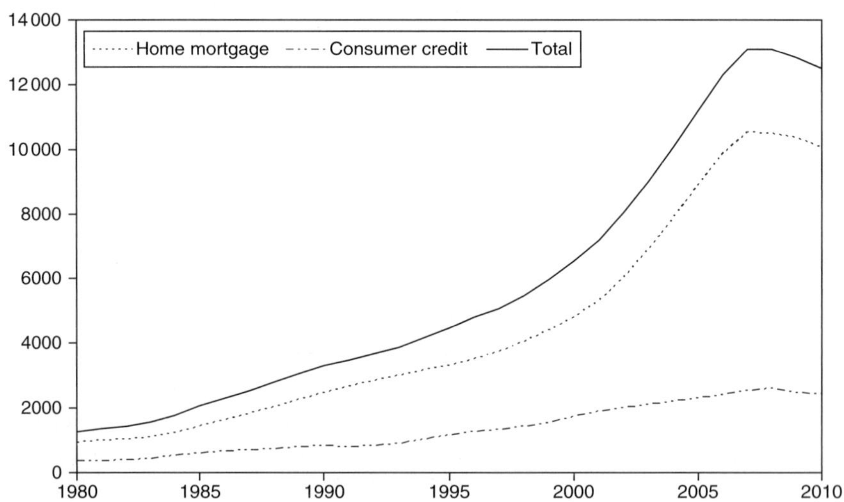

Figure 10.2 Outstanding household debt ($ billion)

vibrant advertising campaigns also contributed to growing consumption and hence debt.

Explaining Saving Behaviour

A question that has confronted economists is why countries save at different rates. Some of the factors that affect the amount people save are culture, differences in saving motives, economic growth, demographics, size of the labour force, insurability of risks, and economic policy (including tax policy). Each of these factors can influence saving at a point in time and produce changes in saving over time. For example, the saving rate in Asian countries is high for cultural reasons and because of the unavailability of a government-sponsored safety net (for example providing financial support for the elderly). In Chapter 8 we saw that these factors are important for explaining the high saving rate in China. In a survey of the literature, Guidolin and La Jeunesse (2007) present seven explanations for the decline in the US personal saving rate: (i) the wealth effect; (ii) the permanent income hypothesis; (iii) financial innovation, which has transformed unrealized capital gains and future incomes into current purchasing power; (iv) social security programmes and macroeconomic stability; (v) demographic factors; (vi) the Ricardian equivalence whereby higher taxes induce households to save less; and (vii) trends in the way companies compensate shareholders (stock repurchases rather than dividends).

Saving behaviour may be explained in terms of the life cycle model of Franco Modigliani (for example, Ando and Modigliani, 1963). According to this model people save – accumulate assets – to finance their retirement, and they dissave (spend their assets) during retirement. The more young savers there are relative to old dissavers, the greater will be a country's saving rate – hence the role of demographics. While most economists believe that the life cycle model provides the main explanation for US saving, Kotlikoff and Summers (1981) show that saving for retirement explains less than half of total US wealth. As an alternative explanation, they suggest the precautionary motive, that is, the motive to save in order to be prepared for future risks such as the loss of a job or sudden large uninsured medical expenses. Kotlikoff (2008) dismisses increased government consumption and disincentives as explanations for the recent decline in US saving, arguing that "the main explanation for the decline in national saving appears to be the major and ongoing government policy of taking an ever larger share of resources from young and future Americans and giving them to older Americans".

The stylized facts exhibited by Figure 10.1 tell us that a good explanation for the decline in the US saving rate in recent years is financial and real estate bubbles – this is the wealth effect. As stock and real estate prices rise, those holding these assets feel wealthy and consequently they indulge in spending sprees. Furthermore, they can use these assets as collateral to borrow money and spend it. Anthony Chan of JP Morgan Asset Management in Columbus, Ohio, is quoted as saying that "when you have massive capital gains, you get people spending more, pushing the savings rate down" (Marks and Scherer, 2005). Lusardi et al. (2001) provide empirical evidence indicating that "the appreciating stock market wealth since 1988 may have reduced the personal saving rate between 3 and 5 percentage points". Bernanke (2005) uses the concept of wealth effect to blame the decline in the US saving rate on China. According to Bernanke, the wealth effect arises from rising house prices, a consequence of the low interest rates caused by the money flooding from foreign (meaning Chinese) savers. For Bernanke, the low saving rate in the US is a "passive response to a global saving glut washing on its shores" (*The Economist*, 2009c). The argument put forward by *The Economist* goes further: "An unsatisfactory implication of the literature on the saving glut is that it paints America as a tragic victim of forces beyond its control. The emerging markets' need for insurance . . . drives them to export capital to America . . . . America, by implication has no choice but to make room for it." The fact remains, however, that China may have provided the rope, but America hanged itself. No one can force you, or anyone else, to take a loan if you do not wish to take it.

An alternative to the wealth effect explanation of the fall in the saving rate is the permanent income hypothesis. While the wealth effect explanation stresses the effect of rising net worth, the permanent income hypothesis relies more on revisions of the expectations of future income.

Figure 10.1 shows that the personal saving rate fell to its lowest level just before the onset of the global financial crisis. Figure 10.3 is a scatter diagram showing the relation between the personal saving rate and stock prices over the period 1959–2010, which seems to be negative (but nonlinear). The negative relation between the saving rate and stock prices was even more conspicuous during the period 1995–2010, as exhibited in Figure 10.4. The negative relation is more likely to be causal than the result of long-term time trends caused by independent factors.

Another suggested reason for the low saving rate, which is also based on the wealth effect, is disparity in income distribution (for example, Naked Capitalism, 2010). Income distribution in this sense means income inequality, which is described by R. Wolf (2010) as "divisive, depressing and dangerous". As the distribution of income becomes more skewed and wealth more concentrated, the saving rate declines. The explanation for the connection between the saving rate and income inequality is straightforward: feeling wealthier, the rich decide to consume part of their

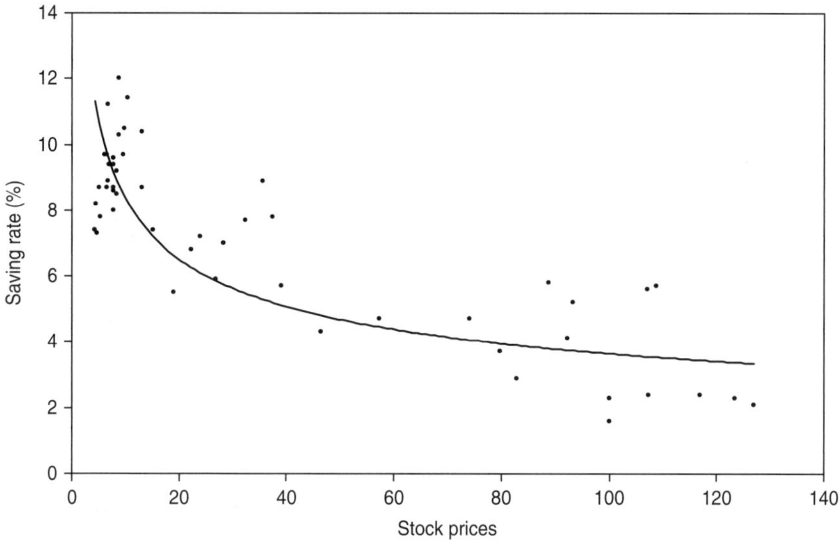

Figure 10.3 *The relation between the personal saving rate and stock prices (1959–2010)*

Figure 10.4 *The relation between the personal saving rate and stock prices (1995–2010)*

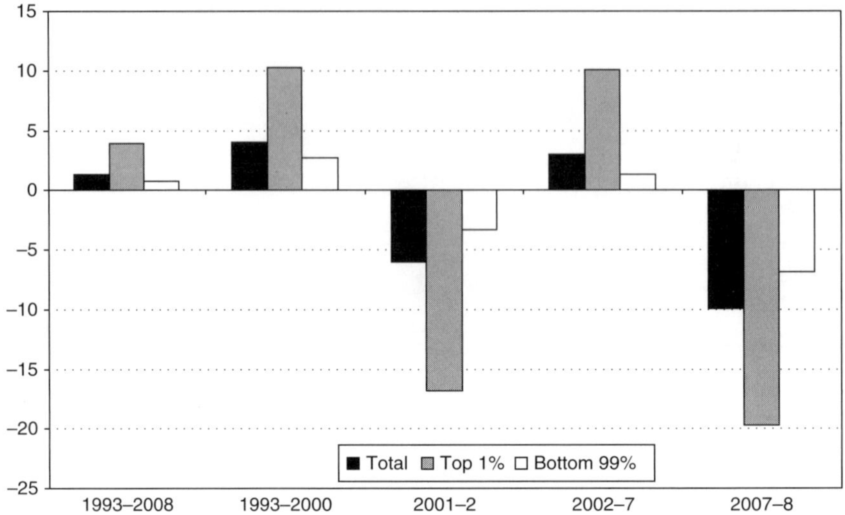

Figure 10.5 Growth of real annual income by groups

capital gains immediately. Since the lower saving rate is applied to a higher income level, the consequent decline in absolute savings for the rich (hence for the country) would be huge. According to Yves Smith, "behaviors on both ends of the income spectrum no doubt played into the low-savings dynamic: wealthy who spend heavily, and struggling average consumers who increasingly came to rely on borrowings to improve or merely maintain their lifestyle" (Naked Capitalism, 2010). Stockman (2010) writes:

> During the last bubble (from 2002 to 2006) the top 1 per cent of Americans – paid mainly from the Wall Street casino – received two-thirds of the gain in national income, while the bottom 90 percent – mainly dependent on Main Street's shrinking economy – got only 12 per cent. This growing wealth gap is not the market's fault. It's the decaying fruit of bad economic policy.

Measures of income inequality are displayed in Figure 10.5–10.8. Figure 10.5 shows the growth of real annual income by groups. The income of the top 1 per cent grew faster than that of the bottom 99 per cent during the period 1993–2008, particularly during the periods 1993–2000 and 2002–7. The period 2001–2 saw a rapid decline of the income of the top 1 per cent only because of the dot.com bubble and the same for the global financial crisis. Figure 10.6 shows the distribution of wealth (net worth) in 2009, with the top 1 per cent commanding 35 per cent of total wealth. Figure 10.7 shows that income inequality (measured by the Gini coefficient) is more severe in the US than in any of the other listed countries, with Norway and

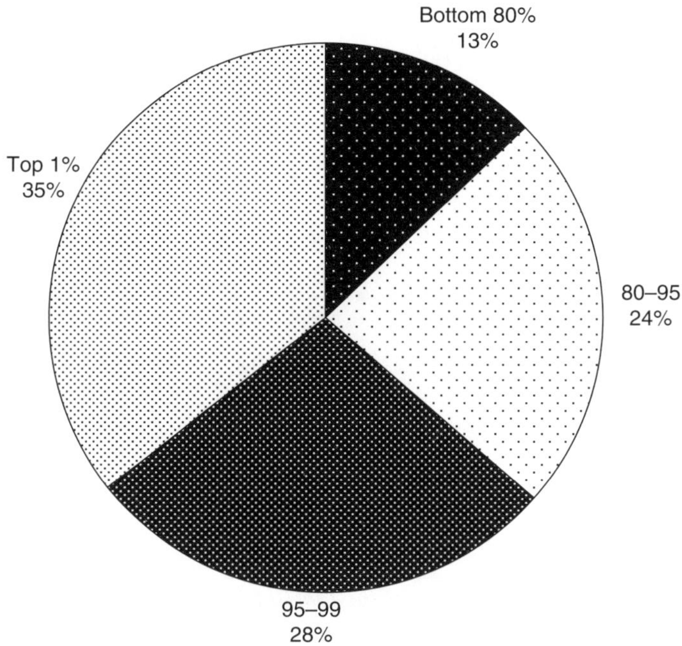

Figure 10.6 *The distribution of wealth*

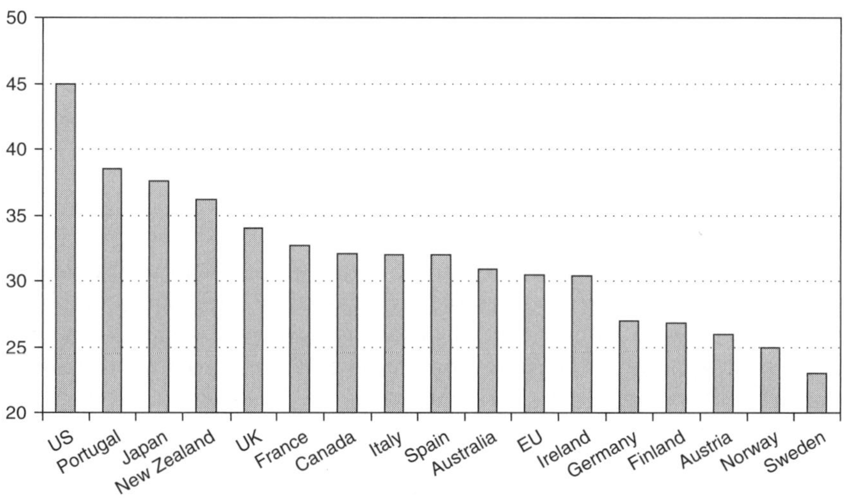

Figure 10.7 *The Gini coefficient for selected OECD countries*

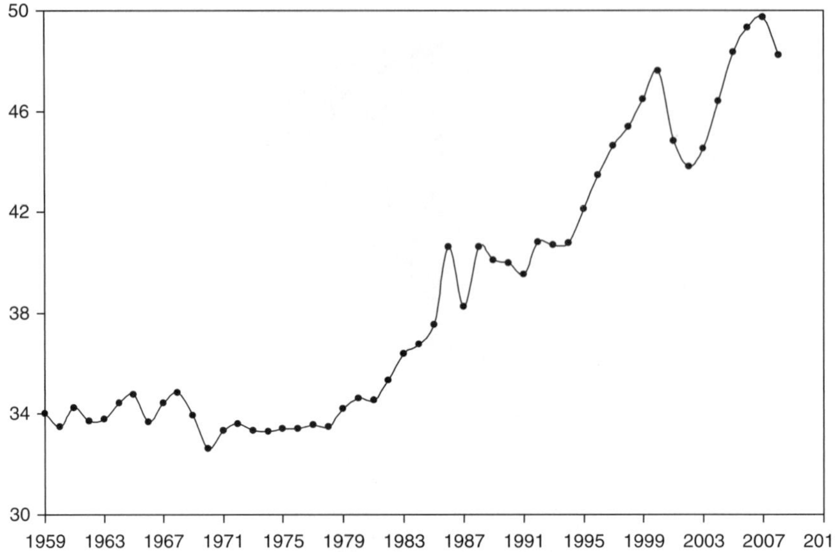

Figure 10.8 The income share of the top 10 per cent

Sweden having the most equitable income distribution. Figure 10.8 shows the income share of the top 10 per cent over the period 1959–2010. While this share was stable during the 1960s and 1970s, it started a rapid upward climb in the 1980s, only declining because of financial crises and stock market crashes. What is more important for our discussion is that Figure 10.9 shows that the relation between the saving rate and income inequality (measured by the income share of the top 10 per cent) is indeed negative.

THE DEMISE OF MANUFACTURING INDUSTRY

An important reason why the US trade deficit is an American problem is that the US no longer produces the manufactured goods imported from China due to the erosion of the industrial base, which free-marketeers consider to be "natural", a phase of economic evolution. These pundits believe that while this change may hurt workers in the doomed sectors, they will over time find more rewarding jobs and benefit from cheap, high-quality imports (Friedman, 2002). Liu (2005c) quotes Alan Greenspan as saying, in a testimony to Congress, that "thinking jobs are better than doing jobs" and that "the US will keep higher-paying jobs in financial services, management, design, development, sales and distribution and let the emerging

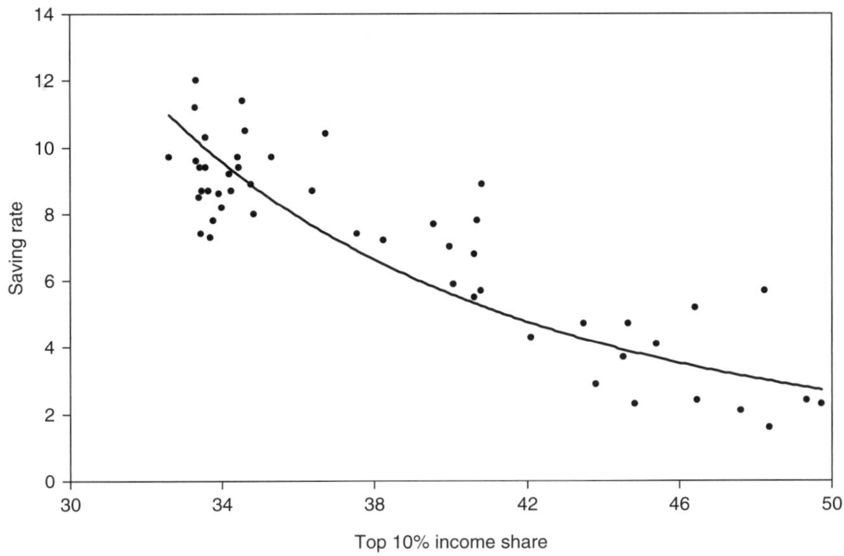

Figure 10.9 The relation between the saving rate and inequality

economies have the low-paying assembly line jobs in factories owned by US companies". If this process is natural and cheap high-quality imports are desirable, why then is China blamed for producing cheap high-quality imports? Liu (2005b) attributes the erosion of the US manufacturing base to "neo-liberal global trade in the last two decades", motivated by dollar hegemony: print dollars and buy the stuff rather than toiling to make it.

Friedman (2002) disagrees with the proposition that it is natural for services to replace manufacturing industry by arguing along the following lines:

> Such beliefs were plausible in 1994–1998, when business-service employment was booming. As millions of jobs in technically demanding work – programming computers, setting up communications systems, for example – were created, business services offset slower growth or job losses in manufacturing. But when manufacturing went into a tailspin in the later 1990s, the business-service growth that powered the healthiest phases of the decade's boom slowed too. Rather than supplant manufacturing, business-service enterprises depended on healthy factories, which, after all, were among their biggest clients.

Friedman is justifiably sarcastic when he points out that "it's hard to imagine how service-sector expansion can play a role in wealth creation if growth in, say, manicurists exceeds that of engineers". And while manufacturing industry lends itself to specialization and economies of scale (hence, rising productivity) the service industry kills productivity because there is no potential for the exploitation of economies of scale and exports.

Krugman (2011b) quotes a Russian immigrant, an engineer by profession, as saying that "America seems very rich . . . but I never see anyone actually making anything". Krugman comments that this statement became increasingly accurate over time, which led him to suggest that "Americans made a living by selling each other houses, which they paid for with money borrowed from China". With respect to manufacturing industry, Krugman asserts that "manufacturing, once America's greatest strength, seemed to be in terminal decline". He actually relates the trade deficit directly to the decline in manufacturing industry by arguing that "the bubble-fueled expansion of the decade's middle years – an expansion marked by a huge rise in the trade deficit – left manufacturing behind". Spence and Hlatshwayo (2011) call for the US economy to find ways to expand employment in traded goods (mostly the output of manufacturing industry) arguing that demand for non-traded goods may not continue to grow at the pace of recent decades. On the other hand, Jagdish Bhagwati thinks that those who argue for boosting manufacturing output suffer from "manufacturing fetish" (*The Economist*, 2011t), arguing that the service industry is as good as manufacturing in generating jobs and boosting exports. This claim, however, is not supported by simple observable facts like the inability of the post-crisis US growth to generate jobs. For the purpose of our discussion here, the following question arises: how can the US, by depending on services, reduce its imports from and boost its exports to China? One wonders if Professor Bhagwati has the answer to this question.

Explaining the Decline

The Congressional Budget Office attributes the decline in manufacturing employment since 2000 to the recession that began in 2001 and the relatively weak recovery in demand that followed (CBO, 2004). The recession, according to the CBO, was "particularly hard on the manufacturing sector, as the demand for goods weakened in both the United States and the rest of the world". The CBO predicted that "even after the economy has fully recovered from the 2001 recession, employment in manufacturing is unlikely to return to its prerecession level". This prediction turned out to be accurate. The CBO identifies a number of long-term factors that have influenced US manufacturing employment, including the following:

- Shift in demand away from manufactured goods, as the share of consumer spending devoted to manufactured goods has declined over time.

- Strong growth in productivity and a slower rate of growth in the demand for manufactured goods have necessarily entailed a decline in the manufacturing sector's share of total employment.
- A portion of the long-term decline in employment in some manufacturing industries can be linked to the expansion of trade and competition from foreign producers. Some observers have specifically attributed recent job losses in manufacturing to a surge in the bilateral trade deficit with China (the usual story).
- The tendency of manufacturing industry to meet short-term fluctuations in demand by hiring temporary workers through agencies and by contracting with outside firms to provide certain support functions (for example, cafeteria, janitorial, and payroll-processing services).

Still, some pundits attribute the decline of manufacturing employment in the US to Chinese policies. For example, Scott (2008) argues that "the growing US trade deficit with China has displaced huge numbers of jobs in the United States and has been a prime contributor to the crisis in manufacturing employment". On the one hand, the shift from manufacturing industry to services is a natural phase in the process of economic evolution. On the other hand, the demise of manufacturing industry, which is caused by China, is regrettable and a blow to the ability of the US economy to create jobs. What are we supposed to believe?

The Facts and Figures

Let us have a look at the facts and figures relating to manufacturing employment and output. Figure 10.10 displays the rise and fall of manufacturing employment over the period 1939–2010 (a trend curve is superimposed). Manufacturing employment reached a high level of 19.3 million in 1978; thereafter it declined persistently to stand at 11.6 million in 2010. Most of this decline occurred between 2000 and 2010 (from 17.2 million to 11.6 million). While it is tempting to think that this decline is "natural", caused by a rise in productivity, the manufacturing output figures do not support this proposition. In Figure 10.11 it is shown that while the dollar value-added of manufacturing industry has been on the rise since 1980, the contribution of this sector to GDP has shrunk to half of its value in 1980. It is surprising, therefore, that the US–China Business Council (2006) casts doubt on the validity of the proposition that US manufacturing industry is in decline on the basis of a rising manufacturing value-added (in dollar terms) and the fact that the US is still the largest manufacturer in the world. The analysis of the US–China Business Council seems to be

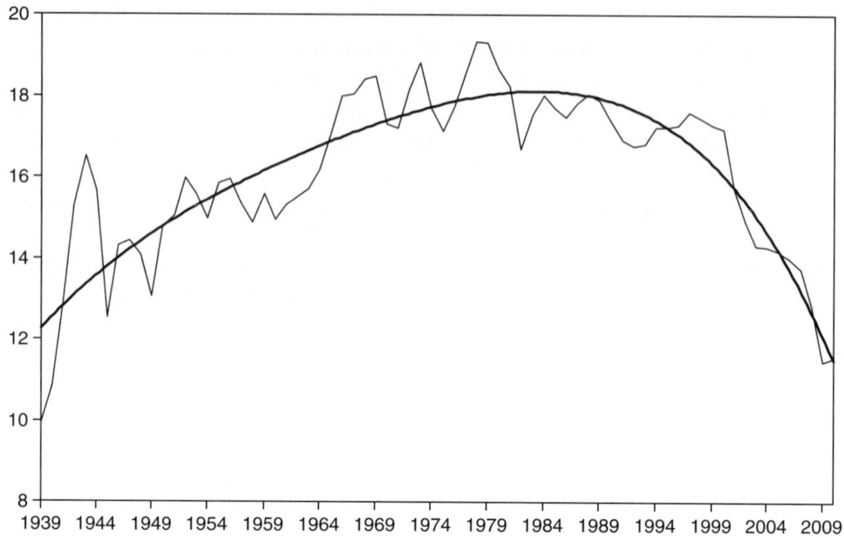

Figure 10.10 Manufacturing employment in the US (million)

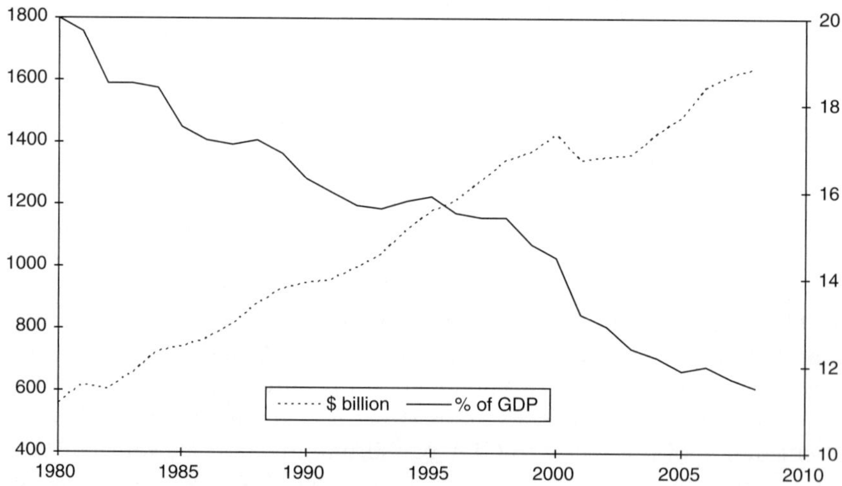

Figure 10.11 Value-added of manufacturing industry ($ billion and as a percentage of GDP)

more diplomatic and reconciliatory than representative of the situation in terms of objective positive economics.

The interpretation of the US–China Business Council is that those who argue that US manufacturing is in decline refer to the long-term decline in manufacturing industry. This is attributed to the "continuing structural economic shift from manufacturing to service industries in the United States, as in all developed nations". Glenn Hubbard, who until March 2003 was chairman of President Bush's Council of Economic Advisers, wrote in *The Wall Street Journal* on 9 September 2003 that "the decline in manufacturing employment resembles that in agriculture in the last century, in which robust productivity growth characterized American performance, and millions of workers exited agriculture for other segments of the economy". This is the natural evolution process referred to earlier. Hawkins (2003) criticizes this view, arguing that the loss of 2.7 million manufacturing jobs between 2000 and 2003 cannot be attributed to higher productivity. In reference to Hubbard's analogy with agriculture, Hawkins argues that "his [Hubbard's] supposed comparison between the pattern of agriculture and manufacturing is cited frequently, but is nonsense when seriously examined". He adds that "the most obvious point is that America has not lost its ability to feed itself, whereas it has lost the ability to provide its people with a substantial share of their manufactured goods". He further argues that "productivity leads to layoffs only if the extra output cannot be sold".

La Botz (2009) argues that "the [US] economy remains stagnant in large measure because during the last several decades the process of globalization has restructured American manufacturing industries in ways that have reduced their weight and significance in the economy and society." He emphasizes the loss of the machine tool industry by arguing that "even more disturbing perhaps than the decline of the auto industry is the decline of the machine tool industry, an industry that stands at the heart of any industrial economy". On the other hand, Butcher (2008) argues that "China's machine tool industry seems to be coming of age globally, driven in large part by the country's rapidly rising machine tool investment, output and exports" and that "in recent years, China's machine tool industry has played an increasingly crucial role in the world machine tool industry". Pope (2009) points out that manufacturing is indispensable, not only in the structure of the American economy, but also in the very culture and fabric of American society. He attributes to manufacturing industry "the tremendous advancement of the American standard of living during a period spanning barely 50 years".

What seems to be a confused understanding of the issue here is that the US remains the world's largest manufacturer, just like it remains the world's largest economy. For example, the *Supply Chain Digest* (2008) quotes John

Engler, the president of the National Association of Manufacturers, as saying that "the US remains by far the world's largest manufacturer, producing nearly one-fourth of the world's industrial output". What matters and what Engler chooses to overlook is that manufacturing industry is shrinking relative to the size of the economy and that America no longer produces the goods that can compete with China. This is how this matter is related to the trade balance issue. Given the current trends, the US will no longer be the largest manufacturer or the largest economy. Maintaining a state of denial will not serve any meaningful purpose.

THE DOMINANCE OF THE FINANCIAL SECTOR

The decline of manufacturing industry in the US, and elsewhere where the American model is cherished, is a consequence of the illusion that as countries mature they shift from manufacturing to services. Financial services, in particular, are thought by some to be an appropriate replacement for manufacturing industry as the backbone of the economy. In the UK, for example, policy makers have been guided (or rather misguided) by the motto "who needs manufacturing industry when we have the City?". There is even the motto "who needs manufacturing industry when we have Wimbledon?". The reality is that a modern economy cannot be run on a sector that is dominated by parasitic activities, which is exactly what the modern financial sector is all about. And while Wimbledon provides entertainment for two weeks every year, it cannot be considered seriously as a major economic "activity" in terms of creating value-added and employment. Let us stick to the financial sector, the US financial sector in particular.

The US economy has changed from a super manufacturing power to one dominated by the financial sector. While the Chinese have been making consumer goods and machine tools, the Americans have been making financial products that have no social value whatsoever and can be destructive as demonstrated by the global financial crisis. While the Chinese have been promoting the products of scientific innovation and engineering, the Americans have been promoting the products of financial engineering: options on futures, futures on options, options on futures on options on swaps, CDOs, CDSs, and so on.

Relevance to the Trade Deficit

The dominance of the financial sector has implications for the trade deficit issue. Consider the following points:

1. Preference for the production of financial assets rather than manufactured goods means that the US does not have import-competing industries. Therefore, even if the revaluation of the yuan works, there is no American substitute for Chinese goods.
2. The outrageous payments received by bankers, financial engineers and traders for engaging in parasitic activities have been a major reason for increasing income inequality. We have already seen that income inequality is associated with a declining saving rate in the US.
3. Excessive private spending has been financed by borrowed funds, which the financial sector provides.
4. Whenever there is a financial crisis caused by financiers and their marvellous products, they claim the "too big to fail" status. The government responds by providing funds to keep failing financial institutions afloat ($750 billion dollars in 2008–9). The result will be rising budget deficit and government debt.
5. Financial crises, which are more severe when the economy is dominated by a disproportionately big financial sector, are typically followed by recessions, during which tax revenue goes down and the government is forced to increase debt.

On the issue of "too big to fail", Alden (2011) points out that "in the midst of the global financial crisis in 2008, the Federal Reserve lent Goldman Sachs, Credit Suisse and Royal Bank of Scotland at least $30 billion each at interest rates as low as 0.01 per cent with no public disclosure of the details". He quotes Dean Baker, co-director of the Center for Economic Policy and Research (Washington), as saying that while the Fed is supposed to be an agency of the government, it has become an agency of the banks.

Sombre Views

Irrespective of whether or not the dominance of the financial sector has implications for the trade deficit, most economists and observers have been alarmed by this phenomenon. Stockman (2010), who is a Republican, describes as "the third ominous change in the American economy" the "unproductive expansion of the financial sector". He expresses his view rather elegantly as follows:

> Republicans have been oblivious to the grave danger of flooding financial markets with freely printed money and, at the same time, removing traditional restrictions on leverage and speculation. As a result, the combined assets of conventional banks and the so-called shadow banking system (including

> investment banks and finance companies) grew from a mere $500 billion in 1970 to $30 trillion by September 2008. But the trillion-dollar conglomerates that inhabit this new financial world are not free enterprises. They are rather wards of the state, extracting billions from the economy with a lot of pointless speculation in stocks, bonds, commodities and derivatives. They could never have survived, much less thrived, if their deposits had not been government-guaranteed and if they hadn't been able to obtain virtually free money from the Fed's discount window to cover their bad bets.

Likewise, Johnson and Kwak (2010) point out that "over the past thirty years, they [bankers] had become one of the wealthiest industries in the history of the American economy, and one of the most powerful political forces in Washington" and that "the ideology of Wall Street – that unfettered innovation and unregulated financial markets were good for America and the World – became the consensus position in Washington on both sides of the political aisle". Johnson (2009) calls the rise to power of the financial sector a "quiet coup".

Cook (2008) argues that "the [US] financial system . . . is bankrupt", describing the situation as a "perfect storm, the result of a 200-year-old financial system where money is largely created by bank lending". He also believes that "the problem politically is that control of the US long ago was turned over to the bankers and the financiers of the Western world". He describes financial deregulation as "the same phenomenon that first created and then ruined the British Empire, and it's what created and is now ruining the American Empire today". Madrick (2011) summarizes his view of the prominence of the financial sector in the title of his book *The Age of Greed: The Triumph of Finance and the Decline of America, 1970 to the Present*. In a review of the book, Cowen (2011) argues that "one can sympathize with Madrick's view that the economic and political ascendancy of finance has been undesirable".

The Obese Sector

The financial sector as a whole has become much larger than can be justified on the basis of its basic function of supporting real economic activity, perhaps too big for the good of the economy – or "too big for its boots", as *The Economist* (2009d) puts it. Philippon (2008) studied the growth of the US financial sector over the period 1860–2007 and concluded that the growth seemed to reflect fundamental economic needs up to 2001, but that it was not clear why the sector kept growing so quickly after 2002. His analysis and consequent conclusion are based on the proposition that financial institutions provide services to households and companies and that the financial sector's share of aggregate income reveals the value that the rest of the economy attaches to these services. Based on a simple model, which attributes changes in the size of the financial sector to corporate demand for financial services, Philippon found that the financial sector was about one percentage point of GDP too big.

The main defect in Philippon's work is the proposition that the size of the financial sector reflects the value that the rest of the economy attaches to financial services. The expansion of the financial sector was sustained even after the wider community started to realize that some products of financial engineering were useless and did not serve any meaningful purpose. This is why Philippon is bewildered by the continued growth of the financial sector after 2001. He actually underestimates the size of the financial sector, and his explanation of its growth in the period since 1980 overlooks an important explanatory factor: financial deregulation.

It is not only the amounts involved that cause concern, it is also the quality of financial services and products that we allocate a tremendous amount of resources to for the benefit of the financial sector and its bosses. Johnson (2009) wonders whether modern finance is more like electricity or more like junk food. "It is more like junk food", Johnson believes. He points out that "there is growing evidence that the vast majority of what happens in and around modern financial markets is much more like junk food – little nutritional value, bad for your health, and a hard habit to kick".

The Government's Love Affair with the Financial Sector

The finance industry, particularly in the US, has lifted itself to super stardom by creating an image, boosted by group think, that a flourishing financial sector necessarily means a flourishing economy. Politicians, including law makers and those in government, have not only embraced this image of the finance industry but also reinforced it. This has been helped by lobbying coupled with political donations and campaign contributions. Igan and Mishra (2011) argue that "lobbying and network connections played an important role in shaping the financial regulatory landscape". The US government contributed to the rising star of finance through changes in monetary policy. In October 1979 the Fed switched policy from interest rate targeting to money supply targeting, making interest rates highly volatile and bond trading rather lucrative, boosting such institutions as Goldman Sachs.

The massive profitability of the finance industry allows financiers to gain political influence, either through the funding of election campaigns or via the desire of the government to protect taxpaying businesses. Johnson (2009) points out that although the finance industry has become one of the top contributors to political campaigns, at the peak of its influence it did not have to buy favours in the way, for example, the tobacco companies or military contractors might have to. Johnson argues that the finance industry "benefited from the fact that Washington insiders already believed that large financial institutions and free-flowing capital markets were crucial to America's position in the world." They were wrong.

One explanation for the love affair between the US government and the finance industry is the movement of personnel from the financial sector to government and vice versa, the so-called "revolving door" between the government and the financial sector. This is what Bhagwati (2009) calls "the Wall Street–Treasury Complex". Robert Rubin, once the co-chairman of Goldman Sachs, served in Washington as Treasury Secretary under Clinton, and later became chairman of Citigroup's executive committee. When he was Treasury Secretary, Mr Rubin was instrumental in the loosening of financial regulation, which made the creation of Citigroup possible by allowing banks to expand far beyond their traditional role and permitting them to profit from a variety of financial activities. He also impeded the tighter oversight of exotic financial products. Rubin is one of many influential figures who have been through the "revolving door", and the man himself is known to have been very harsh on Japan for having a trade surplus with the US.

CONCLUDING REMARKS

In this chapter and the previous one we considered the proposition that the US trade deficit is an American problem, caused by too much debt-financed spending, too little saving, and a changing economic structure away from manufacturing industry. We have also argued that the culture of blaming others for one's own problems is a sign of moral deterioration, which kills the motivation to tackle the causes of the underlying problem (the trade deficit).

Wyplosz (2010) believes that "blaming China today is like blaming Japan in the 1970s and '80s and that every argument that you may hear today about China was made then". At that time, he argues, complaining about Japan manipulating its exchange rate was "a sure vote-getter in the US and pleasure-getter on Capitol Hill". Likewise, Persaud (2010) comments on the same issue by writing:

> We have been here before. Back in the mid-1980s, Detroit blamed its woes not on the inferior quality of American cars, their gas guzzling, or the fact that the Japanese prefer not to carry all their belongings in the back or to have the steering wheel on the left. They blamed the yen–dollar exchange rate.

When Japan eventually caved in and allowed the yen to appreciate, the US current account deficit improved, but only temporarily (and perhaps because of changes in factors other than the exchange rate), while Japan remained in surplus after a temporary reduction. The move, which according to Persaud (2010) "did as little to save Detroit then as a rise in the yuan would do today", has wrecked the Japanese economy, which has not grown since; the Japanese used to call this "the lost decade", and it is now becoming a lost generation. As China emulates Japan's export-led growth strategy, this story is likely to figure prominently on its policy makers' minds, and rightly so (for more detail on this story see Park and Wyplosz, 2010). Ito (2009) discusses the similarities in economic relations with the US of Japan during the 1980s and China during the 2000s.

Wyplosz describes the situation succinctly as follows. While financial deregulation in the US led to a drastic decline in US private savings, which translated in a long-run trend deterioration in the current account balance, China embarked on an export-led strategy. Rapid growth in China put continuously more income in the hands of large firms that started to save more as they could not invest fast enough to absorb their resources. This translated into a long-run trend rise in China's current account. Wyplosz insists that the exchange rate is "not a necessary ingredient in the story". In short, China has been doing what is good for its economy, but the US deficit has been inflicted on America by itself.

11. Concluding thoughts

MYTHS, FACTS AND FIGURES

The title of this book is *The US–China Trade Dispute: Facts, Figures and Myths*. Throughout the ten previous chapters we came across numerous myths, facts and figures, some of which will be spelled out in this chapter. The words "myths" and "facts" are typically used in articles on the US–China trade dispute, but it is frequently the case that the proclaimed facts are actually myths, and vice versa. The transformation of facts into myths and myths into facts follows from the ideologically-driven desire to prove a pre-conceived idea – on this occasion the idea that China is indulging in wrong-doing.

Some of the genuine underlying myths have been identified by *The Economist* (2007b); these myths pertain to the proposition that revaluation of the yuan will work. The four myths are stated as follows:

1. There is overwhelming evidence that the yuan is grossly undervalued.
2. China's sharp increase in trade surplus is due to expansion in cheap imports.
3. Imports from China destroy jobs and harm the American economy.
4. Revaluation of the yuan will greatly reduce America's trade deficit.

The first of the four myths identified by *The Economist* is a myth because the evidence for the alleged yuan undervaluation is weak, fragmented and mixed. For a long time it was established that the yuan was undervalued because *The Economist*'s Big Mac index said so. Not any more: by modifying the Big Mac index to take into account the effect of per capita income, the index no longer indicates undervaluation. Claiming that the yuan is undervalued because things are cheap in China, because China has massive foreign exchange reserves, because China has a large trade surplus, and because China intervenes actively in the foreign exchange market is nothing short of ideologically-motivated travesty. The so-called "formal" evidence for yuan undervaluation is the product of model manipulation, with the objective of proving that the yuan is indeed undervalued.

Myth number 2 is a myth because, according to *The Economist* (2007b), "the main reason for the bigger trade surplus was a sharp slowdown in the annual growth rate of imports". The slowdown can be accounted for by the decline in the imports of steel, aluminium, chemicals and machinery. As to the third myth that imports from China destroy American jobs, it is strange that this claim was made long before the global financial crisis and the Great Recession, when the US unemployment rate was 4.5 per cent. Myth number 4 is described by *The Economist* (2007b) as "the biggest myth of all". The simplest justification for why this is a myth is that "there is little overlap between American and Chinese production, so that American goods cannot replace Chinese imports". Moosa (2011c) suggests seven different reasons why revaluation of the yuan will not work – hence seven different explanations for the "biggest myth of all".

Cline (2010a) uses the word "myth" to describe two observations: (i) the exchange rate does not affect the US–China trade balance; and (ii) the US no longer makes things that can compete with Chinese products imported by the US. By claiming that these facts are myths, he chooses to ignore theory, intuition, stylized facts, empirical evidence and just simple figures. For example, he claims that those who cast doubt on the feasibility of correcting the US–China trade imbalance by revaluing the yuan fail to recognize the lagged effect of the exchange rate in driving trade. He wrongly argues that the improvement of the bilateral trade balance of the US with China in 2009 was caused by the revaluation of the yuan in 2005 and its gradual appreciation since then. It is unlikely that Cline is in a position to use the same twisted logic to explain why the bilateral imbalance deteriorated in 2010, although the explanation does not need a macroeconomist of the calibre of John Maynard Keynes. It was the income effect resulting from the recovery of the US economy that led to the 2010 deterioration of the US trade balance. Cline's second myth is actually a fact used by *The Economist* (2007b) to explain his first myth. He chooses to ignore the fact that US manufacturing unemployment has been shrinking rapidly, not because of rising productivity but because of dwindling contribution to GDP. The fact that the US still produces more manufacturing output than China is irrelevant because what we are talking about here is changes over time. The US will cease to be the biggest producer of manufactured goods, just as it will no longer have the largest economy in the world. Reid (2010) talks about three myths that are truly myths, pertaining to the preposterous claim that tax cuts reduce the budget deficit, as the Republicans try to mislead people to believe.

Now consider some of the proclaimed facts that are actually myths. The following are examples (the facts/myths are in italics, followed by comments or responses):

- *There is no serious debate about whether China's currency is undervalued against the US dollar. There is a general consensus among economists that the Chinese yuan is undervalued by as much as 40 per cent against the US dollar*. This is a myth because there is indeed serious debate about the issue of yuan undervaluation, although China bashers choose to ignore the other side of the story. Putting the yuan undervaluation at 40 per cent has become a tradition, since the figure was first mentioned by *The Economist* magazine on the basis of the conventional Big Mac index. Those claiming this to be a fact overlook the observation that since July 2011, when the modified big Mac index was developed, *The Economist* no longer claims that the yuan is undervalued.
- *China's currency remains substantially undervalued. The reforms adopted by China in July 2005 have resulted in only a small increase in the yuan's value vis-à-vis the US dollar. China still keeps the yuan's value from rising to levels that reflect a market-based value.* This is a myth because the yuan has appreciated by over 20 per cent in nominal terms and some 50 per cent in real terms since 2005. If the market warrants the yuan to be at a higher value, the Chinese authorities cannot prevent that from happening. The foreign exchange market (or that portion involving the yuan) is too big for the resources of any central bank, including the Chinese central bank.
- *China's undervalued currency has serious implications for the global economy. Recognizing this global impact, leaders in the major world economies as well as the International Monetary Fund and the Asian Development Bank have all urged China to infuse greater flexibility into its exchange rate system*. This is a myth because, according to the arguments for and against flexible exchange rates, China has more to lose by adopting flexible rather than fixed exchange rates. Calls on China to infuse flexibility by the IMF and others are politically motivated, the outcome of pressure by the US. At the end, exchange rate regime choice is a sovereign decision.
- *Undervaluation of the yuan has a demonstrable trade effect on US manufactured goods. The low value of the yuan makes Chinese exports cheaper in the US and US exports more expensive in China than they otherwise would be*. This is a myth because the causal link between the exchange rate and the trade balance is not straightforward. It is a fact that Chinese firms use the dollar as the currency of invoicing and this practice on its own is sufficient to sever the link between the exchange rate and trade balance.
- *A broad cross-section of US manufacturers have cited overwhelming evidence of job losses, plant closures, bankruptcies, and weakened*

financial performance due to price constraints influenced by the large influx of low-priced Chinese imports into their markets. This is a myth because the US no longer produces goods that can compete with Chinese exports. Even if that were not the case, Chinese products will still be competitive. Is it not a principle of free trade not to complain about cheap foreign goods? And is it not true that the Washington Consensus, an American-designed set of doctrines, has free trade as one of its commandments?

- *The US administration, lawmakers, and even the Chinese government agree that China's existing exchange rate system is not sustainable and systemic reforms are needed to fix the problem. Delay in introducing additional exchange rate flexibility is unjustified given the strength of the Chinese economy and the progress in China's transition. China needs to move quickly to introduce exchange rate flexibility at a far faster pace than it has done to date*. This is a myth because there is no evidence to indicate that China will benefit from a rapid appreciation of its currency. To be sure of that, just ponder the Japanese experience since Japan yielded to pressure to allow its currency to be excessively strong.

Consider now the following statements that are portrayed to be facts when in fact they are mere rhetoric (Huber, 2011):

- *The cheap yuan gives China an unfair advantage in the export market, encouraging the US growing trade deficit with China and keeping goods in markets like India from competing locally*. China is competitive not because of the exchange rate but because of cheap factors of production.
- *Holding so much US currency gives China a lot of power over the dollar, and thus the US economy. What if China's central bank decided to sell a large amount of US dollars and Treasury notes all at once? The dollar could drop, leaving the US economy gasping for breath.* This is really strange: China is damned if it does and damned if it does not. If China does not hold US Treasury securities, it will be accused of depriving the US from the capital flows necessary to finance its trade deficit. If China holds US securities then it has power over the US dollar. And why complain about the dollar dropping? Is not this what China bashers want? And is it not the case that the dollar has been dropping because of quantitative easing, which has nothing to do with China?
- *Unnaturally cheap goods and services from China hurt growing economies like India. India has a trade deficit of $19.2 billion with China.*

India has the potential to manufacture and sell lower priced goods, if the rupee could compete with the yuan. India crops up again, in the spirit of proclaiming that China is hurting not only the US but the whole of the "international community".

- *By making other currencies relatively expensive, the booming Chinese population is discouraged from importing goods from other countries, including India, the US and Europe, because the cost is artificially inflated. This restricts a balance in trade and increases other countries' trade deficits with China.* Really? How then do we explain the success of Germany in Chinese markets? Simply because the Germans still make good stuff that the Chinese like to buy. China is not competitive because of the exchange rate and neither is Germany. The difference is that China is competitive on a price basis and Germany is competitive on a quality basis. If China and Germany can do it, there is no reason why other countries cannot do it instead of just blaming trade imbalances on China.
- *When currency is kept undervalued it leads to inflation, from which China suffers. As China powers their export economy through a weak yuan, other sectors of their economy suffer. If the Chinese had to compete with goods and services on an even playing field, they may be forced to improve quality and safety. This would be good for their economy in the long run and improve the safety of goods world-wide.* What is difficult to understand is complaining about inflation in China; inflation will, with the passage of time, bring about the currency appreciation that the US is demanding from China.

MORE MYTHS, FACTS AND FIGURES

Consider now some additional facts and figures that we have come across in earlier chapters. Let us start with the myths:

- *A strong yuan is good for China.* This is not necessarily true for a simple reason: the majority of Chinese imports are dollar-dominated commodities. As a general principle, no country wants to see its currency too weak or too strong.
- *A strong yuan is good for the US and the rest of the world.* Assuming for the sake of argument that Chinese firms use foreign currency invoicing, a stronger yuan will make Chinese goods more expensive for everyone. Moreover, US firms will get fewer yuan per dollar of FDI.

- *Expenditure switching policies work.* This proposition is not supported by intuition, stylized facts, theory or formal evidence. For the revaluation of the yuan to work, an incredible set of assumptions must be satisfied, as we saw in previous chapters.
- *Chinese policies are hampering the recovery of the world economy.* China is using policies that all developed countries used when they were in a similar stage of development. If recovery is hampered because the Chinese are exporting too much, then other countries should stop buying Chinese goods. It is up to them.
- *Intervention in the foreign exchange market is currency manipulation.* Intervention is not illegal and it has been used even by countries claiming to adopt free floating. The so-called "manipulation" is in fact a requirement of the adoption of a fixed exchange rate regime, which is allowed by Article IV of the IMF charter.
- *Chinese policies are immoral and illegal.* There is nothing illegal or immoral about adopting a fixed exchange rate arrangement or an export-led growth strategy.
- *A trade surplus indicates undervaluation of the currency.* This is a proposition that is not supported by the stylized facts.
- *The yuan is undervalued because things are cheap in China.* Things are cheap in China because of cheap factors of production. Actually not everything is cheap in China (for example, five star hotels and meals are expensive). The exchange rate has nothing to do with it.
- *The yuan would appreciate if it were not for intervention.* To assert that the yuan would appreciate if left to market forces means that it is necessarily undervalued, but we do not know that. And if that were the case, intervention would not prevent its appreciation.
- *Chinese policies are not good for China.* Only China decides what is good or not good for its economy and its people.
- *China should switch to consumption-led growth.* There is no such thing as consumption-led growth. High consumption means low saving, which would have an adverse effect on investment and growth.
- *A fixed exchange rate is bad for China.* Not in terms of the arguments for and against fixed and flexible exchange rates.
- *Exchange rate misalignment can be measured with a reasonable degree of accuracy.* Formal measures of exchange rate alignments are not the product of science, they are based on models and procedures that are not robust with respect to a number of factors, including model specification.

- *The J-curve effect explains why the US trade deficit has not improved following the revaluation of the yuan in 2005*. The J-curve effect is not even an empirical regularity.

Now consider the facts, where a fact may be a well-supported proposition:

- *Economics is not physics*. We cannot use econometric models to reach the conclusion that the yuan is undervalued and that undervaluation of the yuan is the reason for the US deficit, then start a trade war on that basis. The miserable state of exchange rate economics is not conducive to the enhancement of our ability to determine the equilibrium exchange rate.
- *Blaming others for one's own problems is a major driver for the claims that Chinese policies are responsible for the poor performance of the US economy*. Apportioning blame goes hand-in-hand with the attitude of "do as I say" and ambivalence towards many things such as free trade and fixed exchange rates.
- *A small dose of an effective remedy should produce results*. With a 50 per cent real appreciation of the yuan since 2005 the US trade deficit should have narrowed.
- *The US trade deficit is an American problem*. It is caused by too much debt, too much spending, too little tax revenue, too little saving and the dismantling of manufacturing industry.
- *High saving is symptomatic of catching-up economies, hence the Chinese cannot be blamed for saving too much*. There are numerous specific and legitimate reasons why the Chinese save.
- *China has contributed to the great moderation by suppressing world inflation*. If anything, we should be grateful to China for that.
- *Chinese firms use the dollar as the currency of invoicing*. This on its own provides a formidable reason why revaluation of the yuan will not work.
- *The relation between the trade balance and the exchange rate is ambiguous*. In causal terms the relation could go either way, and when it is contemplated that the trade balance affects the exchange rate, the relation turns out to be positive. For all we know, the association is spurious as both are determined jointly by other factors.
- *There are more reasons to believe that fixed exchange rates are better for China*. Robert Mundell has come up with 12 different reasons why this is the case, many more than what advocates of flexible rates for China have come up with.
- *Pegging the yuan to the dollar has been an important element of the stabilization policies pursued since China opened up to the rest of the*

world. This is because a dollar peg provides a monetary anchor for price stability by linking domestic monetary policy to the inflation rate of a large, non-inflationary economy.

- *China has the last say on its policies, exchange rate and the like*. The Chinese people have the right to determine their consumption–saving balance, to say the least. China's high saving rate has been instrumental for Chinese economic development and the transition from a planned low-income economy to a market-based middle-income economy.
- *The US budget deficit and public debt constitute a major problem that threatens the long-term prospects of the US economy*. The budget deficit is both a spending and a revenue problem, and unless it is recognized as such, America's fiscal mess will persist.

Let us now recall some of the figures we came across throughout this book. Perhaps the most crucial figure is that the yuan has appreciated by 50 per cent in real terms since 2005. China bashers do not realize this, or choose to ignore it. Once the author of this book had a discussion with a self-proclaimed "China expert" who disputed this figure because he had never seen it. While this figure can be found in *The Economist* (2010c), anyone with basic knowledge of economics will not find it difficult to believe. Between 2005 and 2010, the yuan appreciated by over 20 per cent in nominal terms. During the same period costs and prices were rising much faster in China than in the US. Add the nominal appreciation to the inflation or unit labour cost growth differential and you will get the magical 50 per cent. The importance of this figure is that it shows that revaluation of the yuan has not and will not work.

Another set of figures pertains to the extent of yuan undervaluation, which has been put at anywhere between 70 per cent and zero (some studies even found overvaluation). If anything, the dispersion of these figures shows that the yuan's undervaluation is anyone's guess. The figures also show that China's surplus with the US is 3.95 per cent of its GDP, which is higher for Israel (4), Malaysia (4.56) and Mexico (5.58). Even China's total surplus is not that big when measured relative to GDP: for China the surplus/GDP ratio is 3.37, which is lower than that for Thailand (3.76), Germany (5.97), Singapore (12.99) and Norway (19.95). Likewise, China's reserve holdings are not that big if measured relative to the size of the economy: the ratio of China's reserves to GDP is 4.6 per cent, which falls behind Thailand (5.1), Singapore (10.2) and Hong Kong (11.7). Furthermore, numerous figures have been presented to show that changes in exchange rates do not affect trade volumes, indicating that expenditure switching policies, implemented through changes in exchange rates, do not work.

THE FEAR OF CHINA

The trade dispute between the US and China is part of a bigger picture – the fear of China and apprehension about its expanding role in the world economy. All of a sudden, US policy makers have lost their taste for what Liu (2005b) calls the "socio-economic Darwinism of survival of the fittest" because "the US is no longer the fittest and the survival of US hegemony is at stake". To the neo-conservatives, who believe that war is the way out of any dispute, China may have to be stopped by war.

Take, for example, the fuss that was made about the launch in 2011 of the first Chinese aircraft carrier. China's desire to acquire an aircraft carrier is motivated not only by being until now the only permanent member of the Security Council without one, but also because India has one, so does Thailand (Japan has a carrier for helicopters that can be adapted for fighters). The neo-cons choose to overlook the fact that "unlike the Soviets, the Chinese appear not to be trying to match the size and capability of America's huge fleet" (*The Economist*, 2011u).

It is only natural for China to play an important role in the world economy. The country has the world's largest population, an ancient culture and a long history. Furthermore, the Chinese culture commands a close affinity with the population of Asia, the main concentration of the world's population, and is now a revived focal point of global geopolitics. Liu (2005b) correctly argues that "an internationally-engaged China will be a positive force for world peace and prosperity". Liu predicts that China will "impact traditional international economic relations to restructure residual prejudicial racial enmity and Cold War geopolitical alliances and give rise to a new mode of world order free of residual racial phobia and obsolete ideological conflicts". Unfortunately the US is in a state of denial with respect to the growing international role of China, even with regard to what for some are trivial matters. For example, most Americans refuse to acknowledge the fact that China won the 2008 Olympic Games, claiming (on the basis of faulty measures) that the US did.

The US is playing with fire by trying to form a coalition against China. We have already seen that a traditionally faithful ally of the US, Australia, refused to take part in a conference to frame China for economic crimes against humanity. Usually dependable US allies such as the UK, France, Germany, Japan, and even Israel, are experiencing rising conflicts with US policy on China. While the US is demanding unequivocal support from its allies for its anti-Chinese stance, these countries feel that they have a lot to lose by alienating China. It is not only countries but also institutions and people. In the US Goldman Sachs and its former boss, Henry Paulson, have been less antagonistic towards China than others, even when Paulson was the US Treasury Secretary. For this reason he was criticized by the anti-China hawks as being "too soft" on China and for "not standing up to the challenge".

THE MORAL OF THE STORY

The US–China trade dispute is similar to the dispute between a (fictional) friend of mine and his butcher. My friend, who is an economist like me, has been complaining about his trade deficit with the butcher because he buys a lot of meat from the butcher but the butcher does not buy anything from my friend. My friend accuses the butcher of causing the trade deficit because the meat is so reasonably priced that my friend, who really likes meat, buys a lot of it. The deficit of my friend with the butcher has been increasing over time because of his increasing meat intake.

Since my friend believes that the butcher is the cause of the trade deficit, he gives the butcher an ultimatum: "do something about the deficit or else". The butcher is not sure what to do: he can either raise the price of meat so that my friend reduces consumption or start buying economics lessons from his customer, the economist. Neither of these potential courses of action seems to make sense from the perspective of the butcher: raising the price of meat may hurt his bottom line as other meat lovers reduce their consumption, and he is not interested at all in buying economics lessons. The first course of action is unlikely to solve the problem because my friend is an enthusiastic meat lover – meaning that his demand for meat is price inelastic.

What my friend seems to overlook is that the trade deficit with the butcher is a problem of his own making and that he can only reduce the deficit by a drastic change in life style. For him it is unimaginable to become a vegetarian, which is the only way to eliminate the deficit. If he chooses to declare a trade war on his butcher and to buy meat from another butcher, he will still have a trade deficit with the other butcher, because butchers are not interested in spending hard-earned money on economics lessons. I have advised my friend to cut down on the consumption of meat (which will be good for his health) as a measure to reduce his deficit with the butcher. Unless and until my friend is convinced that the trade deficit with the butcher is his problem and that he is the only one who can deal with it, the deficit will persist and so will the acrimonious relationship between him and the butcher.

That is the moral of the story. America must accept the reality that the trade deficit is a problem of its own making and that solving this problem requires a drastic change of lifestyle. Revaluation of the yuan will not correct the deficit, neither will the threat of a trade war. So far the trade war has been a cold trade war. Let us at least hope that it remains so without unnecessary escalation that will benefit no one. Let us also hope that Henry Liu's article title 'Trade wars can lead to shooting wars' remains an article title and does not in time become a description of a fearsome reality.

References

Aaron, H.J., W.G. Gale and P.R. Orszag (2004), "Meeting the revenue challenge", in M. Rivlin and I. Sawhill (eds), *Restoring Fiscal Sanity*, Washington, DC: Brookings Institution Press.

ABC (2010), "World on verge of currency war: Robb", 10 October, accessed at www.abc.net.au/news/stories/2010/10/10/3034176.htm?section=justin.

Agbola, F.W. (2004), "Does devaluation improve trade balance of Ghana?", University of Newcastle School of Policy working paper, accessed at www.isser.org/publications/older/Devaluation_Agbola.pdf.

Ahearne, A., W. Cline, K.T. Lee, C. Park, J. Pisani-Ferry and J. Williamson (2007), "Global imbalances: time for action", policy brief 07-4, Peterson Institute for International Economics.

Ahn, D. (2010), "Is the contemporary Chinese exchange rate regime WTO-legal?", *Vox*, 16 April, accessed at www.voxeu.org/index.php?q=node/4867.

Aiyar, S. (2009), "An International Monetary Fund currency to rival the dollar?", Washington DC: Cato Institute.

Akita, S. and N.J. White (2009), *The International Order of Asia in the 1930s and 1950s*, Farnham: Ashgate.

Alden, W. (2011), "Federal Reserve lending revelations intensify criticism of Central Bank secrecy", *Huffpost Business*, 26 May.

Alexander, S.S. (1952), "Effects of devaluation on a trade balance", *IMF Staff Papers*, **2**, 263–78.

Al-Eyd, A., R. Barrell and O. Pomerantz (2005), "Dollars and deficits: the US current account deficit and its exchange rate consequences", *National Institute Economic Review*, **191**, 31–6.

Allard, G.J. and P.H. Lindert (2006), "Euro-productivity and Euro-job since the 1960s: which institutions really mattered", National Bureau of Economic Research working paper no. 12460, August.

Alloway, T. (2009), "Questioning the J-curve", March, accessed at http://ftalphaville.ft.com/blog/2009/03 /11/53462/questioning-the-j-curve/.

Ando, A. and F. Modigliani (1963), "The life cycle hypothesis of saving: aggregate implications and tests", *American Economic Review*, **53**, 55–84.

Auerbach, A.J. (2002), "The Bush tax cut and national saving", *National Tax Journal*, September.

Backus, D. and T. Cooley (2010), "Global 'imbalances' and the crisis", *Wall Street Journal*, 11 January.

Bahmani-Oskooee, M. and J. Alse (1994), "Short-run versus long-run effects of devaluation: error correction modelling and cointegration", *Eastern Economic Journal*, **20**, 453–64.

Bahmani-Oskooee, M. and S.W. Hegerty (2010), "The J- and S-curves: a survey of the recent literature", *Journal of Economic Studies*, **37**, 580–96.

Bahmani-Oskooee, M. and A. Ratha (2004), "The J-curve: a literature review", *Applied Economics*, **36**, 1377–98.

Balassa, B. (1964), "The purchasing power parity doctrine: a reappraisal", *Journal of Political Economy*, **72**, 584–96.

Bank for International Settlements (2005), "Foreign exchange market intervention in emerging markets: motives, techniques and implications", *BIS Papers*, no. 24, May.

Bank for International Settlements (2010), "Triennial central bank survey of foreign exchange and derivatives market activity in 2010: final results", accessed at www.bis.org/publ/rpfxf10t.htm.

Bartlett, B. (2009), "The 81% tax increase to pay for government's promises on social security and medicare", *Forbes*, 14 May.

Bartolini, L. and A. Lahiri (2006), "Twin deficits, twenty years later", *Current Issues in Economics and Finance*, no. 12, October.

Bastiat, F. (1848), *Selected Essays on Political Economy*, published by The Foundation for Economic Education (1995), accessed at www.econlib.org/library/Bastiat/basEss0.html.

Baxter, M. (1995), "International trade and business cycles", in G.M. Grossman and K. Rogoff (eds), *Handbook of International Economics*, vol. 3, Amsterdam: North-Holland, pp. 1801–64.

Bean, C. (2009), "The great moderation, the great panic and the great contraction", The Schumpeter Lecture, given at The Annual Congress of the European Economic Association, Barcelona, 25 August.

Beattie, A. (2011), "IMF casts doubt on renminbi rise", *Financial Times*, 21 July.

Beattie, A., J. Chaffin and K. Brown (2010), "Wen warns against renmibi pressure", *Financial Times*, 6 October.

Bergsten, C.F. (2007), "The dollar and the renminbi", statement to the hearing on US Economic Relations with China, Committee on Banking, Housing and Urban Affairs, United States Senate, 23 May.

Bergsten, C.F. (2009), "The dollar and the deficits: how Washington can prevent the next crisis", *Foreign Affairs*, **88**, November/December.

Bergsten, C.F. (2010a), "Correcting the Chinese exchange rate: an action plan", testimony before the Committee on Ways and Means, United States House of Representatives, 24 March, accessed at www.piie.com/publications/testimony/testimony.cfm?ResearchID =1523.

Bergsten, C.F. (2010b), "New imbalances will threaten global recovery", *Financial Times*, 10 June.

Bernanke, B.S. (2005), "The global saving glut and the US current account deficit", remarks by Federal Reserve System Governor Ben S. Bernanke at the Sandridge Lecture, Virginia Association of Economists, Richmond, Virginia, 10 March, accessed at www.federalreserve.gov/boarddocs/speeches/2005/200503102/default.htm.

Bernanke, B.S. (2008), "Remarks on the economic outlook", International Monetary Conference, Barcelona, 3 June.

Bernanke, B.S. (2010), "Achieving fiscal sustainability", speech to the National Commission on Fiscal Responsibility and Reform, 27 April, accessed at www.federalreserve.gov/newsevents/speech/bernanke20100427a.htm.

Bernard, A. (2008), "Chinese exporters, exchange rate exposure, and the value of the renminbi", Tuck School of Business at Dartmouth working paper, February, accessed at http://mba.tuck.dartmouth.edu/ pages/faculty/andrew.bernard/xrchina.pdf.

Betts, C. and M. Devereux (2000), "Exchange rate dynamics in a model of pricing-to-market", *Journal of International Economics*, **50**, 215–44.

Bhagwati, J. (2009), "Feeble critiques: capitalism's petty detractors", *World Affairs*, Fall, accessed at www.worldaffairsjournal.org/articles/2009-Fall/full-Bhagwati-Fall-2009.html.

Bibow, J. (2008), "The international monetary (non-) order and the global capital flows paradox", The Levy Economics Institute and Skidmore College working paper 531, April.

Bini-Smaghi, L. (2008), "The financial crisis and global imbalances: two sides of the same coin", speech to the Asia-Europe Economic Forum, Beijing, 9 December.

Bivens, J. and R.E. Scott (2006), "China manipulates its currency: a response is needed", Economic Policy Institute Research and Ideas for Shared Prosperity, 25 September, accessed at www.epi.org/publications/entry/pm116/.

Blanchard, O. and G.M. Milesi-Ferretti (2009), "Global imbalances: in midstream?", *IMF Staff Position Note*, 09/29, 22 December.

Blanchard, O., G. Dell'Ariccia and P. Mauro (2010), "Rethinking macroeconomic policy", *IMF Staff Position Note,* 10/03, 12 February.

Bloomberg (2010a), "Currency tensions may be curbed with IMF help, Strauss-Kahn says", 8 October, accessed at http://www.bloomberg.com/news/2010-10-08/global-currency-tensions-may-be-curbed-with-imf-rep orts-strauss-kahn-says.html.

Bloomberg (2010b), "Global finance chiefs seeking to soothe not solve currency war", 8 October, accessed at http://www.bloomberg.com/news/2010-10-08/global-finance-chiefs-seeking-to-soothe-not-solve-currency-war-at-imf.html.

Bloomberg (2010c), "Finance leaders call for IMF role in averting protectionist currency war", accessed at www.bloomberg.com/news/2010-10-09/finance-leaders-call-for-imf-role-in-averting-protectionist-currency-war-.html.

Boehner, J. (2011), "Washington has a spending problem that hurts job creation, not a revenue problem", 13 April, accessed at http://johnboehner.house.gov/News/DocumentSingle .aspx?DocumentID=236233.

Bordo, M.D. and A.J. Schwartz (1991), "What has foreign market intervention since the Plaza Agreement accomplished?", NBER working paper no. 3562.

Buffett, W. (2003a), "America's growing trade deficit is selling the nation", *Fortune*, 10 November, accessed at http://www.independent.ie/business/world/buffett-trade-deficit-could-pell-turmoil-118449.html.

Buffett, W. (2003b), "Dividend voodoo", *Washington Post*, 20 May.

Buffett, W. (2006), "Trade deficit could spell 'turmoil'", 19 January, accessed at www.independent.ie/business/world/buffett-trade-deficit-could-spell-turmoil-118449.html.

Buiter, W. and E. Rahbari (2011), "The 'strong dollar' policy of the US: Alice-in-Wonderland semantics vs. economic reality", *Global Economic Views*, Citibank, 26 May.

Business Today (2011), "US trade deficit broadens sharply", accessed at www.businesstoday-eg.com/economy-policies/united-states/us-trade-deficit-broadens-sharply.html.

Butcher, D.R. (2008), "China's machine tool industry coming of age", *Industry Market Trends*, 23 July, accessed at http://news.thomasnet.com/IMT/archives/2008/07/china-machine-tool-industry-coming-of-age-investment-output-export.html.

Butler, C. (2010), "Geithner advocates a weak dollar policy", *Daily Reckoning*, 20 October, accessed at http://dailyreckoning.com/geithner-advocates-a-weak-dollar-policy/.

Caballero, R. and A. Krishnamurthy (2009), "Global imbalances and financial fragility", NBER working paper no. 14688, January.

Caballero, R., E. Farhi and P.O. Gourinchas (2008), "Financial crash, commodity prices and global imbalances", CEPR discussion paper no. 7064.

Calvo, G.A. and C.M. Reinhart (2002), "Fear of floating", *Quarterly Journal of Economics*, **117**, 379–408.

Campa, J. and L. Goldberg (2005), "Exchange rate pass-through into import prices", *Review of Economics and Statistics*, **87**, 679–90.

Cantor, E. (2011), "Spending, not revenue, is the problem", 24 February, accessed at www.cbsnews.com/stories/2011/04/13/earlyshow/main 20053445.shtml.

Cappiello, L. and G. Ferrucci (2008), "The sustainability of China's exchange rate policy and capital account liberalization", European Central Bank occasional paper series no. 82, March.

Carney, M. (2010), "Restoring faith in the international monetary system", *Spruce Meadows Changing Fortunes Round Table*, 10 September.

Cavallo, M. (2005a), "Understanding the twin deficits: new approaches, new results", *FRBSF Economic Letter*, no. 2005–16, July.

Cavallo, M. (2005b), "Government consumption expenditures and the current account", Federal Reserve Bank of San Francisco working paper 2005–03, accessed at http://www.frbsf.org/publications/econom ics/ papers/2005/wp05-03bk.pdf.

CBO (Congressional Budget Office) (2000), "Causes and consequences of the trade deficit: an overview", accessed at www.cbo.gov/doc. cfm?index=1897&type=0.

CBO (2001), "The budget and economic outlook: update", August, accessed at ftp://ftp.cbo.gov/30xx/doc 3019/EntireReport.pdf.

CBO (2004), "What accounts for the decline in manufacturing employment?", 18 February.

CBO (2005), "Analyzing the economic and budgetary effects of a 10 per cent cut in income tax rates", *Economic and Budget Issue Briefs*, 1 December.

CBO (2008), "Options for responding to short-term economic weakness", January.

CBO (2010), "Federal debt and the risk of a fiscal crisis", *Economic and Budget Issues in Brief*, 27 July.

CBO (2011), "Budget and economic outlook: historical budget data", January 2011, accessed at www.cbo.gov/ftpdocs/120xx/doc12039/ HistoricalTables%5B1%5D.pdf.

CBS News (2006), "America the bankrupt: GAO head takes fiscal show on the road to warn of trouble ahead", 28 October.

Cecchetti, S.G., M.S. Mohanty and F. Zampolli (2010), "The future of public debt: prospects and implications", BIS working paper no. 300, 26 March.

Chamon, M. and E. Prasad (2010), "Why are saving rates of urban households in China rising?", *American Economic Journal*, **2**, 93–130.

Chang, H-J. (2002), "Kicking away the ladder", *Post-Autistic Economics Review*, no. 15, accessed at www.paecon.net/PAEtexts/Chang1.htm.

Chen, J. (2007), "Behavioral equilibrium exchange rate and misalignment of renminbi: a recent empirical study", paper presented at the 6th

International Conference on the Chinese Economy, 18–19 October, Paris.
Cheng, F. and D. Orden (2005), "Exchange rate misalignment and its effects on agricultural producer support estimates: empirical evidence from India and China", MTID discussion paper no. 81.
Cheung, Y-W., M.D. Chinn and E. Fujii (2008), "Pitfalls in measuring exchange rate misalignment: the yuan and other currencies", NBER working paper no. 14168.
Cheung, Y-W., M.D. Chinn and E. Fujii (2009), "China's current account and exchange rate", NBER working paper no. 14673, January.
Chinn, M.D. (2004), "Incomes, exchange rates and the US trade deficit, once again", *International Finance*, **7**, 451–69.
Chinn, M.D. (2005), "Getting serious about the twin deficits", Council on Foreign Relations special report no. 10, September.
Chinn, M.D., Y.W. Cheung and E. Fujii (2006), "Why the renminbi might be overvalued (but probably isn't)", University of Wisconsin, Madison, September, accessed at www.ssc.wisc.edu/~mchinn/RMB_paper.pdf.
Clark, P.B. and R. MacDonald (1999), "Exchange rates and economic fundamentals: a methodological comparison of BEERs and FEERs", in R. Macdonald and J. Stein (eds), *Equilibrium Exchange Rates*, Norwell, MA: Kluwer Academic Publishers.
Cline, W.R. (2005), *The United States as a Debtor Nation*, Washington, DC: Institute for International Economics.
Cline, W.R. (2007), "The current account deficit and US foreign debt", testimony before the Budget Committee of the United States Senate, 1 February.
Cline, W.R. (2010a), "Estimating the impact of the exchange rate on the trade balance and jobs", Peterson Institute for International Economics, accessed at http://www.piie.com/ realtime/?p=1806.
Cline, W.R. (2010b), "Renminbi undervaluation, China's surplus, and the US trade deficit", Peterson Institute for International Economics policy brief 10-20.
Cline, W.R. and J. Williamson (2009), "Estimates of fundamental equilibrium exchange rates", Peterson Institute for International Economics policy brief 09-10.
Cline, W.R. and J. Williamson (2010a), "Estimates of fundamental equilibrium exchange rates", Peterson Institute for International Economics policy brief PB10-15.
Cline, W.R. and J. Williamson (2010b), "Currency wars?", Peterson Institute for International Economics policy brief PB10-26.
Cline, W.R. and J. Williamson (2011), "Estimates of fundamental

equilibrium exchange rates", Peterson Institute for International Economics policy brief PB11-5.

Cook, R.C. (2008), "The final crash of western civilization: status report on the collapse of the US economy", 16 July, accessed at http://aotearoaawiderperspective.wordpress.com/2008/07/16/status-report-on-the-collapse-of-the-us-economy/.

Cooley, J. (2008), *Currency Wars*, New York: Skyhorse Publishing.

Cooper, R.N. (2009), "The future of the dollar", Peterson Institute for International Economics policy brief PB09-21, September.

Copeland, L. (2005), *Exchange Rates and International Finance*, 4th edn, Harlow: Prentice Hall.

Cowen, T. (2011), "Master of the universe", *Finance and Development*, June, 57.

Crockett, A. (2008, "Commentary", in M. Goldstein and N. Lardy (eds), *Debating China's Exchange Rate Policy*, Washington, DC: Peterson Institute for International Economics.

DeLong, J.B. (2008), "The wrong financial crisis", *Vox*, 10 October.

Deraniyagala, S. and B. Fine (2001), "New trade theory versus old trade policy: a continuing enigma", *Cambridge Journal of Economics*, **25**, 809–25.

Devereux, M.B. and J. Yetman (2008), "Price adjustment and exchange rate pass-through", working paper, accessed at http://faculty.arts.ubc.ca/mdevereux/priceer.pdf.

Dooley, M. and P. Garber (2009), "Global imbalances and the crisis: a solution in search of a problem", *Vox*, 21 March.

Dooley, M.P., D. Folkerts-Landau and P. Garber (2003), "An essay on the revived Bretton Woods system", National Bureau of Economic Research, accessed at http://www.nber.org/ papers/w9971.

Dooley, M.P., D. Folkerts-Landau and P. Garber (2009), "Bretton Woods II still defines the International Monetary System", National Bureau of Economic Research, accessed at http://ideas. repec.org/p/nbr/nberwo/14731.html.

Driver, R.L. and P.F. Westaway (2004), "Concepts of equilibrium exchange rates", Bank of England working paper no. 248.

Duasa, J. (2007), "Determinants of Malaysian trade balance: an ARDL bound testing approach", *Journal of Economic Co-operation*, **28**, 21–40.

Dukes, C.J. (2005), "Nobel Laureates back RMB's dollar peg", 15 June, accessed at www.btmbeijing.com/contents/en/bbonline/2005/articles/nobel.

Dunaway, S. (2009), *Global Imbalances and Financial Crisis*, Washington, DC: Council for Foreign Relations Press.

Dunaway, S. (2010), "China's exchange rate policy: the heat is on", Council on Foreign Relations, 10 February, accessed at www.cfr.org/publication/21455/chinas_exchange _rate_policy.html.

Dunaway, S., L. Leigh and X. Li (2006), "How robust are estimates of equilibrium real exchange rates? The case of China", IMF working paper no. 06/220.

The Economist (2003), "The price of profligacy", 18 September.

The Economist (2005), "The dragon comes calling", 1 September.

The Economist (2007a), "Misleading misalignment", 21 July.

The Economist (2007b), "Lost in translation", 17 May.

The Economist (2008a), "Revaluation by stealth", 10 January.

The Economist (2008b), "Divine intervention", 27 March.

The Economist (2009a), "Burger-thy-neighbour policies", 5 February.

The Economist (2009b), "Birth pains: a new global system is coming into existence", 14 May.

The Economist (2009c), "When a flow becomes a flood", 22 January.

The Economist (2009d), "Too big for its Gucci boots", 12 September, p. 71.

The Economist (2010a), "Fumbling towards a truce", 16 October.

The Economist (2010b), "An indigestible problem", 16 October.

The Economist (2010c), "Nominally cheap or really dear", 6 November.

The Economist (2010d), "Flood barriers", 9 October.

The Economist (2010e), "Learning to crawl", 26 June.

The Economist (2010f), "Where are the profits?", 11 December.

The Economist (2010g), "China buys up the world", 13 November.

The Economist (2010h), "The indispensable economy", 30 October.

The Economist (2010i), "The dangers of rising China", 4 December.

The Economist (2010j), "Repent at leisure", Special Report on debt, 26 June.

The Economist (2010k), "Confronting the monster", 20 November.

The Economist (2011a), "Beefed-up burgernomics", 30 July.

The Economist (2011b), "Birth pains: a new global system is coming into existence", 14 May.

The Economist (2011c), "An anniversary for the world currency markets", 13 August.

The Economist (2011d), "Poor dollar standard", 13 August.

The Economist (2011e), "JFK and quantitative easing: twisted thinking", 2 April.

The Economist (2011f), "Stopping quantitative easing may be harder than starting it", 19 March.

The Economist (2011g), "The Great Depression: blame game", 26 March.

The Economist (2011h), "Learning to like inflation", 19 February.

The Economist (2011i), "Hands slapped", 9 July.

The Economist (2011j), "Coming up short", 22 July.
The Economist (2011k), "Shame on them", 9 July.
The Economist (2011m), "Countdown", 9 July.
The Economist (2011n), "No thanks to anyone", 6 August.
The Economist (2011p), "Central bankers to the rescue?", 13 August.
The Economist (2011q), "Substandard & Poor", 13 August.
The Economist (2011r), "Looking for someone to blame", 13 August.
The Economist (2011s), "The civil war in Washington, DC is damaging American business", 13 August.
The Economist (2011t), "Cash machines: calls to boost manufacturing ignore the gains to be made from services", 2 April.
The Economist (2011u), "China's aircraft carrier: name and purpose to be determined", 13 August.
The Economist (2011v), "The last best hope", 26 November.
Edwards, S. and M.A. Savastano (1999), "Exchange rates in emerging economies: what do we need to know?", NBER working paper no. 7228.
Eichengreen, B. and D.A. Irwin (2009), "The slide to protectionism in the Great Depression: who succumbed and why?", NBER working paper no. 15142.
Ekelund, R.B. and R.F. Hébert (1997), *A History of Economic Theory and Method*, 4th edn, Long Grove, IL: Waveland Press.
Elliott, L. (2003), "Policy made on the road to perdition", *The Guardian*, 13 October.
Elmendorf, D.W. and D.L. Reifschneider (2002), "Short-run effects of fiscal policy with forward-looking financial markets", *National Tax Journal*, September.
Ensinger, D. (2010), "China's WTO entry has been a failure for US", *Economy in Crisis*, 21 November, accessed at www.economyincrisis.org/content/chinas-wto-entry-has-been-failure-us.
Erceg, C.J., L. Guerrieri and C. Gust (2005), "Expansionary fiscal shocks and the trade deficit", Federal Reserve Board international finance discussion paper 825, accessed at www.federalreserve.gov/pubs/ifdp/2005/825/ifdp825.pdf.
Falk, M. (2008), "Determinants of the trade balance in industrialized countries", FIW research report no. 013, Foreign Direct Investment, June, accessed at www.fiw.ac.at/fileadmin/Documents/Publikationen/fiwstudie13.pdf.
Fatas, A. (2010), "Current account imbalances and exchange rates", 7 April, accessed at http://fatasmihov.blogspot.com/2010/04/current-account-imbalances-and-exchange.html.
Feenstra, R.C., W. Hai, S. Yao and W.T. Woo (1998), "The US–China bilateral trade balance: its size and determinants", May, paper

presented at the UNDP-HIID Conference on China's Integration into the Global Economy, 17 January, accessed at www.econ.ucdavis.edu/working_papers/98-9.pdf.

Fernando, V. (2010), "Why China's high savings rate could be a sign of weakness", *Business Insider*, 12 March, accessed at http://www.businessinsider.com/why-chinas-high-savings-rate-could-be-a-sign-of-weakness-2010-3.

Financial Crisis Inquiry Commission (2011), *Financial Crisis Inquiry Report*, Washington DC: US Government Printing Office, accessed at www.knowledgemosaic.com/ papertrail/fcic_final_report_full.pdf.

Frankel, J.A. (2004), "On the renminbi", Kennedy School of Government, October, accessed at http://ksghome.harvard.edu/~jfrankel/On the Renminbi.pdf.

Frankel, J.A. and S-J. Wei (2007), "Assessing China's exchange rate regime", *Economic Policy*, **22**, 575–627.

Franks, J. (2010), "Failed interventions and export prices", *Seeking Alpha*, 12 September, accessed at http://seekingalpha.com/article/224745-failed-interventions-and-export-prices?source =feed.

Fratzscher, M., L. Sarno and L. Juvenal (2007), "Asset prices, exchange rates and the current account", ECB working paper no. 790, accessed at http://ssrn.com/abstract=1003965.

Friedman, D. (2002), "No light at the end of the tunnel", accessed at www.newamerica.net/publications/articles/2002/no_light_at_the_end_of_the_tunnel.

Friedman, M. (1953), "The case for flexible exchange rates", in *Essays in Positive Economics*, Chicago, IL: University of Chicago Press.

Friedman, M. (1997), "The case for free trade", *Hoover Digest*, 4.

Friedman, M. and R. Friedman (1980), *Free to Choose*, New York: Harcourt Brace.

Friedman, T. (2008), "Swedish spoken here", *New York Times*, 4 October.

Fu, Z-Y. (2009), "Achievement, problems and countermeasures of RMB exchange rate system reform since 2005", accessed at http://en.cnki.com.cn/Article_en/CJFDTotal-GXSY200903018.htm.

Fukuyama, F. (2008), "The fall of America, Inc", *Newsweek*, 3 October, accessed at http://www.newsweek .com/2008/10/03/the-fall-of-america-inc.html.

Fuller, D. and D. Geide-Stevenson (2003), "Consensus among economists: revisited", *Journal of Economic Education*, **34**, 369–87.

Funke, M. and J. Rahn (2004), "Just how undervalued is the Chinese renminbi?", Bank of Finland working paper, accessed at http://www.bof.fi/NR/rdonlyres/F3372088-5FE8-4995-A1C7-4D8BCBF18A88/0/dp1404.pdf.

Gagnon, J. and G. Hufbauer (2011), "Taxing China's assets: how to increase US employment without launching a trade war", *Foreign Affairs*, 25 April.

Gagnon, J.E. and M.M. Knetter (1995), "Markup adjustment and exchange rate fluctuations: evidence from panel data on automobile exports", *Journal of International Money and Finance*, **14**, 289–310.

Gale, W.G. and S.R. Potter (2002), "An economic evaluation of the Economic Growth and Tax Relief Reconciliation Act of 2001", *National Tax Journal*, March.

Geiger, K. (2011), "Republicans reject Buffett's tax argument", *Chicago Tribune*, 16 August.

Georgopoulos, G. (2008), "The J-curve revisited: an empirical analysis for Canada", *Atlantic Economic Journal*, September.

Ghosh, A.R. and H.C. Wolf (1994), "Pricing in international markets: lessons from *The Economist*", NBER working paper no. 4806.

Gokhale, J. and K. Smetters (2005), "Measuring social security's financial problems", NBER working paper no. 11060.

Goldberg, L. and C. Tille (2006), "International role of the dollar and trade balance adjustment", Group of Thirty occasional paper 71, Washington, DC.

Goldberg, P.K. and M.M. Knetter (1997), "Goods prices and exchange rates: what have we learned?", *Journal of Economic Literature*, **35**, 1243–72.

Goldkorn, J. (2005), "Greenspan to congress: yuan revaluation won't help America", 24 June, accessed at www.danwei.org/business_and_finance/greenspan_to_congress_yuan_ rev.php.

Goldstein, M. (2004), "Adjusting China's exchange rate policies", Peterson Institute for International Economics working paper 04-1, Washington, DC.

Goldstein, M. (2006), "Paulson's first challenge: can the new U.S. treasury chief confront China's currency manipulation?", *International Economy*, **20**, 10–15.

Goldstein, M. and N. Lardy (2003), "Two-stage currency reform for China", *Asian Wall Street Journal*, 12 September.

Goldstein, M. and N. Lardy (2008), "China's exchange rate policy: an overview of some key issues", in M. Goldstein and N. Lardy (eds), *Debating China's Exchange Rate Policy*, Washington, DC: Peterson Institute for International Economics.

Goldstein, M. and N. Lardy (2009), *The Future of China's Exchange Rate Policy*, Washington, DC: Peterson Institute for International Economics.

Grassman, S. (1973), "A fundamental symmetry in international payments", *Journal of International Economics*, **3**, 105–16.

Gravelle, J.G., T.L. Hungerford and M. Labonte (2009), "Economic stimulus: issues and policies", Congressional Research Service, 10 November.

Greenspan, A. (2010a), "The crisis", presentation to the Spring 2010 Conference of the Brookings Papers on Economic Activity (BPEA).

Greenspan, A. (2010b), "The US debt and the Greece analogy", *Wall Street Journal*, 18 June.

Greenwood, J. (1984), "Non-traded goods, the trade balance and the balance of payments", *Canadian Journal of Economics*, **17**, 806–23.

Gregory, R., C. Henn, B. McDonald and M. Saito (2010), "Trade and the crisis: protect or recover", *IMF Staff Position Note*, 16 April.

Griswold, D. (2007), "Are trade deficits a drag on US economic growth", *Free Trade Bulletin*, no. 27, 12 March, accessed at www.cato.org/pub_display.php?pub_id=10661.

Guidolin, M. and E.A. La Jeunesse (2007), "The decline in the US saving rate: is it real and is it a puzzle?", *Federal Reserve Bank of St Louis Review*, **89**, 491–514.

Harbaugh, R. (2004), "China's high savings rates", paper presented at the conference on the Rise of China Revisited: Perception and Reality, National Chengchi University, accessed at www.bus.indiana.edu/riharbau/harbaugh-chuxu.pdf.

Hartung, W.D. (2007), "Bush military budget highest since WWII", 10 February, accessed at www.commondreams.org/views07/0210-26.htm.

Hawkins, W.R. (2003), "US manufacturing's steep decline calls for new trade policies", 11 September, *American Economic Alert*, accessed at http://americaneconomicalert.org/view_art.asp?Prod_ID=885.

He, X. and Y. Cao (2007), "Understanding high saving rate in China", *China and World Economy*, **15**, 1–13.

Higgs, R. (2004), "The defense budget is bigger than you think", 25 January, *Antiwar*, accessed at www.Antiwar.com.

Hitt, C. (2011), "The global economic crisis: it's China's fault! (Not to mention a few leprechauns and rainbows)", 10 February, accessed at http://blogmosaic.knowledgemosaic.com/2011/02/10/fcic-report-causes-of-economic-crisis/.

Hodrick, R. and E.P. Prescott (1997), "Postwar business cycles: an empirical investigation", *Journal of Money, Credit and Banking*, **29**, 1–16.

Hofman, B. and L. Kuijs (2008), "Rebalancing China's growth", in M. Goldstein and N. Lardy (eds), *Debating China's Exchange Rate Policy*, Washington, DC: Peterson Institute for International Economics.

Hossein-Zadeh, I. (2007), "Escalating military spending: income redistribution in disguise", accessed at www.informationclearinghouse.info/article17552.htm.

Huber, A. (2011), "How China keeps the yuan undervalued", accessed at www.globalfinanceschool.com/Articles/07/26/2011/how-china-keeps-yuan-undervalued-%E2%80%93-5-reasons-care.

Hume, D. (1742), "Essays, moral, political and literary", published by Liberty Fund Inc (1987), accessed at www.econlib.org/library/LFBooks/Hume/hmMPL28.html.

Igan, D. and P. Mishra (2011), "Making friends", *Finance and Development*, June, pp. 27–9.

Ilzetzki, E., E. Reinhart and K. Rogoff (2008), "The country chronologies and background to exchange rate arrangements in the 21st century: which anchor will hold?", working paper, accessed at http://terpconnect.umd.edu/~creinhar/Papers/ERA-Country%20chronologies.pdf.

IMF (International Monetary Fund) (2004), "People's Republic of China: 2004 Article IV Consultation", IMF country report 04/351, November.

IMF (2009), *World Economic Outlook: Crisis and Recovery*, April.

IMF (2011), "Enhancing international monetary stability – a role for the SDR?", IMF issues briefs SM/11/3, September.

Institute for International Economics (1999), "Safeguarding Prosperity in a Global Financial System: The Future International Financial Architecture", report of an independent task force sponsored by the Council on Foreign Relations, Washington, DC, September.

Irwin, D.A. (2011a), "Esprit de currency", *Finance and Development*, June, pp. 30–33.

Irwin, D.A. (2011b), *Peddling Protectionism: Smoot-Hawley and the Great Depression*, Princeton, NJ: Princeton University Press.

Ito, H. (2009), "US current account debate with Japan then, with China now", Portland State University Department of Economics working paper.

Jackson, G. (2003), "Twin deficits fallacy returns", BrookesNews.com, 16 April, accessed at www.brookesnews.com/031604twindeficits.html.

Johansen, S. (1988), "Statistical analysis of cointegrating vectors", *Journal of Economic Dynamics and Control*, **12**, 231–54.

Johnson, S. (2009), "The quiet coup", *The Atlantic*, May.

Johnson, S. (2010), "Time to press China on its exchange rate", *New York Times*, 25 February, accessed at http://economix.blogs.nytimes.com/2010/02/25/time-to-press-china-on-its-exchange-rate/.

Johnson, S. and J. Kwak (2009), "Don't blame China", *Washington Post*, 6 October.

Johnson, S. and J. Kwak (2010), *13 Bankers: The Wall Street Takeover and the Next Financial Meltdown*, New York: Pantheon Books.

Joint Committee on Taxation (2005), "Macroeconomic analysis of various proposals to provide $500 billion in tax relief", JCX-4-05, 1 March, accessed at www.house.gov/jct/x-4-05.pdf.

Kapoor, S. (2010), "Why is saving a top priority for Chinese consumers", *Nielsen Wire*, 29 October, accessed at http://blog.nielsen.com/nielsenwire/consumer/why-is-saving-a-top-priority-for-chinese-consumers/.

Keidel, A. (2005), "China's currency: not the problem", Carnegie Endowment for International Peace policy brief 39, June, accessed at www. carnegieendowment.org/files/PB39.keidel.FINAL.pdf.

Keynes, J.M. (1925), *The Economic Consequences of Mr. Churchill*, London: The Hogarth Press.

Kikuchi, A. and M. Sumner (2002), "Exchange rate pass-through in Japanese export pricing", *Applied Economics*, **34**, 279–84.

Kim, S. and N. Roubini (2004), "Twin deficits or twin divergence? Fiscal policy, current account and real exchange rate in the US", mimeo, Korea University and New York University, accessed at http://econ.korea.ac.kr/prof/sykim/files/fiscalus9.pdf.

Knetter, M.N. (1989), "Price discrimination by US and German exporters", *American Economic Review*, **79**, 198–210.

Knetter, M.N. (1993), "International comparisons of pricing-to-market behaviour", *American Economic Review*, **83**, 473–86.

Kogan, R. (2003), "Will tax cuts ultimately pay for themselves?", Center on Budget and Policy Priorities, 3 March.

Kohn, D.L. (2010), "Global imbalances", speech at the High-Level Conference on the International Monetary System, Zurich, 11 May.

Kotlikoff, L.J. (2006), "Is the United States bankrupt?", *Federal Reserve Bank of St Louis Review*, July/August, pp. 235–49.

Kotlikoff, L.J. (2008), "Saving", accessed at www.econlib.org/cgi-bin/printcee.pl.

Kotlikoff, L.J. and L.H. Summers (1981), "The role of intergenerational transfers in aggregate capital formation", *Journal of Political Economy*, **89**, 706–32.

Kreinin, M.E. (1997), "The effect of exchange rate changes on the prices and volume of foreign trade", *IMF Staff Papers*, **24**, 297–329.

Krugman, P. (1987), "Is free trade passé?", *Journal of Economic Perspectives*, **1**, 131–44.

Krugman, P. (2005), "Bad for the country", *New York Times*, 25 November.

Krugman, P. (2007), *The Conscience of a Liberal*, New York: Norton.

Krugman, P. (2010a), "China is 'really the bad guy' in currency war", 14 October, accessed at www.creditwritedowns.com/2010/10/krugman-china-is-really-the-bad-guy-in-currency-war.html.

Krugman, P. (2010b), "Debt and transfiguration", *New York Times*, 12 March.

Krugman, P. (2011a), "The unwisdom of elites", *New York Times*, 8 May.

Krugman, P. (2011b), "Making things in America", *New York Times*, 19 May.

La Botz, D. (2009), "The decline of manufacturing and machine tools, and the future of American industry and the working class", *Monthly Review*, July, accessed at http://mrzine.monthlyreview.org/2009/labotz240709.html.

Labonte, M. and G. Makinen (2005), "The budget deficit and the trade deficit: what is their relationship?", CRS report for Congress, 24 March.

Lardy, N.R. (2005), "Exchange rate and monetary policy in China", *Cato Journal*, **25**, 41–7.

Lardy, N.R. (2010), "China's exchange rate policy and trade imbalances", testimony before the Hearing of the Senate Committee on Banking, Housing and Urban Affairs Subcommittee on Economic Policy, 22 April.

Larrain, M. (2003), "Central bank intervention, the current account, and exchange rates", accessed at www.entrepreneur.com/tradejournals/article/107199797.html.

Lerner, A. (1944), *The Economics of Control*, New York: Macmillan.

Li, C., S. Chang and J. Chang (2009), "Exchange rate pass-through and currency invoicing in China's exports", *China Economic Issues*, No. 2/09, July.

Liew, K., K-P. Lim and H. Hussain (2003), "Exchange rates and trade balance relationship: the experience of ASEAN countries", *International Trade*, 0307003, Econ WPA.

Lind, M. (2003), "Free trade fallacy", *Prospect*, **82**, 20 January, accessed at www.prospectmagazine.co.uk/2003/01/freetradefallacy/.

Liu, H.C.K. (2002), "Dollar hegemony", *Asia Times Online*, 11 April.

Liu, H.C.K. (2004), "China and a new international finance architecture", September, accessed at www.henryckliu.com/page3.html.

Liu, H.C.K. (2005a), "The coming trade war and global depression", *Asia Times Online*, 18 June.

Liu, H.C.K. (2005b), "Trade wars can lead to shooting wars", *Asia Times Online*, 20 August.

Liu, H.C.K. (2005c), "Scarcity economics and overcapacity", *Asia Times Online*, 18 June.

Liu, H.C.K. (2010), "Labor markets delinked from gold", *Asia Times Online*, 3 December.

Lusardi, A., J. Skinner and J. Venti (2001), "Saving puzzles and saving policies in the United States", *Oxford Review of Economic Policy*, **17**, 95–115.

Ma, G. and W. Yi (2010), "Chian's high saving rate: myth and reality", BIS working paper no. 312, June.

Ma, H. and P. Zhang (2008), "RMB exchange rate pass-through onto prices of China's exports to Euro area", accessed at http://en.cnki.com.cn/Article_en/CJFDTOTAL-JING20080 7006.htm.

Madrick, J. (2011), *The Age of Greed: The Triumph of Finance and the Decline of America, 1970 to the Present*, New York: Random House.

Magee, P.S. (1973), "Currency contracts, pass through and devaluation", *Brooking Papers on Economic Activity*, **1**, 303–25.

Malia, M. (1998), *The Communist Manifesto: Introduction*, New York: Penguin.

Mankiw, G. (2006a), "Outsourcing redux", 7 May, accessed at http://greg mankiw.blogspot.com/ 2006/05/outsourcing-redux.html.

Mankiw, G. (2006b), "Is the US trade deficit a problem?", 31 March, accessed at http://gregmankiw. blogspot.com/2006/03/is-us-trade-deficit-problem.html.

Marazzi, M., N. Sheets, R. Vigfusson, J. Faust, J. Gagnon, J. Marquez, R. Martin, T. Reeve and J. Rogers (2005), "Exchange rate pass-through to US import prices: some new evidence", International Finance discussion paper no. 833, April.

Marks, A. and R. Scherer (2005), "US savings rate falls to zero", *Christian Science Monitor*, 3 August, accessed at http://articles.moneycentral.msn.com/Investing/Extra/USSavingsRateFalls To Zero.asp.

Marsh, I.W. and S.P. Tokarick (1994), "Competitiveness indicators: a theoretical and empirical assessment", IMF working paper no. WP/94/29.

Marshall, A. (1923), *Money, Credit and Commerce*, London: Macmillan.

Marston, R.C. (1990), "Pricing to market in Japanese manufacturing", *Journal of International Economics*, **29**, 217–36.

Matto, A. and A. Subramanian (2008), "Currency undervaluation and sovereign wealth funds: a new role for the World Trade Organization", Peterson Institute for International Economics working paper WP 08–2.

Mazerov, M. (2010), "Cutting state corporate income taxes is unlikely to create many jobs", Centre on Budget and Policy Priorities, 14 September.

McKeever, M. (1996), *Balanced Trade: Toward the Future of Economics*, San Francisco, CA: McKeever Institute of Economic Policy Analysis.

McKinley, W. (1892), speech on 4 October 1892 in Boston, MA, published in *William McKinley Papers*, Washington, DC: Library of Congress.

McKinnon, R. (2007), "Why China should keep its dollar peg?", *International Finance*, **10**, 43–70.

McKinnon, R. and K. Ohno (1997), *Dollar and Yen: Resolving Economic Conflict between the United States and Japan*, Cambridge, MA: MIT Press.

McNally, C.A. (2010), "Defusing tensions over China's exchange rate policy", East–West Center, 18 February, accessed at www.eastwestcenter.org/news-center/east-west-wire/defusing-tensions-over-chinas-exchange-rate-policy/.

Meade, E.E. (1988), "Exchange rates, adjustment, and the J curve", *Federal Reserve Bulletin*, October, pp. 633–44.

Meese, R.A. and K. Rogoff (1983), "Empirical exchange rate models of the seventies: do they fit out of sample?", *Journal of International Economics*, **14**, 3–24.

Merk, A. (2009), "China, US play currency chicken", *Asia Times Online*, 29 January, accessed at www.atimes.com/atimes/China_Business/KA29Cb01.html.

Miles, M.A. (1979), "The effects of devaluation on the trade balance and balance of payments: some new results", *Journal of Political Economy*, **87**, 600–20.

Miller, T. (2008), "China's undervalued currency benefits Americans", accessed at www.heritage.org/Research/TradeandForeignAid/wm1919.cfm.

Modigliani, F. and S.L. Cao (2004), "The Chinese saving puzzle and the life-cycle hypothesis", *Journal of Economic Literature*, **42**, 145–70.

Moffett, M.H. (1989), "The J-curve revisited: an empirical examination for the United States", *Journal of International Money and Finance*, **8**, 425–44.

Moosa, I.A. (2008a), "Risk and return in carry trade", *Journal of Financial Transformation*, **22**, 8–13.

Moosa, I.A. (2008b), "Forecasting the yuan/dollar exchange rate under the new Chinese exchange rate regime", *International Journal of Business and Economics*, **7**, 23–35.

Moosa, I.A. (2010a), *International Finance: An Analytical Approach*, 3rd edn, Sydney, NSW: McGraw-Hill.

Moosa, I.A. (2010b), "The profitability of carry trade", *Economia Internazionale*, **63**, 261–380.

Moosa, I.A. (2011a), "The magnificent seven: reasons why revaluation of the yuan will not work", RMIT working paper.

Moosa, I.A. (2011b), "The failure of financial econometrics: assessing the cointegration 'revolution'", *Journal of Financial Transformation*, **32**, 113–22.

Moosa, I.A. (2011c), "On the U.S.–China trade dispute", *Journal of Post Keynesian Economics*, 34, 85–111.

Moosa, I.A. (2011d), "Not China, not S&P: why the US has only itself to blame", *The Conversation*, 9 August, accessed at http://theconversation.edu.au/profiles/imad-moosa-2097.

Moosa, I.A. and R.H. Bhatti (2010), *The Theory and Empirics of Exchange Rates*, Singapore: World Scientific.

Moosa, I.A., T. Naughton and L. Li (2009), "Exchange rate regime verification: has China actually moved from a dollar peg to a basket peg?", *Economia Internazionale*, **62**, 41–67.

Morrison, W. and M. Labonte (2008), "China's currency: economic issues and options for US trade policy", Congressional Research Service, RL32165, 9 January, accessed at www.fas.otg/sgp/crs/ row/RL32165.pdf.

Mussa, M. (2007), "IMF surveillance over China's exchange rate policy", Peterson Institute for International Economics, accessed at www.iie.com/publications/papers/mussa1007.pdf.

Naked Capitalism (2010), "High income disparity leads to low savings rates", 29 March, accessed at www.nakedcapitalism.com/2010/03/high-income-disparity-leads-to-low-savings-rates.html.

Neely, C.J. (2000), "Are changes in foreign exchange reserves well correlated with official intervention?", *Federal Reserve Bank of St Louis Economic Review*, September/October, pp. 17–31.

Nurkse, R. (1944), *International Currency Experience: Lessons of the Interwar Period*, Geneva: League of Nations.

Obstfeld, M. (2006), "The renminbi's dollar peg at the crossroads", CEPR discussion papers no. 5771.

Obstfeld, M. and K. Rogoff (2009), "Global imbalances and the financial crisis: products of common causes", November, accessed at http://elsa.berkeley.edu/~obstfeld/santabarbara.pdf.

Olivei, G.P. (2002), "Exchange rates and the prices of manufacturing products imported into the United States", *New England Economic Review*, first quarter pp. 3–18.

Ou, Y-M. (2005), "Empirical analysis on the relations between exchange rate and China's foreign export", accessed at http://en.cnki.com.cn/Article_en/CJFDTOTAL-GJMW200509022.htm.

Page, S.A.B. (1977), "Currency of invoicing in merchandise trade", *National Institute Economic Review*, **33**, 1241–64.

Page, S.A.B. (1981), "The choice of invoicing currency in merchandise trade", *National Institute Economic Review*, **98**, 60–72.

Palley, T. (2005), "The China currency problem: a reply to Albert Keidel", accessed at www. thomaspalley.com/docs/research/China CurrencyProblem_Keidel.pdf.

Park, Y.C.P. and C. Wyplosz (2010), *Monetary and Financial Integration in East Asia: The Relevance of European Experience*, Oxford: Oxford University Press.

Paulson, H. (2008), remarks by Secretary Henry M. Paulson on the

Financial Rescue Package and Economic Update, US Treasury press release, 12 November.
Penner, R.G. (2010), "Choosing the nation's fiscal future", The President's National Commission on Fiscal Responsibility and Reform, 27 April.
Persaud, A. (2010), "Why China's exchange rate is a red herring", *Vox*, 10 April.
Peter Peterson Foundation (2010), "State of the Union finances: a citizen's guide", April, accessed at www.google.com.au/search?q=%22State+of+the+Union+Finances%3A+A+Citizen%E2%80%99s+Guide%22&ie=utf-8&oe=utf-8&aq=t&rls=org.mozilla:en-US:official&client=firefox-a.
Pettis, M. (2009), "Why do Chinese save so much?", *Wall Street Pit*, 29 May, accessed at http://wallstreetpit.com/4636-why-do-chinese-save-so-much.
Philippon, T. (2008), "The future of financial industry", Stern on Finance, accessed at http://sternfinance.blogspot.com/2008/10/future-of-financial-industry-thomas.html.
Poole, W. (2005), "Does the US have a current account deficit disorder?", in Philip G. King and S.K. King (eds), *International Economics and International Economic Policy*, New York: McGraw Hill.
Pope, J. (2009), "Democrats and the decline of manufacturing in America", 2 September, accessed at http://pajamasmedia.com/blog/democrats-and-the-decline-of-manufacturing-in-america/.
Portes, R. (2009), "Global imbalances", mimeo, February.
Prasad, E. (2008), "Monetary policy independence, the currency regime, and the capital account in China", in M. Goldstein and N. Lardy (eds), *Debating China's Exchange Rate Policy*, Washington, DC: Peterson Institute for International Economics.
Reid, B.M. (2010), "The three biggest myths about tax cuts and the budget deficit", The Heritage Foundation, 21 June.
Reinhart, C.M. (2010), "Testimony before the senate budget committee", 9 February, accessed at www.scribd.com/doc/58554993/Reinhart-Senate-Testimony-February-9-2010.
Reinhart, C.M. and K. Rogoff (2009), *This Time Is Different: Eight Centuries of Financial Folly*, Princeton, NJ: Princeton University Press.
Richman, R., H. Richman and J. Richman (2008), *Trading Away Our Future*, Pittsburg, PA: Ideal Taxes Association.
Rodrik, D. (2004), "Rethinking economic growth in developing countries", John F. Kennedy School of Government, Harvard University working paper, October.
Rodrik, D. (2006), "Goodbye Washington Consensus, hello Washington confusion? A review of the World Bank's economic growth in the 1990s:

learning from a decade of reform", *Journal of Economic Literature*, **44**, 973–87.

Rose, A.K. (1990), "Exchange rates and the trade balance: some evidence from developing countries", *Economics Letters*, **34**, 271–5.

Rose, A.K. and J.L. Yellen (1989), "Is there a J-curve?", *Journal of Monetary Economics*, **24**, 53–68.

Roubini, N. (2007), "Why China should abandon its dollar peg?", *International Finance*, **10**, 71–89.

Roubini, N. (2009), "A balanced global diet", *New York Times*, 28 January.

Roubini, N. (2010), "A presidency heading for a fiscal train wreck", FT.Com, 28 October, accessed at www.ft.com/intl/cms/s/0/dd140d16-e2c2-11df-8a58-00144feabdc0.html#axzz1MljJh357.

Roubini, N. (2011), "The Confucian consumer: seven reasons why the Chinese save, when they should be spending", *Newsweek*, 17 January, accessed at www.newsweek.com /2011/01/18/the-confucian-consumer.html.

Ruffing, K. and J.R. Horney (2010), "Critics still wrong on what's driving deficits in coming years: economic downturn, financial rescues, and Bush era policies drive the numbers", Center on Budget and Policy Priorities working paper, 28 June.

Samuelson, P.A. (2004), "Where Ricardo and Mill rebut and confirm arguments of mainstream economists supporting globalization", *Journal of Economic Perspectives*, Summer, **18**(3).

Samuelson, R.J. (2007), "China's wrong turn on trade", *Newsweek*, 6 December.

Samuelson, R.J. (2009), "Barack Obama's risky deficit spending", *Real Clear Markets*, 18 May, www.realclearmarkets.com/articles/2009/05/barack_obamas_risky _deficit_sp.html.

Schaefer, K. (2009), "How China's dollar peg keeps oil prices high", *Seeking Alpha*, 11 August.

Scott, R. (2008), "The China trade toll: widespread wage suppression, 2 million jobs lost in the US", EPI briefing paper no. 219, July.

Sekine, T. (2006), "Time-varying exchange rate pass-through: experiences of some industrial countries", BIS working paper no. 202, March.

Sester, B. (2008), "Bretton Woods 2 and the current crisis: any link?", blog entry, Council on Foreign Relations.

Shane, S. and R. Nixon (2007), "US contractors becoming a virtual fourth branch of government", *New York Times*, 4 February.

Shengjun, L. (2010), "China's exchange rate policy: what's really going on", *HBR Blog Network*, 2 July, accessed at http://blogs.hbr.org/cs/2010/07/chinas_exchange_rate_policy.html.

Sicilia, D.B. and J.L. Cruikshank (2000), *The Greenspan Effect*, New York: McGraw-Hill.

Sims, C.A. (1988), "Bayesian skepticism on unit root econometrics", *Journal of Economic Dynamics and Control*, **12**, 463–74.

Sinnakkannu, J. and A. Nassir (2006), "A study on the effect of de-pegging of the renminbi against the US dollar on China's international trade competitiveness", *International Research Journal of Finance and Economics*, **5**, 64–77.

Smith, A. (1776), *An Inquiry into the Nature and Causes of the Wealth of Nations*, reprint of the Clarendon Press edition, Oxford 1976, with Edward Cannan's original index from 1922, Indianapolis, IN: Liberty.

Song, H. (2007), *Currency Wars*, Beijing: CITIC Publishing House.

Spence, M. and S. Hlatshwayo (2011), "The evolving structure of the American economy and the employment challenge", Council on Foreign Relations working paper.

Spruk, R. (2010a), "Renminbi appreciation", *Citizen Economists*, 26 April, accessed at www. citizeneconomists.com/blogs/2010/04/26/renminbi-appreciation/.

Spruk, R. (2010b), "China's growth model", *Citizen Economists*, 16 September, accessed at www.citizeneconomists.com/blogs/tag/currency-manipulation/.

Staiger, R.W. and A.O. Sykes (2009), "Currency manipulation and world trade: a caution", accessed at www.voxeu.org/index.php?q=node/2934.

Stein, J.L. (1994), "The natural real exchange rate of the US dollar and determinants of capital flows", in J. Williamson (ed.) *Estimating Equilibrium Exchange Rates*, Washington, DC: Institute for International Economics.

Stockman, D. (2010), "Four deformations of the apocalypse", *New York Times*, 31 July.

Stutchbury, M. (2010), "Why we won't join currency war on China", *The Australian*, 14 October.

Suominen, K. (2011), "Did global imbalances cause the crisis?", *Vox*, 14 June.

Supply Chain Digest (2008), "Decline in US manufacturing versus China vastly overstated", 19 August, accessed at www.scdigest.com/assets/On_Target/08-08-19-3.php.

Taylor, J.B. (2008), "The financial crisis and the policy responses: an empirical analysis of what went wrong", keynote address at Bank of Canada, November.

Thin, W. (2010), "More on Geithner's currency classifications", 21 October, accessed at www.creditwritedowns.com/2010/10/more-on-geithners-currency-classifications.html.

Thompson, R. (2008), "Twin deficits and the fate of the US dollar: a hard landing re-examined", *Journal of Public and International Affairs*, **19**, 107–23.

Triffin, R. (1960), *Gold and the Dollar Crisis: The Future of Convertibility*, New Haven, CT: Yale University Press.

Truman, E.M. (2010), "The international monetary system and global imbalances", paper based on presentation at International Monetary Fund and the UK Economic and Research Council Conference "Monetary system: looking to the future and lessons from the past", January.

US–China Business Council (2006), "US manufacturing: dying . . . or still going strong?", accessed at www.uschina.org/public/documents/2006/09/us-manufacturing.pdf.

Vistesen, C. (2010), "The global economy – old maids who won't play anymore", 8 September, accessed at www.citizeneconomists.com/bligs/tag/currency manipulation/.

Walker, D.M. (2008), "U.S. financial condition and fiscal future briefing", United States Government Accountability Office (GAO-08-446CG), 17 January.

Wang, J. (2009), "China's intellectual contribution to addressing the 'once-a-century' financial crisis", *China Daily*, 25 March.

Wang, J. and Y. Fu (2010), "No winner in currency war", 11 October, accessed at http://news.xinhuanet.com/english2010/business/2010–10/11/c_13551840.htm.

Wang, T. (2004), "Exchange rate dynamics", in E. Prasad (ed.), *China's Growth and Integration into the World Economy: Prospects and Challenges*, IMF occasional paper no. 232.

Washington Post (2007), "A heckuva claim: Mr. Bush is oblivious to the consequences of his tax cuts", 6 January.

Wei, S.J. and X. Zhang, (2011), "Sex ratios, entrepreneurship, and economic growth in the People's Republic of China", NBER working paper no. 16800.

Whaples, R. (2006), "Do economists agree on anything? Yes!", *The Economists' Voice*, **3**.

Whelan, K. (2010), "Global imbalances and the financial crisis", briefing paper for the European Parliament's Committee on Economic and Monetary Affairs, March.

Wickens, M. (1996), "Interpreting cointegrating vectors and common stochastic trends", *Journal of Econometrics*, **74**, 255–71.

Williamson, J. (1983), "The exchange rate system", *Policy Analyses in International Economics*, Washington, DC: Institute for International Economics.

Williamson, J. (2003), "The renminbi exchange rate and the global monetary system", lecture delivered at the Central University of Finance and Economics, Beijing, 29 October.

Williamson, J. (2009), "Why SDRs could rival the dollar", Peterson Institute for International Economics policy brief PB09-20, September.

Wolf, M. (2008), *Fixing Global Finance*, Baltimore, MD: Johns Hopkins University Press.

Wolf, M. (2010), "Currencies clash in new age of beggar-my-neighbour", *Financial Times*, 29 September, accessed at www.ft.com/cms/s/0/9fa5bd4a-cb2e-11df-95c0-0144feab49a.html.

Wolf, R. (2010), "Rising income inequality in the US: divisive, depressing, and dangerous", accessed at http://mrzine.monthlyreview.org/2010/wolff070210.html.

Wolverson, R. (2010), "Confronting the China–US economic imbalance", Council on Foreign Relations, 18 February, accessed at www.cfr.org/publication/20758/confronting_the_ chinaus_economic_imbalance.html.

Woo, W.T. (2005), "Why is China's savings rate so high?", *Mahalanobis*, April, accessed at http://mahalanobis.twoday.net/stories/611408/.

World Bank (2011), *Multipolarity: The New Global Economy*, Washington, DC.

Wyplosz, C. (2010), "Is an undervalued renmimbi the source of global imbalances?", *Vox*, 30 April, accessed at www.voxeu.org/index.php?q=node/4866.

Xiao, G. (2010), "China's exchange rate policy and what it means for the dollar", *What Matters*, 13 January, accessed at http://whatmatters.mckinseydigital.com/currencies/china-s-exchange-rate-policy-and-what-it-means-for-the-dollar.

Xin, X. and X. Liu (2011), "Why has China's trade grown so fast? A demand-side perspective", *Emerging Markets Finance and Trade*, **47**, 90–100.

Xinhuanet (2010), "Possible 'currency war' to hamper int'l economy recovery", accessed at http://news.xinhuanet.com/english2010/business/2010–10/17/c_13561641.htm.

Yang, Y. (2011), "Structural adjustment needed to cure China's $3 trillion headache", *The Age*, 22 August.

Yazici, M. (2006), "Is the J-curve effect observable in Turkish agricultural sector?", *Journal of Central European Agriculture*, **7**, 319–22.

Yi, J. (2008), "China's exchange rate movements and corporate currency invoicing strategies", University of Nottingham China Policy Institute discussion paper 31, June.

Zakaria, F. (2010), "The real challenge from China: its people, not its currency", *Time*, 7 October, accessed at www.time.com/time/world/article/0,8599,2024090,00.html.

Zhang, Z-B. (2008), "The empirical analysis of the appropriate level of renminbi (RMB) exchange rate", accessed at http://en.cnki.com.cn/Article_en/CJFDTOTAL-BUSI200801046.htm.

Zhou, X. (2009), "Reform the international monetary system", essay posted on the website of the People's Bank of China, 9 April, accessed at www.pbc.gov.cn/english/detail.asp?col=6500&id=178.

Zhu, A. and D.M. Kotz (2010), "The dependence of China's economic growth on exports and investment", working paper, July, accessed at http://people.umass.edu/dmkotz/China_Growth _Model_%2010_09.pdf.

Zhuang, R., R. Won, W. Koo and J.W. Mattson (2007), "Determinants of the US trade balance in consumer-oriented agricultural products", Center for Agricultural Policy and Trade Studies, North Dakota State University, agribusiness and applied economics report no. 607, July, accessed at http://ageconsearch.umn.edu/ bitstream/9079/1/aer607.pdf.

Index